A BROAD CHURCH

VOLUME 2

Gearóid Ó Faoleán was awarded a PhD in Modern Irish History from the University of Limerick in 2014 and currently works in scholarly publishing in London and Belfast. He is a member of the Oral History Network of Ireland and the Irish Association of Professional Historians. His first book, *A Broad Church: The Provisional IRA in the Republic of Ireland, 1969–1980*, was published by Merrion Press in 2019.

A BROAD CHURCH

THE PROVISIONAL IRA IN
THE REPUBLIC OF IRELAND

VOLUME 2: 1980–1989

Gearóid Ó Faoleán

MERRION
PRESS

First published in 2023 by
Merrion Press
10 George's Street
Newbridge
Co. Kildare
Ireland
www.merrionpress.ie

978 1 78537 445 6 (Paper)
978 1 78537 446 3 (Ebook)

A CIP catalogue record for this book is
available from the British Library.

Typeset in Minion Pro 11/15 pt

Cover images © Kaveh Kazemi/Getty Images

Merrion Press is a member of Publishing Ireland.

CONTENTS

ACKNOWLEDGEMENTS

As in my first volume, I wish to acknowledge the support and guidance of my former PhD supervisor, Ruán O'Donnell. I want to acknowledge the support I received from the staff at the National Archives and National Library, Ireland, the British Library and the National Archives of the UK. Much of the research for this book was done in between periods of Covid-19 lockdowns, and the staff at all of these locations were professional and friendly under difficult conditions. I want to thank Mark Dawson at *An Phoblacht* for his great help in sourcing photographs from the archives. A very sincere thanks also to Conor and Wendy at Merrion Press for their support and guidance in bringing this book to completion and publication.

I want to express my sincerest gratitude again to those who consented to be interviewed for this research, both the university dissertation and the book itself. Finally, I want to thank my family and friends for their support throughout the years.

INTRODUCTION

As the 1970s ended and the first decade of the 'Troubles' concluded, a clear stalemate existed between the British state and the forces of militant Irish republicanism. The Provisional Irish Republican Army (IRA) and the Irish National Liberation Army (INLA) were committed to military campaigns to force a British withdrawal from Northern Ireland, and the previous ten years had witnessed bombings and shootings on a scale and intensity not experienced on the island since the early 1920s. More than 2,000 people had been killed by the end of 1979, with a multiple of that number injured. Thousands of people were interned without trial, and tens of thousands more were displaced either temporarily or permanently as a result of the conflict. Politically, the Provisional IRA's campaign had succeeded in proroguing the Northern Irish Parliament at Stormont in 1972, while unionist opposition collapsed its successor two years later.

The conflict was not contained within the borders of that state, however. In Britain, both the Official and Provisional IRA, as well as the INLA, carried out attacks on military personnel and civilians, with some minor activity in continental Europe in the late 1970s also. In the Republic of Ireland, there was a wide range of IRA activity throughout the decade and that state was greatly impacted by the 'Troubles'. During the first three years of the conflict alone, two government ministers were put on trial for allegedly attempting to arm militant republicans, the British Embassy in Dublin was burned down in response to a British Army attack on civil rights demonstrators in Derry city, and juryless courts were introduced to try republican suspects. By the decade's end, many more events of great significance had taken place. A number of gardaí were killed in the line of duty, armed robberies by the IRA became an almost daily occurrence, and hundreds of men and women were incarcerated in Irish prisons for republican activity. Garda brutality, forced confessions and media censorship – self-imposed or otherwise – were already commonplace by the middle of the decade. In addition, the greatest loss of life in a single day during the 'Troubles' took place in May 1974, the result of co-ordinated loyalist bombings in Dublin city and Monaghan town. According to the authoritative 'Troubles'-related website Conflict Archive on the Internet (CAIN), seventy-four people were killed in the Republic of Ireland during the 1970s as a result of the conflict.[1] Richard Fallon, a member of An Garda Síochána, was the first citizen of the Republic to lose his life. He was shot by members of the small far-left republican group Saor Éire during the course of a bank robbery in Dublin city in April 1970. During the 1980s, a mercifully reduced number, twenty people, were killed in the Republic as a result of the 'Troubles', including members of An Garda Síochána, the British Army's Ulster Defence Regiment (UDR) and the IRA, as well as a number of alleged informers shot by republicans.

The Provisional IRA came into being in late 1969. It formed out of a split in the wider republican movement driven largely by its perceived failure to act in defence of the nationalist population of Northern Ireland, who faced attack from sectarian gangs and British state forces in the late 1960s. In January 1970, this division was formalised further when Sinn Féin also split at its Ard-Fheis, ostensibly over the long-standing republican policy of abstentionism (see Chapter 5). The Provisional IRA was established following a meeting of local IRA officers from across Ireland in Birr, County Offaly, although this meeting was seen less as a foundation and more of a reconstitution. Those involved regarded themselves and their structure as a legitimate continuity army stretching back fifty years to the Irish revolutionary period. The Provisional IRA thus maintained a pre-existing military structure, with a General Army Convention of representatives from IRA brigades across the island electing a twelve-person Army Executive. This body in turn chose a seven-person Army Council, usually from among its own members, but not exclusively. The Army Council, as the supreme authority of the IRA, selected a Chief of Staff and Adjutant. While the Army Council and Executive determined strategy to varying degrees, a separate body – General Headquarters (GHQ) – was tasked with prosecuting that strategy. GHQ was divided into military 'departments', primarily: Quartermaster, Engineering, Operations, Finance, Intelligence, Training, Education, Security and Publicity. This structure was largely retained during the 1970s, although there was some variance as more volunteers became involved. And, although Northern IRA units increasingly acted with considerable autonomy as the conflict intensified from 1971, officially the Provisional IRA's only independent command until the mid-1970s was Munster Command in the south-west of the Irish Republic. As discussed in the previous volume of this book series, this area contributed immensely to the Provisional IRA's campaign, logistically and financially, throughout the 'Troubles'.[2] A number of volunteers from that province also saw 'active service' in Northern Ireland, the border region and – particularly in later years – England.

In February 1975, several years into their military campaign, the Provisional IRA declared a ceasefire. With some exceptions, notably South Armagh, some tit-for-tat sectarian attacks and a feud with the Official IRA in Belfast, the ceasefire held until January of the following year. However, the IRA structure in the South never considered itself bound by the terms of the ceasefire (being outside the 'war zone') and so continued its activities throughout 1975. This primarily consisted of training, financing and matériel supply. While the British government had no intention of consenting to the republican demands that accompanied the ceasefire, they allowed negotiations to drag on for most of the year in order to encourage divisions within the republican movement, build up their intelligence on IRA members and have the organisation's support base experience peace, so that a return to conflict became unpalatable. It was a highly effective strategy. By the time the Provisionals officially renewed their campaign in January 1976, the ceasefire had already effectively ended in several areas of the North. However, the IRA struggled with initiative and momentum following the campaign renewal. Indeed, one could argue that the ceasefire nearly broke them: 1977 was perhaps the low-water mark for IRA activity and morale during the 'Troubles'.

Leadership changes and organisational restructuring were deemed necessary for the organisation's survival. To streamline logistics, operations and lines of reporting, two distinct commands were created: Northern and Southern Command. Northern Command comprised the six counties of Northern Ireland and all the bordering counties of the Irish Republic. Southern Command comprised all the remaining counties in the South. A cellular system also replaced the old brigade structure in most areas. However, in areas with relatively large populations of republican support, the cellular structure was only partly implemented or not at all, as with South Armagh and Kerry. The notion of republican 'areas' and where these might be located has been discussed in the previous volume of this series. Certainly, some parts of the Irish Republic seem to have been more supportive of, or sympathetic to, militant republicanism than others. This can be deduced through a collection of factors (the 'how'), from the intensity of IRA activity there to incarceration numbers per county, to electoral support, albeit the latter being less of an indicator. What determinants were involved (the 'why') is more complicated. Historic events, economic factors – past and present – even the presence of a small number of atypically active republican veterans to act as a beacon to others, all of these could play a part. However, it is important to consider the individual and acknowledge their agency in complementing such trends or quantitative analysis. For this, oral history in the form of participant interviews provides a particularly valuable contribution.

A central purpose of this book is to document, discuss and analyse IRA activity in the South during the 1980s. Relative to the North, there is a dearth of research on IRA volunteers from the Republic throughout the 'Troubles'. Therefore, it is important to present a membership and activity analysis of this cohort at the beginning of this study. This analysis, which was also conducted for the 1970s in the previous volume, contributes to our understanding of a number of important factors regarding IRA activity, such as location, age range and occupation, all of which helps build a clearer picture of the profile of militant republicanism in the South. As it is outside the scope of this study to conduct a similar analysis of Northern Ireland, Northerners arrested and tried for IRA activity in the South were excluded from the analysis to provide a clearer presentation of the Southern profile.

For this research, extensive searches were made of newspaper reports of court appearances involving IRA suspects from and in the Republic of Ireland. This research was conducted in order to build a comprehensive picture of IRA membership and its active support base in the South, insofar as can be established through arrests and court appearances. Certain criteria were applied to determine whether court appearances represented militant republicans and, more particularly, militant republicans linked to the Provisional IRA rather than the INLA. For example, the Special

Criminal Court was almost exclusively used to try republican suspects. Where IRA activity intersected with regular criminal activity, as in the case of armed robberies, one can determine whether the defendants were members of the IRA or INLA or not based on what court they were tried in. Although the Provisional IRA changed their policy in the late 1970s to allow their membership to recognise the court system in the South, a number of defendants still refused to do so when on trial. This provides an additional filter. Shouts of 'Up the Provos' or similar from defendants or their supporters in the court galleries indicate Provisional IRA members. Lastly, cases in the Special Criminal Court involving possession of explosives were most likely linked to the Provisionals; the INLA rarely acquired significant explosives.

As noted, the analysis below only considers IRA defendants from the Republic of Ireland. Where it could be established, court reports of defendants living in the Republic but who had moved there from Northern Ireland were discounted. Newspaper reports of republicans from Northern Ireland who were tried in the Special Criminal Court tended to emphasise the defendants' place of origin in those cases. It is thus likely that where a defendant's place of origin was not given, it can be attributed to the Republic with some confidence. In total, this research found 202 court cases for militant republican suspects tried in the Republic who, it appears, were from that state. One additional entry is included in this analysis – that of an Irish man from the Republic tried in the UK under the Prevention of Terrorism Act. This gives a total of 203 defendants. The majority of IRA court trials took place in the first half of the decade and tapered off towards the late 1980s (see Chart 1). Potential explanatory factors include continued streamlining of the IRA as an organisation and a broad trend in reduction of IRA activity, as well as greater counter-surveillance and counterintelligence on the part of the IRA.

On age profiles, and excluding the unknown/not given age range when making calculations, it can be seen that during the 1980s, based on court reports, 42.2 per cent of IRA volunteers from the South were in the age range of 22–29 years (see Table 1). This is remarkably similar to the 1970s, where that same age range constituted 43.9 per cent of defendants. The 18–21 age range represented 10.5 per cent of the total during the 1980s and 23.7 per cent in the previous decade. During the early years of the 'Troubles', many

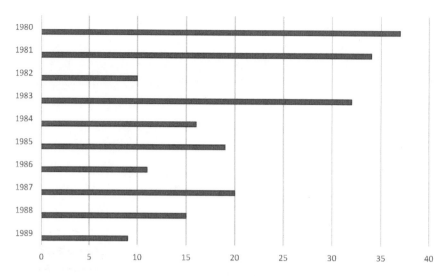

**Chart 1. Number of IRA-related trials of people from
the Republic of Ireland by year**

young men and women on both sides of the Irish border flocked to the ranks of the IRA. Following the post-1975 ceasefire, however, the organisation became more selective of volunteers. In addition, increased internal security likely protected many new members from coming to the attention of the gardaí. Of the other two age ranges, 30–45 and 46–72, they represented 36.6 per cent and 17.2 per cent, respectively, for the 1980s. Considering the 1970s, those same cohorts were 27.7 per cent and 5 per cent.

Table 1. Age range of defendants, 1980–89

Age range of defendants	Number of defendants
Unknown/not given	10
18–21	19
22–29	76
30–45	67
46–72	31
Total	**203**

As seen in Table 1, the average age of Southern IRA defendants profiled from court appearances was thirty-three. This is relatively old for active participation, and indeed five years older than the average age of the same group in the previous decade. It is nearly ten years older than the average age of 1,240 IRA volunteers (not exclusively from the South) posited by a 2013 study. That study analysed data from IRA members spanning 1970 to 1998 and found the average IRA volunteer to be twenty-four years of age.[3] The average age of republican court defendants in the South stands in even greater contrast to those in the North during the hunger-strike period. Anecdotally, speaking of the late 1970s and early 1980s, 'ninety-nine percent of the people … came into the jail when they were nineteen'.[4] This perspective is largely supported by data. According to a major study carried out by universities in Galway, Belfast and Bristol during the 1980s, more than half of republican prisoners in the North were under twenty-one years of age, with barely 11 per cent being older than thirty.[5]

The limitations of relying on reporting of court proceedings is that these only indicate people prosecuted for IRA activity. Court proceedings cannot speak to those active in the IRA who evaded arrest or prosecution. As noted, in the late 1970s the IRA restructured itself, becoming much more streamlined. In effect, it became smaller and more selective. New recruits, more than ever, were encouraged to be 'lily whites' to avoid garda attention, meaning they were under strict instructions not to be seen associating with known republicans, not to attend republican rallies, meetings or funerals, not to sing republican songs in pubs, and so on. The increased age profile in the 1980s is at least partly a reflection of the lack of intelligence the gardaí had on new recruits during this decade. Many of the older defendants during this period had been well known to gardaí for years, if not decades. But even if it is only partially representative of the profile of Southern IRA involvement during the 1980s, the data perhaps indicates the extent to which Southern Command had moved to a support role by this time. Gone were the heady days of the early 1970s, when it was not uncommon for volunteers from Cork, Kerry and Limerick to be engaged in active service around and across the border.

Where the charge was clearly listed, nearly half of Southern IRA defendants prosecuted in the courts during the 1980s faced arms or explosives possession charges (see Table 2). These ranged from possession of a small number of bullets or a pistol to possession of massive quantities of explosives. Given the extensive use of the South for weapons importation and storage, as well as the manufacture of homemade explosive (HME), this is to be expected. Many of those arrested for possession were caught transiting or storing arms, while others were arrested at so-called 'bomb factories'; typically remote outhouses where agricultural fertiliser was converted into HME. This had been a primary activity of Southern-based IRA members since the early 1970s.

The second most common charge for Southern IRA defendants was armed robbery. Again, this is not unexpected given how central the IRA's Southern Command was for funding the organisation as a whole. Taking the other charges that were linked to fundraising – forgery, kidnap, hijacking, robbery – it becomes clear just how important this activity was in the South. In addition, IRA membership charges represent nearly 15 per cent of cases. When used as an isolated charge, this often represented cases where the state felt that other charges would not stick. Of course, many of those

Table 2. Charges proffered against defendants, 1980–89

Principal charge in court	Number of defendants
Explosives or arms possession	96
Armed robbery	38
IRA membership	30
Forgery	9
Hijacking / Robbery	8
Kidnapping / False imprisonment	7
Murder / Conspiracy to murder	7
Harbouring	2
Riotous assembly	2
Incitement	2
Official Secrets Act	1
Prevention of Terrorism Act	1
Total	**203**

prosecuted for the other categories listed above also faced secondary charges of membership; far from insignificant, given that IRA membership could lead to seven years' imprisonment.

In nearly half the cases (90), the defendant's occupation was not listed. Therefore, one must be careful in making statements about the profile of IRA members or supporters based on the remainder (113). Of that latter cohort, 'unemployed' was the largest category, at 32 per cent. The Republic of Ireland faced massive economic challenges and recession during the 1980s. In 1986 unemployment peaked at 17 per cent and over 200,000 Irish people emigrated during the decade as a whole.[6] However, another factor might also be at play here. Analysis of the 1970s in the previous volume of this series demonstrated that the 'unemployed' category jumped significantly following the IRA's organisational restructure. That is, the organisation slimmed its ranks and the number of those who were on full-time active service (and thus unable to be in formal employment) became proportionately higher. This trend likely continued during the 1980s and is reflected in these figures. Those practising a trade became proportionately smaller during the 1980s compared to the previous decade, dropping from 30 to 15 per cent. 'Unskilled' also dropped, from 29 to 17 per cent. The number of those whose profession was listed as 'farmer' in court reports remained quite consistent, at 11 per cent during the

Table 3. Occupation of defendants, 1980–89

Employment status	Numbers of defendants
Unknown / Not given	90
Unemployed	37
Unskilled	20
Tradesman	18
Farmer	13
Service	11
Professional	7
Student / Retired	4
Former soldier	3
Total	**203**

1980s compared to 10 per cent for the previous decade. Most farmers who faced trial for IRA-related activity were from peripheral counties, or counties not generally known for good land, such as Donegal, Monaghan and Leitrim. As demonstrated in the previous study, such people were often the mainstay of militant Irish republicanism during the 'lean years'.

The geographical origin of Southern IRA members during the 1980s, where it is known, provides no surprises, particularly when compared to the previous decade. Nearly one-third of those prosecuted for IRA-related activity were from Dublin, almost entirely from the city and suburbs (see Table 4). During the 1970s, the county and city accounted for over 35 per cent of court defendants. The Provisional IRA historically had a strong presence in Dublin, with a brigade based on each side of the River Liffey, which bisects the city. The next most-represented county is Louth. This is interesting given the county's relatively small size. It seems probable that proximity to the border, family ties and greater exposure to the experiences of Northern nationalists played a part in the high numbers of involvement. Other border counties with relatively small populations (Donegal, Monaghan) are also well represented. Kerry, Cork and Limerick combined make up approximately 15 per cent of cases. This is in line with previous decades where those counties had strong traditions of and representation in militant republicanism. As with the 1970s, Leinster is the most represented province, with 55 per cent of all defendants (see Table 5). Even if Dublin is removed from this category, 25 per cent of defendants were from Leinster, larger than the next most represented provinces of Ulster and Munster, both of whom account for nearly 20 per cent each, with Connacht making up 4 per cent of cases.

It can be inferred that active participation in the Provisional IRA of the 1980s was much like the previous decade. That is, its members transcended boundaries, were geographically representative of the entire island and often confounded class perceptions. Those tried (and acquitted) in Britain for their alleged part in a 1980s bombing campaign included a nephew by marriage of a Fine Gael TD and minister.[7] The same could be said of its active supporters, who probably make up a sizeable number of those profiled in the above analysis. What then of public opinion?

Comprehensive polling to answer this question is a tricky business. The IRA was an illegal organisation. Legislation, censorship and garda

Table 4. County of origin of defendants, 1980–89

County	Number of defendants
Dublin	59
Louth	28
Monaghan	22
Donegal	15
Kerry	15
Cork	11
Limerick	7
Wexford	7
Meath	5
Wicklow	4
Leitrim	4
Westmeath	3
Tipperary	3
Sligo	3
Cavan	3
Waterford	3
Offaly	2
Kildare	2
Roscommon	1
Clare	1
Laois	1
Longford	1
Mayo	1
Unknown / Not given	2
Total	**203**

harassment ensured that actively voicing support for the IRA or even the goal of a united Ireland could mean significant social, legal and professional censure. Generally speaking, only the most courageous or foolhardy of those who held such beliefs actively expressed them. However, we do have some

Table 5. Provincial origin of defendants, 1980–89

Province (excl. N. Irish counties)	Number of defendants
Leinster	112
Ulster	40
Munster	40
Connacht	9
Unknown / Not given	2
Total	**203**

polls and questionnaire results that are near contemporaneous to the period covered by this study. A wide-ranging social survey conducted by Jesuit-cum-sociologist Fr Míchéal MacGréil in 1972 on over 2,300 Dublin-based respondents found that less than 4 per cent of people outright refused to have any social contact with a member of the Provisional IRA. Nearly 40 per cent of respondents were willing to admit a member of Sinn Féin into their family, and 37 per cent would do the same for its military wing.[8] In 1979, the year before this volume begins, a similar study to MacGréil's was published, titled 'Attitudes in the Republic to the Northern Ireland Problem'. This research was notable for the lack of significant changes in attitudes among the population despite nearly a decade of conflict. Indeed, one of the authors acknowledged in a follow-up article how unpleasantly surprised they both were by the results of their polling. The survey noted that 21 per cent of people questioned in the South were in some way supportive of Provisional IRA activities while, given the revelations concerning a 'heavy gang' operating within the gardaí, one-third of those polled were opposed to a tougher line being taken against the Provisionals by the Southern security forces. In addition, 52 per cent of people agreed with the notion that the Provisional IRA was composed of people who were 'essentially' idealists and patriots. While not implying support, such a viewpoint certainly seems to discount outright condemnation.[9] One of the hottest political issues in the South relating to the 'Troubles' during the 1980s concerned the extradition of IRA and INLA members to Northern Ireland or Britain. As will be discussed, there was massive opposition to extradition throughout the decade. While such opposition cannot be translated directly into support for militant republicanism, some portion of it can arguably be taken as proxy for toleration of such activity.

Padraig O'Malley quite succinctly posited that the IRA existed because of the tacit support of a significant number of people North and South who, while possibly disavowing the violent means it employed, nevertheless supported its aspirations.[10] And while some might have disavowed contemporary actions and targets – 'my old idea of the IRA is so shining', in the words of one young schoolteacher in the 1970s – the Provisionals were well aware of the deep emotive basis of their existence.[11] Popular perceptions of the movement were to shift between loathing, apathy and adulation, but republicans knew from past experiences of such mass sentiment that they need not take too seriously the occasional widespread condemnation.[12] While support was rarely, if ever, white-hot among the broader population, practices of active opposition, such as reporting suspected IRA activity to gardaí, even anonymously, still carried a great stigma, and thus the Provisional IRA persevered in the South. It should also be noted, however, that the IRA targeted alleged informers across the island.

As stated in the previous volume, one cannot use electoral support for Sinn Féin as a proxy for measuring tolerance, sympathy or support towards the IRA. Until the 2000s, Sinn Féin never polled anything close to the percentages of people who expressed support or toleration for the IRA in the above surveys. Interviews, published accounts of republicans and, indeed, court appearances demonstrate that men and women of all political backgrounds and none aided the Provisional IRA during their campaign. Since Sinn Féin's electoral support must be viewed at least semi-independently of the IRA, we are left to other devices of measurement. It is the contention of the author that the intensity and longevity of the IRA's campaign strongly points to a high and sustained level of support, sympathy or tolerance among an unknowable but significant percentage of the population of the South. The notion of toleration as being 'easy, comfortable, cost free, traditional and widespread' remains an uncomfortable truth.[13]

There were others in Irish society in the South, however, who did actively oppose the IRA's campaign. Almost bookending this study, in 1976–77 and again in 1993, there were significant public rallies against IRA violence. Although broadcast ostensibly as peace rallies, these were, in practice, directed singularly against republican participants in the

'Troubles'. The latter campaign, the Peace '93 rallies, also took on a distinctly anti-Northern tone. Oftentimes, the greater the Southern attempts at participation in what might have been perceived as 'morally correct' activism, the greater the chasm that was highlighted in their understanding of the situation. In discussing the intentional ambivalence of Southerners in their attitudes to the Northern conflict, Desmond Fennell put it that: 'to the long war [they] contribute yelps of outrage and torrents of sympathy when Protestant or English civilians are killed, indifference or "serves them right" when Catholic Irish are killed, and political mindlessness – "can't bear to think of it".[14] A 1981 description of the funeral wake for a teenage boy shot dead by the British Army in Belfast captured the typical subdued Northern nationalist anger. The thoughts of the adults gathered in the house: 'no kick-up in the papers or the TV … if the 'RA killed a 16-year old you'd hear all about it'.[15] The journalist Fionnuala O'Connor once wrote of the attitudes of Northern nationalists towards a perceived double standard on the part of Southern media: 'it does not surprise them that the state's Radio Teilifís Éireann (RTÉ) should lionise the Ulster Unionist MP Ken Maginnis … and play down loyalist killings of Catholics while emphasising the sectarian aspect of IRA killings'.[16]

The Southern state had long wrestled with how to deal with the considerable body of republican militants, supporters and sympathisers within its borders, native-born or otherwise. Internment was briefly considered in 1970, before being quickly jettisoned after a kite-flying exercise by the Fianna Fáil government revealed an alarming and unexpected level of public opposition. Given internment's effect in galvanising opposition to the Northern Irish state among nationalists, it was a wise decision. Further, the threats facing the state were not sufficient to legally justify internment as per the European Convention on Human Rights. In order to tackle widespread and alarming IRA activity in the state, the Fianna Fáil government did introduce amendments to the 1939 Offences Against the State Act in 1972. This was followed by linked pieces of legislation passed by the Fine Gael–Labour government in 1976: the Emergency Powers Bill and Criminal Law (Jurisdiction) Act. The outcomes of these bills included the extension of the period a republican suspect could be held in custody (from two to seven days), and an extension of the maximum sentence for IRA membership (from two to seven years). In addition, the Criminal Law (Jurisdiction) Act allowed for the courts in the Republic of Ireland to prosecute and imprison people for crimes committed in the United Kingdom. This was an unhappy compromise to the open sore that was the government's refusal to extradite IRA suspects to Northern Ireland or Britain. Demands for extradition were made repeatedly by British politicians publicly and via diplomatic backchannels throughout the 1970s. The failure of these pieces of legislation to stem IRA activity in the South ultimately led to extradition taking centre stage again during the 1980s.

Throughout the first decade of the conflict, the wider politics of the South were notable for the absence of the Provisionals' political wing, Sinn Féin. There were some minor exceptions to this, such as the party's strong campaigning against membership of the European Economic Community (EEC) prior to a 1972 referendum in the Republic. Despite this, the Irish people voted overwhelmingly in favour of EEC membership. Otherwise, Sinn Féin's role in Southern politics was mostly relegated to town and county council level. In the 1979 local election, they won eleven seats or just under 2 per cent of the popular vote. The ceiling on political participation was very much in line with republican ideology during this period. Sinn Féin membership was often viewed by republicans as 'draft dodging', a 'pasture for the harmless and elderly'.[17] Abstentionism, the refusal to 'recognise' or take seats in the parliaments of Dáil Éireann, Stormont or Westminster, had been official republican policy prior to the split of 1969–70 and remained the policy of the Provisionals thereafter. However, by the late 1970s, many republicans viewed abstentionism from the Dáil as a millstone around the neck of the movement and a hindrance to its appeal among the Southern population. This was interlinked with a growth in politicisation within the movement, as well as a membership influx to both political and military wings of the Provisionals around the time of the 1980–81 hunger strikes. An early test of the firmness of republican policy and ideology came in 1976 with the aforementioned Emergency Powers Bill. Simply on the testimony of a Garda superintendent, and with no supporting evidence, republicans could face seven-year jail terms for IRA membership. Many within the movement saw it as an imperative to fight such charges, which meant the courts had to be recognised. After this policy change, numerous acquittals followed, thus proving the success of the change, at least vis-à-vis protecting members from jail sentences. This issue of what was a principle, what was a policy and which of those could be changed for tactical advantage became a recurring discussion at Ard-Fheiseanna during this period, and would come to a head in 1986.

Increased politicisation was intended to supplement the armed struggle, not replace it. Thus, the most significant arms importations in the IRA's history took place in tandem with significant political policy shifts during the mid-1980s. With the acquisition of an array of new weaponry, the IRA increasingly targeted larger and more prestigious British targets, as with the attack on the British border fort at Derryard in the closing weeks of 1989. There was also a return to attacking targets in Britain in a concerted and systematic way for the first time since the mid-1970s. In the South, General Standing Order No. 8, which expressly forbade IRA members from carrying out attacks on members of the security forces of the Republic, remained as official IRA policy. However, it would be broken several times during the 1980s, often with tragic outcomes. A number of IRA initiatives and operations during the decade caused serious concerns to successive Dublin governments, though each of these faced their own limitations. As with the previous decade, at no time during the 1980s did the IRA ever truly represent an existential threat to the Irish Republic. The goal was to use the state's territory first and foremost as a logistical base to prosecute the campaign against the British state to force their withdrawal from Northern Ireland, a campaign which will be considered year by year in the following chapters.

A Note on Terminology

As per the previous volume of this study and recognising that specific terminology can indicate political sympathies to some, please note that the following terms are used interchangeably throughout this work for narrative or stylistic reasons: 'the North' and 'Northern Ireland'; 'the South' and the 'Republic of Ireland'; 'the Dáil' and 'Leinster House'. When the uncapitalised version is used – i.e. 'south' or 'north' – it is meant geographically or directionally rather than referring to either of the two states in Ireland. The 'IRA' and 'Provisional IRA' are used interchangeably. Unless quoting from an interviewee or other source, 'murder' is not used to describe deaths that occurred during the conflict. No consensus exists on many of the deaths in this conflict. Emotive and subjective terms such as 'terrorist' are also avoided. 'IRA member', 'IRA volunteer' and 'militant republican' are all used interchangeably for narrative purposes. The term 'republican' describes those who adhere to the 1916 Proclamation, which asserted the indefeasibility of the Republic and the legitimacy of using armed action to uphold it. 'Nationalists' are all those others who aspire to a united Ireland but do not necessarily support violence.

1

They Made an Awful Lot of Enemies for Themselves: 1980

As the 'Troubles' entered their second decade, the notion of the Republic of Ireland as an alleged 'safe haven' for militant republicans came to the fore once again. In Dublin government circles, the political hot potato of extradition was also back on the agenda. The British government had long pushed for a reconfiguration of Irish policy and law regarding extradition for what were classed as politically motivated crimes. High-profile republican attacks and assassinations in the latter years of the 1970s added to the political and moral pressure on Dublin. These included the IRA's Warrenpoint ambush on British Army paratroopers and the assassination of Louis Mountbatten and MP Airey Neave in 1979, the latter act perpetrated by the INLA.

Ongoing leadership changes during this period within the Provisional republican movement led to a renewed focus, internally as well as among opponents of republicanism, on the movement's political wing, Sinn Féin. Local elections in the Republic in 1979 returned eleven councillors for the party, representing an increase of four council seats. Meanwhile, Northern Ireland Secretary of State Humphrey Atkins initiated talks in 1980 aimed at bringing nationalist and unionist parties to an informal forum, but the Ulster Unionist Party (UUP), the largest unionist party at the time, refused to take part. As with the Sunningdale initiative seven years earlier, Sinn Féin was excluded from participation and the initiative ultimately led nowhere. Amidst these high politic events, heroin had been arriving to Dublin in ever-increasing amounts since the Iranian Revolution in 1979, and it took a strong grip on the inner-city working-class communities in the early 1980s.

This was to have an inadvertent but profound impact on support for Sinn Féin as the decade went on, as will be explored in later chapters.

As it had in the previous decade, government and security policy in the Republic continued to focus on the suppression of militant republicanism. There were further attempts to control supplies of commercial explosives and the material used in HME. As before, such initiatives had limited impact on the IRA's capabilities, much to British frustration. The IRA were suffering from a conventional arms shortage, however, and garda discoveries of several major arms dumps and training camps caused significant disruption in 1980. Furthermore, new tactics to finance the republican movement indicated that security changes introduced in recent years by the government and private organisations were beginning to severely restrict opportunities for the successful armed robberies that the IRA hitherto relied on as a source of income. This failed to completely blunt the organisation's effectiveness, however, and the deaths of several gardaí in 1980 at the hands of republicans starkly demonstrated the continuing impact of the 'Troubles' on the South. Such killings forced Irish society to address its feelings about, and position on, the conflict like never before. For example, for the first time since the eruption of violence in the late 1960s, the Gaelic Athletic Association (GAA) was forced to clarify its own position on militant republicanism or face serious division within the organisation. While garda deaths were one contributing factor there, the other was the worsening crisis in the prisons of Northern Ireland. The republican struggle for recognition of political prisoner status began with the 'blanket protest' in 1976. By 1980, prisoners had been on a 'dirty protest' for two years and had determined that a hunger strike was the only way to break the deadlock. That decision galvanised public support for the prison campaign, in the North and the South, like no other, and major demonstrations would take place across the Republic in the latter part of the year. While the previous decade had witnessed several major events and political campaigns that brought republicans and supporters onto the streets in protest, it was during the 1980s that such activity became more co-ordinated and sustained.

The Political Situation

Throughout the 1970s, there had been public and private calls from Northern Irish and British politicians for a robust extradition treaty with the Republic.

Successive Irish governments resisted these calls, not least due to the general unpopularity of extradition among the wider population. Officially, requests for extradition of republicans were refused with reference to the Extradition Act of 1965, which exempted cases where the actions were 'a political offence or an offence connected with a political offence'. Further:

> … the same rule shall apply if there are substantial grounds for believing that a request for extradition for an ordinary criminal offence has been made for the purpose of prosecuting or punishing a person on account of his race, religion, nationality or political opinion, or that that person's position may be prejudiced for any of these reasons.[1]

These exemptions caused continuous friction between the British and Irish governments, although by 1980 there was a growing feeling among the legal and political establishment in the Republic that the catch-all defence of 'political offence' on the part of IRA and INLA members was wearing thin. Extradition requests continued to be made by British authorities, such as in the case of William Herity, a radio engineer originally from Belfast who had fled to Dundalk following his arrest in Northern Ireland. In February 1980 Herity went before the High Court to challenge an extradition order to Northern Ireland where he would face a charge under the 1883 Explosives Act. Herity had previously stated that at the time of his arrest he was a member of the Belfast Brigade of the IRA, but that he was not, nor had he any intention of becoming, a member of the IRA in the Republic. Addressing Herity, an exasperated Mr Justice Hamilton asked: 'Are there two IRAs? Can you be a member of the IRA in Belfast and not down here? Does that mean that the IRA recognises partition?' Nevertheless, Herity was subsequently discharged.[2] Justice Hamilton's attitude was in contrast to that of several of his peers a decade earlier, such as when a judge acquitted two young Belfast men on IRA membership charges on the basis that they specifically referred to the Belfast Brigade of the IRA, an area outside his jurisdiction.[3]

The increase in extradition requests during this period led to the establishment of anti-extradition committees across the Republic. Areas of particular concern, and thus considerable committee activity, were those with sizeable populations of nationalists or republicans from Northern

Ireland, such as Dundalk and Monaghan town. Further from the border, there was the town of Shannon in County Clare, which also had a large Northern population. As the contemporary booklet, *No Extradition: The Hidden Struggle in Clare*, noted of Shannon: 'there are over 40 people who live in fear of being picked up and handed over to the British occupied Six Counties or to Britain', a fear that led to a particularly vigorous campaign in that county.[4]

In political developments during the opening months of 1980, Northern Ireland Secretary of State Humphrey Atkins hosted multi-party talks in an attempt to bring direct rule to an end and re-establish a devolved government in the North. As noted above, the UUP refused to attend and Sinn Féin were not invited, while the attending parties – Alliance, the Social Democratic and Labour Party (SDLP) and the Democratic Unionist Party (DUP) – failed to reach any lasting agreement. However, Atkins' overtures were said to have increased the level of trust between the Irish and British governments, which would lead, at the end of the year, to a historic summit between Taoiseach Charlie Haughey and Prime Minister Margaret Thatcher.[5]

In the South, Sinn Féin had begun to make modest political gains, as evinced by the 1979 local elections, becoming the fourth largest party grouping in the state. As *Hibernia* noted, this was in spite of the party fighting that election 'without an iota of RTÉ coverage'.[6] An *Irish Times* article in February 1981, entitled 'The respectable face of republicanism', profiled several of the party's elected representatives. One of those was Frank Glynn, the first Sinn Féin chairman of Galway County Council. Glynn's position stemmed from his holding the balance of power in the council and negotiating a voting pact with Fianna Fáil. As the article noted, hostility towards Sinn Féin on a national level, or as gauged from the declarations of TDs (Teachtaí Dála, elected representatives of the Irish parliament) or the media, simply wasn't reflected on the ground: 'local issues can force bizarre voting alliances and the bonds forged between people who share the same home place to the same social background can prove stronger than party political differences'.[7] An article in *An Phoblacht* from the summer of 1980 is also indicative of this: 'John Joe McGirl of Sinn Fein has been unanimously elected chairman of the Leitrim County Council for the coming year. At the annual general meeting of the council on Tuesday 17th June he was nominated for the position by the outgoing chairman [a Fianna

Fáil councillor].[8] That same year, McGirl convinced a majority of council members to sign a resolution calling on the British to end the terrible prison conditions in the H-Blocks. The composition of the council, excepting McGirl, during this period was one independent, eleven Fianna Fáil and nine Fine Gael councillors.

In contrast, some councils still refused to allow Sinn Féin councillors to bring motions, or fellow councillors simply left the chambers when Sinn Féin representatives spoke. The detrimental effects of this practice were noted by *Hibernia* with respect to a case before the High Court in March. Michael Kavanagh had been arrested in Dublin under Section 30 of the Offences Against the State Act, a wide-ranging arrest-and-detention law first introduced in 1939 as a measure to tackle militant republicans. He alleged that, while in custody, he had been burned, kicked, beaten and half-suffocated. As the newspaper concluded: 'The Kavanagh case contains the first serious and detailed allegations of Garda brutality against the Gardaí since the Heavy Gang was disbanded.'[9] The refusal of councils to recognise and discuss such issues ensured that in turn they rarely received media coverage, with the exception of reporting by *Hibernia* and, later, *Magill*. Another Sinn Féin elected representative, and covert IRA volunteer, was subject to significant garda harassment during this period. Jim Lynagh from Monaghan was reportedly arrested eight times in as many months and subject to forcible strip-searching.[10] These incidents were to be a taster of the decade to come.

Another forewarning from 1980, but in this case one which would inadvertently have a positive political outcome for Sinn Féin in Dublin during the following decade, came from the secretary of the Customs and Excise Officers in Ireland, who claimed in December that Ireland was suffering from a drug problem 'of epidemic proportions'.[11] By the secretary's estimation, annual sales of illegal drugs, chiefly heroin arriving to Ireland from Iran via the United Kingdom, amounted to £25 million. The garda commissioner's report for 1980 also noted an increase in drug activity.[12] In April of that year, heroin valued at more than £250,000 had been seized at Heathrow Airport from a Tehran airliner, and some media were warning of dramatic increases in the use of heroin in Ireland that summer.[13] As will be discussed, the major political parties in the state failed to address or acknowledge the extent of this growing heroin problem, which would prove particularly beneficial, albeit unintentionally, to the Provisional republican movement later in the decade.

Arms, Explosives and Training Camps

Speaking in Blarney in March 1980, Minister for Labour Gene Fitzgerald confidently declared that new government regulations controlling the use of dangerous substances were 'making it harder for subversive organisations in the North to get their hands on bomb-making materials like sodium chlorate and nitro glycerine'.[14] Increasingly strict legislation regarding such materials was likely welcome news to the British, whose military had suffered devastating casualties the previous year as a result of IRA HMEs. Already in January 1980, gardaí had made a significant discovery at Grangebellew, near Dundalk, when a 'bomb factory' was discovered containing thirty primed bombs and enough material for a further 450 bombs. Gardaí also found a number of stolen cars and ammunition. Two men subsequently appeared before the Special Criminal Court on explosives charges.[15]

At the beginning of April, gardaí in County Louth made another major discovery, this time near Drogheda, where a specially made bunker was discovered. It was found under a cowshed on a small farm, and gardaí had to dig through two feet of manure and hay to get to the trapdoor leading to it. Inside, they found full bomb-making facilities, with several different kinds of rifles laid against a wall. Surgical masks, apparently used during bomb-manufacturing, were also found, along with twenty-two rifles, seventy-two primed blast-bombs, two rockets, thousands of rounds of ammunition and detonators. Several weeks later, again in Louth, though not far from the County Monaghan village of Inniskeen, gardaí uncovered arms and explosives, described as 'one of the biggest' arms discoveries in the north Louth area to date. This find included mortars, rockets, rocket-launching equipment, assorted explosives and some rifles, which were stored in several dugouts on a farm.[16]

Elsewhere in the state, gardaí made a number of important discoveries that would help to disrupt IRA activities. In May, an unemployed County Westmeath man was arrested at a disused farmhouse outside Mullingar in possession of a large quantity of ammonium nitrate. Gardaí had stumbled upon the scene while conducting follow-up operations after an armed robbery in the vicinity. Along with this matériel, several barrels and other containers were discovered, as well as a gas ring and four forty-gallon drums, three of which were mounted on cement blocks and had evidently been used to extract the ammonium nitrate from agricultural fertiliser. At the time of discovery, over 3,000lbs of ammonium nitrate had already been extracted and was stored in bags ready for transportation. The arrested man, thirty-seven-year-old John Creagh, had previously served a twelve-month prison sentence for IRA membership in 1974. While initially denying any connection to the find, Creagh later said that he would 'take responsibility for the stuff' and was sentenced to seven years' penal servitude.[17]

In Donegal, gardaí disrupted another major explosives' supply line in September. It began when uniformed members of the gardaí were operating a routine checkpoint and had stopped a car to check the registration. They noticed that another car and trailer further back up the road suddenly stopped and turned up a side road. Gardaí gave chase but, after exiting their patrol car, were forced to lie on the ground as four men who emerged from the vehicle armed with machine guns and revolvers fired shots over their heads before taking off again. An intensive search of the area later uncovered the trailer buried under hay in a shed near the village of Kilmacrennan. The trailer contained twenty-eight bags of nitrobenzene and ammonium nitrate with some diesel oil, amounting to perhaps one ton of explosives or, in the words of a garda spokesman, 'sufficient to blast a medium-sized town'. One man from the county was subsequently sentenced to seven years' penal servitude, while another was given a five-year suspended sentence. According to court reports, this second man had 'shot his mouth off' with republican pub talk over a period of time before being approached by two masked men who asked him to store some 'stuff' in his hayshed, which he agreed to out of fear.[18]

That same month, gardaí and British troops made a number of substantial discoveries on the border between Counties Monaghan and Fermanagh. The Monaghan cache was found in a steel drum in a ditch near Ballybay and contained five rifles, a revolver and ammunition. A follow-up search uncovered several more assault rifles, handguns and 10,000 rounds of ammunition buried in a large tank at what was described as an IRA 'training camp' in the woods at Capragh Lake, outside Carrickmacross. Five local men were arrested and brought to Castleblayney Garda Station for questioning.

Over the border in Fermanagh, the British Army discovered 1,000lbs of explosives.[19] The total amount of arms, ammunition and explosives seized by gardaí in the Republic of Ireland in 1980 is detailed in Table 6.

The IRA's ongoing use of the Southern state for training camps also came under the spotlight a number of times in 1980, with several camps discovered or disrupted by gardaí, as at Ballybay above. On the evening of 12 July, gardaí manning a checkpoint at remote Maam Cross in Connemara stopped a van containing three men. Dissatisfied with the responses given to their questions, they conducted a search of the van and discovered a number of IRA training documents. Two of the men, aged nineteen and twenty-four, were arrested, while the third managed to exit the van and escape across fields. The men had been in the process of hurriedly moving equipment from a storage area following a regional garda security clampdown, itself introduced in the wake of the shooting of a garda in neighbouring Roscommon several days earlier. The captured IRA documents from the van indicated the extent to which the Republic was being used for training camps. According to one document, there were five camps at that time in Counties Galway and Mayo,

Table 6. Garda seizures of arms, ammunition and explosives, 1980[20]

Quantity	Type
189	Firearms (including rifles, shotguns, machine guns, pistols, revolvers, etc.)
31,911	Rounds of ammunition (assorted)
3,941	Shotgun cartridges
9	Hand grenades
14,280lbs	Explosive mixture
148lbs	Gelignite/gelatin
81 pints	Nitrobenzene
138	Bombs (various homemade types)
15	Incendiary devices
69	Rockets (including 2 RPG-7 Russian rockets)
1,010	Detonators (assorted)

codenamed Eagle, Hawk, Falcon, Kestrel and ASU. One of these was possibly in the Letterfrack area. Early one morning several years later, two farmers inadvertently stumbled upon a number of armed men in combat gear in that locality while searching for sheep, while a newspaper reported that 'hitch-hikers travelling through the remote mountain areas claim to have heard the sound of gunfire'.[21]

Following the capture of the IRA documents at Maam Cross, gardaí in Mayo were quick to discount the idea of permanent or even semi-permanent IRA training camps in the county, claiming that even camps lasting thirty minutes were unlikely. However, an IRA defector in 1982 described to gardaí how Mayo was extensively used by the IRA for training; he also spoke of how he had visited 'training camps throughout Ireland'.[22] In May 1984, firemen dealing with gorse fires in a remote area of Mayo near Kiltimagh discovered another IRA training camp, described as a firing range 'dug into the mountain top and covered over to avoid detection'.[23]

Among the matériel captured by gardaí at Maam Cross in July 1980 were posters describing marksmanship techniques and intelligence-gathering; these were found concealed under a black plastic bag in the back of the van. Also discovered were allowance sheets and diaries giving details of expenditure on petrol and ammunition. Another document included a list of car numbers and descriptions which, upon investigation, were found to refer to vehicles owned by members of the gardaí. One document on intelligence instructed volunteers to 'get a bum name and get to know all about it'. It stressed the importance of building up a false identity with driving licences and student cards, and of learning the details associated with the 'bum name'. Indeed, both arrested men gave false names to gardaí at the time of their arrest and also refused to recognise the court when they were tried. One was sentenced to three years' imprisonment; the other received a five-year sentence.[24]

Another document discovered in the van was titled 'Instructions for training officers, Irish Republican Army, 1979', indicating continuing sophistication and role delineation within the organisation. Indeed, IRA training during the 1980s was categorised by increasing specialisation, including sniper training camps, and particularly in the establishment of dedicated active service units (ASUs) for the England department.[25] Later in the decade, the current affairs publication *The Phoenix* reported on a two-man unit arrested in London. The article described the men as 'all-rounders', between them being 'bomb-maker, driver, reconnaissance, bomb-layer, armed guard and communication liaison'.[26]

A lengthy article entitled 'Five days in an IRA training camp' published in the Provisionals' magazine *Iris* detailed the form of IRA training camps during this period. Although clearly a propaganda piece intended to demonstrate the professionalism of IRA training, the article does align with accounts of interviewees, as well as garda intelligence and discoveries. Given the changed atmosphere and attitudes among the Southern establishment since the early days of the 'Troubles', security was paramount. The author of 'Five days' described the means by which he and his comrades reached their billet:

> We had left Belfast about twelve hours earlier, travelling separately to avoid the risk of being arrested together if anything went wrong. We reached our first pick-up point in the Free State without incident, however, and made the pre-arranged contact with the local IRA … Night fell at last, thankfully, and we were smuggled out of the house and into a car … Two changes of car later … an endless succession of winding country lanes behind us, we were just beginning to appreciate how the IRA is able to organise a regular flow of training camps for Volunteers across the North.[27]

The author and those travelling with him were brought to 'a semi-derelict farmhouse … thought locally to be uninhabited' with 'black plastic sheeting tacked up across the window'. The article details how the first few days of training involved a repetitive cycle of stripping, cleaning and reassembling all weapons. One of the primary motives for this was psychological: 'constant handling of the component parts helps to "demystify" the guns, which most of us haven't handled before, and so to feel comfortable with them'. Training weapons differed in each camp. In this case, trainees were given instructions in the following: Colt .45, 9mm Browning pistol, .357 Magnum, M1 carbine, Ruger mini-14, AR-15 (the weapon most commonly associated with the Provisional IRA), AK-47, .22 rifle, Beretta sub-machine gun, Uzi 9mm, a shotgun and a Gewehr 43 rifle. This represents an unusually wide range of firearms for a training camp and it is likely that the article was used to demonstrate the breadth of the organisation's armoury for propaganda purposes. Despite firing ranges being located in remote areas, further precautions were often taken. The author of 'Five days' noted how the training officers had constructed a device referred to as an 'acoustic tunnel' to blanket the sound of the firing:

> The 'tunnel' on this occasion consists of a triangular wire frame with narrow wooden supports, placed on top of a large flat rock several feet high ... The wire frame is covered by strips of foam, with our sleeping bags laid over the top. The whole structure is about ten feet long and eighteen inches at its apex.[28]

The article mentions a similar method involving a series of car tyres attached rim to rim. In fact, such a method was in use at the training camp discovered by gardaí near Kiltimagh in 1984.

While useful in suppressing the sound of many firearms, these constructions could not mask the sound of an AK-47. When fired, that weapon produces a distinctive cracking sound, which is not easily masked. As the IRA acquired more of these weapons during the 1980s, means were sought to circumvent this problem. In 1988, gardaí in County Laois discovered that long, horizontal abandoned mineshafts were being used for arms training. *The Irish Times* noted of one find, that it was 'regarded as being of some significance by the Gardaí as it confirms intelligence reports that the IRA has a network of such underground "training areas" in the Republic.'[29] Forty-foot trailers and remote cattle sheds were also used for arms training, as they could muffle the sound of an AK-47 if sufficiently soundproofed with sacks of hay.

The purpose of these camps was not purely weapons training. Education, intelligence and counterintelligence played an increasing role in IRA training from the late 1970s and 'Five days' noted how arms training was interspersed with political discussions, while the last day of training was focused entirely on intelligence-gathering. For those travelling to training camps, security became even tighter from the late 1980s. Upon arrival at a prearranged drop-off point, volunteers were picked up and brought to a farmhouse or remote location, stripped naked and checked for bugging equipment. They were then given different clothes to wear, tracksuits or 'normal wear', with a few pairs of socks, and brought to the training camp. Upon returning, their clothes were washed and the lint traps dispersed in the open air. The local

IRA regularly varied the people they used to wash the clothes, to minimise the chance of forensic evidence building up in any machine from gunpowder residue transferred to trainees' clothing. When volunteers arrived back to their own command area in the North, they were then debriefed by their intelligence officer. Specifically, they were asked questions such as 'Did you know where you were?'; 'What landmarks did you see?'; 'Did you see any road signs?' Following the debriefing, a report was written up and the training area unit was censured or commended by GHQ, depending on what was revealed. One interviewee maintained that north Munster had very good anti-surveillance techniques, while the Kerry IRA, in the main, was rather more lackadaisical. However, they could get away with it as there were such high levels of support in that county for militant republicanism.[30]

In August 1980 another IRA training camp was disrupted by gardaí, this time near the village of Inniskeen in County Monaghan. According to contemporary reports, four rifles and one partly assembled weapon, as well as more than 1,000 rounds of ammunition, were seized. A garda spokesman said that there were signs of a firing range and other weaponry-training facilities at an old railway embankment where the arms cache was uncovered. A tip-off from IRA informer Sean O'Callaghan had led Special Branch detectives and uniformed gardaí to the scene, and it is understood that a number of men made their escape from the area before the police net closed.[31] The following month, a joint army–garda force raided a farmhouse in the remote countryside near Ballyduff in north Kerry, acting on another tip-off from O'Callaghan. Five men and a woman were arrested, three of whom were from the North, while the others were from Cork, Dublin and Westmeath. All six initially tried to escape, as recounted by the female member, Deirdre McDonnell:

On that day the gardaí surrounded the vacant, unfurnished house we were staying in. We were upstairs when I heard the sound of motor cars. I ran into one of the front bedrooms and saw the cars. I shouted to the others and we all bolted out the back bedroom window to escape. We scattered in all directions. I tried to run between the two houses. There was a wall separating them. I thought the gardaí would run round either side of the two houses so I got over the wall thinking, 'Happy days,' but one of the gardaí backtracked and gave chase.[32]

McDonnell had suffered a broken foot when jumping from the bedroom window and so was easily caught by the pursuing garda. One of the men was shot in the leg by gardaí as he tried to flee.

Information from O'Callaghan indicated that this IRA unit was planning to mount a multiple bank raid operation on nearby Listowel at the end of the annual Listowel races. The safehouse thus seems to have been both a training camp and staging point for local IRA fundraising operations given the various documents captured in the security operation. One booklet, detailing recruiting and training for the IRA, had a page headlined 'Camp report', which detailed the training in arms of five people. It noted that 'Barry' was very good as he had used weapons before, but his political attitudes were not very good, although he was interested. Another trainee was good at 'handling', with average shooting, but needed to learn more on politics. A third had good 'pick-up' and 'handling', and his shooting was very good. It was suggested that he should be given extra training 'as he would make a very good shot'. A number of maps and posters were also found in the house, one of which was subsequently shown in court. This gave instructions to 'never sight your weapon on the target for less than 20 seconds'. Seven firearms and over 4,000 rounds of ammunition were discovered in the house, as were targets used in firing practice. During the trial, all the defendants refused to recognise the court. A number of their supporters and family members attended the trial and caused disruption from the galleries, with one sentenced to a month in prison for contempt of court. Four of the men were given seven-year prison sentences, while the fifth, a Dublin bus driver, received eight years. McDonnell was sentenced to eighteen months, which she considered 'an overnighter in comparison to the sentences the lads received'. Shouts from the gallery of 'Up the IRA' and 'This is worse even than Belfast' accompanied the sentencing.[33]

IRA Financing

The garda disruption and arrest of this IRA unit revealed that ambitious armed robberies were still very much a part of IRA strategy. The previous year, nearly £2.25 million had been taken in 250 armed robberies throughout the state, much of which went to Provisional IRA coffers. There were 237 armed robberies in 1978, with £837,000 taken, while in 1977 there were 217 armed robberies, with £1,989,731 taken.[34] The number of armed robberies declined to 194 in 1980.[35] In April of that year, the Allied Irish Bank (AIB) in New Ross, County Wexford, was raided by five armed men who fired shots during the robbery. Just over £67,000 was stolen. A twenty-one-year-old father of two from the town – described by the judge as being 'on the periphery of the crime' – received a five-year prison sentence in the Special Criminal Court. None of the other participants, believed to be from Northern Ireland, were apprehended.[36] That same month, two young men from the North took part in an armed robbery at a plastics factory at Annagry, County Donegal. The robbery was planned in order to take the Friday wage packets, worth £14,000. The two men were arrested following a car chase involving gardaí and workers from the factory. When arrested and charged, they refused to recognise the court. Both men were sentenced to twelve-year prison terms: seven years for intent to endanger life and five years for IRA membership. As the sentences were read out, there were cheers and applause for the men from the gallery of the court. Both gave clenched-fist salutes and shouted 'Up the Provos' as they left the dock.[37]

Over the course of the summer, there were several other significant armed robberies likely carried out by IRA units. That June, also in Donegal, a raid on a branch of Northern Bank by four armed and masked men netted £20,000, while in Killarney another AIB was targeted. The two men involved in the raid, both armed with pistols, padlocked the doors to the bank upon leaving, locking two dozen customers and employees inside. According to a garda spokesman, they were reported as shouting 'something like "Up Roscommon" as they were leaving'.[38]

There had been several fatalities during the course of IRA armed robberies in the late 1970s, with a number of other people, including a garda, injured. In September 1980, during the pursuit of several suspected armed robbers near Merrion Gates in south Dublin, a Special Branch detective fired two bursts from a sub-machine gun over the heads of the fleeing men, as well as a number of civilians on a beach. Several months earlier, a three-man INLA unit opened fire on two gardaí after a double bank robbery in Kells, County Meath. According to reports, the gardaí had rammed the raiders' intended getaway vehicle while they were engaged in the second robbery. When they emerged, they fired on the gardaí in their patrol car before hijacking another vehicle and making their escape. The hijacked vehicle was later found burned out in Rathkenny, about a dozen miles from the town. Dessie Grew was later charged and imprisoned in Portlaoise prison in connection with the Kells robberies, having received some of the stolen money. He was acquitted of the charge of participating in the robbery. The evidence for that charge was based on fingerprints found on the licence plate of the original getaway car, which had been stolen in Monaghan town. According to Grew, he had on many occasions made up number plates for customers as part of his profession. Bernadette McAliskey also provided an alibi for the defendant, claiming that he and another man were in her home discussing a planned Anti H-Block march around the time of the robbery. Grew was a member of the INLA at this time, though he subsequently joined the Provisional IRA. He was shot dead along with another IRA volunteer, Martin McCaughey, by concealed British soldiers as they approached an arms dump in County Armagh in 1990.[39]

July 1980 marked a grim month for An Garda Síochána, as two serving members of the force, Henry Byrne and John Morley, were shot dead in County Roscommon during a shoot-out with armed robbers. The two were the first gardaí to be killed in the line of duty in that decade. It was also the first time since 1940 that two gardaí had been killed in the same incident. In the wake of the shooting, gardaí and the army began an intensive manhunt for the culprits across the northwest of the country, one outcome of which was the capture of the two IRA volunteers at Maam Cross noted earlier. A man was arrested shortly after the killings, having sought aid at a rural home due to injuries sustained in the shoot-out. A second man in a dishevelled state was arrested several days later near Frenchpark, County Roscommon, having evidently been living rough since the incident, while a third man was arrested over a week later in Galway city. The trial of the three men was heated, with senior gardaí openly calling for the death penalty: all three were charged with capital murder, though only for the killing of Garda Byrne. As Garda Morley had been in civilian clothes at the time of his death, it was felt that the case for deliberate killing of a garda would be less clear-cut to prosecute. The men were found guilty and sentenced to death, although this was later commuted to forty-year terms of imprisonment without remission. One of the men was freed in 1995, however, after it emerged that there were conflicting testimonies among gardaí during the trial. At the time of the shooting, the INLA was wrongly believed to have been responsible.

Its political wing, the Irish Republican Socialist Party (IRSP), claimed that only one of the men had links to the organisation dating back five years; this was the man released in 1995. It is now accepted that a splinter group from the small, far-left republican Saor Éire organisation was responsible for the robbery and deaths of the two gardaí. That organisation was believed to be defunct by 1980 but had simply split into several small groups of varying political principles.[40]

On 13 October 1980, two armed robberies took place in the town of Callan, County Kilkenny. Rightly suspecting that the IRA were responsible, gardaí were ordered to check on the movements of known republicans in neighbouring counties. Gardaí Seamus Quaid and Donal Lyttleton were tasked with locating and questioning Peter Rogers, a Belfast man who had settled in Wexford. Rogers was an IRA member and prominent republican, having been involved in the celebrated IRA escape from the *Maidstone* prison ship in 1972. After fruitlessly searching for Rogers for most of the day, the two gardaí happened upon his van close to a quarry at Cleariestown that night. Rogers and the two gardaí were acquainted so, when the van pulled over, no particular precautions were taken in confronting him. Unbeknownst to the gardaí, however, he was in the process of transporting arms and explosives that night and was armed with a pistol. According to the official garda account:

> When the Gardaí went to search the van, which was subsequently found to contain explosives, the driver suddenly drew a gun. He demanded the two Gardaí should let him go, firing a shot over their heads. Detective Garda Quaid drew his gun. Shots were exchanged. The gunman was injured in the left leg in an attempt to disable him. The gunman shot Detective Garda Quaid who subsequently died from the injuries he sustained.[41]

Rogers retreated to a nearby house, from where a local priest later arranged his surrender to gardaí. In 2014, Rogers claimed to have been acting under orders from Martin McGuinness and Gerry Adams that night to transport explosives to England. The explosives were considered unstable, and Rogers was carrying out the order reluctantly. This claim was rejected by Sinn Féin. While he was sentenced to death for the murder of Garda Quaid, this sentence was later commuted to forty years' imprisonment. During his incarceration in Portlaoise prison, Rogers left the Provisional republican movement, joining with unaligned republicans such as Dessie O'Hare, as he claimed that the movement was not doing enough for republican prisoners serving life sentences.[42] Rogers was released under the terms of the Good Friday Agreement.

The events leading up to the killing of Garda Quaid in October 1980 were one of the consequences of the IRA adopting a cellular structure in the latter part of the previous decade. Had Rogers known an armed robbery was due to take place in a neighbouring county on that October day, it is unlikely that he would have been moving arms and explosives, as it was common practice for gardaí to check on local republicans when events such as armed robberies took place in the locality. As one interviewee recalled:

> Very often a robbery would happen, you know, and right in the same area a camp could be going ahead. People had been caught because the guards had been everywhere, and you'd be there 'What the hell happened?' and somebody would hear on the radio that there'd been a robbery so it'd be 'Why didn't they tell us about it?'[43]

Referring specifically to the incident involving Rogers, the interviewee stated:

> I'd say it all happened because there was a robbery in Kilkenny a hundred miles away, or less even, seventy miles away. But anybody acting suspicious, and this guy who was later accused of shooting the Garda did look suspicious, but he was doing something else, you know. He didn't know about the robbery taking place. See the trouble, too, is that there was a change back in the seventies, late seventies. A lot of it was run in cities like the old flying columns, ASUs and all that. But they changed it all into something new … They developed smaller units that were given certain jobs to do, then nobody else would know. And there'd be certain units specifically for fundraising we'll say and others for different operations. Then there was other units, they had to be really tight, the ones that went to England, you know, completely independent of each other. But the problem with that system, that's fine, but somehow or other there could be two operations going side by

side. One goes wrong then the rest get caught … A lot of near misses. The boys might just have gone down one road and the guards would go whizzing by another and neither of the twain would meet by pure luck. By pure luck.

Although uninvolved in the shooting or connected bank robberies, the interviewee was in Wexford at that time and was caught in the security net:

Of course, there was some fierce bad jobs done as well, you know. Yeah, behind the scenes, when I was on the run, I was involved in organising supplies and I was always, kind of, behind the scenes and doing different things that way. So, there was a guard, a detective shot in Wexford in 1980 and I was in Wexford at the time so I didn't get out in time so I was caught … Of course, there was all sorts of people, they [the IRA] made an awful lot of enemies for themselves in Wexford that time, you know.

The GAA and the 'Troubles'

The conclusion of the above excerpt hints at the local backlash against republicans following the shooting of Garda Quaid. This was to be expected in the event of any garda being killed in the line of duty. However, Quaid's prominence in the community was heightened by his athletic reputation. Both he and Garda John Morley had been prominent GAA athletes in their youth. Morley had been on the winning team in the National Football League with County Mayo in 1970, while Quaid had been part of the All-Ireland Senior Hurling title-winning Wexford team in 1960. The killing of these gardaí in 1980 brought into sharp focus the GAA's ambiguous relationship with militant republicanism.

As an all-Ireland organisation, the GAA had maintained a benign position on the concept of militant republicanism for much of the twentieth century. Insofar as the association's constitution took any quasi-political stance, its stated goal was to strengthen the 'national identity in a thirty-two county Ireland'.[44] Ultimately, this aspiration was politically limited and although the GAA's broad nationalist agenda was no secret, it was generally not acted upon. Overall, the association did its best to prevent any nationalist political dimension interfering unduly in its running.[45] The difficulty for the GAA, in terms of the realities of partition and any conflict sparked by that political reality, lay in the fierce independence of local and county boards. This local independence, coupled with the reality of the association's celebrated historic links with militant republicanism, means one could rarely speak of any definitive stance on the part of the GAA as a body. Four of the seven founding members of the GAA had been in the Irish Republican Brotherhood, the precursor to the IRA, while numerous clubs across the country are named after local or well-known Irish republicans. During the IRA's campaign of 1956–62, the funerals of several Southern IRA volunteers witnessed what could at best be described as an ambiguity towards militant republicanism on the part of GAA clubs and members. The funerals of Sean South and Fergal O'Hanlon – the biggest funerals of their generation – are indicative. O'Hanlon's funeral procession was led by members of the Monaghan senior football team, while South's was attended by senior GAA dignitaries.[46] The Sunday after the funerals of those two men, two minutes' silence was observed in Croke Park at a hurling match attended by 6,000 people 'as a mark of respect to the memory of the two raiders who lost their lives'.[47] Later that year, local GAA clubs in County Wexford were formally represented at the funeral of IRA volunteer Paddy Parle, one of those killed when an IRA landmine exploded prematurely at Edentubber, County Louth.[48]

During the early years of the 'Troubles', a number of branches of the GAA had openly expressed support for the Provisional IRA and rallied around its imprisoned members, most notably in 1973, following the capture of the ship *Claudia* carrying five tons of weapons to the IRA from Libya. When Donal Whelan lost his teaching job for his role in that attempted importation, the GAA national congress voted to use every means necessary to have him reinstated.[49] Throughout the 'Troubles', there was a strong overlap of membership between the GAA and militant republican groups. Prior to the IRA split of 1969–70, older veterans in Cork city often made use of their GAA contacts in order to sound out potential sympathisers for the provision of safe houses, for example.[50] The central position of the association within many communities across the state ensured a sense of identity and helped build up relationships and bonds of trust that transcended political boundaries and allegiances. Speaking of his imprisonment during the 1980s, Martin Ferris – a notable Kerry footballer in his youth – put it thus:

> I live in Ardfert. Ardfert would not have been seen as a Sinn Féin village, or a Sinn Féin area. It would be Fianna Fáil, Fine Gael, Labour area … But the GAA clubs, hurling or football, in Ardfert and the football club in Churchill, the youth club, various people of the various political parties, all rallied behind my family … Now I'd been involved in the GAA all my life, I've played a lot of football and I played soccer and everything, it's constant contact with people. And no matter how I was demonised in the press, people saw me in a different light.[51]

A sequence of events beginning in Belfast in 1979 served to bring the conflict forcefully home to Southern members of the GAA, forcing the organisation to confront its previously ambiguous position. In August of that year, a Sinn Féin rally held in the GAA's Casement Park in Belfast erupted into cheers at the appearance of several masked IRA volunteers armed with newly imported automatic weapons. What was essentially a republican photo opportunity for propaganda purposes fixed the GAA directly at the centre of controversy given the use of its land for the rally. Some within the ranks of the association called for a denunciation of IRA-specific violence following this controversy. Casement Park had previously been requisitioned by the British Army in 1972 and it is likely that ill-feeling towards the military, as well as the strong support for the IRA in west Belfast, were factors in the internal disputes and led to local rejection of the calls for denunciation.[52] Another noteworthy event, which took place the following year, was an RTÉ *Frontline* special on the GAA's links with militant republicanism at this time. The episode covered issues such as the Casement Park controversy, the Tyrone county board's support for the 'Smash H-Block' protests and the Provisional republican movement's funeral escort for John Joe Sheehy (discussed later in the chapter). The broadcasting of the *Frontline* episode caused uproar among association members and was described as a 'witch-hunt'.[53]

For those who understood the situation for GAA clubs in Northern Ireland, it was difficult not to be sympathetic to their support for militant republicanism. It was widely reported that GAA members in that state were the subject of frequent harassment by the Royal Ulster Constabulary (RUC) and British Army, ranging from roadblocks outside Gaelic grounds to threats and even violence. In 1988 a British soldier shot dead a young man, Aidan McAnespie, as he walked across the border between Counties Tyrone and Monaghan. McAnespie, a member of his local GAA football team, lived in Tyrone but worked in Monaghan and crossed the border daily. He had been subject to intensive British Army and RUC harassment and threats for some time prior to his death. In Armagh, throughout the 'Troubles', club and county teams were given an unwritten additional allowance of time to arrive at matches due to team members being held up by British forces at checkpoints. It was widely believed that these checkpoints were there purely for harassment. Internal resistance to outrage from the moderate wing of the GAA was strengthened by the ongoing British occupation of the GAA grounds at Crossmaglen, which had witnessed a protest demonstration of forty clubs from across the North in 1979.[54]

There was dissension within the ranks, however, at the association's continued soft stance towards the IRA. This was starkly highlighted by two IRA operations, which took place just days after the Casement Park rally: the bombing attack on Louis Mountbatten and several other civilians, and the Warrenpoint ambush on the British Army's parachute regiment. A member of the Tipperary county board, who subsequently resigned his position, described himself as a 'shamed onlooker at a decade of congresses passing motions parallel to republican purposes – and never once even mentioning the existence of the IRA'.[55] Such controversies called into question a recent amendment to rule seven of the GAA's constitution. Until 1979, that rule declared that 'the Association shall be non-political and non-sectarian'. A one-word amendment at the 1979 Congress changed the rule to 'the Association shall be non-party political and non-sectarian.' This change allowed for engagement in all forms of political activity that wasn't specific to any one party and allowed for any amount of interpretation as far as republicans were concerned.

Because the Anti H-Block campaign was not a formal party-political action, activity in support of it was not prohibited. In May 1980 the Cork H-Block Action Committee held a meeting attended by upwards of 100 people in the Mitchelstown GAA hall.[56] County-convention motions in early 1980 included one from Kerry calling for the GAA's condemnation of the conditions in the H-Blocks. Wexford went one step further, calling for a full British withdrawal from Northern Ireland. In response, the Sligo convention unanimously approved a call for the banning of all political discussions by GAA bodies. Three other counties – Dublin, Leitrim and Galway – threw their weight behind this campaign. In addition, a number of clubs across other counties had been calling for a reversion to the old rule seven since the 1979 Congress. Although that motion did not pass, opposition to the amendment was described as strong. Such was the level of tension among the association's members regarding what stance to take on the conflict in the North that GAA President Paddy McFlynn opened the 1980 Congress with an appeal to members to approach the issues 'in a spirit of charity and forbearance'.[57] Unsurprisingly, the political aspect of the association's 1980 Congress was dominated by the H-Block issue. *Hibernia* had anticipated the possibility of '3,000 GAA clubs with about half a million members throwing their support behind the prisoners in the rapidly-deteriorating situation in the jails' and indeed a motion did pass condemning, on humanitarian grounds, 'the torture in H Block, Long Kesh'.[58]

That same month, January 1980, there was a major political controversy after the funeral of Kerry GAA legend, John Joe Sheehy. Considered one of the greatest footballers of all time, Sheehy was also a lifelong republican and supported the Provisional IRA when the 'Troubles' broke out. His funeral was attended by prominent figures in public life and local politicians, as well as many republicans and GAA members, including a number of top GAA officials, past and present.[59] The first major outrage on the day of the funeral occurred as the hearse left the Bon Secours Hospital in Tralee. A masked and uniformed man stepped from a car and fired three shots into the air from a pistol before disappearing into the crowd. As the cortège made its way to the parish church of St John's, the crowd of several thousand were led by an IRA guard of honour. The republican movement also took control of directing traffic in areas where the cortège passed, while it was reported that gardaí stood in the background.[60] Among those attending the funeral were Fianna Fáil TD and Minister of State, Tom McEllistrim, and Taoiseach Charlie Haughey's aide-de-camp, Commandant Michael Harrington. Despite rubbishing reports of gardaí relinquishing traffic control duties to republicans, Minister for Justice Gerry Collins nevertheless established an inquiry to look into the matter. In rebuttal to the minister's denial, *The Irish*

Times reported that their 'correspondent in the area confirmed that traffic had been directed by known members of the Provisional Movement during the removal of the remains from St John's Church'. Deputy McEllistrim denied being aware of any paramilitary displays: 'I was there and there was no guard of honour that I was aware of.' His fellow Fianna Fáil TD Timothy 'Chubb' O'Connor merely said of the event that, when it came to certain issues, people in the area had their own way of doing things. Despite McEllistrim's claims, numerous newspapers had already published very clear photos of the republican guard of honour. Fine Gael TD, Michael Begley, commented that McEllistrim ought to 'apply immediately to the relevant authority for disability benefit as his sight and hearing are obviously both impaired'. The Fine Gael front bench released a statement accusing the Taoiseach of 'insulting the army', while the National Union of Journalists (NUJ) expressed concerns at RTÉ suppressing video footage of the funeral.[61]

While British officials in the Dublin embassy did not take news of a local TD's attendance too seriously, they noted in a report to London:

> More surprising still was the fact that the Taoiseach was represented at the funeral by his ADC, Commandant Michael Harrington. It seems almost inconceivable that Mr Haughey should have been unaware of Sheehy's sympathies and we are inclined to interpret the presence of Commandant Harrington at the funeral as further evidence of Mr Haughey's desire to keep well in with the Republican backwoodsmen of the West. For what it's worth, the Garda in Tralee are apparently investigating the 'para-military display'.[62]

In November 1981, in an attempt to avoid a repetition of events in Tralee, more than a hundred armed detectives and uniformed gardaí attended the funeral of Kildare IRA veteran, Frank Driver. According to contemporary reports, 'one in five at the well-attended ceremony on Saturday was a Garda and squads of Special Branch detectives from Dublin Castle were drafted in to virtually seal off the graveyard'.[63]

Although the GAA, along with other public bodies, had condemned the murder of Garda Seamus Quaid and expressed their sympathies, the association refused to denounce all 'Troubles'-related violence. A league hurling match at

Enniscorthy between Wexford and Cork a fortnight after Quaid's death began with a minute's silence and the flying of the tricolour at half-mast. However, it became a scene of ignominious disrespect when rebel songs were played over the loudspeaker at half-time. Many of the 1,700-strong crowd joined in the singing. Despite GAA President Paddy McFlynn unequivocally condemning 'the men of violence', *The Irish Times* quite accurately summed up the situation, stating: 'it was shown, once again, that the GAA speaks with many voices'.[64] The contradictions behind McFlynn's condemnation were highlighted in a letter to that paper where the author, a GAA player, pointed out: 'The furthest the GAA leadership was prepared to commit the GAA in the face of violence was that the association didn't condone it – whatever that meant. Only after the Provisional IRA occupation of Casement Park in August 1979 did the GAA president condemn violence and then only in response to a public challenge to do so.'[65] Following the Enniscorthy incident, the Rathmines garda GAA branch (some seventy police officers) withdrew their participation in association affairs. The branch also discussed the possibility of refusing to carry out any assigned stewarding duties in future, a level of interference which *An Phoblacht* claimed 'points to a police state'.[66]

The day after the incident at the Wexford–Cork match, seven republican prisoners in the H-Blocks began a hunger strike. This event, and another hunger strike the following year, ensured that the prison situation in the North would continue to be a topic of contention and division within the GAA for some time.

Further Killings in the South

The shooting dead of gardaí in two separate incidents shook the state in 1980. However, they were not the only 'Troubles'-related killings to take place in the Republic that year. Over the course of the summer, two men linked to the UDR were killed south of the border. In June, George Elliot (48) was shot dead at a cattle mart in Ballybay, a small town in County Monaghan. According to witness accounts, the mart had just concluded, and Elliot was looking at cattle in one of the pens when a man in his early twenties approached him and fired at least five shots before escaping on foot to a waiting car containing two other men. Elliott was a Tyrone native and leading member of the UUP in the region. He had reportedly resigned from the UDR over a year prior to the attack. An IRA statement in the aftermath of his killing alleged that he continued to operate in an 'undercover capacity', gathering intelligence on republicans in border areas.[67] In January 1981, a Monaghan man was put on trial in Dublin for the murder of Elliot. During the trial, it emerged that the defendant had been interrogated for thirty hours following his arrest. As a result, statements made by him at that time were ruled as inadmissible and he was acquitted.[68]

Two months after the killing of George Elliot, three men stopped the car of UDR member, William John Clarke (59), near the village of Pettigo – which straddles the Fermanagh–Donegal border – with their own vehicle and shot him a number of times. The men subsequently hijacked a third car to make their escape. The owner of that vehicle later reported that he, his sister and three young children were coming from Lough Derg when they spotted two cars parked on the roadway with three men in combat uniform standing nearby. They thought it was an army checkpoint until one of the men, with a black scarf wrapped around his face, ran towards them with an automatic rifle and ordered them out of the car before commandeering it. Gardaí from Pettigo station were involved in a high-speed car chase with the men and, at one point, two gardaí in a patrol car were held at rifle-point in an isolated laneway. The men then abandoned the hijacked car and made off into the surrounding hills. A nineteen-year-old Derry man subsequently stood trial on murder and hijacking charges related to this killing. In his trial the following year, statements he had made while in garda custody were ruled inadmissible due to his being sleep-deprived at the time. The presiding judge, Mr Justice D'Arcy ruled that there was no prima facie case against the defendant in relation to the murder charge, but he was tried and sentenced to five years' imprisonment on the hijacking charge.[69]

A number of deadly border attacks on members of the British Army and RUC took place during the year. In February, the IRA killed two members of the RUC in a remote-controlled landmine attack on their Land Rover near the Fermanagh town of Rosslea. Command wires were found on a small hill overlooking the road and it was believed that the IRA unit responsible escaped over the border just a few miles away. The use of remote-controlled bombs, particularly in rural areas, was a deadly addition to IRA tactics in the late 1970s.[70] This attack was the third in the area in the space of a fortnight. The previous week, a UDR corporal was shot dead as he worked on his farm while, several days earlier, another UDR member was shot and seriously wounded in a gun attack as he returned home from work.[71] The IRA also shot an alleged informer in the border area later that year. The victim, Ross Hearst (56), was abducted in County Monaghan and later discovered shot dead next to his burnt-out car near the Armagh border village of Middletown. While the IRA claimed that Hearst was an informer, others believed that his political sympathies and family connections lay behind his death. His daughter was a member of the UDR and Hearst himself had been attending a meeting of the Royal Black Preceptory – an Orange Order-linked organisation – on the evening of his abduction.[72]

In July 1981 a Monaghan man went on trial in Dublin for the murder of Hearst, as allowed under the Criminal Law (Jurisdiction) Act. However, several days into the trial, the defence objected that the defendant had not been asked at the outset whether he wished to stand trial in Northern Ireland or the Republic, as was his right under that Act. The judge acknowledged his error in not informing the defendant of his choice in the matter and the case was thrown out. However, following a retrial in 1983, the accused was found guilty and received a life sentence.[73] In a rare reversal of border activity, two Northern Irish men, members of the Ulster Defence Association (UDA), went on trial in the Special Criminal Court in Dublin in February 1980 charged with conspiracy to murder. The two had been arrested in Swanlinbar, County Cavan, in December 1979, having been reported to gardaí by several locals as acting suspiciously. It was believed they were en route to assassinate Francis McGirl, the nephew of veteran republican John Joe McGirl, at the time of their arrest. Francis McGirl had earlier been acquitted for his part in the murder of Louis Mountbatten. The two defendants were found guilty and sentenced to seven- and five-year jail terms, respectively. Francis McGirl died in 1995, in a road traffic accident, when his tractor crashed into a ditch.[74]

H-Block Protests and Hunger Strike

Spring of 1980 marked the four-year anniversary of the revocation of the special category status previously afforded to republican prisoners in Northern Ireland. Since then, hundreds of IRA and INLA prisoners in the prisons of the North had refused to wear prison clothing and instead used the blankets provided in their cells as clothing. This refusal to wear prison clothing, instigated by nineteen-year-old IRA volunteer Kieran Nugent, was referred to as the 'blanket protest'. The protest gradually escalated after a dissenting prisoner was badly beaten by prison officers during a forced strip-search and put in solitary confinement. When word of this spread within the prison, other republican prisoners smashed their cell furniture in protest. After that, authorities removed all remaining items from the cells save mattresses, blankets and Bibles. Republican prisoners claimed that, whenever they left their cells, they were subject to violent beatings from the warders. Violence also typically accompanied the 'mirror searches', where naked prisoners were forcibly spread-eagled over a mirror during searches. As the cells did not contain toilet facilities, prisoners used buckets and had to 'slop out' in the mornings. It was alleged that warders were deliberately spilling buckets of urine and faeces on the prisoners' mattresses, which were on the floor of the prison cells. In March 1978, IRA and INLA prisoners thus began refusing to leave their cells. They poured their urine out under the cell doors and spread their faeces on the walls of the cells, initiating the 'dirty protest'. During this period, there were regular reports of assaults by prison warders: often several men in full riot gear would beat isolated, naked prisoners. At this same time, the British interrogation centre at Castlereagh was coming under increasing censure from human rights groups for the alleged ill-treatment of republican detainees. Locals referred to Castlereagh as 'the conveyor belt', with the H-Blocks being the final destination for those processed through the centre.[75]

In response to the escalation of the prison crisis in the North, the IRA and INLA began to target prison officers for assassination. Between the revocation of special category status in March 1976 and the beginning of a hunger strike on 27 October 1980, nineteen prison officers were killed by republicans in the North. This was in contrast to the situation in the Republic where, with the exception of one shooting (discussed in Chapter 3), the IRA did not target prison officers. It was against the backdrop of this increasingly worsening prison situation in the North that the newspaper *Hibernia* commented sardonically on a conference hosted in Dublin by the Union of Students in Ireland (USI) on the subject of 'repression in Ireland': 'It must be difficult for radically-minded people, or anyone for that matter, to discuss "Repression in Ireland" for a whole afternoon without even a single reference to H-Block.' Indeed, it had been reported earlier that year that there was conflict within the

USI over manipulation of the union's policy by members who were affiliated with Sinn Féin–The Workers' Party, with allegations of 'secret manoeuvres and undemocratic methods' to ensure the leadership remained composed of anti-republicans.[76] In the week prior to the USI conference, the student union of Queen's University Belfast had passed a motion in favour of supporting special category status, setting it at odds with both the USI and the British National Union of Students.[77] Just how representative student unions were of the broader student population regarding issues and groups related to the 'Troubles' remains a topic of debate. In December 1981, Galway University's Political Discussion Society had its highest ever turnout when Anti H-Block MP Owen Carron was invited to speak.[78]

The atrocious conditions for republican prisoners in Northern Ireland, including in the women's prison in Armagh, continued throughout 1980. Bobby Sands, a leading republican prisoner at the time, understood the British position on the prison crisis and articulated it through his 'Breaker's Yard' thesis to fellow republicans. By demoralising the prisoners and forcing them to accept criminalisation policies, the British government hoped to break the back of support for the militant republican campaign on the outside.[79] As a former prisoner remarked of this view: 'what the Brits are into building here isn't just for breaking us. What's happening here is that the Brits have a closely worked out psychological approach ...'[80] Sands and others within the republican prison leadership understood that their struggle was simultaneously interlinked with the broader republican campaign, while also being a drain on its resources and a distraction from what was taking place on the outside. In an attempt to break the deadlock, a decision was taken by the prison leadership to start a hunger strike in late October 1980. The strike would involve seven men – six IRA prisoners and one INLA prisoner; three female republican prisoners in Armagh would join the strike in December. The hunger strike galvanised support North and South for the prisoners, who were campaigning on a slogan known as the 'Five Demands'. These were:

1. The right to wear their own clothing instead of prison uniform.
2. The right to abstain from prison work.
3. Freedom of association with other republican prisoners.
4. Restoration of visiting, parcel and letter privileges.

5.   Restoration of all prison sentence remissions which had been lost during the protest.

For a time in the late 1970s, the prison campaign in North Ireland had resonated strongly with people living in the South and there was significant turnout for demonstrations in support of the prisoners. However, by the end of that decade, numbers had dwindled as the crisis continued without resolution. In December 1979, in an effort to re-engage people, a meeting of over 500 people, including a number of leading trade unionists and several solicitors, convened to elect a Southern-based sub-committee to co-ordinate H-Block activity in the Republic.[81] Large protests were again organised throughout the state and, in March 1980, it was reported that 1,000 people took part in a rally in Dublin, with 500 attending an Anti H-Block meeting at the Connolly Hotel in Cork city.[82] In June, 'the largest crowd ever mobilised in Dublin on the H-Block issue' were treated to a concert where Christy Moore played, among others. Two years previously, Moore had produced a compilation album entitled *H Block*. The launch party had been raided by gardaí and the album's single '90 Miles from Dublin Town' received no airplay, despite selling thousands of copies and entering the Irish charts. On occasion, radio stations played the single's B-side, 'The Rights of Man, Repeal the Union'. In September 1980, the second Dublin conference of the National H-Block Committee took place, with 800 people attending. The following month, campaigners were given a stimulus when Taoiseach Charlie Haughey met with several families of imprisoned republicans. An additional morale boost came from the endorsement of Nora Connolly O'Brien, daughter of executed 1916 leader James Connolly, who congratulated the H-Block prisoners on their 'heroic stance'.

On 9 November, over 600 Anti H-Block protestors marched in Limerick city while an angry scuffle developed outside a church in Sligo between several elected representatives, the local priest and members of the Anti H-Block committee who were collecting funds in the churchyard.[83] Later that month three relatives of hunger strikers fasted outside Leinster House in Dublin for three days, while 200 students from the Students Against H-Block group marched from College Green to the USI headquarters, demanding that the student body make a statement in support of the prisoners' campaign. Several days later, more than 10,000 people from all over Ireland marched in

Dublin in support of the hunger strike. Among the speakers at the meeting was TD Neil Blaney.

As November slid into December, and the conditions of the hunger strikers deteriorated, the protest took on added urgency. On 5 December, a march was organised to the British Embassy in Ballsbridge in south Dublin. The protestors were stopped several hundred yards short of the embassy and there was some intermittent stone-throwing from a younger section of the crowd. The protest was largely peaceful, however, though effigies of Margaret Thatcher and Secretary of State for Northern Ireland Humphrey Atkins were burned. Of the attendees, number estimates range widely. Bernadette McAliskey claimed that there were 60,000 people in attendance, while the gardaí asserted 12,500; journalists estimated perhaps 15–20,000. While the impact of the Dublin march in March 1980 was downplayed by claims that most attendees were from the North, it was clear that citizens of the Republic were strongly represented in this later march.[84] The following week, there were work stoppages and further demonstrations in support of the hunger strikers. Newspapers reported over 1,000 marchers in Sligo and 'thousands' in Dundalk, while at the major refinery plant at Aughinish in County Limerick, 400 workers downed tools for a protest where they were addressed by a shop steward from the site. Several days later, there were further protests in Carlow town, as well as the cities of Cork, Dublin and Galway.[85] During this period, a Dublin City Council motion to express humanitarian concerns for the hunger strikers was voted down by Fine Gael and Labour members supported by Sinn Féin–The Workers' Party President Tomás Mac Giolla.

On 18 December, after fifty-three days, the hunger strike was called off by Brendan Hughes, Officer Commanding (O/C) of the IRA prisoners in the H-Blocks and one of the hunger strikers himself. The decision to end the strike came from a combination of two factors. The first was an understanding that the British would accede to the 'Five Demands', based on discussions between the republican leadership and key British authorities during the strike. The formal acknowledgement of this was in an apparent memorandum of understanding, a document that had not yet been produced by the British but was expected at any time. The second consideration was that Sean McKenna, one of the hunger strikers, was very close to death. Ultimately, though, the British reneged on the deal and the momentum of the protest campaign was halted with no gain, demoralising activists and campaigners North and South. In a 1980 review of the Republic of Ireland, British Ambassador Leonard Figg wrote:

> The ending of the hunger strike in the Maze prison on 18 December was received with immense relief in the Republic. I have no idea what might have happened if one or more of the hunger strikers had died. The Irish Government were certainly very worried. And it is likely that many who had been indifferent to the protest would have blamed the British for any troubles which dead hunger strikers might have caused. However, the murder in the Republic of two policemen in July and one in October by terrorists had hardened opinion against militant Republicanism. While the Irish Government took a close interest in our handling of the hunger strike their attitude was sympathetic and helpful throughout this difficult period. And public opinion remained indifferent or openly critical of the activities of the Anti H-Block Committee. There was little support for the marches. There has been a shift of opinion in the South and the man in the street now takes a more sympathetic view of the problem facing the British Government in its handling of Northern Ireland.[86]

Figg was certainly correct in identifying a 'hardened opinion' in the South towards militant republicanism as a result of garda deaths in 1980. His assessment of public opinion towards the prison campaign, and particularly people's attitudes to the 'problem facing the British Government', seem rather more fanciful and optimistic in hindsight. The prison issue remained unresolved and a second hunger strike, beginning in March 1981, would harden Irish attitudes towards Britain in ways not seen since Bloody Sunday nearly nine years earlier.

2

This Is the Real Thing,
We Are the IRA: 1981

In 1978 a British Army report drawn up by Brigadier General Glover, the most senior British Army officer in Northern Ireland, was intercepted by the IRA. Among the claims in the report was that: 'Republican terrorists can no longer bring crowds of active sympathizers onto the streets at will as a screen for gunmen … there is seldom much support even for traditional protest marches.'[1] By the latter part of the 1970s, a war weariness and despondency had indeed settled in many nationalist areas of Northern Ireland. However, the Anti H-Block campaign created a new cause to rally around and the increasing numbers on the streets during the 1980 hunger strike attested to the will of the people to demonstrate when there was a specific and timebound need. Perhaps such a development could not have been anticipated by the author of the 1978 report. And it is unlikely that anybody could have predicted the state of affairs North and South as 1981 drew to a close. By year's end, IRA prisoners had been elected to both British and Irish parliaments, and the nationalist areas of Belfast and Derry in particular had become politicised to a point hitherto unimaginable. In the Republic, the government and media looked on warily at a population which defied the long-settled narrative of no sympathy or support for the republican cause.

The hunger strike of 1981 represented a paradigm shift in a number of ways. It caused a policy reassessment within the IRA and Sinn Féin, and led to the passing of new legislation in Westminster barring convicted criminals from holding parliamentary office. It also precipitated a climax on the policy dispute that had wracked the embattled GAA surrounding political activity and the prison crisis. The IRA was also undergoing tactical appraisals in 1981.

Increased and improved security measures for banks and cash transit vans were continuing to reduce Southern Command's success in armed robberies. At the same time, the need for money within the republican movement was greater than ever. The prison campaign was not cheap, the considerable number of IRA prisoners across several jurisdictions had dependants in need of financial support, and weaponry was being depleted due to improved garda intelligence and collaboration with the RUC across the border. What seems to have been a trial fundraising operation, successfully implemented by the South Armagh IRA, subsequently kicked off a new avenue of IRA financing in the South. Kidnappings would become one of the hallmark activities of the IRA's Southern Command as a result. The success of that first kidnapping-for-ransom operation highlighted again how central the border regions were to the IRA's campaign and, in 1981, there were several high-profile attacks on civilian and military targets around this porous zone.

Border Attacks

Amidst the fallout from the failed 1980 hunger strike, as discussions were underway within the H-Blocks for a second campaign, the new year opened with several high-profile IRA attacks in the border region. In January, prominent unionists Norman Stronge (86) and his son, James (48), were shot dead by the Provisionals at their home in Tynan Abbey, County Armagh. The house, originally a thirteenth-century abbey, was situated just three kilometres from the border with County Monaghan. On the night of 21 January, an IRA unit of up to ten men in military clothing, including some of the most experienced operators in that area, approached the house in two stolen cars. The families who owned the cars were held captive in their homes by other armed men dressed in similar clothing. The IRA unit at the Stronge home used grenades or explosives to break through the abbey's heavy, locked doors. Father and son were then shot dead in the library, but not before having launched a flare, which alerted the nearby British Army and RUC. The explosions which had blown in the front doors caused a fire and the abbey was engulfed in flames. In the midst of this chaos, British forces arrived and set up a roadblock close to the burning building. They then engaged in a firefight with the IRA unit. After an exchange of up to twenty minutes, the IRA were able to disengage and escape towards the

Monaghan border in the vicinity of Glaslough. The land around Glaslough, particularly the Leslie Estate, was made up of forest, hills, bogs and small lakes so that, despite the Garda Special Task Force joining the hunt for the men, they were able to escape entirely. In a later search of the grounds of Tynan Abbey, the RUC found half-eaten sandwiches and lemonade cans, believed to have been left behind by IRA members who had been watching the house for some time.

According to the Provisionals, the Stronge family had been targeted as 'symbols of hated Unionism', with the attack being 'a direct reprisal for the whole series of Loyalist assassinations and murder attacks on Nationalist people and Nationalist activists which has gone on far too long. Our operations against these targets have been based on their involvement in the Crown forces.'[2] James Stronge had briefly been a member of the Northern Ireland Assembly and was a member of the RUC Reserve, while Norman had held a string of high-profile political positions in Northern Ireland, including Speaker of the House of Commons of Northern Ireland, though he had long since retired. The killings caused shock and despair locally. It has been alleged that among those involved in the attack on Tynan Abbey were veteran republicans Jim Lynagh and Seamus McElwaine.[3]

One man was later arrested in connection with the killings. Seamus Shannon (25), originally from Dungannon in County Tyrone, was arrested at his mobile home at Balbriggan, County Dublin, in July 1983. An order for extradition was subsequently processed and a lengthy legal battle and appeals process began. Ultimately, the extradition request was acceded to and Shannon was handed over to the RUC at the border near Newry in the summer of 1984. In delivering judgment, the Chief Justice said that the circumstances of the murder were so brutal, cowardly and callous that it would be a distortion of language if they were to be accorded the status of political offences or offences connected with political offences.[4] Shannon was charged with the murder of James and Norman Stronge, the prosecution evidence resting on two thumbprints found on one of the cars alleged to have been used in the attack. The defence counsel argued that this evidence established only that Shannon had been in contact with the car sometime prior to the finding of the prints and that there was ample opportunity for the prints to have gotten there entirely innocently. In an unsworn statement, Shannon claimed that he often drank in bars around Glaslough and had occasionally helped move cars that were parked haphazardly on the road. The owner of the vehicle said that, at some time before the vehicle was hijacked, he had been drinking in a bar at Glaslough and when he left the bar he found that his car had been moved. Shannon was acquitted in December 1985, with the judge remarking that 'while he had reservations about the incident having occurred, he could not overrule the possibility that Mr McQuade [the owner of the car] was telling the truth … The fingerprints did not therefore prove sufficiently satisfying to uphold a conviction in his case.'[5]

While the prime focus during 1981 was understandably on the prison crisis, British concerns over cross-border attacks were also very much to the fore. At the beginning of the conflict, the British Army had carried out a policy of blowing up minor roads that crossed the border. The intention was to channel traffic through a small number of army checkpoint crossings. The policy caused mass resentment in the border region and significantly disrupted economic and social life there. It was not uncommon for locals to repair the cratered roads after the British Army withdrew, and clashes between soldiers and locals often took place. Rubber bullets were used by the army during such clashes. Due to its ineffectiveness and alienating impact, this policy had been largely scaled back by the mid-1970s. However, in 1979 the Northern Ireland Office (NIO) wrote to London that the army have 'a growing feeling on their part that a number of crossings which have been by-passed should be re-cratered and that consideration should be given to the closing of some routes which have hitherto remained open'. The recommendations of the NIO memo were occasionally followed up on, with minor border roads blocked or cratered in the early years of the 1980s though never on a scale matching the previous decade. The memo also noted that the closing of these roads is 'admittedly, almost totally psychological, to the border farmers and townsfolk on the other side of the border', so the closures were intended to 'prod the south, by disrupting their citizens'.

A security assessment at the time stated that British forces were 'threatened by the existence in Co Donegal, Monaghan and Co Leitrim of three PIRA [Provisional IRA] Active Service Units [ASUs] based on Bundoran/Ballyshannon; Clones and Swalinbar/Ballyconnell'. These ASUs were described as being made up of around twenty-one terrorists, all of whom are described as 'dedicated' and eight of whom are believed to be explosives 'officers'. There was reported to be no shortage of explosives and the ASUs were 'believed to have the ability to achieve a high degree of coordination in any action they may plan'.[6] In May 1981, there was a major gun battle between IRA volunteers and the British Army near Crossmaglen when an IRA road checkpoint drew the attention of a British Army patrol. In the subsequent exchange, an army helicopter came under fire from an IRA heavy machine-gun crew. Two lorries and a car were hijacked by the IRA unit and set on fire in order to help cover their escape. A fortnight later, a twenty-three-year-old man was arrested just south of the border following another gun battle between the IRA and British Army. The man was discovered by Irish security forces concealed in a hole in a field with a black mask and a loaded rifle. His brother was arrested shortly afterwards, on the northern side of the border.[7]

In the early weeks of 1981, the IRA also targeted British-registered shipping in Lough Foyle, between Counties Donegal and Derry. On the night of 6 February, up to eight IRA men had taken over the pilot station outside Moville, County Donegal, and held the pilot and two visitors at gunpoint. The pilot was ordered to ferry an IRA unit out in the pilot boat to the *Nellie M*, a British-registered coal ship, which had been waiting for improved weather and tidal conditions to reach Coleraine in County Derry. According to a republican report of the event: 'Aboard the "Nellie M" the captain and chief engineer were watching the war film *Kelly's Heroes* on television, when suddenly the Volunteers, who had quietly boarded the boat, burst into the cabin and said, "This is the real thing, we are the IRA."'[8] After ordering the crew off the boat at gunpoint, the IRA planted two bombs before returning to land. The IRA unit, the pilot and his visitors then travelled over the border to Donegal in several cars. Sometime later, around 11 p.m. and 2 a.m., the two bombs exploded. The ship suffered a breach in the bulkhead, with a substantial hole in its shell plating. The wreck lay in shallow waters for several months before being raised and brought to Derry, where her cargo was discharged and repairs began.

The sinking sparked disputes centred on compensation for the ship's owners – who lodged claims in both jurisdictions, the Republic of Ireland and Northern Ireland – due to disagreements regarding culpability and territorial demarcation. As reported at the time: 'If insured by a war risks clause, the underwriters will cover the damage and try to recoup money by the sale of the ship and cargo ... It is not clear whether the local authority or the Government would be open to a compensation claim.'[9] While neither the British nor the Irish governments particularly wished to pay the large claim, both felt that to allow the other side to do so would be to concede territorial claims to Lough Foyle. The two governments were also opposed to the ship's owners receiving a double pay-out, due to an anticipated public outcry over spending waste. The issue of sovereignty regarding this sea lake had never been truly clarified. During the seventeenth century, the waters of the lough were consolidated into the county of Derry. However, in the 1930s, the Republic of Ireland (then the Irish Free State) claimed that the whole of Lough Foyle was in its jurisdiction. Thirty years later, at the 1964 International Law of the Sea Conference, both states agreed that where there was less than twenty-four miles of water, it was to be evenly divided between Britain and Ireland. Whether this applied to tidal waters was a matter not resolved at the time. Now, with the issue back on the agenda, an internal Irish government memo noted:

> [The view of the Attorney General was that] in the event of a delimitation dispute between Britain and Ireland in relation to the waters, fisheries or seabed of Lough Foyle it would be very much to the disadvantage of this State's claims (based on Article 2 and 3 of the Constitution), if it were to concede that there was or, even could have been, a valid "Northern" claim to some form of jurisdiction within 300 yds. of the Southern low-water mark.

Furthermore:

> As you are aware[,] it has long been maintained by a number of lawyers, North and South, that the territorial seas of the whole island, which were included in the territory which passed under the Government of Ireland Act, 1920 did not and could not 'opt out'; only the administrative areas of counties could – and six did – opt out. The territorial seas around these counties remained territorial seas of the new State and still do so.[10]

The British demurred. It was for this confusing reason that the owners of *Nellie M* lodged compensation claims with both the Northern Ireland Office and the Irish government.[11] There was some local panic in Donegal, as the claim had to be lodged directly with Donegal County Council. The state swiftly assured the council that they would reimburse them for any payment made. Referring to the dispute in the Dáil on 10 February 1981, Minister for Justice Gerry Collins insisted that *Nellie M* was sunk in the Republic's waters and ordered that a 25-inch map be placed in the library of the Dáil showing the line between British and Irish waters. On hearing this, the British Embassy in Dublin responded, in a message to Whitehall, that this would be a difficult feat for Minister Collins as no such map existed showing that line. Unionist MP for Derry William Ross wrote to Margaret Thatcher requesting that she claim the boat as being in British waters in order to settle the broader jurisdictional dispute.[12] Months passed without a resolution.

The IRA was aware of the disrupting effect the attack had had on British–Irish political relations. On the night of 23 February 1982, almost exactly a year after the sinking of *Nellie M*, it struck again. In this instance, the 2,000-ton coal ship *St Bedan* was boarded and sunk by a ten-man IRA unit in the same area, the men having commandeered the local pilot boat themselves this time to bluff their way on board. The IRA members also posed for propaganda photographs with the crew before ordering them into a lifeboat. The photographs were for distribution in the US, the crew was told. The owners of the *St Bedan* followed those of the *Nellie M* and lodged compensation claims in both jurisdictions. This second set of claims prompted British Ambassador Leonard Figg to urge his Irish counterparts to take some action, noting that the attack on the *St Bedan* 'highlighted publicly the fact that decisions remain to be taken on the MV *Nellie M*. Secondly, there is very considerable pressure from the claimants in the case of MV *Nellie M*, which is entirely understandable in view of the lapse of time and the sums involved.'[13]

The British had previously suggested to their Irish counterparts that each government pay half the claimed compensation amount, discreetly and with no statements or claims one way or the other over jurisdiction. There was silence from Dublin for several months to this suggestion. The relatively rapid turnover of Irish governments during this period undoubtedly contributed to the delays. When relevant British officials did get to meet their counterparts, they reported that the Irish delegation was entirely uninformed of their briefs. Eventually, during the summer of 1982, the British gave notice that they had already been making payments in instalments to compensate the ship owners and, by 21 July, these had reached £250,000 for the owners of the

St Bedan, with another £250,000 due imminently. The final payment for the owners of the *Nellie M* was 'close'. This prompted speculation in the media about the Irish government ceding sovereignty over the lough, causing panic in the corridors of government.[14] Suddenly discovering the energy to address the matter, the Irish government began pressing the British weekly through diplomatic channels for answers as to why they were paying anything at all. Internally, there were some disputes among governmental departments at being caught on the hop by the British.[15] The Attorney General's office was particularly piqued, noting in an internal memo: 'This matter has dragged out far too long. Had the advice of the Attorney-General's Office, supported by this Department, been taken in June, 1981, the matter would have been disposed of long since.'[16]

Finally, at the end of September 1982, the Irish government indicated that they would be willing to contribute 50 per cent of the costs of the two claims. As the claim had to be processed through Donegal County Council, it wasn't until 1985 that the government were in a position to begin making payments. Awkwardness ensued, as the NIO had already paid out over 65 per cent of the total amount.[17] The two sides eventually reached an agreement whereby the Irish government made direct financial transfers to the British Exchequer in return for the NIO completing the full payments to the two ships' owners. The matter was seemingly resolved following the settling of these payments. Fortunately for both governments, the IRA did not revisit the targeting of ships in Lough Foyle after the February 1982 bombing, as relations between them were already at a low ebb as a result of the Northern prison crisis.

The 1981 Hunger Strike and its Fallout

In its annual review, the Provisionals' newspaper *An Phoblacht* quite rightly summarised 1981 as being 'dominated by the grim and heroic struggle of republican prisoners for political recognition'.[18] The hunger strike in the winter of 1980, although galvanising hitherto flagging support for the prisoners, had ultimately failed to achieve the 'Five Demands'. For the IRA prison leadership, now led by Bobby Sands, the evident weakness in that hunger strike was that all participants began at the same time. As one man weakened, there was significant moral pressure on the others to end the strike, as happened with Sean McKenna in December. So, in March 1981, a second hunger strike of IRA and INLA prisoners began in the H-Blocks. This time, prisoners would begin in a staggered procession, at two-week intervals, beginning with Sands himself. Despite the fact that the previous hunger strike had ended only recently, support for this second one quickly gained momentum across the island, helped by the fact that the organisational infrastructure of the last campaign was still in place. On 20 April, three TDs visited Bobby Sands in prison. Deputies Síle de Valera, Neil Blaney and Dr John O'Connell spent some time in private discussion with Sands and came out in public support of the prisoners' demands. Dr O'Connell declared that the British 'standing firm on these issues is ridiculous'.[19] He also stated that his principal reason for visiting Sands was as a doctor to persuade him to give up the hunger strike. Four days later, a number of Irish journalists – a grouping that, with a few exceptions, had been distinctly non-vocal on prisoner rights and the 'Five Demands' – handed a letter into the British Embassy in Dublin in support of the prisoners.[20] The following week, at the annual general meeting of the Local Government and Public Services Union, a motion was carried condemning the treatment of H-Block prisoners on humanitarian grounds.[21] The republican youth group, Fianna Éireann, took over a pirate radio station in Dublin during this period and broadcast appeals to support Sands and the hunger strike. Some days later, a combined group of Fianna Éireann and Students Against H-Block members, a dozen strong, occupied the Dublin stock exchange for over five hours. Another group of students occupied the Labour Party headquarters in Gardiner Street, calling on the party to 'catch up with socialist realities and speak out against the H-Blocks'.[22]

Not all protests were peaceful during this period. In March, a British businessman was shot in the leg three times in Trinity College Dublin while addressing a conference. According to a contemporary account:

[T]hree men, two of whom were armed, burst in through the back door of the lecture room. The three, who were of slight build and in their early twenties, were wearing military-style combat jackets and balaclava helmets ... One turned to the audience and shouted in a nondescript accent 'Everybody freeze, nobody move. This action is in support of the H-Blocks'.[23]

The perpetrators were members of a small Marxist group, Revolutionary Struggle, unrelated to either the INLA or IRA.[24] There were understandable British fears for the safety of their embassy staff in Dublin during the hunger strike. The IRA had previously demonstrated their capabilities, having assassinated the British ambassadors to the Republic of Ireland and the Netherlands in 1976 and 1979 respectively. As reported by Ambassador Figg, Garda Special Branch had already conveyed warnings to him, from a 'delicate source', regarding plans to 'mount an attack on [my] military attaché as he enters his house (possibly by taking over one of the adjacent houses). The Garda assess this information as reliable and they are taking the threat very seriously.'[25] Ultimately, nothing came of this apparent threat.

Shortly after Bobby Sands began his hunger strike, Frank Maguire, an independent nationalist MP for Fermanagh–South Tyrone, died of a heart attack. The republican movement decided to put Sands forward as a candidate in the subsequent by-election.[26] On 9 April, in the sixth week of his hunger strike, he was duly elected as MP for Fermanagh–South Tyrone, defeating the UUP candidate by 30,493 votes to 29,046. The straight competition between the two candidates was a result of other nationalist and unionist parties withdrawing from the election in order not to split the respective votes. In a collected work on the hunger strikes, compiled on its twenty-fifth anniversary, journalist Paddy Prendiville reflected on attitudes in the South on the night of Sands' election victory:

[T]hat elite layer, the self-appointed guardians of public morality and 'modern' values (academics, journalists, establishment politicians, captains of industry) could not hide, did not even try to hide their antipathy to Bobby Sands and his comrades. Whereas among the silenced majority, censored republicans and the great mass of Irish people, the sense of solidarity was palpable. This solidarity was sometimes hidden from view, sometimes fractured and atomised, sometimes helpless … I sat in a Dublin city-centre pub as the television newscaster announced that Bobby Sands had won the Fermanagh and South Tyrone by-election. My own elation was an insipid drop in the emotional tsunami that engulfed the rest of the room in a display of fervour that would have surprised the Falls Road. Every so often, 'southern' Irish people express themselves in a manner and with a force that completely contradicts the desiccated media image of a people who are supposed to have matured beyond such backward, nationalist sentiments. The industrial strikes that broke out spontaneously on building sites, in Dublin bus depots and in factories; the walk-outs and protest marches across the country; the seas of black flags that festooned working-class estates everywhere … a dark, malevolent silence descended on the Dublin-based media in 1981 as editors looked away (and worse) and journalists kept quiet for fear of damaging their careers. But as the cheers of people in pubs and elsewhere around the country rang out, that evening showed that most Irish people knew what Sands and his comrades were doing; they knew the hunger-strike was another chapter in the great drama that is our history.[27]

Veteran 'Troubles' journalist Ed Moloney recounted something similar during the summer of 1981, after hunger strikers had begun dying:

That summer the author regularly and repeatedly drove around Northern Ireland and around the Border counties and down to Dublin, in the Republic, covering the protest for the *Irish Times*, and there was scarcely a crossroads in a nationalist area in either jurisdiction that was not draped with mourning black flags or did not have rows of telephone poles adorned with protesting placards.[28]

Bobby Sands died in the early hours of 5 May and news of his death filtered out from the prison shortly afterwards. In west Belfast, residents came out in the pre-dawn gloom to say the rosary in groups and bang dustbin lids in scenes reminiscent of the early days of the 'Troubles'. Youths also began preparing petrol bombs and a day of rioting ensued across the North. In Dublin, a crowd of sixty or so demonstrators protested on O'Connell Bridge on the afternoon following Sands' death. The demonstration passed peacefully.

However, the capital was just beginning to experience a range of responses to the deaths of hunger strikers in the H-Blocks. Later that evening, a large crowd of perhaps 2,500 gathered outside the General Post Office (GPO) on O'Connell Street. Dáithí Ó Conaill, Rev. Piaras Ó Duill and Joe Stagg addressed the crowd. Joe was the brother of IRA prisoner Frank Stagg, who had died on hunger strike in England in 1976. Songs were sung and poems recited. A decade of the rosary was also said. Later, as the attendees dispersed, groups of youths – eventually numbering close to 200 – broke off from the main crowd. As the youths passed gardaí on O'Connell Street, missiles were thrown. Making their way across the river to St Stephen's Green via Grafton Street and Dawson Street, they smashed the windows of numerous shops. Six cars were overturned and two set alight. At the Hibernian Hotel, a number of windows were also smashed and gardaí made several arrests. Most of the gardaí were still policing the remains of the peaceful GPO commemoration, however, and so the crowd of youths was able to rampage largely unchecked. Around St Stephen's Green, up to forty cars were attacked and their windows smashed. Slowly losing numbers, the crowd eventually made its way towards the British Embassy in Ballsbridge. A large garda presence there discouraged any further acts of violence or vandalism. According to contemporary news reports, the rampaging crowd, made up of youths 'dressed in punk and skinhead gear', had begun their attacks on property despite the attempts of the organising H-Blocks/Armagh Committee to prevent them from doing so. *The Irish Times* said, 'Throughout the meeting gangs of teenagers circulated around the edge, unable to, or uninterested, in hearing what was being said from the platform.'[29] Following the riot, the H-Blocks/Armagh Committee called off a demonstration that had been scheduled for the following evening in the capital. The Lord Mayor of Dublin, Fine Gael TD Fergus O'Brien, called for a ban on demonstrations in the city centre, referring to the rampaging youths as 'bloody thugs' engaged in 'marauding terrorism'. O'Brien witnessed the rioting first-hand, near City Hall, and his wife's car was one of those smashed up.[30]

Bobby Sands' funeral on 7 May was yet another tense date in the Republic. Major turnouts in public displays of sympathy and support were expected in many urban areas, and on a scale not witnessed since Bloody Sunday in 1972. Five Irish Members of European Parliament (MEPs) attended the funeral in Belfast, along with many republicans from the South. In Dublin, despite a torrential downpour, a crowd of perhaps 5,000 marched through the city centre. There were no incidents of unrest reported. As with 1972, a number of businesses closed for the day to allow staff to join the marches or religious services for Sands. The Quinnsworth chain of supermarkets closed during the afternoon for this reason, while a number of Córas Iompair

Éireann (CIÉ) staff did not report for duty that day, severely disrupting early morning bus services in the capital. Disagreement remains regarding the extent to which these closures were voluntary. *The Irish Times* intimated that there was an element of intimidation at CIÉ, where 'men wearing black armbands spoke to the staff when they arrived for work'.[31] Garret FitzGerald, then leader of the opposition, made similar claims, although Minister for Justice Gerry Collins reported that gardaí had no knowledge of any such intimidation. Other media reports carried claims that warnings to close had been received in Dublin, Louth, Monaghan, Donegal, Cork and Waterford.[32] Republicans dispute these claims. One interviewee, speaking about Limerick city, stated:

> It was a very emotional period for all Irish people. The second biggest outflow of grief was in Limerick at the time, where we had it well organised. We went around to every factory and shop, and we asked them – we didn't stop them, we asked them to stop – you know, we got all black flags up everywhere. So, it was just an outflowing of grief for Bobby Sands.[33]

A few days after the funeral of Bobby Sands, the IRA in Dublin abducted, interrogated and killed Daniel McIlhone, a young man originally from Andersonstown in Belfast but then residing in Ballymun. According to an IRA statement, McIlhone was suspected of taking weapons from an IRA arms dump for personal use and was reportedly shot during a struggle with his captors. McIlhone was one of the 'Disappeared', victims of republican violence who were secretly buried and whose whereabouts remained unknown for years or continue to be unknown. The IRA deliberately kept his death and burial a secret, and his body was not discovered until 2008, in a remote area of moorland in County Wicklow.[34]

One week after Sands' death, Francis Hughes, the second of the republican prisoners to embark on the hunger strike, died. A commemoration at the GPO that evening was attended by approximately 1,000 people, numbers certainly down on the gathering for Sands. Dáithí Ó Conaill urged the crowd not to allow their anger and frustration to be 'misdirected into futile confrontation'. However, a full-scale riot broke out later in the evening as up to 1,000 protestors attempted to attack the British Embassy. Hundreds of gardaí fought running battles with the protestors and there was also scattered disruption and attacks on property and vehicles elsewhere in Dublin over the following two days. A bus was hijacked by young teenagers on Sean McDermott Street in the inner city and set alight, while CIÉ withdrew bus services in Ballymun after 10 p.m. after one of their vehicles was hijacked and driven into several parked cars. According to gardaí, there was clear evidence that the riot was planned, following the discovery of 'a cache of petrol bombs in Henry Street, ready for use'.[35] The army was put on full alert in anticipation of supporting the gardaí. While there was no need for army deployment this time – a planned march to the British Embassy was called off for fear of further rioting – the H-Blocks/Armagh Committee spoke of attempting to organise a large protest march in Dublin for an as-yet unspecified date in June.

Dublin Chamber of Commerce estimated that the riots over the preceding fortnight had cost the city £250,000 in damages. Garda Chief Superintendent John Robinson accused some speakers at the rally of inciting trouble: 'Everything was reasonably well behaved until the last few speakers made their speeches. The stewards abdicated on every principle of responsibility.'[36] Two of the speakers had indeed urged the crowd to attack the British Embassy, the aforementioned Joe Stagg, and Gerry Roche of the IRSP, the political wing of the INLA. Elsewhere in the state there were attacks on property following the announcement of Hughes' death, with the *Evening Herald* reporting: 'The Donegal and Cavan summer homes of Official Unionist MP Jim Kilfedder and Lord Farhnam were gutted by fire. The courthouse in Monaghan Town was burned down by arsonists.'[37]

Just as the 1981 Fermanagh–South Tyrone by-election upended traditional electoral politics in Northern Ireland, the collapse of the Fianna Fáil government in late May led to a gripping general election in the Republic. The leadership of both the Provisionals and the Irish Republican Socialist Movement (IRSM) (the collective of the INLA and the IRSP) agreed to run candidates across the state under a collective Anti H-Block banner. Candidates would be republican prisoners, male and female, in the H-Blocks and Armagh prison, although not all of them were on hunger strike. It was agreed that members of both organisations would campaign for whatever candidate was in their constituency, regardless of affiliation. For the Provisionals, this electoral strategy had been made possible due to a motion proposed by Sinn

Féin's Tom Hartley and passed at the 1980 Ard-Fheis allowing for formal Sinn Féin participation in an Anti H-Block broad front organisation.[38] That motion had met with bitter opposition from within the republican movement as the prison campaign sought to mobilise support on a human rights platform and did not ask that demonstrators endorse the armed struggle. There was thus a concern that Sinn Féin involvement in a broad campaign with such people risked diluting Provisional republican principles that support for the 'armed struggle' must be unequivocal.[39] Gearóid MacCárthaigh spoke of this occurring in Cork city, referring to those who joined the movement at this time as 'H-Block republicans'. MacCárthaigh refused an invitation to join the Cork branch of the prison campaign due to the involvement of people whose commitment to republican principles he doubted.[40]

The candidates and constituencies chosen by the Anti H-Block campaign for the 11 June 1981 Dáil elections are outlined in Table 7.

Veteran campaigner and former MP Bernadette McAliskey was heavily involved in the campaign, touring all the constituencies. In Sligo, she shared a platform with Joe Keohane, the celebrated footballer and former Irish Defence Forces officer.[41] The children of republican candidate and hunger striker Joe McDonnell were introduced to the crowd at this event. In Longford town, 2,000 people turned out for a rally, while heavy rain in Mullingar did not prevent another 2,000 from going to hear McAliskey speak there. Similar numbers were reported in Ballybunion and Waterford city.[42]

Table 7. Anti H-Block candidates in the 1981 Irish general election

Candidate	Organisation	Constituency
Kieran Doherty	IRA	Cavan–Monaghan
Tom McAllister	INLA	Clare
Mairéad Farrell	IRA	Cork North–Central
Anthony O'Hara	INLA	Dublin West
Sean McKenna	IRA	Kerry North
Martin Hurson	IRA	Longford–Westmeath
Paddy Agnew	IRA	Louth
Joe McDonnell	IRA	Sligo–Leitrim
Kevin Lynch	INLA	Waterford

The Sligo appearance of Keohane opened up another round in a long-running dispute within the GAA regarding their stance on militant Irish republicanism, given his standing within that organisation. Throughout that year, the Dublin Civil Service GAA club had increasingly looked for a complete and unequivocal condemnation of violence to be written into the association's constitution. In this, they were joined by the Kilmacud Crokes and the Fermanagh and Sligo county conventions.[43] An unsatisfactory compromise was reached at the 1981 congress, where the motion calling for such a condemnation and change to the constitution were not allowed to go forward to vote. Instead, 'it was agreed that the congress could express the association's attitude simply by reaffirming the condemnation of political violence made several times by the GAA president, Mr Paddy McFlynn'. However, the GAA did begin to crack down on activities that might have been ignored in previous years. The involvement of its members in the Anti H-Block campaign was prohibited on the grounds that the association now considered it 'party political activity'.[44]

The GAA's attempted neutral stance during the hunger strike ensured the hostility of sections of the republican movement and the families of prisoners. Many IRA and INLA prisoners, including men who were to die during the hunger strike, had been active in local GAA clubs for much of their lives. Many Northern clubs simply ignored the association's ban and took part in IRA and INLA funerals in an official capacity. Although the GAA leadership was strongly criticised at the funeral of INLA man Kevin Lynch for their reticence, local GAA members from Dungiven, County Derry, formed an honour guard at the funeral.[45] At the GAA's 1982 annual congress, it finally and unanimously condemned 'all violence'.[46] Later that year, an investigation was begun into four Belfast clubs following the use of their names in an advertisement supporting Sinn Féin for the Assembly elections.[47] As one historian of the GAA noted, where politically contentious issues involving the North were concerned, the nine Ulster counties 'paid scant regard to the views held by GAA members in the other twenty-three counties'.[48] A later example occurred during the 1986 senior football final when, on television, several of the Tyrone players dedicated their performances to the republican prisoners in the H-Blocks.[49] Of the fifty-eight volunteers on the Tyrone Provisional IRA's roll of honour, twenty-nine were locally or provincially prominent GAA members.[50] In the South, some prominent GAA members also continued to walk a fine line in their political activities. The Clare anti-extradition committee in the late 1980s, for example, was headed by the secretary of the west Clare hurling board, Michael Ryan.[51]

As the Irish general election results came in on 12 June, there was both celebration and disappointment among Anti H-Block campaigners. In Louth, Paddy Agnew topped the poll with 2,500 more votes than his nearest rival. Kieran Doherty was also elected to Dáil Éireann in the Cavan–Monaghan constituency. In Dublin West, Tony O'Hara – brother of hunger striker, Patsy – outpolled both Sinn Féin–The Workers' Party leader Tomás Mac Giolla as well as the Labour candidate, Mary Robinson, and came within 200 votes of unseating incumbent Liam Lawlor. Joe McDonnell came sixth in the Sligo–Leitrim constituency, polling particularly strongly in the south Leitrim area. Altogether, Anti H-Block candidates garnered an average of 15 per cent of votes in the constituencies they contested. Given the lack of an organisational canvassing structure, as well as the short window of time from the calling of the election to polling day, the achievements of the Anti H-Block campaign were quite remarkable.[52] The joint canvassing agreement between Sinn Féin and the IRSP was a broad success.

However, in County Clare not all Provisional supporters or members came out for the INLA candidate Thomas McAllister. According to one account, the O/C of the IRA's Munster Command put out the word that IRA volunteers were not to canvass for him.[53] Additionally, the candidate's involvement in a Provisional–Official IRA feud in Belfast during the 1970s alienated some Belfast Provisionals now based in Shannon who had first-hand experience of McAllister during that time.[54] Gerry Adams wrote a campaign diary for *An Phoblacht* during this period and his accounts of the turmoil in Clare are quite blunt. He described 'local disunity' and 'confusion' as being 'fairly depressing': 'divisions among H-Block activists had obviously damaged election hopes. For my part, we spent the night, all night, trying to settle the differences, speeding into the small hours back and forth across the county.'[55] Despite these local quibbles, McAllister received a respectable 2,120 first-preference votes, with one report referring to his 'polling surprisingly well in the Ennis–Shannon area.'[56]

On 2 August, several weeks after being elected to Dáil Éireann, Kieran Doherty became the eighth hunger striker to die. The new Taoiseach, Garret

FitzGerald, extended his sympathies to the family, adding: 'I have also learned with sorrow of the deaths of the two RUC constables murdered today in the course of their duty in Co. Tyrone. This deplorable act brings only further disgrace on the organisation which carried it out.'[57] In Cavan town, part of Doherty's constituency, a crowd of several hundred took part in a demonstration led by two pipers and six men in military uniform. Among those attending a rally in Dublin that same day, in which a letter of protest at a perceived lack of government action around the hunger strike was handed in to FitzGerald, was the TD and MEP Neil Blaney. The following evening, gardaí maintained a low profile in Monaghan town as a crowd of up to 1,500, including dozens of masked and uniformed IRA and INLA members, took part in a march. No intervention was attempted as three IRA volunteers stepped forward from the crowd and fired a volley of shots over an empty coffin draped with a tricolour. There was a token closure of shops for several hours in the towns of Cavan and Monaghan that same day. In Shannon, several weeks earlier, a similar demonstration had taken place. The procession marched through the town to the airport and finished by placing two empty coffins on the counters of the British Airways offices. En route to the airport, a masked and uniformed man had emerged from a laneway beside the road and fired several shots over the coffins. Gardaí were late on the scene, much to the participants' surprise. When asked later that day about the incident, gardaí said that there had been no official report of shots fired and refused to comment further.[58]

The climax of the major Anti H-Block demonstrations in the Republic during the hunger strikes was a planned march to the British Embassy on 18 July. Just five days earlier, Tyrone IRA volunteer Martin Hurson became the sixth hunger striker to die and tensions were very high. Somewhere between 12,000 and 20,000 protesters set off from St Stephen's Green and marched towards Merrion Road and the embassy in the summer heat. Among those attending were the President of the Irish Transport and General Workers' Union, the General Secretary of the Amalgamated Transport and General Workers' Union and politicians Neil Blaney and Kevin Boland. The aftermath of Bloody Sunday, when the British Embassy – then situated in the city centre – had been burned to the ground by an angry crowd, was on many people's minds. Now, nine years later, the gardaí were taking no chances. They set up barriers well forward of the embassy and were present in their hundreds, sometimes ten deep. Many were in riot gear or mounted on horseback. At least 100 soldiers were also on duty around the embassy.

As the crowd approached the barriers, amidst shouts of 'Gardaí-RUC', a shower of material was launched at the gardaí: stones, bricks, railings and a small number of petrol bombs. A deputation of the demonstration's organisers did actually meet with gardaí at this time, though it did not influence the more raucous element of the crowd. While most demonstrators did not take part in the violence, it was reported that those who did numbered around 500. Several gardaí were injured by missiles, at which point a formal request was made to nearby troops that CS gas be fired into the crowd. This request was denied.[59] After enduring the barrage of missiles for some twenty minutes, gardaí in riot gear launched a baton charge at the demonstrators. The ensuing riot was unlike anything the state had witnessed during the 'Troubles' thus far. Pitched battles broke out between rioters and gardaí, and gardens in the surrounding area were destroyed as men and women smashed up pieces of walls and paving stones to throw. Flag poles and palings from garden fences were also used. More petrol bombs were thrown and twice the gardaí were driven back to their barriers. Finally, at 4.22 p.m., a concerted garda baton charge succeeded in breaking up the main body of the crowd. Panic struck many people, who ran and screamed in terror into gardens and down side streets. A number of demonstrators were trapped in doorways and surrounded by gardaí, who beat them unconscious. A truck with a loudspeaker, which had been directing the demonstration at the beginning, was trapped on the road by the surging crowd. Gardaí smashed the windows and began beating the occupants.

The violence became indiscriminate at this point, perhaps fuelled by reports that the most senior garda present, Chief Superintendent John Robinson, had been injured along with many of the rank and file.[60] A number of journalists were also attacked by gardaí during this part of the riot, with one suffering four fractured ribs and another requiring five stitches. The crowd broke into smaller knots, fleeing in every direction, many taking off across playing fields towards a train track. Gardaí moved quickly to block their escape. A doctor who was driving through Ballsbridge told reporters of witnessing a young man attacked by gardaí: 'I think he may have shouted something at them. But it certainly didn't justify rushing across and beating him with their batons until blood literally ran out of him.'[61] One journalist saw a group of gardaí on motorcycles, with one waving his baton over his head and roaring, 'Let's go, let's go, let's go get them.' Peter Murtagh, a reporter for *The Irish Times*, saw one man staggering along an otherwise empty street with blood on his torn shirt: 'Two gardaí approached the man with their batons drawn. One of them, a sergeant, punched the man in the stomach with this baton. They both beat the man until he fell to the pavement on his face.' By the day's end, up to 200 people were hospitalised, including scores of gardaí. Damage was estimated at £250,000, with another £310,000 in costs for garda overtime.

There is no doubt that many of those who set out from St Stephen's Green earlier that day had violent intent. A number of hand weapons were found in the aftermath among the debris, including an iron bar wrapped in barbed wire, a slash hook and some garden tools. The National H-Blocks/Armagh Committee declared: 'Full responsibility for the riot rests completely with the gardaí,' while Taoiseach Garret FitzGerald pointed out that the gardaí endured up to twenty minutes of a barrage of missiles before charging: 'Anyone who was still around must have been aware they were in danger.'[62] In December, twenty men went on trial for their part in the riot.[63] One of them, a young Englishman named Patrick J. Kehoe, received a three-year prison sentence – the maximum sentence possible – on the charge of preventing gardaí from carrying out their duties. The other nineteen men ultimately faced a range of sentences, including monetary fines, suspended sentences and eighteen-month prison sentences.[64] Despite the intensity of the violence on 18 July, the government allowed another demonstration to take place in Dublin later that month, which passed off peacefully.

Throughout the long summer of 1981, the deaths of hunger strikers punctuated the news and the lives of those living in the Republic. Sales of *An Phoblacht*, which had been averaging 20,000 per issue during the 1970s, more than doubled to 45,000 in 1981.[65] However, as has been noted in another study of the period, the numbers who participated in even the largest Anti H-Block marches that year were a fraction of those who took part in the major tax protests in 1978–80.[66] One interviewee, even while describing the declining public engagement, put high numbers of attendance at Limerick marches: 'by the time the last hunger striker had died, Mickey Devine, it had probably whittled down to a thousand or two people on the streets in Limerick. So, it was kind of, you know, it was going down, the momentum was never really kept up …' However, it is clear that 'republicanism did gain from it. They started a new wave of building on a political level, I'd say, more than anything.'[67] The hunger strike also re-engaged some former activists. Kieran Conway had been a young Dubliner when he joined the IRA during the early 1970s, serving with the Derry Brigade. He left the republican movement later that decade, but a chance encounter with the head of Southern Command on a Dublin street during the hunger strike led to him rejoin. Conway went on to become the IRA's Director of Intelligence. Coming from a middle-class background, he had built a network of sympathetic affluent south Dubliners during his earlier period of activity. According to Conway, this middle-class support circle was easily reactivated in 1981.[68]

The 1981 hunger strike ultimately ended on 3 October after several families intervened to save their sons' lives as they passed into unconsciousness. By that time, ten of the participants had died. Several days after the cessation, the British government conceded on four of the five prisoner demands. The fifth, the right to refrain from prison work, was granted sometime later.

Disrupting Supply Lines

Throughout 1981 gardaí made a number of major arms and explosives finds. During the tense month of May, a garda car was hijacked at gunpoint by armed and masked men after gardaí inadvertently stumbled upon them in mid-transit of weaponry near Bunbeg, County Donegal. There were major follow-up searches in the area over the following days by gardaí supported by the Irish Army, leading to the discovery of two arms dumps. One, in a vacant house near Annagry, turned up two rifles and a considerable amount of heavy-calibre ammunition, while in a field near Gweedore, a sawn-off shotgun and fifty cartridges were uncovered.[69] That same month, three men – Dessie Ellis (28), Thomas Hughes (44) and Leonard Hardy (26) – were arrested and charged with having explosives in their homes in Finglas, Bray and Cabra respectively. In the case of Ellis, a television repairman, it was reported that gardaí raided his home on the morning of 13 May and found three bags of electronic timing remote-control devices. Ellis was granted (and subsequently skipped) bail, travelling to the USA where he was arrested the following year and extradited back to the Republic for trial and sentencing. Hughes, a laboratory technician and electronics expert working at University College Dublin (UCD), was later cleared in court of possession of explosive devices. Hughes had joined the Irish Army in 1956 and later spent some time abroad before returning to Ireland in 1967. He then worked with the Phillips Company in Clonskeagh but was made redundant in 1980 and obtained employment in UCD a short time afterwards. The presiding judge ruled that the prosecution had failed to convince the court that the objects found in Mr Hughes' home could not have been used for a lawful purpose: Hughes had told the court that he was a fan of Citizen Band (CB) radio, had repaired hundreds of CB radios and that there was nothing sinister about homemade electrical circuit boards. The prosecution had argued that these CB radio transmitters were used extensively by the IRA in the North to trigger remote control bombs but failed to convince the judge.[70]

In the same month that Ellis, Hughes and Hardy were arrested, a thirty-nine-year-old County Wexford man appeared in the Special Criminal Court charged with possession of explosives, ammunition and a firearm. The man, who was not legally represented, said he did not recognise the court. He subsequently pleaded guilty to having a quantity of charcoal, assorted lengths of aluminium piping, a radio transceiver, a sporting rifle and several dozen rounds of assorted ammunition in his possession, and received a three-year suspended sentence.[71] The man's seventy-year-old father received a two-year suspended sentence after he was found guilty of possessing explosive substances at his farm. During a search of the farmyard, gardaí had found two rolls of detonating fuse wire, bell wire and multi-core wire. The father admitted he had been keeping parcels for the IRA for the past two or three years and, as far as he knew, the parcels contained explosives destined to cause explosions in Northern Ireland. The last parcel he received was two or three weeks previously, and it had been collected after a few days. He thought the explosives were left on his farm by Wexford men, but he did not know the names of those who collected them. The judge suspended the elderly defendant's sentence due to age and previous good character. He was a widower – as was his son – with another son in An Garda Síochána and a daughter working in the missions in Nigeria. In suspending his sentence, the presiding judge remarked that there were many subversive elements throughout Irish society, and they would not be able to continue to operate without the sort of help that people like the defendant gave them.[72]

In November, gardaí arrested a young man on the street in Ballybough, Dublin, having followed him by foot and in an unmarked car. The man, a twenty-one-year-old welder, was found in possession of detonators, fuse wire, ammonia nitrate sawdust and nitroglycerine. The explosive components were wrapped inside a cellophane bag inside the man's pockets. He refused to recognise the court and was sentenced to eight years' penal servitude: five years for explosives possession and another three for IRA membership.[73] The following month, there were a number of significant arms seizures in border counties. Gardaí discovered a large quantity of weapons, ammunition and paramilitary clothing hidden under sods of grass in sand dunes beside a makeshift firing range near Burtonport, County Donegal. The cache included ten rifles, several thousand rounds of ammunition, an assortment of uniforms and sketches of military tactics, which appeared to be part of a training manual. The gardaí were reportedly acting on a tip-off from the RUC and had searched the area intensively for several days. However, this was denied by Garda Headquarters in Dublin, who claimed that the discovery 'was the result of intensive investigation over a long period'.[74] One report noted that an IRA defector was linked to the find but that senior gardaí were cagey about revealing his involvement, while another garda spokesman claimed the stash was found by chance as gardaí were searching for the body of a fisherman linked to the sinking of a fishing trawler, the *Skifjord*.[75] In the following days, arms and ammunition were also discovered near Loughglas and Dundalk. A week later, another arms cache was discovered at an outhouse at Carrigart, near Milford in County Donegal, comprising six heavy rifles 'in good condition'.[76]

The British reported that, in the aftermath of the hunger strike, 'co-operation with the Garda remains excellent and there have been many valuable arrests and finds in the Republic this year'.[77] Indeed, since the previous year, the newly established Garda Special Task Force had been operating with significant efficiency in the border areas. Due to its alleged ill-treatment of republicans and harassment of suspected sympathisers, this branch of the gardaí earned regular condemnation in *An Phoblacht* during the following years. In one case, it was reported that a Cavan Sinn Féin county councillor's home was raided and private documents relating to his constituents were 'carefully scrutinised and may have been copied'.[78] In another piece, titled 'Donegal Brutality', the newspaper documented a series of allegations against the task force in that county, including burning men with cigarettes during interrogation and placing plastic bags over their heads. In one instance an arrested man, a gaelgoir (native Irish speaker), was told by a garda: 'Before we're finished, you'll be an English speaker.'[79] He was then punched in the stomach. A doctor from Falcarragh allegedly ignored clear bruising on the arrested man during a cursory examination and announced that no force was used. The following month, a man had his nose broken and was knocked unconscious during an arrest in Letterkenny following a public meeting on the H-Block issue. There were also allegations in *An Phoblacht* that the task force engaged in physical and verbal abuse of two middle-aged women during Anti H-Block protests. In 1984, one of these women, Vera Bannon, received a £5,223 compensation pay-out for an assault carried out on her at a protest in Ballyshannon in August 1981. Bannon had been thrown to the ground by a garda and kicked in the face, suffering a broken nose.[80] Several years later, she received a five-year suspended sentence after admitting IRA membership in Dublin's Special Criminal Court. Bannon, a forty-one-year-old mother of three, was reported to be 'the officer in charge of the Provisional IRA in Co. Donegal for some period of time'.[81]

The total amount of arms, ammunition and explosives seized by gardaí in the Republic of Ireland in 1981 is outlined in Table 8.

Despite their many successes during the year, gardaí came under criticism in June following the surprise appearance of Paul 'Dingus' Magee at Bodenstown cemetery in County Kildare, during the annual republican commemoration at the graveside of Wolfe Tone. Magee had been imprisoned in Northern Ireland as part of the 'M60 gang', an elite IRA unit which had carried out several attacks on British soldiers with a general-purpose machine gun from 1978 onwards. He was part of a group of eight IRA remand prisoners who shot their way out of Belfast's Crumlin Road Gaol on 10 June 1981, when a gun that had been smuggled into the prison was produced in the visiting area. Ten warders were locked into a cell while a number of prisoners were released. The group then proceeded to lock up several dozen other warders, along with visitors and solicitors. As reported by *An Phoblacht*:

Two warders and a solicitor were ordered to strip and three of the IRA Volunteers, dressed in two uniforms and a suit respectively, calmly walked to the main gate which was opened for them. They then pulled guns on the real warders in this key security area, and made them lie on the ground until their five comrades ran across a small courtyard to join them ...[82]

Table 8. Garda seizures of arms, ammunition and explosives, 1981[83]

Quantity	Type
211	Firearms (including rifles, shotguns, machine guns, pistols, revolvers, etc.)
17,349	Rounds of ammunition (assorted)
4,964	Shotgun cartridges
23	Magazines
45lbs	Gelignite (approximately)
90	Detonators
2,541lbs	Explosive mixture
3	Rockets
49	Bombs
5	Hand grenades
14	Timing devices
865 yards	Fuse wire

Outside, the alarm was finally raised and the prisoners engaged in a gun battle with British soldiers stationed in a prison watch tower. The prisoners managed to escape uninjured from this and made it to a nearby car park where a number of cars were waiting for them. As *An Phoblacht* reported: 'All eight men reached safe houses within the hour and after lying low for a short while were spirited over the border to begin new lives "on the run".'[84] According to one account, all of the escapees ended up in County Kerry for some time before being split up and moved to other parts of the country.[85]

Magee's sudden appearance on the rostrum at Bodenstown twelve days after the breakout took gardaí and Irish Army units by complete surprise. He took off his hat to the 5,000 or so delighted republican attendees, signed several autographs and walked in parade back to the town of Sallins, a mile from the cemetery. A senior garda later remarked to the press that it would have been too dangerous to attempt to arrest Magee during the parade. Magee was believed to have made his escape from the massive ring of roadblocks subsequently thrown up by the security forces by running along a railway line in the fields outside Sallins as crowds dispersed.

Three months later, another of the Crumlin Road escapees, Robert Joseph Campbell, was arrested during a routine garda patrol in Dundalk. Michael Ryan of Ardboe, County Tyrone, the only non-Belfast escapee, was picked up in Monaghan in October. Campbell and Ryan were subsequently put on trial in Dublin. This was allowed under the Criminal Law (Jurisdiction) Act, passed in 1976, which provided for persons to be tried in the Republic for alleged offences committed in Northern Ireland. Both men were charged with escaping from prison and a separate charge of using firearms in the attempt, as well as a charge of attempted murder: an RUC officer was shot and wounded outside the prison while attempting to apprehend the escapees. The two were acquitted of the attempted murder charge, but were found guilty of the other two charges, in the first successful application of the Criminal Law (Jurisdiction) Act. They were sentenced to concurrent sentences of eight and five years' imprisonment, which they served in Portlaoise.[86] By January 1982, seven republicans were serving prison sentences in the South 'in respect of convictions obtained in the Special Criminal Court' in application of this act.[87]

IRA Financing and Political Developments

It is possible that the hunger strikes of 1980 and 1981 led to a significant injection of funds to the Provisional republican movement far beyond the average annual income in the preceding years. By one account, $250,000 was raised in the USA during the hunger strikes. However, according to another account, the US-based Irish Northern Aid Committee (NORAID) was raising an average of $300,000 annually during the early 1980s, in which case the former figure would be unremarkable.[88] Comparing these examples does, however, illustrate the level of guesswork that exists about IRA finances, which is an issue for historiography.

Armed robberies continued to be one of the primary activities of the IRA's Southern Command, with one foiled robbery of a post office in Togher, County Cork, leading to the arrest and imprisonment of three men in 1981. It was during this period that the IRA began to contemplate the use of kidnappings as a means of financing their campaign. Previously, kidnappings had been used intermittently and without Army Council approval to try to effect political or other change. In 1972 the IRA's Belfast Brigade kidnapped the German industrialist Thomas Niedermayer, seeking to use his kidnapping as leverage in negotiations for the transfer of republican prisoners from Britain to Northern Ireland. Niedermayer was inadvertently killed by his captors, allegedly during an escape attempt. Three years later, a rogue IRA unit in the midlands kidnapped Dutch businessman Tiede Herrema in order to demand the release of several IRA members imprisoned in the South. Herrema was later freed, and his captors were jailed after a two-week siege in the County Kildare town of Monasterevin.[89] Unlike these previous kidnappings, the new strategy was leadership-approved and intended to raise funds through ransom payments.

In October 1981, Ben Dunne of the Dunnes Stores multinational retail chain was driving north on a County Louth road. A green car suddenly appeared from behind a lorry heading in his direction and swerved in front of Dunne's car. The lorry was forced to stop abruptly, while Dunne also hit his brakes and turned sharply before stopping about 100 yards up the road. The green car turned and drove towards Dunne, who waited for it, thinking there had been an accident and they had come to apologise. Four men jumped from the vehicle, at least one of whom had a rifle, and bundled Dunne into their car before speeding away. All of this was witnessed by the lorry driver, who quickly alerted customs officers at the Killeen border post. Dunne was taken over the border to South Armagh, where there was a vehicle swap, and he was then held in an unknown house for several days. The two vehicles used in the kidnapping were later found burnt out near the village of Forkhill, County Armagh. Dunne was held for just under a week before being released near the parochial house at Cullyhanna, where journalist Eamonn Mallie, who had received a tip-off, picked him up. Although the Dunne family maintain that no ransom was paid for his release, Tim Pat Coogan has written of the credible accounts he heard discussed in republican circles regarding a sum of £750,000. Indeed, Minister for Justice Jim Mitchell less-than-convincingly stated at the time that 'while it was not possible to be 100% certain that no ransom was paid for the release of Mr Dunne, there was absolutely no reason for believing that any money had been handed over to the kidnappers'. Upon his release,

Dunne was gifted with three bullets by his captors; one each from the two Armalites and one from the revolver used to guard him.[90]

Given his profile in Irish society, Ben Dunne's kidnapping and captivity provoked a media flurry, albeit one which quickly died down following his release. Other events that took place in 1981 received less attention as the Northern prison crisis and hunger strike dominated media coverage. One of these was the not insignificant political germination which took place that year between the Dublin and London governments, with the establishment of the Anglo-Irish Intergovernmental Council. This body was formed to discuss the possibility of institutional links between the two states vis-à-vis Northern Ireland. While the council had no impact that year, largely owing to alienation from the hunger strike, it set the stage for what would become the Anglo-Irish Agreement in 1985.

Within the Provisional republican movement, the successful election of Bobby Sands and, subsequently, Owen Carron for Fermanagh–South Tyrone, as well as two Anti H-Block TDs elected to the Dáil, caused a major rethink of political strategy. Former IRA volunteer Pat Magee noted of the movement's prior experiences of political involvement and politicisation: '[our] greatest weakness must be turned into our greatest strength.'[91] The hunger strike demonstrated the huge potential that existed to turn that recently generated momentum into a lasting political movement. While the evolution of that strategy is largely outside the scope of this study, it is worth noting a few points. It was at Sinn Féin's 1981 Ard-Fheis that Danny Morrison voiced the new thinking, asking the delegates if they would object to the movement taking power in Ireland with a ballot paper in one hand and an Armalite in the other. While many saw in this statement, and other similar remarks that weekend, the first steps towards ending the abstentionism policy, the crowd largely agreed with the sentiment.[92] Although the emerging leadership centred around Gerry Adams may have been contemplating such a policy change, it was not yet being voiced explicitly. At this stage, any direct challenge to abstentionism might lead to a bitter and even bloody split in the movement.[93]

The first order of business was to end the federalism policy of Éire Nua, the official policy of Sinn Féin since the early 1970s and particularly associated with the leadership of Ruairí Ó Brádaigh, Dáithí Ó Conaill and Seán MacStiofáin. Attacking that policy was an indirect way of attacking the old leadership. The IRA had already abandoned federalism as a policy in 1979, but it remained the official policy for Sinn Féin, though the Éire Nua policy had long drawn criticism from within the party also. At the 1977 Ard-Fheis, for example, speakers complained of the difficulty party members had in understanding it and a motion was even passed calling for its publication in a simpler form.[94] Notes from a Sinn Féin Coiste Seasta (standing committee) meeting following the 1981 elections also included one on the 'difficulty in explaining abstentionism'. An attempt to abolish Éire Nua was narrowly defeated at the 1981 Ard-Fheis. Such a motion required two-thirds of a vote to pass and, while this was not forthcoming, the vote was so close as to render Éire Nua a dead-duck policy. Adams and his allies were certainly in the ascendant from a public relations standpoint; *An Phoblacht*, under the editorship of Danny Morrison, even published a letter condemning party President Ó Brádaigh for speaking against the Éire Nua resolution at the Ard-Fheis.[95] The previous year, the newspaper had taken several digs at the policy, referring to 'much-needed up-dates' being required.[96] Despite tensions, both the military and political movement saw out the year with increased confidence in itself as well as strong internal cohesion. As *The Irish Times* noted of the Ard-Fheis: 'Some of the country's larger political parties would be surprised at the degree of overt democracy in its ard-fheis procedures; they might, too, have felt at least mildly alarmed at the confidence of a movement which views 1981 as perhaps the most significant in its history.'[97]

Indeed, other forces certainly felt the same and sought to disrupt the party's growth. In the space of six days, the Sinn Féin headquarters in Belfast and Dublin were both attacked by loyalist paramilitaries, the latter on 25 November, when the UDA launched a brazen attack on the party's offices on Dublin's Parnell Square. According to a Sinn Féin spokesman, a man 'came into the hall and seemed a bit incoherent. He shouted something like "I'm gonna get you" and then there were a couple of shots aimed at the floor.'[98] Two men working in the offices at the time were injured in the shooting; one was Pat Magee, who was shot in the leg. According to his account, the attacker had panicked and fired a burst from a machine gun before fleeing.[99]

As well as facing violent attacks, party members were also under legal threat in the South. A week after the Parnell Square shooting, two Sinn Féin councillors – Jim Lynagh and John Joe McGirl – were charged with IRA membership in the Special Criminal Court.[100] The period between McGirl's arrest and his trial witnessed a general election in the Republic in which he was the Sinn Féin candidate for Sligo–Leitrim, the constituency where hunger striker Joe McDonnell had missed out on a Dáil seat by 315 votes. McGirl's alleged IRA status was highlighted by outgoing minister Patrick Cooney as one of the reasons why the broadcasting ban on Sinn Féin should be upheld during that election. The case against McGirl, who was sixty years of age at the time of his arrest, was thrown out six months later. At the trial, no evidence for IRA membership was offered against McGirl, other than a garda claim that he appeared to be 'very nervous' when stopped by a garda while driving to the village of Killeshandra one evening in November 1981. Lynagh was also acquitted, but later rearrested on other charges (see Chapter 6).[101]

3

Sticks of Gelignite in
Their Lunch Boxes: 1982–83

As 1982 opened, all parties to the conflict were reeling from the passions and impacts of the previous year's hunger strike. The IRA continued their attempts to disrupt co-operation between the British and Irish governments, blowing up another ship in Lough Foyle that February in an attempt to replicate the minor sovereignty crisis of the previous year. Elsewhere, the year began quite disastrously for the organisation. A string of garda successes in capturing arms and explosives around the Monaghan area was linked to community outrage following the death of a local man during a botched 'punishment shooting'. Yet, despite severe disruption to IRA supply lines up to and over the border, republicans still managed to launch a massive bombing campaign in Northern Ireland in April. Later that summer, a gun battle between IRA volunteers and British soldiers in South Armagh lasted nearly an hour, calling to mind an intensity of IRA activity not seen in nearly a decade. The following year, a mortar attack on Crossmaglen barracks narrowly missed a Royal Air Force Wessex helicopter, demonstrating the continued effectiveness of training in that weapon going on in the Republic of Ireland.

But lines of supply and travel did not just run south to north. In September 1983 thirty-eight IRA prisoners staged the largest prison breakout in British penal history. Of the escapees, nearly twenty successfully made their way across the border to the Republic. Additional developments in the South during this period included increasing tension within Portlaoise prison, where the majority of IRA and INLA prisoners in the state were incarcerated. In breach of long-standing policy, IRA members targeted a prison officer in the Republic in March 1983. The security forces of the state became increasingly willing to confront the IRA with force, as happened during a failed kidnapping attempt by the IRA in County Wicklow in August. There, armed gardaí opened fire on the ASU involved, wounding several. Truly subversive republican fundraising attempts, such as a state-wide counterfeit money-laundering campaign, may have contributed to this hardening attitude. Increasingly, during this period, media reports of garda ill-treatment of republican suspects began to sound a note of alarm akin to the mid-1970s. Two other botched fundraising attempts through kidnapping led not only to the removal of the IRA's Director of Operations, but nearly caused a ban on the Sinn Féin party. It was truly a long way from the triumphalist political feeling with which the Provisionals had closed out 1981.

Political Developments and Arms Discoveries

Two general elections took place in the Republic of Ireland in 1982. The first came nine months after the June 1981 general election, which saw two Anti H-Block candidates elected to Dáil Éireann. The election had been called following the collapse of a Fine Gael–Labour coalition due to the government's failure to pass a budget. Given the electoral boost and mass sympathy that had been witnessed the previous year in the South for republican prisoners, Sinn Féin were hopeful that they might further capitalise. They ran seven candidates across the state, including in Louth and Cavan–Monaghan, which had elected Kieran Doherty and Paddy Agnew the previous year. This time around, several locally prominent republican activists were selected as candidates. In Dublin Central, former IRA prisoner Christy Burke was the candidate, while in Longford–Westmeath, Sinn Féin councillor Sean Lynch was selected to run. Veteran republican and Sinn Féin councillor John Joe McGirl ran in Sligo–Leitrim.[1] Lynch made headlines when he challenged the constitutionality of the long-standing Section 31 of the Broadcasting Act, which forbade members of Sinn Féin from appearing on broadcast media i.e., television or radio. The act prohibited RTÉ from broadcasting anything that could be interpreted as supporting the aims or activities of organisations that 'engage in, promote, encourage or advocate the attaining of any political objective by violent means.'[2] In practice, Sinn Féin members could not speak on any subject, political or otherwise, as they were simply not allowed to appear on radio or television.

In a surprise move, the High Court ruled that the Act was in fact unconstitutional and ordered that it be removed from the statute book. The Attorney General immediately appealed the decision to the Supreme Court, who upheld the Act. According to Garret FitzGerald, it was the 'ballot box and Armalite' speech made by Danny Morrison several months earlier that decided the issue. Sinn Féin were not to receive any broadcasting time as part of the general election campaign. During the election, Sinn Féin member Patsy Wright of Athy debated Section 31 with Labour TD Alan Dukes, who said that Sinn Féin would be allowed on the radio whenever they handed over their guns. According to *Magill*, Wright argued that Sinn Féin had no guns, to which Dukes responded, 'Would you ever fuck off.'[3] In an early example of guerrilla marketing, the party's Dublin Central election team circulated a campaign video featuring party Vice President Dáithí Ó Conaill, which was broadcast in a number of pubs in the city in the run-up to the election.

Ultimately, though, the election was a grave disappointment for Sinn Féin. They failed to retain either seat won by Anti H-Block candidates in 1981. Indeed, all seven of their candidates collectively polled just 16,984 votes: less than 40 per cent of that of the Anti H-Block candidates the previous year. Their best result was in Cavan–Monaghan, where imprisoned IRA volunteer Seamus McElwaine received 3,974 votes. While the reaffirmation of Section 31 likely impacted on Sinn Féin's vote, the issue of abstentionism also raised its head. Speaking to a reporter in the aftermath, Dáithí Ó Conaill acknowledged that the policy may have influenced voters. When asked if any consideration was being given to rethinking that policy, he replied: 'I always rethink, that's my nature. But I recognise that, fundamentally, Sinn Féin was founded on the principle that nobody but the Irish people acting as a unit had a right to set up an institution in this country.'[4] Fianna Fáil leader Charlie Haughey was able to form a government when several left-wing TDs agreed to critical voting support. It was short-lived. When that government in turn collapsed in November 1982, Sinn Féin declined to run any candidates, instead focusing their energy unsuccessfully on lobbying for the abolition of Section 31. The previous month, they had put forward candidates in the elections for the newly constituted Northern Ireland Assembly, where they had much greater success, winning five seats and narrowly missing out on two others.

Regardless of which party ruled in the Republic, and aside from the occasional hiccup, such as the sinking of the *St Bedan*, security co-operation with the British remained steady. In March, garda intelligence led to the British Army discovery and defusing of two large beer-keg bombs on the border at Glassdrummond, near Crossmaglen. Command wires from the two bombs were discovered leading across the border into County Louth.[5] Co-operation between gardaí and the RUC around the border during this period was so effective that Minister for Justice Seán Doherty could arrange for the RUC to arrest a man travelling from Northern Ireland to the Republic to testify in an assault case. The man had been due to testify that the garda brother-in-law of Minister Doherty, himself a former garda, had assaulted him. As the plaintiff failed to appear in court, the case was thrown out.

Two escapees from the 1981 Crumlin Road Gaol breakout were recaptured in the South in the early months of the year. Paul 'Dingus' Magee had been a top priority for gardaí following his appearance at Bodenstown the previous June. In the early hours of 6 January 1982, he was arrested in Tralee, County Kerry, when Special Branch detectives accompanied by uniformed gardaí raided a house. That same week, Anthony Gerard Sloan was arrested in a house on the north side of Cork city.[6] Two months later, another IRA prison escapee Gerard Tuite was picked up by gardaí in Drogheda, County Louth. Originally from County Cavan, he had been one of nine republicans arrested in co-ordinated police raids in London and Merseyside in 1979. Charges against the nine included conspiring to cause an explosion and unlawful possession of weapons. Tuite had escaped from the high-security wing of Brixton Prison in 1980 while on remand and had been on the run since that time. He was charged in an Irish court for offences committed in England, under the 1976 Criminal Law (Jurisdiction) Act, receiving a ten-year prison sentence in Portlaoise.[7]

Gardaí had a number of security successes in the early months of 1982, particularly with arms discoveries around the border. In early February, farmer and father-of-four Patrick Corrigan of Emyvale, County Monaghan, was arrested when gardaí discovered five rifles, 40,000 rounds of ammunition and a number of explosive devices in a large steel box concealed in a hedge on his land. Corrigan appeared in court later that year charged with numerous offences and received a prison sentence of ten years' penal servitude. Leave to appeal was rejected.[8] Over the course of several days at the beginning of February, gardaí made no fewer than eleven discoveries of arms, explosives and other military paraphernalia in the border area, particularly in County Monaghan. During the previous month finds had included over 600 rounds of ammunition and an Armalite rifle with ammunition at Scotstown, with 510lbs of explosives also being found in the area. At Emyvale, just prior to Corrigan's arrest, gardaí discovered blast bombs, detonators, gelignite and other bomb components, while in Dundalk that same day, eight mortar bombs with 116lbs of explosives in each were discovered. Just outside Clones, County Monaghan, a bomb with command wires was found near the border. All of these losses represented a considerable blow to the IRA's capabilities in the border region in the short to medium term.

While it is not certain what set this chain of discoveries in motion, they were believed to be linked to a fatal shooting just outside Emyvale on New Year's Eve 1981. In the early hours of that morning, five armed and masked men called to the home of Gabriel Murphy, a married man and part-time bouncer at the Hillgrove Hotel in Monaghan town. Murphy was shot several times in the lower part of his body as he stood in his doorway in what was believed to be a 'punishment shooting'. As a form of 'non-fatal' punishment, the attack was extremely excessive, with up to ten shots being fired, several hitting him in the waist. Murphy died shortly after arriving at Monaghan General Hospital. The circumstances surrounding the shooting remain unclear, although it was believed to have been carried out by local IRA members. According to local accounts, Murphy was one of several staff members at the Hillgrove Hotel who assaulted local IRA leader Jim Lynagh during a confrontation on the premises at Christmas time. While the IRA in Belfast released a statement from the Republican Press Centre denying any involvement in this attack, and its leadership announced their intention to conduct an inquiry into the shooting, it is not clear whether this took place, and gardaí and the general population in Monaghan tended to believe that the killing was the work of several local volunteers. Following Murphy's killing, one of his colleagues was arrested on a Monaghan street with a loaded rifle, which he fired at the feet of a garda detective as a warning. The man had received the weapon from a friend as he feared an attack from the same republican punishment squad. The disgust that the attack on Murphy provoked in the locality was believed to be behind several tip-offs the gardaí received in the following weeks.

Four men were arrested in the aftermath of the New Year's Eve shooting, one of whom was seventeen-year-old Colm Lynagh, younger brother of Jim. He was charged with the murder of Gabriel Murphy and shooting with intent to cause grievous bodily harm in March 1982. Found guilty, he was sentenced to life in prison. A second man, Oliver Barry Kerr, originally from Coalisland, County Tyrone, faced the same charges later in the year, although the murder charge was withdrawn by the state at the opening of the trial. Kerr had been arrested in April when he fled from a farmhouse near Scotstown with several other men at the approach of detectives. While in custody, he allegedly remarked to gardaí, 'You know we didn't mean to kill him. It went wrong.' He also alleged that gardaí struck him during his detention. Kerr received a seven-year prison sentence in December 1982.[9] Two other Lynagh brothers, who were both living in Dublin and unconnected with republican activity, were subject to continuous garda attention around this time. One of them, Michael Lynagh, was regularly arrested, harassed and subject to ill-treatment from gardaí while in custodial detention. While Michael had pre-existing mental health problems, chiefly depression, family and friends attribute a worsening of his condition to garda harassment during this period. Following yet another arrest and detention in Mountjoy prison in September 1982, Michael hanged himself in his cell with a bed sheet.[10]

Increased garda attention in the border region in 1982 had a noticeable impact on the IRA's activities. Another security success at this time was the breaking up, in part, of an ASU in the Louth–South Armagh area. Patrick McNamee (25) of Hackballscross, County Louth, Francis Quigley (30) of Belfast and Francis McCabe (24) of Crossmaglen, County Armagh, were travelling in a van near Hackballscross when they encountered a checkpoint manned by gardaí and Irish Army personnel. The van reversed away from the checkpoint, at which point an army vehicle began a pursuit. The van then suddenly accelerated, colliding with the army and garda vehicles. Two of the men then fled the vehicle and sought to escape across fields, occasionally turning to fire shots at the pursuing gardaí. They were discovered and arrested in a house about half a mile from the checkpoint, while the third man was picked up in the vicinity later. Inside the van, which bore a false number plate, gardaí found three milk churn bombs, two beer-keg bombs, a self-loading rifle and seventy rounds of ammunition. The three arrested men were experienced IRA volunteers and subsequently received prison sentences ranging from six to eight years on arms and explosives charges. McNamee later served as a local councillor for Sinn Féin.[11]

In late March, gardaí searched a farm near Stradbally, County Laois, following an intelligence tip-off. They discovered a small arsenal of eighteen sticks of gelignite, a grenade, a handgun and assorted ammunition. Gardaí reported that nobody lived at the farm, which had been purchased recently by a local man. The RUC congratulated the gardaí on this and several other recent finds.[12] However, not all garda discoveries during this period were so timely. Just two weeks earlier, and after several days' delay, they issued a warning to the RUC that 'large quantities' of gelignite had been stolen from the Mogul mines in County Tipperary in what was described as a *Mission Impossible*-type operation. According to an internal garda report, 'investigations here have established that an unauthorised entry to the underground area was effected by means of an escape shaft which breaks surface in an isolated area about one mile from the mine proper'.[13] The raiders then walked a mile underground before acquiring a 'transport car' for the return journey with the explosives. The total amount taken was reported to be '14 cases of Fragex [*sic*], 6 reels of cordtex (two abandoned), 195 electronic dets and thirty fuse caps', with the amount of detonators and fuse wire taken exactly matching the needs of the amount of explosives stolen. According to the report, 'the mine was last seen intact shortly before 7.00pm on Sunday 14th March 1982 when visited by shift boss … It was this same employee who discovered the interference with the reserve station between 8.00 and 9.00am this morning'.[14] The following week, a garda superintendent dismissed reports that the stolen explosives had been used in a wave of bombings in the North several days earlier, stating: 'these explosives were not taken until Sunday night and it is doubtful they could have got them over the border in time for use on Monday'.[15]

While the theft may have occurred as reported, an alternative account is that shift workers had been taking small amounts of explosives from the mines incrementally over a long period of time. This was possible due to lax record-keeping practices. When a long overdue inventory did take place, revealing the extent of the missing explosives, the decision was taken to report the theft as one single operation.[16] It is worth noting that, during the 1970s, a number of mine workers and soldiers tasked with guarding explosives supplies in mines were arrested and charged with their theft.[17] These incidents took place particularly in the Mogul mines, as well as the Arigna mines in County Roscommon. Indeed, in discussing the 1982 Mogul explosives theft, one garda told journalists, 'Many times we have caught employees trying to smuggle sticks of gelignite out in their lunch boxes.'[18] Elsewhere, in a 1989 obituary for Tom Lavin, a republican and coalminer from Arigna, it noted that 'the miners of Arigna were always to the fore in the cause of human liberty.'[19] While the above alternative account for the Mogul mines theft cannot be proven, it is certainly not improbable. And, while the explosives were never recovered in any great amount, in August that year the RUC did successfully intercept another load of IRA explosives being transported in a lorry near Banbridge, County Down. In the lorry, which had come from the Republic, were discovered sixty large bags of HME.[20]

According to a British Home Office report, by 1981 commercial explosives from mine 'leaks' accounted for just 0.7 per cent of bombings in the North. Commercial explosives were in use in both Northern Ireland and the Republic, and their point of origin could not be traced following an explosion. However, the provenance of this 0.7 per cent was believed to derive entirely from the Republic, 'where supervision by the Gardaí is not nearly so extensive as that applied in NI.'[21] The report asserted that 88 per cent of the IRA's bombs were HME derived from fertiliser. There were serious efforts underway during the early 1980s to limit paramilitary access to material used in HMEs. Since the beginning of the previous decade, the IRA had relied on commercial fertiliser for the majority of the explosives used in its bombing campaigns. The Republic of Ireland was historically a predominantly rural country, and farming was still a major part of the economy in the latter part of the twentieth century. Fertiliser was easily available for purchase across the state and was not subject to controls. The fertiliser for sale in the Republic was a three-quarters ammonium nitrate to one-quarter calcium carbonate mix, and it was the ammonium nitrate which the IRA needed. Prior to 1972, fertilisers were available that were almost pure ammonium nitrate, but these were removed from sale in the early years of the 'Troubles'. Efforts to reduce the ammonium nitrate percentage further were resisted by agricultural interests in the Republic. This was due to Irish livestock needing a high-nitrogen supplement which the fertiliser brought to grasslands. The ammonium nitrate from the fertiliser could be extracted by spreading it across a trough or other container, heating it gently but continuously and turning it. This method was known as 'boiling' and was a key activity of the IRA's Southern Command. As the British report noted, the ammonium nitrate was then mixed with fuel oil to form a blasting explosive known as ANFO (ammonium nitrate and fuel oil).

The last time the British and Irish governments had discussed controls on or modifications to fertiliser was in 1978. In 1982 the British Ministry of Defence began pushing other government departments to restart these discussions. An internal communication on the subject read:

> One point which has been brought home to me very strongly indeed in my visits to the Armed Forces in Northern Ireland, not least by GOCNI [General Officer Commanding Northern Ireland], is how concerned they are at the ease with which terrorists can manufacture their own explosives … in the last year some two in three of the deaths and injuries caused by terrorist bombs have been caused by homemade rather than commercial explosive. In addition the terrorists' continuing capability to manufacture the kind of very large bomb which is put in a culvert or at a roadside seriously hampers the Army's freedom of movement, particularly in the border areas … As this explosive is derived from agricultural fertiliser manufactured in the Republic, the key to the problem does seem to be to persuade the Irish authorities to stop manufacturing fertiliser based on the present 74% ammonium nitrate 26% calcium carbonate mix. In order to do this we must be able to offer some alternative fertiliser which is satisfactory from the industrial and agricultural point of view but which cannot be rendered into explosive.[22]

While discussions did indeed begin again in 1982, it was to be several years before any progress was made.

Elsewhere, the IRA's low ebb continued in terms of arms losses. There were major interceptions in the USA of arms bound for the IRA throughout this and the previous year. In May 1981, the US Customs

Service and special agents of the Bureau of Alcohol, Tobacco and Firearms examined a crate found at the Aer Lingus cargo terminal at JFK airport in New York and discovered eight semi-automatic rifles and 120 rounds of ammunition. The following month, another arms shipment was discovered in the city prior to embarkation. This one included a 20mm cannon with shells, a flamethrower, twenty-one rifles and handguns, 12,500 rounds of ammunition and booby-trap components. Michael Flannery of NORAID was arrested in follow-up operations. In the summer of 1982, the Federal Bureau of Investigation (FBI) smashed a million-dollar arms operation by the IRA in New York. Two men were charged with conspiracy to purchase and export weapons and munitions including five surface-to-air (SAM) missiles (each costing $10,000) and a large number of assault rifles. One of the accused, Belfast man Gabriel Megahey, had told FBI agents posing as arms dealers that his organisation had $1 million to spend on the purchase of weapons. The loss of the money and arms was a huge blow to the IRA's finances. In a final case, the FBI arrested two Irish brothers on charges related to the shipment of arms and ammunition to the Republic. One of these shipments was sent in a container marked as containing roller skates and blankets.

Working with US officials, gardaí were able to identify this container when it arrived at Ringsend in Dublin on 13 June. Rather than intercept it at the port, it was decided to track the container in the hopes of arresting more than just the pick-up man. The container was put in a truck and driven to Carew Park, on Limerick city's south side. When gardaí confronted the driver and another man, shots were fired from both parties, with the driver and his accomplice fleeing. One of the two – Patrick McVeigh (31) from Belfast – was apprehended, while the other escaped. The owner of a nearby house, Limerick man John Moloney (52) and his brother Father Patrick Moloney (54), were also arrested. Father Moloney, a member of the Greek Malachite Order, was a US citizen but born in Ireland and had been back on holiday at the time of his arrest. He and the two others were charged with possession of an Armalite rifle and several hundred rounds of ammunition. Father Moloney was initially refused bail as a potential flight risk. However, in a surprise move during his trial, the Director of Public Prosecutions dropped the charges against him. The same judge who had opposed bail then declared that charges should never have been brought in the first place. Bail was then granted to Moloney's brother but refused for McVeigh as a flight risk.[23] John Moloney and McVeigh received three- and seven-year prison terms respectively on arms charges.[24]

A report on arms, ammunition and explosives seizures by gardaí in 1982 listed the following:

Table 9. Garda seizures of arms, ammunition and explosives, 1982[25]

Quantity	Type
238	Firearms (including rifles, shotguns, machine guns, pistols, revolvers, etc.)
47,641	Rounds of ammunition (assorted)
1,164	Shotgun cartridges
47	Magazines
6	Sticks of gelignite
88	Detonators
2,409lbs	Explosive mixture
1	Rocket
4	Rocket shells
27	Bombs
11	Hand grenades
34	Timing devices

As with other years, some of the above might have been linked to the INLA and Official IRA, but the majority were likely weapons captured from the Provisional IRA. Co-operation between the gardaí, RUC and British Army was reported to be 'excellent' during this period, and the British commended the 'many valuable arrests and finds in the Republic'.[26] What may have been another significant IRA arms importation attempt was disrupted in France the following year. In August 1983, French police arrested an Irishman at Le Havre as he was about to drive an Irish-registered lorry onto a ferry bound for Rosslare. Hidden in a false tank beneath the trailer, they discovered twenty handguns, over 10,000 rounds of ammunition, magazines for AK-47 assault rifles, Russian-made grenades, detonators and nearly 30lbs of explosives. The lorry driver, Michael MacDonald (27) from County Louth, had run a small haulage business for three years prior to his arrest. While French authorities claimed that the arms found in the lorry were bound for the IRA, gardaí discounted that notion, claiming that MacDonald – while known to them – was not known to have any connections with subversive organisations. This perhaps indicates their belief that the arms were bound for some other group or gang.[27] Overall, the near three-fold increase in ammunition seized in 1982, as well as an increase in arms captured, compared to the previous year can be seen as a significant garda success and was bound to increase pressure on the IRA.

Tension and Clashes with Security Forces

In February 1982, the gardaí suffered a tragic loss when Garda Patrick Reynolds became the eighth member of the force to be killed on duty as a result of the 'Troubles'. He and several colleagues had been dispatched to investigate reports of suspicious activity at a house in Tallaght, County Dublin, late one night. Arriving at the building and seeking to enter, the gardaí spied armed members of a gang inside. As the unarmed gardaí withdrew, they were pursued by the gang, who shot Garda Reynolds in the back before fleeing. He died at the scene. It is believed the gang were using the house to count the proceeds of a recent bank robbery carried out in Askeaton, County Limerick.[28] The INLA was initially suspected and a number of homes in Cork and Dublin belonging to IRSP members were raided in the aftermath.[29] For their part, the INLA rejected the connection. In a statement, the organisation said:

> The Irish National Liberation Army since its inception has never been involved in the shooting of either gardaí or civilians in the 26 counties. We will no longer tolerate, or accept responsibility for, the actions of rejects from our organisation. These same elements have in the recent past been responsible for the attempted assassination of leading members of the IRSP.[30]

This was one of the first apparent public cracks in the INLA; the organisation would tear itself apart during the 1980s.

In June 1982, the INLA was responsible for the assassination of leading Official IRA member, Jim Flynn, at his barber shop in Cabra, north Dublin city. Shortly before this killing, the current-affairs magazine *Magill* had published a lengthy exposé on the links between the secretive Official IRA and Sinn Féin–The Workers' Party. Although it had not explicitly named Flynn, it did refer to him obtusely in connection with the assassination of INLA Chief of Staff Seamus Costello in 1977. Workers' Party TD Proinsias De Rossa stated publicly that *Magill* bore responsibility for the death of Flynn, and editor Vincent Browne received death threats in the aftermath of the killing.[31] The INLA themselves claimed that they carried out the revenge attack because the recent publicity about the continued existence of the Official IRA made such an action more publicly acceptable. Vincent Browne and *Magill* condemned the shooting of Flynn, claiming that it entirely undermined the IRSP's campaign for the release of Nicky Kelly, a member of their organisation.[32] Kelly had been one of several IRSP members arrested in 1976 and beaten into confessing their role in a train robbery at Sallins. The confessions were entirely false and in fact it was the Provisional IRA who carried out the robbery.

This garda practice of physical assaults on suspects in custody and the forced extraction of confessions was particularly prevalent during the Fine Gael–Labour coalition of 1973–77. It partly subsided during the tenure of Jack Lynch's Fianna Fáil government but began to make a return during the early 1980s. In 1981 the chairman of Amnesty Ireland accused the gardaí of using torture, and the government of doing nothing to prevent it.[33] That same year, four young men were arrested in County Cavan on suspicion of an arson attack on the Billyhill Orange Order Hall near Shercock. The men all signed confessions and immediately recanted them following their release, claiming to have confessed under duress. Two of the detectives involved in that investigation had also been assigned to the Sallins robbery case, with three of them later working on the 'Kerry babies' case, discussed in the following chapter. In 1982, garda conduct during interrogations at Shercock Garda Station again came to national attention when a man was found dead in his cell at the station. The man, Peter Matthews, had been taken to the station for questioning regarding the theft of post office books. When his wife saw him later that day, she reported that 'his hair had been torn out, there were lumps of hair on his shoulder and sleeve … he had a black eye and blood on his cheek'. A friend of Matthews who saw his body claimed that 'it appeared that hair had been pulled out and the ears were swollen'.[34] Writing of this case, Gene Kerrigan summarised the situation at the time:

> There was a lot of disquiet over the fact that a man could die violently in a police cell and his death could remain unexplained and no one would be made accountable. But no further avenues were explored, no further charges were laid … Pressing too hard on such an issue might bring whispers of anti-police tendencies, perhaps even suggestions of a whiff of subversion.[35]

In the case of Peter Matthews, he had not actually been under arrest but had voluntarily accompanied gardaí to the station to assist with their enquiries. To those unfamiliar with their legal rights, such a garda request might not actually be perceived as one that could be refused. The ambiguity of this garda practice was criticised in a report by Justice Barra Ó Briain commissioned by the government in 1978. The government had rejected or deferred two-thirds of the Ó Briain report's recommendations, including ending the policy of gardaí taking people to stations to 'assist with enquiries'.[36]

Section 30 of the Offences Against the State Act continued to be the chief tool used by gardaí to hold republican suspects. In 1972, there were 229 arrests under Section 30. This figure increased to 602 in 1974 and 1,015 in 1976. Each year, as the numbers of those arrested under the Act increased significantly, the number of charges proffered dropped dramatically.[37] By the 1980s the ratio of arrested to charged flipped, with just over 10 per cent of those being arrested subsequently facing a charge.[38] In 1981, in Dublin alone, there were 1,255 arrests. Across the state that year there were 2,303 arrests but only 323 charges, while the following year the figures were 2,308 arrests and 256 charges, respectively.[39] In 1983, there were 2,234 arrests under the Act, with just 15 per cent of cases resulting in charges.[40] As *Magill* pointed out, it was 'quite striking that the bulk of Section 30 arrests occurred not when the Provisional IRA was engaging in the greatest amount of violence but when Sinn Féin began using electoral methods to gain support'.[41] In considering the figures for arrests as against prosecutions from the early 1980s onwards, it appears the Act was increasingly being used in a proxy form for temporary detention of republicans and other subversives.

One arrest and interrogation in Cavan in 1982 resulted in a massive pay-out six years later. Thomas Martin of Kingscourt, County Cavan, was arrested in December 1982 on suspicion of the theft of guns, ammunition and cash from a firearms dealer in County Meath. Martin's testimony, supported by two doctors, was that during interrogation detectives subjected him to considerable violence. This included being punched, pulled by the hair, having his head banged and his arms twisted behind his back. At one point, a detective allegedly took a bullet from his pocket and placed it in the hollow of Martin's neck. He was awarded £24,360 in the High Court in 1988.[42] In the same month that the Meath firearms dealer was raided, £100,000 was taken in a post office raid in Tallaght. One of those interrogated on suspicion of involvement in that robbery was twenty-one-year-old Amanda McShane. McShane was subsequently put on trial for her part in the robbery. In a surprise move, mid-trial, the prosecution announced that they were dropping charges against her and she walked free. This sudden about-face followed on from McShane's solicitor producing a 'highly irregular' document in court, which he had discovered in the interrogation room at Crumlin Garda Station. The document was a written statement purportedly made by McShane and simply awaiting her signature. McShane had in fact made no such statement. Following the document's production and the subsequent acquittal, there was no garda inquiry.[43]

During this same period, the prison regime in Portlaoise, which had been relatively peaceful in the preceding years, turned increasingly hostile. According to the Portlaoise Prisoners Relative Action Committee, in February 1982 assaults against republican prisoners became more commonplace, particularly during strip-searches, which were also now occurring with more regularity. Remand prisoners were being searched in this manner before and after court visits, with one prisoner alleging in court that men were being hung up by their ankles in the prison. This followed on from the discovery of several ounces of explosives in the handicrafts section of the prison on 3 February.[44] In October of that year, a major search operation was undertaken by prison authorities, during which eighty prisoners were injured, some as a result of forced strip-searches. Relatives claimed that no doctors were allowed into the prison for two days in order to 'give bruises a chance to disappear'.[45] It was further alleged that many off-duty prisoner officers and gardaí were called in to assist during the operation, several of whom had been drinking and proceeded to use significant violence. In 1983, prison officers acknowledged the treatment meted out to republican prisoners, which was blamed on the prison governor and his assistant. According to the Prison Officers' Association, the majority of the brutalisation was ordered and overseen by the leadership of the prison administration, 'and officers who expressed disapproval of the battering of prisoners were called "Provo lovers" and were blatantly victimised by the prison management'.[46]

The following year, a number of members of the Prison Officers' Association again raised concerns about the beating of prisoners in Portlaoise. Minister for Justice Michael Noonan maintained that there was insufficient evidence to prosecute any of the culprits. In response, prison officers claimed they were not even interviewed by gardaí about the allegations. They also accused the minister of turning a blind eye to reports of such incidents. According to the Assistant General Secretary of the association, staff in Portlaoise had been incited by senior officers to use excessive force against prisoners. Noonan confirmed in November 1984 that there would be no criminal prosecutions against prison officers for attacks on prisoners during October of the previous year.[47]

In March 1983 members of the IRA carried out an unprecedented shooting of a prison officer based at Portlaoise, the first such armed assault on a prison officer in the history of the state. Chief Prison Officer Brian Stack was shot in the neck and seriously injured as he left the National Stadium in Dublin on 25 March. His assailants fled on a motorcycle and were never apprehended. Stack remained in a coma for several months without recovering and died after eighteen months in a Dublin hospital. In the immediate aftermath of the shooting, there was much speculation about the attackers and their motives. One newspaper spoke of 'a hitherto little-known paramilitary group called The Alliance, composed of the INLA and the Provisional IRA', attributing the attack to 'increased unrest among prisoners in Portlaoise, particularly over search techniques'.[48] Liz Walsh later attributed the attack to the IRA, saying it was retaliation 'for what they claimed was his hard-line attitude towards republican prisoners'.[49] In

2013 the Provisional IRA belatedly claimed responsibility, albeit insisting that it was carried out without Army Council knowledge or approval.[50] In a statement released by the organisation and addressed to the children of Brian Stack, they asserted:

> This was a secret guerrilla army. It kept no records of its military operations. During the 30 years of war activists were killed, many thousands were imprisoned and leaderships at all levels were constantly changing. Reliable information is therefore not readily available and sometimes not available at all. The IRA did have rules and regulations, including a rule which prohibited any military action against Irish state forces. Regrettably at times these rules were breached … This is the context in which IRA volunteers shot your father. This action was not authorised by the IRA leadership and for this reason the IRA denied any involvement … The IRA was responsible for your father's death. This operation should not have taken place.[51]

The following year a list containing the names and addresses of 120 Irish prison officers was found in Bushy Park, Terenure, south Dublin.[52] Ultimately, warders in Northern Ireland were the only body of prison officers to be officially designated as 'legitimate targets' by the Provisional IRA for several years during the conflict.[53]

In 1984 the families of republican prisoners in Portlaoise stepped up their campaign to bring public awareness to conditions within the prison. In September, the Portlaoise Prisoners Relatives Action Committee toured the country with a life-sized reproduction of a prison cell for people to view and step into. A rally in Dublin city centre in November of that year attracted a large crowd, which was entertained by some of the best-known Irish musicians of the period. One protestor was arrested after scuffles with gardaí. The awareness campaign continued into the following year. In Cork, a number of homes were raided by gardaí and three Sinn Féin members arrested in March 1985, after posters had been pasted across the city relating to conditions within Portlaoise prison. Two months later, 350 people were reported as attending a march and public meeting in Finglas as part of Finglas Prisoners Week. According to *An Phoblacht*, eight men from that area were then serving prison sentences in Portlaoise for IRA activity and 'the rally was a timely reminder of the ongoing contribution which Finglas has made to the republican cause'.[54]

On the Ropes

While garda practices were coming under greater scrutiny during this period, the IRA was also feeling the pressure. In February 1982 three experienced volunteers from Southern Command received lengthy prison sentences for their part in an armed robbery in County Cork the previous October. Stephen Gibson (22), a Belfast native, and Edward Gerard Leahy (24) from Cork were part of a three-man unit that took part in a raid on the post office at Togher. Fleeing from the building with £2,293, they were confronted by three detectives. The detectives managed to block in the escape car and fired shots into the air and at one of the tyres of the raiders' car to immobilise it, before arresting the men. During their trial, Gibson and Leahy refused to recognise the court. They were later given additional three-year concurrent prison terms for IRA membership. Their accomplice had already been sentenced to eight years' imprisonment having pleaded guilty to the armed robbery charge.[55] According to IRA informer Sean O'Callaghan, it was information provided to gardaí by another IRA informer, John Corcoran, which led to these arrests.[56] The detectives had received a tip-off in advance from Corcoran and had not simply happened upon the scene as per the official account.

Later that summer, another IRA ASU was dismantled when five volunteers were arrested at St Johnston, County Donegal, a short drive from Derry city. The men, from Counties Donegal, Tyrone and Derry, had commandeered a house in the area on 17 July and held its occupants captive, seemingly while an IRA operation took place in the locality. The occupation continued into the following day and, at one point, the husband in the house was allowed into the nearby village to pick up supplies. A courier also delivered supplies to the IRA unit. At some point, however, the gardaí were alerted and they surrounded the house with support from the Irish Army. A priest negotiated the surrender of the men, who each received eight-year prison sentences. The charges were for hijacking, false imprisonment, IRA membership and possession of arms with intent to endanger life, though the combined sentences were to run concurrently.[57]

Despite these setbacks, the Provisionals continued to prosecute their campaign. On 20 July 1982, they carried out bombings in London's Hyde Park and Regent's Park, which caused a wave of condemnation across the UK and the Republic. The Hyde Park bomb was targeted at members of a British Army cavalry regiment as they took part in a daily changing of the guard. The gelignite and shrapnel device used in the attack was placed in the boot of a car parked on the road along which the horsemen passed. Four soldiers and seven horses were killed. The latter attack took place as bandsmen of the Royal Green Jackets played at a bandstand in Regent's Park. That bomb had been placed underneath the bandstand in advance of the advertised performance. Seven soldiers were killed. While the revulsion was understandable, particularly as a number of civilians were also injured, Tim Pat Coogan noted that the deaths of army horses seemingly 'elicited more outrage from the British tabloids than did the deaths of the soldiers'.[58] The British Embassy in Dublin reported back to London on the numerous letters of support they received in the aftermath of the attacks from people across the Republic of Ireland. Frank O'Reilly, chairman of the Royal Dublin Society (O'Reilly also served as chairman of Ulster Bank at this time), contacted the embassy to offer £45,000 that he and a number of other Irish businessmen had collected to pay for the replacement of the horses. This would be done under the aegis of the Royal Dublin Society in order to preserve the anonymity of the donors. The money was turned down as, according to a British memo, 'One does not need the prejudices of a *Daily Express* or *Daily Telegraph* leader writer to realise, however, that it is open to misinterpretation as showing more concern for the dead horses than the dead humans ...'[59] The money was ultimately donated to the widows and children of those killed.

IRA activity in the South faced another serious disruption with the arrest of two members of an ASU engaged in armed robberies in the Munster area in November and December. George Hayes (23) of Limerick city and David Douglas (21) of Cabra were each sentenced to twelve years' imprisonment on charges of attempted murder, armed robbery and firearms possession. The two were part of a four-man unit which entered the Allied Irish Banks (AIB) sub-branch, part of Wang Laboratories, at a technology park in Annacotty, just outside Limerick city. They shouted at staff to get down on the ground and filled a bag with cash. The total amount taken was £24,500. During the raid, a shot was fired through the roof of the building. Following the robbery, they fled in the direction of Limerick city. However, while en route the escape car's engine cut out. A blue HiAce van then inadvertently blocked the car. Detectives, who had received a call about the incident at the bank, were on their way there when they spotted the accidental roadblock. One of the raiders fired several shots at the detectives' car, striking the bonnet and windscreen but missing the occupants. The IRA unit then commandeered the blue van and fled, with gardaí giving chase. They lost sight of the van after a short pursuit, finding it abandoned some distance away. Meanwhile, the raiders had overshot the location selected as the drop-off point for the money and weapons, and when they did arrive, the 'pick-up man' was not there. In a panic, the men split up, with three of them fleeing down a local canal while the fourth man made off across the same canal. Douglas was arrested later that day in People's Park in Limerick city. The rest of the unit appeared to have gone underground, as two of them were never captured. Hayes, meanwhile, confessed his part in the robbery following his arrest in Tullamore the following month on suspicion of being a member of an unlawful organisation.

Accounts in court of the build up to the armed robbery give a valuable insight into the operational compartmentalisation of the IRA's cell system, adopted in the latter half of the 1970s. According to Douglas, he received instructions while living in Dublin to travel to Limerick on the night of 16 November. There, he would meet a man with a red scarf named 'Dave' in the St George's pub. 'Dave' took Douglas to a house, where he stayed the night. The following morning, 'Dave' arrived at the house with three other men. They were given a briefing and told that they would be going to Wang's [Laboratories] where there would be 'twenty grand'.[60]

Not all major armed robberies carried out by republicans during this period ended so badly. For example, five raiders wearing paramilitary uniforms and dark glasses escaped with £50,000 from the Bank of Ireland branch in Askeaton, County Limerick, in February 1982. In December of that year, an IRA unit from Kerry made off with £24,000 from a factory in County Waterford, evading pursuit by taking a boat across the River Suir.[61]

On the whole, however, the number of bank robberies taking place in the Republic of Ireland began to drop off significantly from 1982 onwards. Indeed, one of the Sunday newspapers had run a piece titled 'Where have all the bankrobbers gone?' in August 1981.[62] The decrease was largely the result of additional security precautions introduced by banks, under strong pressure from the government. These included metal doors, time locks on doors and safes, surveillance cameras and screens. Collectively, the measures cost Irish banks £5 million. One of the outcomes of these changes was that paramilitaries and crime gangs began to shift towards softer targets, such as cash transit vans, from 1981.

Estimates on IRA finances – its needs and what it managed to raise – vary during this period. In one history of Sinn Féin, the author puts annual costs for the Provisional republican movement as a whole at £3 million in the mid-1980s, with the IRA's fundraising capacity in the very broad range of £5–8 million.[63] Another estimate is that the IRA took over £2 million in armed robberies in the Munster area alone in the six years up to 1983. This estimate is supported by the account of a leading IRA officer in the region at that time.[64] According to a British report from 1983: 'The Provisional IRA alone requires between £3 and £4 million a year to finance their campaign'. It claimed that NORAID had raised $3 million since its inception in 1969 and that 'between 1971 and 1982 over £7 million was stolen in armed robberies in Northern Ireland, the largest proportion being taken by the Provisionals. In the Irish Republic, it's estimated that the Provisional IRA takes some 50 per cent, 400,000 of the cash stolen each year.'[65]

From the early 1980s, an increasing number of gardaí began routinely carrying firearms, which posed an additional risk for armed robbers. In June 1982, an INLA unit was involved in a gun battle with armed gardaí in the centre of Tipperary town during the course of a double bank robbery. According to contemporary accounts, four men armed with handguns entered the AIB and held up the staff inside, forcing the manager to open the safe vaults. Two other men, one with a rifle and one with a pistol, kept guard in the market area alongside the bank and took advantage of an AIB mobile unit arriving to take some of its cash load, though staff were able to hide most of it. When two gardaí arrived on the scene they were ordered to lie on the ground. Shots were exchanged when four more gardaí arrived in a patrol car, though nobody was hurt. As the INLA unit began to make its escape, they ordered the driver of a lorry to block the street behind the mobile AIB unit. Gardaí did manage to give chase but lost the getaway car after some distance. A Belfast native living in Dublin received a six-year prison sentence in January 1983 for his part in the robbery.[66] Other members of the unit were more locally based, being from the Limerick–Shannon region.[67]

In the same month as the sentencing for the Tipperary bank robbery, the INLA were outlawed in the Republic of Ireland, having been a legal organisation since their foundation in December 1974. The proscription of the INLA followed several attacks, most notably the Droppin' Well bombing in County Derry in which eleven British soldiers and six civilians were killed, as well as their bomb attack on the radar station at Schull in west Cork. The Schull bombing was due to the erroneous belief that it was a NATO radar station, with the damage estimated at £1.5 million. A fireman from Castleconnell was subsequently sentenced to nine years' imprisonment for his part in that attack.[68] At the time of their proscription, the INLA and its political wing, the IRSM, were facing significant leadership disputes, as well as persistent funding issues. While their support base was never more than a fraction of that held by the IRA, raising funds during this period was an increasing challenge for both movements.

Dire Financial Straits

When the IRA began to transition from bank robberies as a principal source of income in the early 1980s, they did not rely entirely on targeting post office and bank deliveries. Indeed, these potential sources of cash also began to benefit from increased security, such as more regular armed garda escorts. As a replacement, the potential dividends of ransom pay-outs from kidnapping proved particularly tempting. According to one account, from the beginning of 1980 to the end of 1982, nearly £400,000 had been paid out in ransom payments in the Republic, although it should be noted that the IRA was not provably linked to any of these kidnappings (it excludes the Dunne kidnapping).[69] For the IRA, however, any replication of the successful kidnapping of Ben Dunne in 1981 would prove alluring, particularly as funds were needed for future arms importations and other avenues of fundraising were looking increasingly risky. That kidnapping had taken place without a hitch and, if replicated, the dividends for the movement could be very lucrative. Even better if the target would not attempt to escape and could not later identify his captors.

On the evening of 8 February 1983, an IRA unit abducted the world-famous racehorse Shergar from the Ballymany Stud in County Kildare. The four-man unit entered the home of Jim Fitzgerald, Shergar's groom, and held his family at gunpoint while Fitzgerald was forced to take some of the men to Shergar's stable. Horse and groom were then bundled into a horsebox and car respectively. Fitzgerald was released several miles from the stable, having been given a password that the kidnappers would use in negotiations.[70] Despite the potential pay-off from this kidnapping, the IRA's decision to carry out the operation is baffling on several levels. Shergar was possibly the world's most recognisable horse, with a distinctive white muzzle marking, making him very difficult to hide. The IRA also didn't seem to have given thought to the ownership structure of the horse. Shergar was owned by a syndicate, making any possibility of ransom payment inherently complicated, if not impossible. Lastly, if the Provisionals were hoping that the kidnap of a horse would arouse less public anger than that of a person, they were mistaken. Tens of thousands of Irish Farmers' Association members conducted a two-day search for Shergar, while calls flooded in from across the country with possible information on the horse's whereabouts. A spokesperson for the Thoroughbred Breeders' Association stated: 'I don't think the Irish mentality would lend itself to doing anything to harm the horse.'[71] At one point, a week after the abduction, several dozen gardaí converged on the countryside near Tynagh, County Galway. They had intercepted a two-way radio conversation which indicated a possibility that Shergar was about to be transported through that area. The search took in a number of isolated farms, heavily wooded hills and a disused mine, all without success. When Galway was ruled out, the focus of the search shifted to Mayo, then Leitrim. At one point, it was even claimed that clairvoyants were brought in by gardaí to assist them where conventional policing techniques had failed. Whether solicited or not, some psychics did suggest possible locations for the search, including the area around Castlecomer, County Kilkenny.[72] By 25 February, with hopes fading of Shergar ever being found, the 100,000 members of the Irish Farmers' Association committed to searching every horsebox, barn and field in the state.[73] They had no more success than on the previous occasion.

While hoping to net £2 million from the ransom, the IRA never received any money for Shergar and the fate of the horse remains a mystery. The most common theory is that the high-strung animal injured itself while being led out of the horsebox and was shot by its captors and secretly buried. Suggested burial sites are numberless. If the prevailing theory is true, the IRA likely kept it a secret for fear of the inevitable disgust and hostility that the killing would arouse in much of the population – as well as still hoping to extract a ransom payment from Shergar's owners. Former IRA member and informer Sean O'Callaghan claimed to have intimate knowledge regarding the fate of Shergar. Like many of O'Callaghan's claims, however, this was never verified.[74] Ed Moloney attributed the kidnapping to leading Tyrone IRA member Kevin Mallon, stating that the disastrous outcome of the operation contributed to his downfall within the republican movement.[75] Tim Pat Coogan cryptically claimed that the kidnapping was 'associated with one particular maverick IRA man whose daring exploits have often been in the news'.[76] Another former IRA volunteer stated that a Limerick-based member of Southern Command was responsible for the idea and planning of this operation, though he was not a participant himself.[77] Similarly, Liz Walsh believed it was the work of the same south-west unit that would later carry out the Don Tidey kidnapping (discussed later in this chapter).[78]

The Provisional IRA also experimented with counterfeit money as a means of fundraising in the 1980s. In this, they were following in the path of their former rivals, the Official IRA. Having printed upwards of £1 million-worth of fake £10 notes in early 1983, the Provisionals intended to circulate them among the general public cash flow. The operation necessitated considerable planning and co-ordination, as it was to be carried out over the course of just one April bank holiday weekend and involved activists across the country.[79] If the plan had been carried out successfully, hotels, shops, pubs and bookmakers would all have been surreptitiously inundated with a huge number of these counterfeit notes. A garda spokesman described the forgery operation as 'one of the largest ever in this country'.[80] The distribution of the counterfeit notes went beyond active IRA members and, in fact, involved a wide network of republican supporters across the state.

As it was, the operation fell short of the ambitious original goal. In the early hours of 13 April, gardaí raided a home in the Cronan Park area of Shannon town and arrested a man and woman living there. The man was subsequently charged at a 'special court' in Lahinch Garda Station with possession of 150 forged £10 notes. As one newspaper remarked, the

'Cronin [sic] Park district has a large population of "settlers" from the Six Counties'.[81] According to a *Magill* article, published two years later: 'At the beginning of April 1983 Special Branch detectives decided to search homes in the Shannon area, suspecting arms and explosives were concealed there. Dawn raids on eight houses instead turned up an unexpected bounty'.[82] That raid in Shannon town occurred on the Thursday prior to the designated weekend for the state-wide dispersal of the bank notes, throwing the whole operation into doubt.[83] Official accounts paint the discovery of the counterfeit notes as a lucky accident, as per the *Magill* article. An alternative account is that an informer had tipped gardaí off about the cash and the arms raids were carried out by them as a cover. According to one interviewee, a republican sympathiser tasked with dispersing some of the counterfeit notes in Limerick city during the bank holiday weekend had used one of them in the Royal George Hotel to pay for a drink on the preceding Wednesday night. Evidently, this forgery was discovered and word of the plan, already involving more and more participants state-wide, leaked. Whether gardaí then utilised informers or simply relied on existing intelligence of potential participants is unknown. The following morning, when they raided the Shannon home, a locally based member of the Special Branch ran up the stairs of the house directly into one particular bedroom and opened a wardrobe where the counterfeit notes were stored.[84] This local disruption in Munster was followed by several more garda discoveries in Dublin city, Arklow and Enniscorthy during the week.

Despite this, the IRA's dispersal operation went ahead, though at a much-reduced level, in counties as far apart as Cork, Monaghan, Mayo and Wexford.[85] Gardaí worked to defeat the IRA's plans by circulating descriptions of the counterfeit money, noting that, although they were good enough to escape immediate detection, they were slightly smaller and paler than their legitimate counterparts. They also felt limper and creased easily.[86] Intermittently, throughout the year, gardaí continued to make significant seizures of up to £5,000 or even £10,000 at a time, and even a year later forged notes were being discovered, as in Monaghan in July 1984.[87] In fact, *Magill* reported in April 1985 that 'the notes are still being offered for sale in north Dublin bars at forty percent of face value'.[88] Arrests and prosecutions continued throughout 1983. In May, twelve people appeared in a Dublin court following the discovery of £10,000 in forged notes when gardaí stopped a car in the city. The following month, another man appeared in court in Dublin, and three men were in court in Carrickmacross, County Monaghan. In November, a father of six from Finglas was sentenced to five years' imprisonment for possession of £9,000 worth of forged notes. Elsewhere, a Wexford man (25) was sentenced to three years' penal servitude for possession of ten of the notes. A Dublin man pleaded guilty to buying a quantity of the notes for £5 each and received a £100 fine.[89]

This form of external money-laundering showed that the Provisionals were willing to adapt to new methods of financing provided they seemed likely to pay off and reduced the likelihood of volunteers being arrested and imprisoned. However, the operation alienated quite a few supporters across the country. The 'washing' of the money into the system was to be done through such people and their businesses, and many got burned as a result of the early detection.[90] April 1983 might have been an even greater disaster for the Provisionals when gardaí raided a home in Drumcondra and arrested nine men, including three members of the Sinn Féin Ard Comhairle. The arrested men were: Liam Connolly (25), Drumcondra; Gerard O'Neill (29), Ballybough Road; Brendan Swords (40), Mourne Road; Patrick Doherty (35), Carrigart; John McCallan (28), Sillogue Road; Martin Ferris (33), Tralee; Patrick Bolger (34), Dromawling Road; Gerry Fitzgerald (32), Bray, and Noel McLaughlin (26), Clondalkin. O'Neill, Fitzgerald and McCallan were all originally from Belfast, while Swords, Bolger and Doherty were members of the Sinn Féin Ard Comhairle. The list reads like a veritable who's who of senior republicans, including IRA members. According to later court reports, as gardaí entered the room where the men were meeting, Gerry Fitzgerald was seen putting something in the fireplace and setting it on fire. Gardaí managed to put out the fire and recovered a brown packet with scraps of paper inside. The scraps contained various notes on Sinn Féin cumainn throughout the country, as well as the note: 'check embassy videos'. Asked about this in court, counsel for the defence stated that it referred to existing videos of the 1981 embassy riots. Luckily for the republican movement, all nine men were subsequently acquitted of IRA membership.[91]

Things would not work out so well for the IRA later that year. On 15 August 1983, St Colmcille's Hospital at Loughlinstown in south Dublin was described as resembling a fortress, policed by armed members of the Garda Special Task Force. Within the hospital, three highly experienced members of the IRA's Southern Command were recovering from wounds they had received in a shoot-out with gardaí the previous week. One of the three had been so badly injured that a garda had whispered the Act of Contrition in his ear as they waited for ambulances to arrive. The situation at the hospital was awkward, as the men were not actually under arrest. They had initially been arrested following the gun battle and held for forty-eight hours, under Section 30 of the Offences Against the State Act. Gardaí had every intention of re-arresting and charging the men when they were sufficiently recovered from their injuries but had not yet done so. In the meantime, they could ill afford to allow their comrades to rescue them from the hospital. The three men had been part of a larger IRA unit which had gone to the Wicklow home of British-Canadian businessman Galen Weston intent on kidnapping him. They had all been wearing boiler suits and balaclavas, with most armed with sub-machine guns. Unbeknownst to the men, gardaí had received advance intelligence about the operation and were lying in wait. Weston himself was out of the country, in the UK. As the IRA unit walked across the courtyard of the large home, a detective shouted, 'Gardaí. Drop your guns.' According to garda testimony, the men pointed guns in the direction of the detective and fired, although it was later acknowledged that only one of the unit opened fire. In return, twelve gardaí fired a total of 185 rounds. Several of the men were hit before five of them surrendered. At least one of the unit escaped arrest and injury.

Three months after the failed operation, the five captured men appeared in court, where a number of supporters including Gerry Adams were present in a show of support. Of the five, three were from Belfast, though with the same Dublin address at the time of their arrest: John Hunter (39), Gerry Fitzgerald (32) and John Stewart (26). Peter Gerard Lynch (33) was originally from Dungiven, County Derry, while Nicky Kehoe (27) was from Dublin. Fitzgerald had been one of those arrested in Drumcondra in April and acquitted of IRA membership. The five men faced a range of firearms offences and were found guilty of the same. They received sentences of up to fourteen years' imprisonment. As they were being led out of the court to shouts of support from the crowded public gallery, they gave clenched fist salutes and shouted 'Up the Provos!'[92]

The shoot-out between the IRA and gardaí in Wicklow was to have a profound impact on how some IRA members viewed subsequent interactions with Irish security forces. The IRA's constitution contained an explicit prohibition of attacks on members of Irish state forces: General Standing Order No. 8, which was largely adhered to by its volunteers.[93] However, some began to question the wisdom or practicality of this order in the face of what seemed like increasing garda aggression in encounters with IRA members. An internal British memo commenting on IRA activities in the Republic of Ireland noted that 'Weston appears to mark a change in policy by PIRA which had earlier abandoned this type of crime because of the damage caused by bad publicity.'[94]

While the IRA had lost key operators and risked loss of life in the shoot-out with gardaí, they remained committed to the policy of kidnapping as a means of fundraising. Additionally, it could occasionally be used tactically for other reasons. During the early years of the 1980s, both republican and loyalist organisations were rocked by a series of 'supergrass' trials. These trials typically involved a former member of an organisation providing testimony against large numbers of his former associates in exchange for immunity from prosecution. Over two dozen supergrasses emerged between 1981 and 1983, and hundreds of alleged members of the IRA, INLA and Ulster Volunteer Force (UVF) were put on trial on the word of these people. Legally and morally questionable, the supergrass strategy was ultimately abandoned by British authorities as most convictions obtained in this way were overturned on appeal. Raymond Gilmour, a former INLA and IRA volunteer from Derry city, was one such supergrass. In November 1982, upwards of 100 alleged members of the IRA and INLA were being held on remand due to his testimony. On the night of 17 November, three masked men claiming to be from the IRA entered the Gilmour family home in the Creggan area of Derry city. The men abducted his father, Raymond senior, who was held captive for nearly a year at various locations in the Republic in an apparent effort to have his son retract his testimony. In late September 1983, Fr Piaras Ó Duill, chairman of the National H-Blocks Committee, received a phone call from Gilmour senior's captors. Ó Duill was instructed to go to a location in the Republic where Gilmour senior was handed over to him. This location has never been revealed. Mr Gilmour was reported to be in good health following his ordeal, though he had lost some weight. From the beginning of this episode, however, suspicion hung over the kidnapping. The family had to publicly deny claims that they acted in concert with the

IRA to orchestrate a kidnapping in order to have Raymond junior retract his evidence.[95]

Politics and Republican Policy

While the IRA may have faced various setbacks during this period, politically Sinn Féin was on the up. In 1983 Gerry Adams was elected MP for the Westminster constituency of West Belfast, unseating SDLP member and long-time Provisional critic Gerry Fitt. Alex Maskey became the first Sinn Féin representative elected to Belfast City Council since the 1920s. That year also saw several significant changes within the political wing of the republican movement. Ruairí Ó Brádaigh stood down as President of Sinn Féin and was replaced by Adams. Ó Brádaigh had led the party since its foundation in 1970. At the Ard-Fheis in November 1983, federalism – the central pillar of the Éire Nua policy – was abolished as Sinn Féin's official position. Also abandoned was the ban on discussions regarding abstentionism from the European Parliament. For some, this was the first step towards addressing the abstentionist policy in the Republic, with Dáithí Ó Conaill resigning his position as party vice president as a result of the changes. The previous year, an important ally of Ó Brádaigh and Ó Conaill had been ousted: Christine Ni Elias was a highly articulate member of the Sinn Féin Ard Comhairle and had played a key role in the organisational side of the Anti H-Block campaign. Her commitment to the Éire Nua policy and her criticisms of the Belfast Sinn Féin leadership made her a dangerous element to that emerging leadership. While the exact details of her expulsion from Sinn Féin and subsequent move to Canada remain murky, Ni Elias's ousting had sent a clear signal to others within the party who considered opposing the new political trend.[96]

Despite some internal turmoil, members of Sinn Féin entered that year's Ard-Fheis on a high owing to a recent prison breakout from the H-Blocks. On 25 September 1983 thirty-eight IRA prisoners escaped from what was one of the most high-security prisons in Europe. While some escapees were captured in the vicinity in the aftermath of the breakout, eighteen men made it to South Armagh, from where a number of them were spirited across the border. At a Sinn Féin function in 2003 to commemorate the thirtieth anniversary of the escape, Gerry Kelly spoke of how he and other escapees stayed in the homes of prominent Fianna Fáil and Fine Gael members when they made it safely into the Republic.[97] Gardaí inadvertently aided the IRA's later kidnapping of supermarket executive Don Tidey during the ensuing security sweeps for the H-Block escapees. According to a report in *The Phoenix*, garda raids on known or suspected republican safe houses following the prison breakout helped the IRA understand which safe houses were still unknown to the gardaí, a boon in later months.[98]

In a further boost for Sinn Féin's public profile and the IRA's campaign, Gerry Adams was invited as guest speaker for the 1983 annual commemoration of the Kilmichael Ambush, an event in remembrance of the IRA West Cork Brigade's successful ambush of British forces in November 1920. There was much concern in the media over Adams's invitation. Professor John A. Murphy, a friend of former Official IRA Chief of Staff Cathal Goulding, referred to it as 'obscene'. The secretary of the Kilmichael committee, Donal Mac Giolla Phoil, responded to the furore by stating that there was nothing unusual in the decision to invite Adams: 'He was invited as an MP, as an elected representative.' The decision on the invitation was not universal, however. One committee member, Con Cahalane, a member of the Fianna Fáil national executive, resigned over the invitation, while another – a Fianna Fáil councillor – boycotted the commemoration. The organising committee threatened to take disciplinary action against these dissenting members. In a break with tradition, Minister for Defence Patrick Cooney refused to allow the Irish Defence Forces to provide guns or blank ammunition for the 'Old IRA' firing party at the commemoration due to Adams's presence. This led to unfounded fears that the Provisional IRA might provide their own firing party for the event. The committee criticised Minister Cooney's decision, accusing the government of denying the surviving members of the IRA's West Cork Brigade the right to honour and salute their dead comrades. Mac Giolla Phoil continued: 'This is in stark contrast with Mr Cooney's decision to have the Irish Army represented recently at the memorial service in Dublin, organised by the British Legion, to honour their comrades who died in the First World War.' The Bishop of Cork and Ross, Dr Michael Murphy, refused calls to ban Mass being said at the commemoration.

At the event, surprising nobody but enraging many, Adams defended the killing of British soldiers and RUC members in Northern Ireland as 'legitimate' actions. On accusations of encouraging people to join the IRA, Adams said, 'I have never advised people to join the IRA; I think the presence of British soldiers on the streets and the situation that's there provides the only invitation they need.'[99] Adams also condemned the recent INLA sectarian attack on the Pentecostal Church at Darkley, County Armagh, as well as declaring that the Provisional republican movement represented no threat to the Southern state. According to a local newspaper, there was a much larger crowd than usual at the annual event, with estimates ranging from 500 to 750 people.[100]

'A cold and tiring vigil'

The relative high within the republican movement due to Sinn Féin's electoral progress towards the end of 1983 was shattered in December as a result of two IRA operations, one in the Republic of Ireland and another in the UK. Three weeks after five of its members were sentenced for their part in the failed kidnapping of Galen Weston, an IRA fundraising unit struck again, this time at an associate of Weston. Don Tidey, an Englishman and widower with two children, was working as a senior executive for the grocery company Quinnsworth and living in the Rathfarnham area of Dublin. Shortly before 8 a.m. on the morning of 23 November, he was driving his daughter, Susan, to school, while his son, Alistair, followed behind, driving a second car. As the small convoy reached a junction leading out of their quiet cul-de-sac, they were stopped by what appeared to be a garda checkpoint. Between five and six men were standing next to two cars, one of which had a flashing blue light on the roof. At least two of the men were wearing garda uniforms, or very convincing fakes, while others wore balaclavas. (Earlier in the year, in an incident that may have been linked to this, a number of garda uniforms had been stolen from Fenit Garda Station in County Kerry.)[101]

As Tidey slowed down and lowered his window, one of the uniformed men approached and quickly drew a sub-machine gun, pointing it at Tidey's head and ordering him out of the vehicle. Others rushed the passenger side, where his daughter sat, and the car behind carrying Alistair, hustling the two out onto the side of the road. Alistair's keys were confiscated as were the keys of Tidey's own car. Tidey was bundled into one of the parked cars and the two cars were driven off at speed in a southerly direction, towards the Dublin mountains. The whole operation was over in a matter of minutes.

Sometime later, the cars used in the kidnapping were abandoned in Maynooth, County Kildare, and subsequently the kidnappers swapped over to several other vehicles. Tidey was kept prostrate and face downwards, with a hood covering his head, during this second part of the journey. According to later court accounts, he was struck on the head and ribs by his captors. After the car journey, the party marched cross-country to a location in 'deeply-wooded country' where Tidey was tied to a tree in a hide, bound at the ankles, knees and wrists. The hide was a camouflaged polythene tarpaulin stretched over a dugout on the southern slopes of a wood in County Leitrim, just twenty yards from open fields which commanded a clear view of a nearby road. Tidey was to remain a captive in this hide for the next twenty-three days.[102]

It may have seemed sensible to abandon the kidnapping tactic as a means of fundraising following the failure of the Shergar and Weston operations, particularly given the loss of such experienced men during the latter. In fact, one early theory was that this kidnapping had actually been carried out to secure the release of the Weston five.[103] The IRA's Director of Operations, whose brainchild all three kidnappings were, evidently felt one last attempt was needed to secure much-needed funds, particularly given an anticipated major arms importation the following year. While the Weston kidnapping debacle had removed some key operators from Southern Command in August 1983, the H-Block prison escape the following month returned a number of highly experienced IRA volunteers to action, and several of them may have been involved in the Tidey kidnapping.

Garda attention quickly focused on several possible areas for Tidey's captivity: particularly counties Galway, Leitrim and Kerry. One of the cars used in the kidnapping had been stolen from the town of Newcastlewest in County Limerick, just twelve miles from the Kerry border. Another of the cars was revealed to be a rental, hired by a William Kelly of Tralee in that same town shortly before the kidnapping. Kelly was arrested for false imprisonment when the car was traced to him, with bail denied. He had been arrested in the past for republican activity but told gardaí that he had 'not been involved in the IRA for years'. Kelly refused, or was unable, to provide any information to gardaí at the time of his arrest, stating: 'If I give any names my life won't be worth living. I will have to live in the shadows for the rest of my life. I would rather spend the rest of my life in jail than give names and be called an informer.'[104] The activity around south-west Munster was in fact a ruse to influence garda focus and, with no information forthcoming from Kelly, they were forced to erect checkpoints across the state, follow up on hundreds of leads and carry out laborious investigative and search work.

In late November there was a flurry of concentration on the Ballinamore area of County Leitrim, after a man was seen running from a remote farmhouse as heavily armed gardaí searched the surrounding area, but neither the man nor Tidey were found.[105] This area had long been considered a strong 'republican area', with veteran IRA member and former Sinn Féin TD John Joe McGirl at its centre. Gardaí had regularly conducted searches and house raids in the area during the previous decade.[106] For the next two weeks, searches were conducted across the state, including the Ballinamore area. It is still unclear how gardaí eventually tracked Tidey and his kidnappers to Derrada Wood, just north of Ballinamore. Some accounts credit IRA-volunteer-turned-informer Freddie Scappaticci, while basic detective work is also credited. The chief superintendent of the Cavan–Monaghan district had repeatedly warned Garda HQ of unusually heightened republican activity in the area, including the presence of outsiders. In fact, the area around Derrada Wood had been searched twice already prior to the evening of 13 December.[107] The large numbers of gardaí temporarily stationed in the area as part of the search were not always welcomed. One elderly local republican spotted a familiar face among them. He later recalled:

It was that same fellow who put the Branch on to me in Bray when I got sacked. When they were looking for Don Tidey, and that was thirty years after, the same fellow arrived down here one night; he had heard that I had a pub here. So I said; *look friend, get the bus now and get out of here fast.*[108]

The Irish Defence Forces were drafted in to support gardaí during the search for Tidey. As part of the seasonally named 'Operation Rudolph', ten teams set out to search the Derrada Wood area on the morning of 13 December. Each team consisted of a garda inspector, two sergeants, a local garda, two members of the Special Branch with knowledge of border intelligence, seven detectives armed with Uzi sub-machine guns, and a group of ten cadet gardaí temporarily seconded from the Garda Training College at Templemore. A soldier armed with an FN rifle would accompany each group as an extra safeguard.[109] Irish Army rangers were stationed at various points on the perimeter of the search area with listening equipment, though they did not take part in the actual searching, a decision that was later questioned.

The wisdom of putting raw garda recruits into a position where they might encounter an armed and experienced IRA unit, particularly following the shoot-out at the home of Galen Weston, was also questioned. Irish soldiers already had reservations about gardaí who'd been involved in joint operations, viewing them as too 'laidback, informal and casual'.[110] One journalist on the scene described the garda cadet element of the party as 'terribly young looking'. One of those recruits recounted his view of the operation as they set out: 'We were all excited when we were told we were being sent to Ballinamore – thought it would be like a nature trail.'[111] However, set against the risks was a need born of necessity, given that the state-wide extent of the search operation required considerable manpower.

The actual events which immediately preceded Tidey's rescue remain unclear. Visibility in the search area was hugely reduced given its low and thick growth of the conifer forest plantations, with a mid-December evening coming on fast. In many parts of Derrada Wood, effective visibility was down to mere feet. As one of the teams searched the thick woodland, several members spotted what looked like another party member just ahead and called out, 'There's a man here.'[112] In an instant, there was pandemonium. Gunfire erupted, then more gunfire, possibly from several locations, and at least one loud bang was heard. Early reports claim this was a fragmentation grenade, though it was in fact a non-lethal stun grenade. It is also claimed that, during those few moments of noise and panic, all members of the search team dropped their weapons.[113]

During the confused aftermath, Tidey himself managed to get loose and ran in the first direction available to him. After fleeing several dozen yards, he was tackled by members of another of the search teams and held at gunpoint until he could convince the men of his identity. Meanwhile, the four-strong IRA unit who'd been guarding him split into two. One pair escaped towards a narrow road where they hijacked a car. The other two managed to overpower three soldiers and four gardaí – three of whom were trainees – and took these new hostages deeper into the thick undergrowth. When they reached the edge of the woods, all seven were released, while another two soldiers who had been acting in support in the area were overpowered and disarmed. The kidnappers then regrouped at the hijacked car, speeding past Don Tidey and his rescuers at one point, where there was a further exchange of gunfire. A garda car then blocked the road, forcing the IRA unit to exit the vehicle and make their way cross-country. As they escaped across nearby fields, they took turns covering each other and returning fire on members of the search teams who had converged on the area. One of the IRA volunteers had been shot in the foot, while a detective who was accompanying Tidey was struck in the leg. Owing to the falling darkness, the continued sounds of gunfire in the area and the lack of communication between teams and headquarters, confusion reigned for some time. At one point, a car driven by two civilians was fired on by soldiers as it approached an army checkpoint. The driver was shot in the head, though he survived.[114] Back at the hide where Tidey was discovered, Trainee Garda Gary Sheehan and Private Patrick Kelly of the Irish Defence Forces lay dead.

Gardaí and the Irish Army set up roadblocks across Leitrim that evening, with senior gardaí referring to it as a 'ring of steel'. This would go down as a particularly unfortunate phrase owing to the subsequent exposure of the porousness of the security operation. In reality, the 'ring of steel' was put in place more than eight hours after Private Kelly and Trainee Garda Sheehan were killed, and involved just 300 members of An Garda Síochána and the Irish Defence Forces, not the 2,000 claimed by the gardaí at the time. The kidnappers were outside the security cordon before it was even established and would breach it three times in total. They were aided in this by their ability to eavesdrop on the poorly secured radio communications operated by the Irish security forces.[115]

Six men in the Ballinamore area suspected of aiding the kidnappers were arrested in the days after the rescue of Don Tidey. These included John Joe McGirl and one of his sons. By late January 1984, eighteen local people had been arrested on suspicion of aiding or taking part in the kidnapping. The owner of the land where Derrada Wood was situated was charged with falsely imprisoning Tidey and refused bail at a sitting of the Special Criminal

Court on 29 December. John Curnan (58) told the court he was 'as innocent as a lamb' and knew nothing of the kidnapping. He said he had seen a strange man in the area of the woods two weeks prior to Tidey's discovery and had given the man two flasks of boiling water.[116] Curnan was later sentenced to seven years' imprisonment while a co-accused was acquitted.

An account of the kidnappers' escape was published in a local republican history in 2014 and seems to be based on insider knowledge. According to that account, the four IRA volunteers again split into pairs once outside the immediate vicinity of the search parties. Local republican Francis McGirl met with two of the men and brought them to County Mayo, via Sligo, on foot over the course of that evening and night. The other two men remained in safe houses in the Leitrim area, before eventually making their way to north Longford, where they stayed for several months.[117] For some days, gardaí and soldiers remained in the Ballinamore vicinity in the belief that the kidnappers were sleeping rough there. The search focused on the area between Ballinamore and Cuilcagh Mountain, where it was reported that two men were spotted crawling into a wooded area. British Army counterparts across the border in County Fermanagh also maintained a close watch but were privately of the view that the IRA volunteers had long since escaped. On several occasions, flares were fired into the night sky to illuminate the landscape while Irish Army rangers kept watch. Hopes were renewed when a quantity of blood was found near a bridge in the area, but forensic tests later revealed that this was not human blood.[118]

On 20 December, as the rangers prepared to resume an intensive search of the area north of Ballinamore, gardaí manning a checkpoint near Ballycroy, County Mayo, nearly 100 miles away, were overpowered by three armed men with northern accents. The men had approached the checkpoint in a Mercedes Benz driven by a female. The car, which had been stolen, was later found in Charlestown, seventy miles away. Shortly afterwards, a woman from that town, Mary McGing (26), was arrested under Section 30 of the Offences Against the State Act and taken to Ballina Garda Station for questioning. McGing was subsequently sentenced to twelve months' imprisonment in Limerick Gaol for 'harbouring criminals'.[119] While imprisoned, McGing ran as the Sinn Féin candidate for the Connacht–Ulster constituency in the European Parliament elections.[120] The evening after the Ballycroy checkpoint incident, acting on a tip-off, gardaí approached a remote bungalow near the town of Claremorris, also in County Mayo. Three men armed with rifles or shotguns were seen fleeing the building. Despite cries to halt and shots fired over their heads, the men all escaped. Another garda dragnet failed to capture them.

The British Embassy was less than impressed with what was termed repeated 'Garda ineffectiveness'.[121] There was also massive discontent within the force, with local gardaí referring to the Claremorris raid as a 'fiasco'. Seemingly, the decision to raid the house at dusk was made only after a heated argument. It was undertaken by the Special Task Force, and gardaí at Claremorris Garda Station, just a mile from the house, were not informed in advance.[122] The owner of the Claremorris house, a teacher and officer in the local Fianna Fáil cumann, was acquitted of charges similar to those proffered against McGing. According to the accused, he had allowed McGing to use his home for what he understood to be a Sinn Féin meeting. The court accepted that the armed men who actually showed up were there without his permission.[123]

One upshot of the gardaí search for the IRA unit was the discovery of an underground concrete bunker in County Monaghan on 21 December. The bunker, discovered in the garden of a house near Inniskeen, was six feet in depth and ten-foot square, with the roof covered with earth in order to blend in with the garden. Within the bunker were found several thousand rounds of ammunition, stored in sacks, and an explosive device. The find was linked to the INLA and two men were arrested. In Derrada Wood, during follow-up searches, gardaí also discovered three rifles and ammunition wrapped in polythene.[124]

On the same day that gardaí in Ballycroy were held up at their checkpoint, the funerals of Private Kelly and Trainee Garda Sheehan took place in Moate, County Westmeath, and Carrickmacross, County Monaghan. Garda recruits formed a guard of honour as the body of Gary Sheehan was removed from his family home. As per the request of Private Kelly's widow, there were no shots fired over her husband's coffin. In the aftermath of these killings, blame was understandably placed on the IRA for the deaths of the two men. In a statement released several days after the shooting, the IRA claimed that their members 'were acting in defence of their lives and had in their minds the Task Force's attempted massacre of IRA volunteers at Roundwood [the failed Galen Weston kidnapping]'.[125] However, it did not take long for doubts to emerge regarding the fatal shootings in Derrada Wood, and indeed for questions to arise over which side fired first. Lieutenant Colonel Pat Dixon, the military commander of the search, was vehement that 'the first shots were definitely not fired by us. Our men were shot down in cold blood.'[126] Spent cartridges from firearms used by the IRA, gardaí and Irish Defence Forces were all found at the scene, confusing the matter. The government only released a minimal ballistics report several weeks after the shooting. This was in contrast to the RUC, who typically released reports within forty-eight hours of such an incident.[127] No public inquest took place and there were reports that the Irish Defence Forces blamed the gardaí for the deaths and refused to operate joint patrols in future, although this was strongly refuted by spokespersons from each side.[128] In late 2021, Assistant Garda Commissioner John O'Driscoll stated that a review of the case would conclude in 'a short period of time', which would prove beyond doubt that Private Kelly and Trainee Garda Sheehan were not killed by 'friendly fire' or state weapons. At the time of writing, this review has not yet been published.[129]

While there was great shock in the locality following the Derrada Wood killings, the elusiveness of the IRA kidnappers introduced an element of farce.[130] Adding to this were the contemporaneous exploits of INLA leader Dominic McGlinchey, who was being sought by gardaí and British forces. On several occasions during this period, McGlinchey held up and stripped gardaí at roadblocks across the Republic. These exploits were celebrated in a musical recording titled 'Hands up, pants down'.[131] One senior garda decried the attitude held by Southerners in 'many circles', pointing out that militant republicans were all too often considered 'the Robin Hoods of the twentieth century'.[132] Such attitudes may not have been restricted to the general population. In his account of the period, one former IRA volunteer wrote of staying with a man who had previously had McGlinchey billeted with him:

> As the net on Dominic closed, the chap had gone for a drive and found that every road seemed to have a Garda checkpoint. When stopped at one a uniformed Garda, who he knew through the local GAA club, and who knew that Paddy was not unsympathetic to people like Dominic, basically told him how someone might avoid the checkpoints by

taking certain backroads. Of course, neither let on why anyone might want to do so. Perhaps the Garda was even acting out of a personal concern should McGlinchey happen to be stopped at a checkpoint he was manning.[133]

The fallout within the IRA following the Tidey kidnapping was significant. According to a contemporary *Magill* report, the IRA 'regard the Tidey episode as one which started efficiently and then graduated to disaster … [the] kidnapping strategy is being re-evaluated'.[134] The IRA's Director of Operations lost his position in the aftermath. Hitherto a dominant force in the organisation, he began to play an ever-decreasing role within the IRA. Ultimately, this was perhaps a boon for the IRA. According to one account, this man had resumed his old position after being released from prison a few years previously but had continued to exist and operate in a 1970s mentality. Technological advances that made surveillance much more acute and insidious had passed him by and he refused to heed warnings that he was under surveillance.[135] Despite the disastrous and tragic climax to the Tidey kidnapping, rumours persisted in the months following that Associated British Foods, the parent company of Quinnsworth, had in fact made a payment of £2m to the IRA in December 1983. It is unclear whether this represented a ransom payment or a payment in response to threats by the IRA of further kidnappings of the company's executive staff, or indeed whether any such payment was made. In 1985 a British Labour MP called for the prosecution of Associated British Foods under the Prevention of Terrorism Act for allegedly making this payment to the IRA, although the matter did not proceed further as the UK's Attorney General stated there was no proof of any such payment.[136]

The Don Tidey kidnapping came again to national attention in 1985 when Michael Burke, a father of three from Cork, went on trial for his part in it. Burke had previously served in the Irish Defence Forces and had also worked as a prison officer at Portlaoise. He had been on the run for some time before surrendering himself at Tralee Garda Station in August 1984 in the presence of his solicitor. He was subsequently picked out of two identification parades by a neighbour of Mr Tidey. When notified of this by a detective, Burke responded: 'I recognise him too. I didn't think he'd recognise me too after so long. That still doesn't say I killed any garda or soldier. I'm

not going to admit anything to you.' During the trial, Burke claimed that
he stayed with friends in Cork after leaving home prior to 23 November
1983 but could not name them as he did not want them implicated in the
trial. He had heard that gardaí were calling to his home looking for him
and so he turned himself in to clear his name. Burke was found guilty of
the kidnapping and sentenced to twelve years' imprisonment without leave
to appeal.[137] According to veteran Cork republican, Gearóid MacCárthaigh,
Burke had visited him regularly during his time on the run and had kept him
updated on events and activity within the republican movement.[138]

In 1998 a former IRA volunteer from Belfast, Brendan 'Bik' McFarlane,
was arrested in the Republic of Ireland and charged with the kidnapping
of Don Tidey as well as possession of a firearm with intent to endanger
life at Derrada Wood. McFarlane had been one of the IRA prisoners who
escaped from the H-Blocks in the mass breakout of 1983 and had served
as O/C within the prison during the 1981 hunger strike. Following a
lengthy appeals process, McFarlane's trial went ahead in Dublin in June
2008. During the trial, two key pieces of evidence were expected to be
presented by the prosecution: fingerprints from McFarlane had been found
on a milk carton, a plastic container and a cooking pot, all recovered from
Derrada Wood. In addition, gardaí claimed that certain statements made
by McFarlane following his arrest in 1998 would be used as evidence. In a
surprise decision, the case against McFarlane was thrown out of court. The
alleged items discovered with his fingerprints on them had gone missing
from Garda Headquarters and could not be located. Following intense
legal debate, an alleged admission made by him while in garda custody
was ruled inadmissible as evidence. In addition, the former head of Garda
Intelligence refused to reveal to the court the source of information that
led to McFarlane's arrest. In 2010 the European Court of Human Rights
ordered that McFarlane be awarded €15,500 in compensation and costs for
the delay in bringing him to trial.[139]

In the aftermath of the shoot-out at Derrada Wood, the *Irish Independent*
ran an editorial entitled 'Ban Sinn Féin', and reported on Minister for Defence
Patrick Cooney's remarks:

For far too long ambivalence to the men of violence, fuelled alike by
political opportunism and the unbalanced view of history inbred in

generations of our young people has resulted in tepid indifference at best
... to their foul deeds ... Mr Cooney extended his remarks to encompass
Provisional Sinn Féin, their active members and tacit supporters and
even those members of a trade union who tolerated a member of
Provisional Sinn Féin as their leader.[140]

This last remark was aimed at Phil Flynn, a prominent trade unionist and
recently elected vice president of Sinn Féin. Flynn had previously acted as a
mediator in the 1974 kidnapping of Tiede Herrema.[141]

There was discussion within government and media circles regarding
the potential outlawing of Sinn Féin at this time. Former Labour government
minister Conor Cruise O'Brien also called for internment to be introduced in
the Republic. Speculation regarding proscription extended across the sea to
Westminster. The day after the Derrada Wood killings, the IRA had exploded
a bomb outside the upmarket Harrods department store in London, killing
six people and injuring scores more.[142] There was considerable public outrage
in the South as a result of this bombing, particularly coming on the heels of
Derrada Wood. On 20 December, the *Irish Examiner* carried a story about
Gerry Adams's refusal to condemn the bombing alongside a story of 1,500
gardaí taking part in a cortège at the funeral of Gary Sheehan.[143] Sinn Féin
Director of Publicity Danny Morrison also had to officially deny there was
any split between the IRA and Sinn Féin, as there was some speculation that
the attack was an attempt to embarrass the party and halt the politicisation
of the movement. In fact, Phil Flynn condemned the Harrods bombing on
the same day, in a move *The Irish Times* interpreted as a sign of tensions
within the party at such operations.[144] Limerick-born actor Richard Harris
landed in hot water following his remarks in a US interview, describing the
bombing as 'horribly wrong but understandable', and stating that Prime
Minister Margaret Thatcher simply viewed the deaths as a means to ensure
the IRA lost support.[145]

While the IRA's actions undoubtedly contributed to speculation
regarding the proscription of Sinn Féin, fears of the party's electoral progress
also likely played a role. The party was steadily increasing its number of
elected representatives, north and south of the border, and was expected to
represent an electoral challenge at the next general election in the Republic.[146]
Charles Haughey, serving time as leader of the opposition, supported a ban

on Sinn Féin if the government decided to proceed. Ultimately, both British and Irish governments decided not to proscribe the party, feeling that such a move would be counterproductive, but the end of 1983 was a time of great uncertainty for the republican movement.[147]

4

The Rule of Law
Must Be Observed: 1984

While Sinn Féin were ostensibly treated as pariahs in the South throughout much of the 'Troubles', this was never more so than at the dawn of 1984. Indeed, with the Harrods bombing and the deaths of Irish security force members in Leitrim still fresh in people's minds, the party was the closest to proscription that it had ever come. Perhaps encouraged by this low-water mark of public tolerance or sympathy for militant republicanism, the Dublin government finally succeeded in pushing through several high-profile extradition cases in the early months of the year.

The pariah status of the Provisionals was bound to be ephemeral and patchy, however. During this same period that Irish media and political circles were discussing the potential outlawing of Sinn Féin, local activists from that party were instrumental in organising community resistance to heroin dealers in inner-city Dublin. By all accounts, these community groups were filling a vacuum left by garda inability or unwillingness to address the extent of this societal scourge. Sinn Féin would reap the electoral dividends of their members' involvement in the soon-to-be-established Concerned Parents Against Drugs and, later, Coalition of Communities Against Drugs well into the 1990s.

Despite a relative lull in armed robberies in previous years, the IRA had not ceased to rely on this tactic as a significant fundraising activity. There was a brief spike in such operations in 1984, likely at least in part linked to a major arms importation operation scheduled for that autumn. On 29 September, a joint garda–navy operation intercepted this importation, the largest since the capture of five tons of Libyan weaponry on board the *Claudia* in 1973. The cargo of the ship, the *Marita Ann*, was one-and-a-half times the amount found on board the *Claudia*. Among those arrested on board the *Marita Ann* was senior IRA Southern Command officer Martin Ferris. A major bomb attack on the UK Conservative Party's annual conference several weeks later, which shook the British establishment profoundly, only partially covered for the despair wrought by the capture of the *Marita Ann*. The annual Sinn Féin Ard-Fheis several weeks later exposed further the increasing divisions within the republican movement. Following that Ard-Fheis, while abstentionism remained a policy for both the IRA and Sinn Féin, it was clearly only a matter of time before it was jettisoned.

Political Events and Extradition

Following the debacle that was the Don Tidey kidnapping, and the deaths of three civilians and three police officers in the Harrods bombing, there was widespread public outrage directed at the Provisional republican movement in the South. The Irish government ultimately ruled out proscribing Sinn Féin, believing that this would simply push militant republicanism further underground, as well as increasing an overburdened garda workload. However, the Fine Gael–Labour coalition did agree a policy of refusing to deal with any political delegation containing members of that party. In February, Minister for the Environment Liam Kavanagh refused to meet a delegation of Donegal county councillors that included the elected Sinn Féin representative Eddie Fullerton. The following week, Kavanagh did the same with a Longford delegation, which included Sinn Féin councillor Michael Nevin. Government resolve with respect to this policy came up against impracticalities quite quickly, however, and by March two government ministers had met with a Galway County Council delegation, which included among its number the long-time Sinn Féin representative Frank Glynn.[1] Despite this, for the year's St Patrick's Day parades, Minister for Defence Patrick Cooney refused to allow Irish Army units to take part in any parades where members of Sinn Féin were involved in its organisation.[2]

The politicians were not the only ones to act. In January gardaí raided Sinn Féin's Dublin offices on Blessington Street and confiscated kegs, crates and bottles of alcohol that were used to supply a drinking club on the premises. According to a party representative, the club had been in operation since 1969 and the gardaí were aware of it all that time; the representative added that the alcohol had not yet been paid for and, 'when we get the bill, we will send it to the gardaí.[3]

Security cooperation between Britain and Ireland continued to be positive going into 1984. One British defence attaché, who toured the border region that year, reported back a 'summary of impressions' to Whitehall, noting that Irish security forces were not hostile to the British Army. On the contrary, they were 'full of professional admiration for the British actions on the other side of the border'. The attaché in turn was 'impressed by the Gardaí I met on the border' adding, in an observation on the complementary nature of that force and the Irish Army, 'their effectiveness [Irish Army] seems to depend entirely on what the Gardaí are asked to do, because wherever the Garda go the Army will go along to protect them'. In a tour of the border region later that same year, the attaché claimed there was even greater cross-border co-operation than during his previous visit.[4]

One area of co-operation in which the Irish government finally felt strong enough to participate was the extradition of republican militants. Back in 1982, when the government first seriously considered the possibility of extradition, the notion was discussed at the annual general meetings of the Association of Garda Sergeants and Inspectors, as well as the rank-and-file Garda Representatives Association. The former group expressed some dissension (British officials commented that 'presumably some were Fianna Fáil supporters'), while the latter were even more stridently opposed.[5] Public opinion was also quite divided on the matter. In the aftermath of the 1979 IRA attacks at Warrenpoint and Mullaghmore, an agency contracted by RTÉ carried out a large poll on attitudes to extradition. Members of the public were asked: 'It has been suggested that the Constitution should be changed to allow for the extradition or handing over of people accused of politically motivated crimes. Do you agree or disagree with this suggestion?' The responses were: Agree (48 per cent); Disagree (31 per cent); Don't know (21 per cent). In August 1982, following the IRA's Hyde Park and Regent's Park bombings, the same question was put to members of the public. The responses this time were Agree (47 per cent); Disagree (32 per cent); Don't know (21 per cent).

Despite the polling numbers changing little between 1979 and 1982, the republican movement was aware that extradition was a very real and imminent threat. Activists began building a public campaign of resistance against any such attempts. A mass demonstration in Monaghan set for early February 1984 was prominently advertised on the front of *An Phoblacht*, with another protest organised for Navan the following month.[6] Extradition was understood to be a highly sensitive issue for the general population, which was what led to the compromise legislation of 1976, allowing for the prosecution of people in the Republic for crimes committed in Britain or Northern Ireland under the Criminal Law (Jurisdiction) Act, a neat political side-step for the time. By the 1980s, however, the Fine Gael–Labour coalition government of the time was committed to addressing the issue head-on, tearing off the band-aid quickly as it were, with a precedent-setting extradition. Given public sensitivities, this first extradition would need to be one with no ambiguity as to the guilt of the person, or with respect to the horror of the crime committed.

In the early months of 1984, INLA Chief of Staff Dominic McGlinchey was the number-one priority for the gardaí. A warrant for his arrest and extradition had already been approved in December 1982, at which point McGlinchey went on the run. His jaunts around the country during the following fourteen months proved particularly humiliating for the gardaí. McGlinchey had previously been a member of the Provisional IRA but left that organisation with perhaps a dozen other volunteers while imprisoned in Portlaoise during the late 1970s and early 1980s, following a dispute with the prison leadership. He subsequently joined the INLA while still imprisoned. During his time on the run, McGlinchey made use of his old network and stayed with a number of IRA supporters, including a prominent former local commander in Carrigtwohill, County Cork. Gardaí actually called to this man's house while McGlinchey was there, and it has been claimed that McGlinchey had to convince him not to shoot the gardaí.[7] On another occasion, he was said to have bivouacked in the hills of north Tipperary and while it was common knowledge among the locals of the area, nobody spoke to the gardaí.[8]

By the middle of March 1984, McGlinchey was staying in the Shannon area of County Clare. His wife and two children were staying in the town itself, being looked after by prominent Derry republican and socialist activist Brigid Makowski. McGlinchey and three other INLA members were staying in a rural house nearer the village of Newmarket-on-Fergus. It remains a matter of dispute how gardaí tracked McGlinchey to this house. One source claimed that there was an informer among the INLA network in this part of Munster, although the visible presence of McGlinchey's family in Shannon may have alerted gardaí to the fact that he might be nearby.[9] The house where he was staying was surrounded by members of the Garda Security Task Force at dawn on St Patrick's Day and a stand-off and shoot-out ensued. McGlinchey and his men eventually surrendered following mediation by a local priest.

In a late-night emergency session of the Supreme Court several hours after his capture, a new extradition order for McGlinchey was approved and he was taken by armed escort to the border checkpoint at Killeen, near Newry, where he was handed over to the waiting RUC.[10] The speed of the process took many people by surprise. Danny Morrison, then Sinn Féin Director of Publicity, was addressing an anti-extradition rally at Silverbridge in County Armagh, just a few miles from Killeen, as these events took place unbeknownst to him.[11] *An Phoblacht* subsequently referred to the event as 'one of the blackest spots in all the long years of Free State collaboration'.[12] Two months later, when Taoiseach Garret FitzGerald visited Monaghan, he received a letter from local Sinn Féin activist Caoimhghín Ó Caoláin 'on behalf of the concerned people of Monaghan Town', referring to 'the shameful act of handing over an Irishman to the most discredited police force and judiciary in Western Europe … We demand, as Irish men and women, that you cease this despicable treachery immediately'.[13]

It has since emerged that there was a questionable legal basis for McGlinchey's extradition. The Supreme Court was willing to put forward the ambiguous claim that, for an offence to be considered 'political' – and thus protected from extradition – it must be 'what reasonable, civilised people would regard as political activity'. McGlinchey was extradited for his alleged role in the attack on the house of an RUC reservist in which the intended target's elderly mother was killed. Moreover, while McGlinchey dropped the claim that his offence was political upon appeal, the court indicated that it was willing to proceed with extradition even if the crime had been committed against a member of the British forces. The summarising remarks of Justice O'Higgins in the McGlinchey case in December 1982 are worth reproducing. They seem to demonstrate that the extradition was due to McGlinchey's actions being outside the bounds of what could be considered a political offence, while at the same time stating that the depths of McGlinchey's actions were not criteria for precedent in future cases:

> I would like to point out, however, that it should not be deduced that if the victim were someone other than a civilian who was killed or injured as a result of violent criminal conduct chosen in lieu of what would fall directly or indirectly within the scope of political activity, the offence would necessarily be classified as a political offence or an offence connected with a political offence. The judicial authorities on the scope of such offences have in many respects been rendered obsolete by the fact that modern terrorist violence, whether undertaken by military or paramilitary organisations, or by individuals or groups of individuals, is often the antithesis of what could reasonably be regarded as political, either in itself or its connections. All that can be said with authority in this case is that, with or without the concession made on behalf of the Plaintiff, this offence could not be said to be either a political offence or an offence connected with a political offence. Whether a contrary conclusion would be reached in different circumstances must depend on the particular circumstances and on whether those particular circumstances showed that the person charged was at the relevant time engaged, either directly or indirectly, in what reasonable, civilised people would regard as political activity.[14]

O'Higgins asserted that an attack of this nature, where an elderly civilian was shot dead, could not be classed as a 'political offence' and so the responsible person – or suspect – could be extradited. In addition, however, an attack where a civilian was killed should not be the benchmark of activity that was outside the bounds a 'political offence', effectively establishing a precedent that any violent republican activity could subsequently lead to extradition. This seems an extraordinary admission in the context of what previous Irish legal and political administrations had been willing to pursue. Fifteen years later it emerged that one Supreme Court justice who was contacted to attend the 1984 emergency sitting agreed to do so but voiced his opposition to the extradition. According to a letter in The Irish Times: 'The judge [Mr Justice Brian Walsh] confirmed his availability but indicated that he was opposed to the extradition. He was not contacted again in this regard' as his services were 'not required'. Given that 'time was of the essence' for this hearing, turning down Justice Walsh although he had confirmed his availability indicates that the court was only seeking those who would confirm McGlinchey's extradition.[15]

Concerns were subsequently raised in the Dáil and elsewhere regarding the RUC's conduct once they had McGlinchey in custody. He was not charged immediately; he was questioned about other offences and he was not brought to court within forty-five days. All three of these represented breaches of the conditions for extradition. Suspects were only to be extradited when the case was clear-cut, thus where a speedy charge and trial seemed assured, and extradited persons were only to be questioned about the offences for which they had been extradited. Eventually, McGlinchey was charged and put on trial for the murder of Hester McMullan but was acquitted due to the failure of the British authorities to present any meaningful evidence. This proved quite embarrassing for both the British and Irish governments. Some unionist politicians sought to blame the Dublin government for this, with one member of the short-lived 1982–86 Northern Ireland Assembly stating: 'As far as I am concerned, the extradition of McGlinchey was nothing but a con trick on the people of Northern Ireland. McGlinchey was becoming too hot to handle in the Irish Republic. Too many policemens' [sic] uniforms were being lost at his hands.'[16] McGlinchey was subsequently re-extradited to the Republic of Ireland and successfully prosecuted for firearms offences linked to the shoot-out outside Newmarket-on-Fergus, receiving a ten-year prison sentence in Portlaoise.

Despite the debacle of McGlinchey's extradition and trial, a precedent had been set, marking a new reality for republicans on the run in the South for offences committed in Northern Ireland or Britain. Many now faced the possibility of being escorted to the border if captured by gardaí. Later that year, IRA volunteer Seamus Shannon – brother-in-law to Monaghan IRA leader Jim Lynagh – was extradited to face charges linked to the killing of James and Norman Stronge, based on the claims of an RUC informer.[17] As detailed in Chapter 2, Shannon was also acquitted. In June 1984, the Supreme Court ruled against the extradition of another man, Philip McMahon, wanted in Northern Ireland on a charge of escaping from Newry courthouse in March 1975. The ruling was made on the ground that four others charged with the same offence as McMahon had not been extradited in 1976 because of the political nature of their offences. The government privately conceded that, 'if McMahon were extradited it would mean that contradictory declarations in relation to the same incident had been issued from our courts.'[18] Why extraditions were necessary, given the existence of the 1976 Criminal Law (Jurisdiction) Act, was never adequately explained by the Irish government or the legal establishment to the broader public. An article in *Magill* titled 'The Extradition Fiasco' noted that 'Dominic McGlinchey, Seamus Shannon and John Patrick Quinn could all have been charged in the Republic with the offences they were wanted for in the North.'[19] Indeed, the government privately acknowledged in a later extradition fiasco concerning Belfast woman Eibhlin Glenholmes that 'these provisions [the Criminal Law (Jurisdiction) Act] could have been used as an alternative to extradition procedures.'[20] While not expressing such an explicit position publicly, the government was aware of limits in the efficacy of the Criminal Law (Jurisdiction) Act, noting in a January 1982 internal memo that there was an 'inherent difficulty in securing evidence' for prosecutions. This stemmed in large part from the lack of RUC involvement in cases pursued in the South for offences committed in the North. While the government may have addressed the hot potato of extradition by March 1984, allowing RUC officers to question republican suspects in the Republic was still too unpalatable.[21]

Concerned Parents Against Drugs and the Republican Movement

The ascendancy of Gerry Adams to the national leadership of the republican movement presaged a focus on political growth to match the IRA's campaign. This focus was bolstered by the extensive public support and sympathy for the hunger strikes of 1980 and 1981. While support for Sinn Féin was on the increase in the North – as evinced by the 1982 Northern Ireland Assembly elections, for example – its popularity in the South remained relatively stagnant. In large part this was due to the party's abstentionist policy, as well as its perceived focus on 'the North' rather than on local issues. However, events in Dublin in the early 1980s provided an opportunity for the party to demonstrate its relevance to a most impactful local issue. The relatively sudden influx of inexpensive and high-quality heroin to western Europe in 1979 has been attributed to two events which took place on the other side of the world that year. In Iran, an Islamic revolution overthrew the ruling Shah of that country in January, while later that year, Soviet Union forces invaded neighbouring Afghanistan to prop up a socialist government there. Many wealthy Iranians who were fleeing their country following the revolution sought to convert their assets prior to confiscation and turned to investment in poppy cultivation in the region. Rebel forces in neighbouring Afghanistan were eager to accommodate this to help finance their guerrilla war against the Soviets. There was thus massive investment in the growth and harvesting of opium in Afghanistan, which was smuggled to Europe via newly established Iranian émigré channels.[22]

With a history of significant unemployment and an almost total absence of youth amenities, working-class areas of Dublin were particularly vulnerable to this heroin influx. A commentator in the previous decade had noted of conditions in the Ballymun flats complex, for example, that for 6,000 children there were no cinemas, no swimming pools, no community centre, no playing fields and no nursery. For the thousands of adults there were 'two pubs'.[23] Other working-class areas of Dublin were in similar doldrums, economically and socially. Ballyfermot, for example, had an unemployment rate that was twice the national average in 1980.[24] In one of its last issues before circulation ceased, the current-affairs publication *Hibernia* had noted forebodingly that 'the misuse of hard drugs like heroin is increasing dramatically in Ireland, as more and more heroin finds its way into Western Europe'.[25]

Initially, the influx was restricted to south of the River Liffey and it wasn't until the summer of 1981 that it infiltrated the north inner city. Tony Gregory was an independent councillor for the Inner-City North ward, having been elected in the 1979 local elections. His recollection of the period was of increasing numbers of concerned parents approaching him about this silent epidemic and the widespread availability of heroin. While sharing their concerns, he felt that some accounts were being exaggerated, until, after being directed to certain areas of the north inner city, he witnessed ten-year-old children taking heroin. Throughout the early 1980s, Gregory and others made regular appeals to politicians, the gardaí and health authorities, to no avail. A government report commissioned in 1983, which recommended a detailed and progressive response to the drug problem, was never published.[26] Addiction levels by this time were running in some areas at 12 and 13 per cent of the teenage population. In fact, the heroin addiction rate amongst teenagers in Dublin was higher than it had been in Brooklyn, London and Paris during the previous decade.[27] Expressing the local frustration, one study of this period noted that 'thousands of garda hours were wasted in an unsuccessful battle to suppress illegal trading [on Moore Street] while a few hundred yards away drug pushers slipped unhampered through the flat complexes of the north inner city'.[28]

In desperation, parents in inner-city areas on both sides of the Liffey considered extreme measures. At first, a request was made to local Official IRA members to attack or intimidate drug dealers, but this appeal was rebuffed. Previously, some parents had considered approaching representatives of the Provisional IRA with the same request but did not follow through. At that same time, however, leaflets ostensibly published by the Provisional IRA had been circulated in west Dublin warning that drug dealers would be 'punished' if they continued their activities.[29] It has also been alleged that, in 1981, the Provisional IRA's Dublin Brigade was authorised to carry out punishment shootings and beatings of petty criminals in the Cabra and Coolock areas. It was in these areas that Sinn Féin candidate and former IRA prisoner Christy Burke received his highest vote in an unsuccessful Dáil campaign in the February 1982 election.[30]

By November of that year, Burke was operating three advice clinics in north inner-city Dublin and was a prominent community activist.[31] There were some minor successes in the Hardwicke Street area of Burke's ward in 1982, with drug dealers either ceasing their activities or leaving the area upon request. On the south side, the first glimpse of an organised community response to the drugs crisis occurred in the summer of 1983, when approximately seventy people met at the St Teresa's Gardens housing complex just outside the Liberties area. Amid much talk and debate, a vote was taken to approach three drug-pushing families and give them a week's ultimatum to leave the area. Following the ultimatum, which the families ignored, a crowd of nearly 300 people entered the flats and formed a human chain, passing all their furniture down the stairs. This was done to distribute any criminal culpability among the protestors. Sometime later a dance was held in the nearby Our Lady's Hall, which locals referred to as the 'Victory Dance'.

Similar spontaneous community reactions began to take place in other areas of the city around this time. Up to 500 people attended a meeting in Crumlin following reports of two women handing heroin packets to children outside a school. The men of that area established nightly roadblocks and patrols to prevent drugs entering the area. Further west, in Tallaght, residents formed the Tallaght Drugs Action Committee and elected local Sinn Féin activist John Noonan as chairman. In an attempt to emulate the St Teresa's Gardens success, they planned to march to the home of a local drug dealer but were prevented from doing so by gardaí and detectives in squad cars and on foot. In the flats of Hardwicke Street a number of local mothers, along with a resident Jesuit priest and Christy Burke, began using the name 'Concerned Parents' and regularly protested outside the homes of known drug dealers. The area soon became known as a difficult place to push heroin.[32] By February 1984, there were various unofficial branches or groups of such community activist groups scattered throughout the city and suburbs. A contemporary report on the conditions leading to the formation of one such group in March 1984 indicates the imperative for such action:

> When the people of Dublin's Lower Crumlin heard that drug pushers had been in the grounds of Scoil Iosagain offering drugs free to the schoolkids, they decided that some action had to be taken … At about half past one in the afternoon, a car would pull up. The car would have the effect, as one resident put it, of the Pied Piper, as up to 30 heroin users bought their supplies from the occupant of the car. Some of them would be in such a bad way for a fix that they would inject themselves straight away and throw the used syringe on the ground. The kids from Scoil Iosagain would pass the spot a couple of hours later on their way home from school.[33]

A coalescence and co-ordination of the various local groups began and the grassroots popularity of the movement was revealed that month when thousands of people marched through the city centre to hand in a letter of concern to Taoiseach Garret FitzGerald. Banners at the march indicated representation from areas such as Dolphin House, Tallaght, Ballyfermot, Ballymun, Crumlin, Clondalkin and Coolock, among others.[34] The following month, the newly co-ordinated groups announced the establishment of a central committee and began to refer to themselves as Concerned Parents

Against Drugs (CPAD). Over the course of the spring and summer of 1984, branches sprang up across Dublin and as far south as Bray, County Wicklow.[35]

There were immense profits to be made in the heroin trade in Dublin. Inevitably, those involved in that trade would react to the major disruption to their business caused by CPAD. Several days before the massive Dublin rally, anti-drugs activist Joey Flynn was shot in both legs in daylight at Donore Avenue near St Teresa's Gardens.[36] A shadowy group soon emerged, rather mockingly self-labelled 'Concerned Criminals'. This group claimed to be 'ordinary decent criminals' whose activities were outside the remit of CPAD, but who claimed to feel threatened by that group's increasing vigilantism. Up to this point, neither the Provisional IRA nor Sinn Féin were officially involved with CPAD, although the prominence of local republicans such as Burke and Noonan in the movement carried a whiff of association. This perceived association of the IRA with the anti-drugs movement was referred to at the time as 'the big bluff'. While not being actively associated with CPAD, in 1983 local IRA members in Dublin city had indicated to key anti-drugs activists that they would provide support if the organisation came under serious threat. A newspaper distributed in Dublin in November 1983, titled *Inner City Republican* and endorsing Christy Burke as Dublin Central by-election candidate, published an interview with an IRA spokesperson. While the spokesperson put responsibility for dealing with the drug problem firmly on the shoulders of each individual community, they went on to say of the drug dealers themselves: 'They are totally cynical and callous business people who will exploit unscrupulously to fill their own pockets and we issue a strong warning to those people that they will not be safe no matter where they live … we are keeping a constant watch on them.'[37] With the shooting of Joey Flynn, the IRA's bluff had been called.[38] It wouldn't take long for members of the Dublin Brigade to respond.

Several days after the mass rally in Dublin city centre, four men entered the Park Inn public house near Harold's Cross on the south side of the city. At least one of the men was armed. They approached Thomas Gaffney, a local man with criminal associations, pulled him out of the building and bundled him into a red HiAce van. The van and its occupants disappeared before gardaí arrived on the scene. Several days later, friends and relatives of Gaffney met with a prominent Tallaght Sinn Féin representative who told them that a Dublin unit of the Provisional IRA may have been involved in the kidnapping, although acting outside of GHQ's sanction. That the unit was acting outside of command orders was very probable. Many IRA members, particularly in the North, were utterly opposed to involvement in the anti-drugs campaign, viewing it as a potentially resource-draining 'second front'. Gaffney's captors held him for twelve days and interrogated him about drugs and the shooting of Joey Flynn. They informed him that they were dissatisfied with garda inaction on the drugs issue and so had felt the need to act themselves. At one point during his captivity, friends of Gaffney marched to St Teresa's Gardens to demand his release. Gardaí had to form a barrier between them and community leaders in the housing complex.[39] At the end of his captivity, Gaffney was dropped out of a van on the Kerry side of the Feale river, about four miles from the County Limerick town of Abbeyfeale. One of his captors told him that they accepted his claims of non-involvement in drug pushing and the shooting of Flynn. Following his release, Gaffney wandered country roads for several hours, being told to 'push off' from the first house he approached, before eventually arriving at the Abbeyfeale parochial house. The local priest made contact with gardaí and Gaffney was eventually reunited with his family in Dublin, shaken but otherwise uninjured. It was later alleged that the kidnapping was requested by members of the Crumlin-Cork St branch of CPAD, who had approached local members of the IRA.[40]

While Gaffney was still in captivity, a second kidnapping attempt was made, this time on Martin 'the Viper' Foley, a close associate of Gaffney's. Foley had been prominently involved in several physical clashes between CPAD members and the 'Concerned Criminals' in previous weeks. At around 7 a.m. on 22 March, five men entered his home in Crumlin, brought him outside at gunpoint and put him into a HiAce van. One of the men had posed as a postman in order to get to the door without arousing suspicion so early in the morning. Foley managed to scream for help before being gagged, alerting neighbours who then called the gardaí. As the van passed near Rialto, a garda walking his beat spotted it and, being suspicious of the number of occupants, radioed it in. This allowed the Special Task Force to zero in on the van's location. Foley's brief ordeal ended in a high-speed chase and a shoot-out between gardaí and IRA members near the Wellington Monument in the Phoenix Park. Four of the five captors surrendered and were apprehended. A shotgun, a rifle and two handguns were recovered from the scene, while

Foley was found bound and gagged in the back of the van. The four arrested men, from Ballyfermot, Finglas and Dún Laoghaire, subsequently received sentences ranging from five to seven years' imprisonment on kidnapping and arms offences. As they were led from the dock following sentencing, one of them raised a clenched fist in the air and shouted 'Up the Provos' to cheers from the public gallery.[41]

With the failed kidnapping of Foley, a very public connection was made between the IRA and the anti-drugs campaign in Dublin. CPAD came under increasing attack from politicians and elements of the media, who denounced it as a front for the Provisionals. Barry Desmond, the Labour TD and Minister for Social Welfare, accused Sinn Féin of 'exploiting the drugs war' for political gain, while conceding that only 15 per cent of illegal drugs coming into the state were being intercepted by gardaí. Minister for Justice Michael Noonan accused Sinn Féin of infiltrating the anti-drugs movement and claimed that 'Dublin is no longer the drugs capital of Europe', the first such government admission that it had in fact been the drugs capital of Europe at any time.[42] The slurs on CPAD were not new. In late 1983, as the disparate anti-drugs groups began to consolidate, the RTÉ current affairs show *Today, Tonight* broadcast a special report on the phenomenon. The editorial slant strongly implied that Sinn Féin had infiltrated the organisation to the extent of dominating it and that it was merely a front for the republican movement. The programme was slammed by community groups. Sister Elizabeth O'Brien, a nun who was involved in the production of the episode, wrote to the *Irish Independent* to express her disgust at the manner in which it was edited to convey a particular political agenda.[43] It should be noted that the Workers' Party, the political wing of the Official IRA, had near total editorial control of *Today, Tonight* during this period.[44]

In other departments of RTÉ, the restrictions of Section 31 of the Broadcasting Act impacted coverage of the anti-drugs movement. The reality was that many Sinn Féin members lived in working-class flat complexes and housing estates, and were involved in CPAD in an individual capacity. Each time a reporter was sent to cover an anti-drugs story, they were instructed to ask the interviewee specifically whether he or she was a member of Sinn Féin. A combination of the difficulty in finding non-Sinn Féin members to interview and the inevitable annoyance those questions would raise for any interviewee, led to CPAD being covered less and less by RTÉ.[45] In the Dáil, Workers' Party TD Proinsias De Rossa was particularly vocal about the CPAD, referring to it as 'simply a front for the Provisionals' and compared their activities to those of the Ku Klux Klan.[46] In an interview with *In Dublin* during this period, Gerry Adams refuted the infiltration allegation, asking how it could be considered infiltration when people approach you and ask you to help.[47]

Provisional–CPAD connections were far from black and white. In a series of articles on the matter, Padraig Yeates (who associated with members of the Workers' Party at the time) concluded that 'Sinn Féin involvement in the Concerned Parents Against Drugs committees began more by accident than by design … Sinn Féin members sit on it [the central committee] as delegates from anti-drug groups, not party members.'[48] In reality, Sinn Féin activists in the CPAD were 'very much in the minority on both local committees and the Central Committee. They were also very much a minority of Sinn Féin members in the city.'[49] One community activist claimed that the tabloid elements of the media played up the Provisional involvement because 'it makes a good read', while the more politically motivated journalists did so as they were terrified of the Provisionals becoming involved in community organisations. The activist spoke of the ironic consequences of this, in that the media 'were exposing something that didn't exist. And in doing so they helped create the very phenomenon which they wished to avoid.'[50] In the second part of Yeates' report into the Provisional–CPAD connection, he wrote: 'The gardaí, and some politicians, are so frightened that people in these areas are organising themselves that they claim they are being manipulated. They can't conceive that ordinary working-class people can organise themselves.'[51]

Media vilification was the least of the anti-drugs movement's worries as time went on. *An Phoblacht*, which because of the proximity of Dublin Sinn Féin members to the drug epidemic had been covering the organising of communities long before the mainstream media gave it due focus,[52] reported: 'Since the disappearance of Thomas Gaffney from the Crumlin area on Sunday, March 11th, the Concerned Parents Committees (formed to combat drug pushing in Dublin) has once again become a target for threats, garda harassment and media sensationalism.'[53] Gardaí began to devote a great deal of time to the harassment of CPAD members. Demonstrations and marches were regularly broken up, and those involved found themselves being arrested for the dubious charge of 'watching and besetting'.[54] Gardaí regularly harassed and arrested leading CPAD members, including Christy Burke and TD Tony Gregory. During this same period, deaths from heroin overdoses increased dramatically, with seven people dying in Dublin in one June week alone.[55] One local publication recounted the experiences of anti-drugs activists during the 1980s: '[Gardaí] used to flood Ballymun with over 100 uniformed and plain-clothes officers when there was a CPAD meeting or march on a pusher. Several parents were arrested, then freed by juries, but the government transferred CPAD (not drug-pushing) cases to non-jury courts and two parents were jailed for moving three pushers out of McDonagh Tower'.[56]

One republican who was involved in the anti-drugs campaign in later years recalled the experiences of non-political members of the CPAD and the consequences of such treatment:

> [T]he cops came in fairly heavy-handed. They used to drive up to people's houses, up the driveway … blaring the lights full-blare on and off in their sitting-room windows. They'd come out and they'd drive off. So, they'd ring the cops, and that was the cops, you know. So, they felt very intimidated by what was going on. So, the cops were basically trying to turn them against doing good work in their own communities. So, there was a lot, we lost a lot of people over that. They were saying 'Ah, jeez, I can't get involved in that, the cops are onto me. I'm only trying to help my kids'.[57]

Tony Gregory tried to inject some perspective into the anti-drugs campaign stating that, while gardaí were 'running women traders off the streets they are not dealing with heroin pushers who are operating within a stone's throw of Store Street station'.[58] At that time, as previously mentioned, there was a major garda clampdown on unlicensed street-market trading in Dublin's north inner city. Gregory contended that the goal of the gardaí was to 'contain the community, not prevent crime within it'.[59]

It is worth noting that initial garda responses to community activism were not hostile. In the Garda Commissioner's annual report for 1983, for example, there was a guarded positivity:

The year saw the emergence of concerned groups of citizens coming together to consider trends and similar problems particularly those relating to drugs in the Dublin City area. While the interest of such groups has to be welcomed and encouraged, a note of caution has to be expressed. These groups need to be ever alert in maintaining their independence and integrity in the interest of community welfare and in avoiding the encouragement of particular ideologies. The Rule of Law must be observed and the Gardaí have a duty to see that this is done.[60]

In November 1984, CPAD held its first annual conference at Liberty Hall. By the spring of the following year, however, there were claims that the movement was running out of steam. This was rubbished by *An Phoblacht*, which pointed to a protest march in Dublin city centre in March 1985 made up of branches from across the city. However, the attendance of 300 or so people was a far cry from the monster rally of the previous year. Ultimatums to, and evictions of, drug dealers continued that year. Six months after the city-centre demonstration, over 600 residents of Ballyfermot marched on the home of a local drug dealer and forced his eviction. The following month, CPAD members – including former IRA member Rose Dugdale – squatted in the home of alleged drug kingpin 'Ma Baker'. They were forcibly evicted by gardaí clad in riot helmets and armed with shields and batons, and more than twenty people faced criminal charges as a result of the squat.[61] CPAD effectively ceased to operate as a protest group in the mid-1980s, after a short but impactful existence. According to one analysis, part of its demise was due to it descending into 'an aggressive, vigilante movement with loose paramilitary associations, and some confusion with respect to its punitive attitude towards drugs'. The problem of domineering personality clashes was also quite a significant factor on a local and central committee level.[62] Ultimately, groups such as CPAD were perceived as a threat to society. Whether this was due to their ambiguous approach to what they saw as a very faulty judicial system or because they represented the potential of working-class unity remains a continued source of debate. As Sinn Féin TD and former IRA volunteer Dessie Ellis said of the rise and fall of CPAD:

> any government, and no matter what it is, if they see a group of people who are doing the work of the police, or they're doing, you know, they're

actively involved in their communities and trying to deal with issues that are genuinely law and order issues in many ways, whether it's drug dealers or whether it's anti-social elements, the state always clamps down on those issues. And anyone who naively thought that they wouldn't, you know, found out in the long run that the state was going to react.[63]

While Sinn Féin and the IRA may not have been centrally controlling the anti-drugs movement in Dublin, they certainly benefited in some ways from their association with it. As one history of the period notes, the Foley and Gaffney kidnappings did not harm the Provisionals' image: 'if anything, it heightened their anti-drugs profile amongst the general public and the crisis welded them closer to the Concerned Parents movement.'[64] In a 1982 interview with *Magill*, Gerry Adams understood that identification of and involvement with working-class issues in the Republic of Ireland was crucial for the republican movement's growth and consolidation, noting: 'You can't get support in Ballymun because of doors being kicked in in Ballymurphy.'[65] Adams's view that community organisation rather than militant intervention was the preferred method for effective action and in building a stable base of support were repeated in a 1995 book. There, he wrote:

Of course, the republicans could have intervened independently – armed IRA interventions against the main drug suppliers or pushers would undoubtedly have enjoyed widespread support in areas blighted by drugs – but the militant actions of Concerned Parents ... have had a more lasting and deeper effect ... in instilling a consciousness of their own power in working-class communities.[66]

Christy Burke, the Sinn Féin member most associated with CPAD, saw his vote increase in every local election during the 1980s, and was first elected to Dublin City Council in 1985. Many of the 14,604 first preference votes that John Noonan received in the 1984 European Parliament election for the Dublin constituency likely came from his prominence in the anti-drugs campaign.[67] In the following decade, more than half of the Sinn Féin councillors elected in Dublin city in 1999 were also to the fore in anti-drugs campaigns in their local communities.[68] Conversely, the constant attacks by the Workers' Party on CPAD were identified by a splinter group from that party as contributing to the drastic electoral decline of the party throughout the 1990s: 'The drugs campaign of the 1980s in Dublin saw the end of grassroots working class support for the WP [Workers' Party]. The WP chose to ignore the working class in Dublin when they had decided to "take on" the dealers who were making people's lives a living hell in working class parts of the city.'[69]

As further evidence of the nuance surrounding the CPAD movement, it should be noted that Workers' Party activist and later High Court Judge Mick White had worked with Christy Burke on a CPAD committee. This was at the same time that his party colleagues were vilifying that organisation in the press.[70]

IRA Financing

While, in later years, elements of the media and security sources would allege links between the Provisional IRA and the drugs trade, no evidence was ever brought forward to support these claims. Indeed, unlike for other republican and paramilitary groups, the Independent Monitoring Commission did not list drug income as a revenue source for the Provisionals.[71] While drug dealing may have been off the cards for the IRA, the organisation's coffers were regularly strained and so various other tactics were considered to help boost them. Despite rumours that the Don Tidey kidnapping had earned the IRA £2 million in a ransom payment, kidnappings were considered high-risk from beginning to end, as well as likely being lengthy operations.[72] As a result, there was a return to more regular armed robberies by the IRA in the Republic during this period, despite the inherent dangers there also. The O/C of Southern Command at the time was a Belfast man. The second-in-command (adjutant) was from Kerry, and also served as O/C for the Kerry Brigade. According to the then-IRA Director of Intelligence, and speaking of this period, there were a lot of armed robberies conducted and Southern Command was 'professional' and 'well run', with Kerry seen as the most effective area.[73]

On 28 January 1984, an IRA unit of up to a dozen armed and masked men raided the large rural home of the Coddingtons, a young couple living just outside Drogheda at Oldbridge. The mansion belonged to Major Richard Coddington, a retired British Army officer and father of the man of the house.

It was reportedly the second robbery at the house in two years; previously, a gang had broken in and stolen £600,000 in paintings and antiques. The Oldbridge estate encompassed some 1,500 acres, including lands on which the 1690 Battle of the Boyne had been fought. In this second raid, the young couple were tied up in an upstairs bedroom while the house was searched for silverware, paintings and prints, all of which were loaded into a vehicle. In all, over £100,000-worth of items were stolen. Following the raid, the Coddington family sold the house and much of the estate, leaving Ireland for good. While the raiders had claimed to be from the INLA, this was treated with scepticism by gardaí, who initially believed it to be the work of 'a highly professional Dublin gang', likely that led by Martin 'the General' Cahill.[74] However, the profile of those subsequently arrested and charged indicates IRA involvement.

In February 1985, two men were jailed by the Special Criminal Court for their part in the robbery. One of the men, a thirty-eight-year-old coal vendor and father-of-four from Dundalk, was sentenced to ten years' imprisonment. The other, a sixty-two-year-old farmer from County Westmeath, pleaded guilty to holding the stolen goods and received prison sentences of three and four years with penal servitude for various firearms charges. This man made a statement to Detective Sergeant Owen Corrigan after his arrest, claiming that he had only agreed to act as a driver on 'a job' and that he had since left the IRA. Corrigan told the court that he believed that the sentenced man 'had been used by ruthless people'.[75] A third man, a thirty-one-year-old truck driver from Rush, County Dublin, was also charged for his part in the robbery, having initially been arrested on suspicion of involvement in the shooting of Garda Frank Hand at Drumree, County Meath (see following page). While in custody, the man reportedly told gardaí: 'I appreciate I have to go for the Coddington job. Make no mistake about it, I'll have to serve years in Portlaoise for it, but what can I do, I have no option. I have nothing to do with Drumree. You appreciate I cannot make a statement.' The defendant was acquitted by the Special Criminal Court. The presiding judge Mr Justice Doyle stated that, while the court was satisfied that the defendant had made certain voluntary admissions to gardaí and that these had demonstrated a degree of complicity in the offences, the prosecution had failed to provide sufficient evidence to prove his involvement in the crime.[76]

In mid-April, two masked men armed with handguns and reported as having 'Northern accents' hijacked a CIÉ lorry as it left the factory gates of the P.J. Carroll cigarette factory on the outskirts of Dundalk. The lorry had been packed with cigarettes with an estimated market value of £250,000. The raiders brought the lorry to a side road near Togher, County Louth, where the cigarettes were transferred to a waiting vehicle. The CIÉ lorry was then abandoned. Six months later Noel Fergus (43), a former-CIÉ driver from Dundalk, was arrested and charged with providing information to the IRA that led to the hijacking of the truck. The defendant claimed he had been approached by a man who asked him to help 'the cause' and had asked him about P.J. Carroll timetables and locks on the containers of the lorries. The presiding judge, Mr Justice McMahon, said the court was satisfied that Fergus had not acted under duress, but also took account of his unblemished record and family situation – he was a father of eight – and sentenced him to a five-year suspended sentence. Two years later, three other men were jailed for their part in the robbery. Thomas Reynolds (25) of Dundalk, Michael Rooney (35) of Dunleer and Joseph Farrell (41) of Dundalk received sentences ranging from two to nine years' imprisonment in January 1986.[77]

The surge in armed robberies after the relative lull of previous years increasingly made physical confrontations with gardaí likely, and a young Detective Garda, Frank Hand, would pay the price of this renewed policy. He was shot dead at Drumree, County Meath, in August 1984, while escorting a post office van delivering pension packets to rural post offices. His colleague, Detective Garda Michael Dowd, was also injured and the raiders – at least six men wearing masks and boiler suits – made off with over £200,000 in cash. According to one account:

The gang struck at 8.03 a.m. just after the Post Office van pulled into the driveway of the post office. The Garda car halted about six feet from the rear of the van, and the two armed men emerged from behind the garden wall. They immediately fired two shots through the rear door of the Garda car. Then the man with the Sten moved to the front of the Fiat and fired a burst at the detectives. Six bullets hit the windscreen, one of them striking Detective Dowd on the forehead and forcing him to drop his Uzi … Meanwhile, Garda Hand was opening his door and trying to draw his revolver. He succeeded in getting out of the car but there was another burst of gunfire and he was fatally wounded by a bullet entering his chest … During the operation the leader of the gang gave orders and was heard to shout 'Shoot him, fucking shoot him.'[78]

The account claimed that the IRA unit responsible was based out of Dundalk. It was reportedly led by a Cork man living in Dublin and a Northern Irish man 'on the run' and living in Dundalk. The cigarette theft and Coddington raid were also attributed to this unit. Garda Hand, a native of County Roscommon, had only returned to work that week, having been away on honeymoon with his new bride, herself a member of An Garda Síochána.

It has been suggested that elements within the IRA had recently introduced an unofficial change of policy regarding the use of firearms in interactions with the gardaí in response to the shooting of several IRA volunteers during the failed Weston kidnapping the previous year. The IRA had claimed that their volunteers were fired on without warning in that incident and so had urged that henceforth no chances should be taken in encounters with armed gardaí.[79] However, this claim cannot be confirmed. Officially, the IRA's General Standing Order No. 8, which stated that security forces in the Republic were not to be targeted and volunteers were to dump arms and seek to escape any confrontation rather than engage them, was still in operation. It is possible that the unplanned shooting at Drumree panicked the perpetrators, as they appear to have dumped the weapons and cash rather than caching them. Following the robbery and shooting, gardaí surrounded a barn at Brownstown, several miles from the site of the attack, where men had been reported as acting suspiciously. Inside, they found what was reported to be a 'substantial portion' of the stolen cash as well as guns – including the Uzi belonging to Michael Dowd – in addition to ammunition and walkie-talkies.[80] Following the death of Garda Hand, army escorts were made mandatory when large amounts of cash were being transported.

Eventually, four men were found guilty of the murder of Frank Hand, although the judge acknowledged that the actual 'trigger man' was not before the courts. Thomas Eccles and Brian McShane, both of Dundalk, and Patrick McPhillips of Lurgan, County Armagh, were sentenced to death in March 1985.[81] Another man, Paddy Duffy of County Louth, received a life sentence, while a fifth, Brendan Treacy of Ballymun, Dublin, was acquitted after the court found that statements he made in custody could not be accepted as evidence as the defendant was 'suffering from grave mental infirmity' at the time. A range of highly qualified psychiatrists supported the view that Treacy suffered from paranoid psychosis at the time of his confession.[82] A sixth man, Thomas Owen Taaffe, received a suspended sentence for transporting the weapons to be used by the IRA unit on the evening before the shooting. Taaffe had previously served in the Irish Defence Forces, where he had risen to the rank of sergeant before being honourably discharged after thirteen years of service. During his trial, Taaffe maintained that he was not involved in subversive activity and had moved the guns as a 'favour'. Detective Sergeant Owen Corrigan told the court that Taaffe had been used by 'more ruthless people'.[83] In February 1986, President Hillery commuted the death sentences of Eccles, McShane and McPhillips to forty years' imprisonment without remission.

From 1980 to the end of 1984, seven members of An Garda Síochána died violently, six of whose deaths were directly linked to the 'Troubles'. Understandably, such attacks on members of the force caused a lot of anger within the ranks, and for some, there was a feeling that more should be done to challenge directly the paramilitaries whose organisations were the cause of such violence.

The Return of the Heavy Gang

During a Dáil debate in February 1984, Fianna Fáil TD for Sligo–Leitrim John Ellis voiced his concerns regarding the recent arrest of two people in Monaghan and of house searches in the Leitrim area since the beginning of the year. Referring to the detention of the two men in Monaghan, Ellis said he was 'beginning to wonder whether Monaghan Garda Station was about to become the "Castlereagh of the South"'. This was a reference to the British interrogation centre outside Belfast, sardonically referred to by republicans as 'the conveyor belt' for the ability of its interrogators to rapidly extract forced confessions from detainees. Ellis claimed that the 'Heavy Gang' had been 'born again'.[84]

The so-called 'Heavy Gang' was a loose grouping of detectives, primarily from the Dublin-based murder squad, who earned a reputation for brutal interrogations of republican suspects during the tenure of the Fine Gael–Labour coalition government during the mid-1970s. Following the election of a Fianna Fáil government in 1977, the group had been broken up and reassigned. Several weeks after Deputy Ellis' contributions to the Dáil, a number of those linked to the 'Heavy Gang' were assigned to a murder investigation in County Kerry. The 'Kerry babies' case was an investigation into the discovery of the body of a newborn baby on a beach in south Kerry. The infant appeared to have died of numerous stab wounds. Suspicion fell on a woman living nearly fifty miles north of the beach. The suspect, Joanna Hayes, had recently been pregnant with the child of a married man, though that baby had been stillborn. The body of Joanna's child was belatedly located and exhumed on the Hayes family farm. However, investigating gardaí maintained that she could have given birth to both babies – the baby buried on the farm and the baby found on the beach – through the statistically highly improbable phenomenon of heteropaternal superfecundation, where a mother gives birth to twins who are from different fathers. It can occur when a second egg is released during the same menstrual cycle which is fertilised by the sperm of a different man in a very short period of time from the time that the first egg was fertilised.

Despite the improbable nature of the case against Joanna Hayes, her most intimate sexual activities were detailed for public consumption in a court trial. A number of commentators, then and since, have accurately attributed her ordeal in large part to the contemporary social environment which sought to punish unwed mothers. It should also be noted that the Murder Squad was an entirely male unit of An Garda Síochána. *Magill* later concluded that there was 'no credible suggestion that the Gardaí bore any malice to the Hayes family nor that they conspired to frame them'. However, their reporting on the trial added: 'these were no ordinary Gardaí. They had for a decade been at the centre of controversial methods of policing. Many allegations had been made of oppressive questioning by detectives in search of questions.'[85] Joanna's eldest brother reportedly suffered psychological abuse while in garda custody. Other family members reported physical abuse. Two of the detectives involved in the investigation would later be accused of beating, choking and forcing a poker into the mouth of a suspect in a Roscommon murder case. Both were later acquitted of any wrongdoing in that case by presiding judge Justice Kevin Lynch. Justice Lynch also presided over the case against Joanna Hayes. Two other detectives involved in the investigation had the Shercock and Sallins train-robbery investigations –

two infamous cases involving severe beatings to successfully extract false confessions from suspects – as part of their records.[86]

One theory to explain the dogged persecution of Joanna Hayes by detectives concerns political differences, ultimately stretching back sixty years. Hayes was the grand-niece of Stephen Fuller, the only survivor of the Ballyseedy massacre in 1923, when Free State soldiers tied eight anti-Treaty IRA prisoners around a landmine in north Kerry and detonated it.[87] Fuller also had a nephew interned in the Curragh during the Second World War, indicating an intergenerational involvement in militant republicanism.[88] As noted by an authoritative book on the 'Kerry babies' case, with the death of Joanna's father and uncle in 1975 and 1979 respectively, 'the Hayes family was vulnerable. There was no grand patriarchal figure to defend the honour of the family.'[89] The involvement of three Dublin-based detectives, all originally from north County Kerry, in this implausible prosecution – the vindictiveness of the case against a vulnerable young woman from a republican family in a county with perhaps the bitterest Civil War legacy – certainly raises questions of motive behind the push for a prosecution in the face of overwhelming scientific evidence.[90]

The Marita Ann

In the early hours of Saturday morning, 29 September 1984, the Irish navy vessel LE Émer, supported by LE Aisling and LE Deirdre, intercepted a fishing trawler near the Great Skellig Rock, off the coast of County Kerry. The navy ships and crew, including armed gardaí, had been at sea for several days, awaiting the return of the fishing trawler. The trawler, the Marita Ann, had rendezvoused with another ship, the Valhalla, 120 miles off the Irish coast, in a relatively shallow part of the Atlantic known as Porcupine Bank. There, over seven tons of arms and military equipment were transferred from the larger to the smaller vessel. The shipment comprised thirteen shotguns, ninety rifles and carbines, six heavy machine guns, seventeen pistols, thirty-four revolvers and 71,000 rounds of ammunition, telescopic sights and webbing and a box of hand grenades. The heavy machine guns had been adapted with special mountings to be used as anti-aircraft weapons. The transfer completed, the Marita Ann then started on its return journey to Ireland. On board were five men: Gavin Mortimer (23), Johnny McCarthy (26), Michael

Browne, the trawler's owner (42) – all from Fenit, County Kerry – Martin Ferris (34) from Ardfert and a former US Marine, John Crawley (27). Once the *Marita Ann* was safely within Irish territorial waters, the Irish navy struck. The LE *Émer* made to intercept it with the two other ships acting in a supporting role. At first, the *Marita Ann* tried to outrun the navy but, after several shots were fired across its bow, the crew accepted the inevitable and surrendered. According to gardaí, as they boarded the boat a hand grenade rolled across the deck, a dangerous albeit almost comical confirmation of the security forces' suspicions of the trawler's cargo. They had just intercepted the largest known arms shipment to the IRA to date.[91]

The weapons originated in the USA, where they had been loaded onto the *Valhalla* for shipment to Ireland. As the *Valhalla* returned to port in Boston, it too was being monitored and its crew was arrested by US law officials. On the US side, the importation had been organised and overseen by several Irish-Americans, including crime boss and FBI informant James 'Whitey' Bulger, working with Belfast republican Joe Cahill. The captain of the *Marita Ann*, Michael Browne, had been involved in discussions with the captain of the *Valhalla* to arrange the rendezvous, while Cahill had travelled to the US earlier in the year to make the necessary arrangements for the shipment before being deported on immigration charges.[92] The loss of the arms and the crew of the *Marita Ann*, as well as the smashing of the arms importation network, was a severe blow to the IRA, particularly since garda and RUC operations had already led to the capture of significant quantities of IRA arms during the preceding years. In addition to the loss of weapons was the financial cost. According to one estimate, the shipment would have cost £1.5 million.[93] Although there are claims that it was financed entirely by Bulger, who extracted the funds through intimidation of Boston-area criminals, it is likely that at least some of the finance was fronted by the IRA's Southern Command. In Kerry alone, between 1981 and 1983 nine armed robberies were attributed to the Provisionals.[94]

In the fallout from the seizure of the *Marita Ann*, those involved on both sides of the Atlantic sought to discover the source of the leak that led to its capture. In Boston, Bulger later had *Valhalla* crew member John McIntyre killed. McIntyre had confessed his role in the gun-running operation to Boston police. However, this was after the fact. Reports in the aftermath of the seizure claimed that the tip-off to gardaí came from British intelligence services, although this may simply have been a way to throw the IRA off the scent of the real source of information. A British spy plane did allegedly photograph the transfer of cargo between the two ships at sea; photographs they then supplied to the gardaí, which might have confused matters.[95] The most plausible explanation is that information provided by IRA informer Sean O'Callaghan led to the capture of the trawler, with the Irish security forces subsequently tipping off their US counterparts about the return of the *Valhalla*. Had the information originated in the US, it is highly unlikely that officials there would have allowed the arms to leave Boston. Not only would it place unacceptable risk on the shipment being successfully tracked and intercepted off the Irish coast, it would also mean a pass on receiving the majority credit for the importation disruption. In the biography of Martin Ferris, it is claimed that Ferris' brother suspected O'Callaghan of being the source of the information to gardaí: 'My brother Brian told me months later on a visit to Portlaoise, "All the papers are running around saying that this informer is in America, but", he said, "the fucking man is alongside of you. You're fucking blind. He is alongside of you."'[96]

The capture of the *Marita Ann* was a major achievement for the Irish security forces. As British officials noted, it served to bolster the morale of gardaí after their 'muddled attempts earlier this year to capture the terrorist kidnappers of Don Tidey were less than reassuring'.[97] At the time of the trawler's capture, the IRA's Director of Intelligence was in Kerry monitoring garda airwaves. Also onshore were 'ten to twelve' IRA volunteers ready to receive the shipment and transport it to waiting arms dumps.[98] The IRA had received garda radio frequencies from a sympathetic journalist some time previously and their eavesdropping had hitherto proven effective for evading gardaí.[99] In this instance, however, Sean O'Callaghan claimed to have alerted gardaí to this practice. Evidently, they switched frequency for the sensitive discussions around this operation.[100] It's also possible that the gardaí simply adapted counter-surveillance techniques, having discovered an IRA walkie-talkie in Derrada Wood the previous year that was tuned into their frequencies.

As standard practice, the five captured IRA volunteers from the *Marita Ann* were debriefed in prison. The Intelligence Officer in Portlaoise at this time was Jim Lynagh, then serving a prison sentence for IRA membership. The five crew were put on trial in the Special Criminal Court in November

1984, charged with arms and explosives possession and importation offences. In addition, they faced charges of possession of firearms and ammunition with intent to endanger life. This latter charge related to the fact that there were several firearms and explosive material to hand when the trawler was intercepted. The defendants claimed that this was because they intended to scuttle the trawler rather than allow it to be captured. At no time during the security operation had the ship's crew used any weapons against gardaí. During the trial, counsel for the defendants sought acquittal on a technicality: the five men had been arrested at the time of interception off the Great Skellig Rock. Following this, they were brought to the naval base at Haulbowline, County Cork. If they had been brought outside Irish territorial waters during that voyage, it would have invalidated the arrest and thus the trial. However, requests to see the logbook of the Irish Navy's LE *Émer* were refused by that ship's captain, as it was a 'confidential document'. All five men were found guilty of all charges, including the contested 'intent to endanger life' charge. Ferris, Browne and Crawley were each sentenced to ten years' imprisonment, while Mortimer and McCarthy received five-year suspended sentences. The three men due to be imprisoned gave clenched fist salutes as they were led away to cheers, handclapping and shouts of 'Up the Provos' from the public gallery.

Among those who sat in the gallery during the trial was Joe Cahill. Eleven years earlier, Cahill had been in the same dock charged with smuggling five tons of arms and ammunition into the country from Libya. Largely unremarked upon in the minor reporting of Cahill's deportation from the US earlier in the year was that he was charged with 'misusing a passport'.[101] This passport was in fact one of 100 blank passports stolen from the Department of Foreign Affairs that year. They had been intended for distribution to various Irish embassies abroad before they went missing, and the IRA was to make full use of them in subsequent years.[102] As for the *Marita Ann*, the boat was in the news a year later, again for all the wrong reasons. After its owner Michael Browne was jailed, the trawler was bought by a Dublin-based solicitor and leased out locally. Gardaí suspected the trawler was being used for illegal salmon trawling and a violent clash involving the Naval Service, a fisheries inspector, gardaí and the *Marita Ann* fishermen and supporters erupted on 18 June 1985, when officials tried to board the boat as it returned to Fenit harbour. A hostile crowd prevented officials from reaching the boat, having built barricades of lobster pots and other objects, while the fishermen were reported to have been masked and wielding iron bars, chains and slash hooks. Gardaí eventually withdrew from the scene as 'there was no point in a head-on confrontation with these persons'.[103]

As the trial of the *Marita Ann* crew was ongoing, the IRA suffered yet another blow to their arms stockpile. On the night of 26 November, three men and a woman travelling in two cars were arrested at a garda checkpoint outside Athy, County Kildare. A search of one of the cars revealed 53lbs of commercial explosives, detonators and a Browning pistol with ammunition. Two of the group later appeared in the Special Criminal Court on charges related to the discovery: thirty-six-year-old Joseph Curran was a Sinn Féin member, while his co-defendant, thirty-seven-year-old Noel Tidd, was a former soldier. According to court reports, detectives noticed that the two cars were travelling together and, as the lead car approached the checkpoint, the rear car pulled into a gateway about thirty yards back. Armed detectives approached the rear car and ordered the two men to get out and lie on the ground. The Browning pistol was found tucked into Tidd's waistband and he was subsequently sentenced to a seven-year prison sentence for unlawful possession of explosive substances with intent to endanger life. Tidd was also given concurrent sentences of five and three years for possession of the pistol with intent to endanger life and unlawful possession of the pistol and ammunition. Curran had claimed that he met with some of the party in a pub prior to attending a Sinn Féin meeting and had left his car parked outside while in the pub. He was acquitted on an explosives possession charge after the court ruled that the prosecution failed to prove the charge beyond reasonable doubt. He had earlier been acquitted on firearms charges, as there was not adequate proof that he knew his co-defendant was carrying the pistol while he was in the car.[104] The total amount of arms, ammunition and explosives seized by gardaí in 1984 is shown in Table 10 overleaf.

Closing Out the Year

If the IRA was seeking any solace from a dismal year for its campaign, the Brighton bombing in October and the dismissal of the Raymond Gilmour supergrass trial in December might have sufficed. Although the targeting of Margaret Thatcher at the Conservative Party's conference at the Grand

Table 10. Garda seizures of arms, ammunition and
explosives, 1984[105]

Quantity	Type
314	Firearms (including rifles, shotguns, machine guns, pistols, revolvers, etc.)
3,142	Rounds of ammunition (assorted)
1,062	Shotgun cartridges
24	Magazines
1,005lbs	Assorted explosives
101	Detonators
725	Shotgun shells
13	Bombs of various types
9	Hand grenades
4	Rockets

Hotel in Brighton was not successful, it brought renewed political focus to the conflict and ultimately led to a renewal of secret talks between the IRA and British government. It also led to a serious reconsideration of IRA strategy with regard to the England Department. A week before Christmas, Gilmour's supergrass testimony was entirely rejected in a Northern Irish court, with the presiding judge declaring that Gilmour was a man 'to whose lips a lie comes more naturally than the truth'.[106] No doubt this was a relief to the IRA and INLA as nearly three dozen of their members were still facing charges based on Gilmour's testimony. It is worth noting that, in addition to the IRA's ability to eavesdrop on garda communication during this period, it is claimed that Southern Command were also tapping the family phones of supergrasses. Indeed, as the supergrass informants themselves were often based in England, IRA intelligence units were sent there to locate them.[107]

In one of the closing weekends of the year, many of the republican faithful made the annual trip to Dublin for the Sinn Féin Ard-Fheis, where the abstentionist policy was reaffirmed. However, public criticism of this line was becoming increasingly common, and more brazen. A delegate from Ballymun stated that the party's electoral policy should be based on realism: 'A majority of the electorate in the 26 counties saw the institutions of the State as legitimate and if Sinn Féin did not understand that they were burying their heads in the sand.' Rebutting this, Councillor Joe O'Neill of Bundoran reminded attendees to ask themselves what Leinster House had ever given republicans: 'It had shot, hanged and jailed Republicans. More than 200 Republicans were in jail at the present time. Participation in the activities of Leinster House was not the way forward.'[108] Ironically, the Ard-Fheis was being held in Leinster House and in fact there was condemnation of the government, including from Fine Gael TDs, for allowing Sinn Féin to use the building.[109]

On the military side of the republican movement, plans were already seemingly afoot to jettison support for the abstentionism policy. Former IRA volunteer Eamon Collins later wrote that local IRA 'forums' in South Armagh and Down were being 'encouraged' to discuss ending the policy in 1984.[110] As part of the moves towards influencing policy with the republican movement, the Northern leadership established a 'Revolutionary Committee' that year. Ostensibly, this was a forum for discussing and debating policy and strategy, whereas in practice its goal was to provide a balance to and perhaps supersede the IRA's Army Executive through new policy and strategy proposals, a role that the Executive traditionally held. While the seven-person Army Council was numerically favourable towards Gerry Adams's strategy of politicisation, the twelve-person Army Executive remained hostile or suspicious. IRA Director of Intelligence Kieran Conway was part of the committee and suggested that they co-opt Ruairí Ó Brádaigh and Dáithí Ó Conaill, a suggestion that was 'met with a stony silence'. According to Conway, this marked the end of his own upward trajectory within the movement.[111]

Both parties to the abstentionist debate would also have been mindful of the results of the European Parliament elections earlier in the summer. While there were some surprisingly high votes for Sinn Féin, there was perhaps the perception of the party as one of protest rather than participation at the European level also. Sinn Féin had run candidates in all six constituencies: Danny Morrison (Northern Ireland), Eddie Fullerton, Mary McGing and Caoimhghín Ó Caoláin (Connacht–Ulster), John Noonan (Dublin), Martin Sharkey, John Carroll and James Dwyer (Leinster) and Richard Behal (Munster). Morrison received 91,476 first-preference votes (FPV), coming in fourth place. The combined FPV for Sinn Féin in Connacht–Ulster was 16,050, with Leinster on 11,189, while Richard Behal received 12,829 FPV, coming last out of all candidates. In Dublin, John Noonan received a more respectable 14,604 FPV or 5.2 per cent of the vote. As noted above, a large part of this was attributed to his prominence in the anti-drugs campaign in the city. It was clear that political participation at an activist- or street-level paid dividends in terms of electoral support. Proponents of dropping abstention could point to the possibility of greater dividends through parliamentary participation, while the opposition could argue that such activities would dilute street activism as well as revolutionary principles. As 1984 came to a close, it was clear that this debate had much more mileage in it.

A march in support of the hunger strikers proceeds down O'Connell Street, Dublin. (Courtesy of anphoblacht. com)

Gardaí successfully prevented rioters from reaching the British Embassy in Dublin during a hunger strike protest in July 1981. (Courtesy of anphoblacht.com)

Protests against conditions in Portlaoise for IRA prisoners were a regular occurrence during the 1980s. The strip-searching of prisoners in Portlaoise before and after visits was a particular grievance. (Courtesy of anphoblacht.com)

A Concerned Parents Against Drugs march in Dublin. The perceived connection between the IRA and CPAD was referred to as the 'Big Bluff'. (Courtesy of anphoblacht.com)

A gesture of defiance from Martin Ferris as he is led away by gardaí following his arrest on board the *Marita Ann*. (Courtesy of anphoblacht. com)

Electoral Strategy

162 That this Ard-Fheis drops its abstentionist attitude to Leinster House. Successful Sinn Fein parliamentary candidates in 26-County elections:

    a. Shall attend Leinster House as directed by the Ard Chomhairle.

    b. Shall not draw their salaries for personal use. (Parliamentary representatives shall be paid a Sinn Fein organiser's subsidy, and the Leinster House salary shall be divided at the direction of the Ard Chomhairle to defray national and constituency expenses.)

Motion 162 at the 1986 Sinn Féin Ard-Fheis. The IRA voted the previous month to drop the policy of abstaining from Leinster House. (Courtesy of anphoblacht.com)

Leitrim IRA veteran John Joe McGirl addresses the 1986 Sinn Féin Ard-Fheis as Gerry Adams, Danny Morrison and others look on. (Courtesy of anphoblacht.com)

The extradition of republicans in the South to face trial in Northern Ireland often led to protests at the border. (Courtesy of anphoblacht.com)

The extradition of Belfast IRA member Robert Russell in 1988 led to a wave of violence across the North in August of that year. (Courtesy of anphoblacht.com)

While serving a life sentence in Portlaoise for several murders, Thomas McMahon was involved in two high-profile escape attempts. (Courtesy of PA Images/Alamy Stock Photo)

We Will Lead You to the Republic: 1985–86

A fter the success of the *Marita Ann* operation, the following two years would see continued triumphs for garda intelligence in relation to the capture of considerable amounts of IRA weaponry, as well as the arrest of a number of Southern Command volunteers. Such successes would only have increased the ever-present fear of informers within IRA ranks, and a number of alleged or admitted informers were killed during this period. To this day, the death of one confessed garda informant in Cork in 1985 casts a shadow over the state's complicity in this shadowy arena of the conflict. The IRA also stepped up its campaign of targeting 'collaborators': building contractors who worked on British Army or RUC barracks and installations.

The determined campaign of the families of Portlaoise prisoners to have a more humane system in place for visits finally bore fruit in 1985. The decade-long system of tight controls on visitors was loosened and families could enjoy a degree of physical contact with imprisoned relatives. This more liberal system was not to last, however, and the easing in prison brutality was never reflected in treatment of republicans on the outside. Republican activists continued to face harassment and physical abuse, and gardaí operated with seeming impunity. The promotion of a detective while an investigation was ongoing into his firing multiple shots on a busy Dublin city street only served to highlight this.

At one point, however, even the government feared it had overstepped the mark. When emergency legislation was introduced in the form of an amendment to the Offences Against the State Act allowing for the seizure of what was believed to be significant IRA funding, the government was worried that it too would be successfully challenged on this assumption. Although this did not come to pass, the government's suspicions that such transactions presaged large-scale IRA arms purchases were not unfounded. During the early 1970s, the IRA acquired some of the first modern armaments of the campaign from Colonel Gadaffi's Libya. While that source had dried up by the mid-1970s, a series of international events led to its reactivation in this decade. As a result, a number of ever-increasing arms shipments began arriving in Ireland from late 1985 into 1986. That latter year would finally see the issue of abstentionism dealt with decisively, when first the IRA and then Sinn Féin voted to end the long-standing policy in the South. As 1986 concluded, the republican movement was in a strong position: the IRA had vast amounts of modern weaponry and material, with more expected in the following year, while Sinn Féin were laying the groundwork for what they expected to be continued growth and possibly even parliamentary representation in the Republic.

Arms

The capture of the *Marita Ann* in 1984 was a major blow to the IRA in their arms-acquisition drive. However, unbeknownst to all but a handful of senior leadership, attempts were already underway to rekindle a previous relationship with Libya, dormant since the mid-1970s. Due to a number of international crises and rising tensions between the UK and Libya, these efforts paid off in the mid-1980s. A series of events and police discoveries in 1985 and 1986 indicated that, despite the *Marita Ann* failure, the IRA were still acquiring modern weaponry, though how much and from what source would remain a mystery.

In late February 1985, three IRA volunteers were en route to an arms cache in Strabane, County Tyrone, when they were ambushed and killed by members of the British military elite Special Air Services (SAS). Among the weapons discovered were two homemade grenade launchers, a recent creation of the IRA's engineering department designed for close-proximity attacks in urban environments. This weapon had been distributed to a number of Northern Command units just prior to the Strabane killing.[1] The discovery of such a homemade armament led to an erroneous belief that the IRA was struggling to acquire sufficient weaponry from abroad. However, also found was an AK-47, an assault rifle that the IRA had rarely been known to use before this time. Another weapon discovered near the bodies was the relatively new Belgian rifle, the FN FNC-80. Both weapons hinted that the IRA had new arms supply chains, and the latter was believed to be connected to the theft of rifles from a Norwegian Reserve Force base near Oslo in May 1984.[2] In the twelve months following the deaths of the three IRA volunteers in Strabane, gardaí made huge seizures of IRA weaponry in Counties Sligo and Roscommon, further pointing to the likelihood that they had indeed acquired significant new arms shipments from abroad.

As well as discoveries of new weaponry, there was an element of business as usual for gardaí in 1985, including the discovery of a 'bomb factory' in Donegal in July of that year. That month, gardaí also arrested H-Block escapee Anthony Kelly, along with a Donegal man, thirty-four-year-old fisherman and father-of-three James Boyle, at a remote house near Inver in County Donegal. Gardaí had been keeping the house under observation, having discovered two empty beer kegs and two empty gas cylinders there previously. Kelly and Boyle arrived at the house shortly after 10 p.m. on 5 July carrying boxes containing a rifle and various bomb-making equipment and were promptly arrested.[3] Kelly was granted bail and failed to appear at his trial, having gone on the run. He would not be recaptured for another two years. The following year, another prison escapee was apprehended near Drumshanbo, County Leitrim. Oliver Thomas McKiernan had in fact escaped from Portlaoise prison over ten years earlier, in a mass breakout of nineteen IRA prisoners in 1974 and was arrested with another man at a house in December 1986.

At the beginning of that year, Special Task Force detectives uncovered three major IRA arms dumps, reportedly some of the largest yet discovered in the state: at a farm at Carrowreagh near Carrick-on-Shannon, in Mullaghroe, near the County Sligo village of Gurteen, and at Coolera, also Sligo. Such was the level of secrecy involved in the security operation that local gardaí were not informed about the intended raids until they had already taken place.[4] Samuel Cryan (52), a bachelor farmer, was sentenced to seven years' imprisonment for the Carrowreagh find. Dozens of AK-47s and more than 12,000 rounds of ammunition were discovered concealed under hay bales in a shed on his farm. The judge dismissed the claim that the defendant knew nothing about the weapons. Cryan had one previous conviction. Many years earlier, he had served a month's prison sentence for refusing to pay a £50 fine for the unauthorised sale of Easter lilies.[5] At Coolera, thirty AK-47s were discovered in the attic of a small farmer and father-of-three. The weapons were packed in clear plastic bags, and each came with a bayonet, scabbard, magazines and cleaning kits. Also discovered in the attic were over 12,000 rounds of ammunition marked 'Libyan Armed Forces' and 'Destination Tripoli'. In court, the defendant claimed that a man whom he did not know called to his home at 11.30 p.m. about two weeks before the garda raid. He asked the defendant to keep some 'stuff' and the defendant 'guessed he was from the IRA'. The presiding judge handed out a five-year prison sentence.[6] The largest discovery during this period was in Roscommon, where gardaí uncovered sixty AK-47s wrapped in plastic and boxes of ammunition hidden behind bales of hay. Two brothers who lived in the house were arrested.[7]

Several months after these seizures, the IRA shot dead a Derry city native and local IRA quartermaster, Frank Hegarty, for allegedly providing information which led to the garda operations. Hegarty's body was discovered just inside the North, on the border with Donegal close to Castlederg, with his hands bound behind his back and his eyes covered with tape. According to an IRA statement released after the killing, Hegarty had been a British informer for seven years and had been assured by his handlers that the Roscommon and Sligo arms would not be seized until they had broken into smaller dumps. This would help disperse suspicion as to the source of the leak. However, the attraction of large seizures proved too great for the British and Irish officials 'who were anxious to demonstrate the security value of the Anglo-Irish Agreement to Loyalists'.[8] Hegarty had fled to England in the aftermath of the seizures, but it is alleged that he returned to Ireland after receiving a personal guarantee from Martin McGuinness of his safety. This claim was strongly refuted by McGuinness and Sinn Féin.[9]

A 1985 British Home Office report on the IRA's use of explosives noted that, in the previous year, more than six tons (12,793lbs) of explosives had been intercepted or detonated across Northern Ireland. The report estimated that 98 per cent of this was HME derived from agricultural fertiliser.[10] As discussed in Chapter 3, the British were keenly aware of the importance of the IRA's fertiliser boiling activities in the South to the bombing campaigns in both Northern Ireland and England. In 1985, a series of meetings took place in London between officials from the Republic's Department of Justice and the British Northern Ireland Office. As noted in a contemporary British report:

The main purpose of the meeting was to take stock of progress being made in the UK and ROI [Republic of Ireland] on the joint programme of research into ways of preventing the use of agricultural fertilisers in the manufacture of HMEs. We also used the opportunity to raise various points of concern on the control of commercial explosives and related materials in the ROI.[11]

As in 1982, officials sought to alter the make-up of fertiliser to serve three aims:

(a) (ideally) capable of commercial production, using existing manufacturing processes in the fertiliser industry;
(b) agronomically acceptable; and
(c) of no, or limited, value as an explosive to the terrorist.

The British put enormous resources into research and development, through leading manufacturer Norsk Hydro, to meet these aims. Tests on the explosive capabilities of the new fertiliser were scheduled for late 1985.

Earlier that year, gardaí had recovered a large quantity of chemicals from a house in Tallaght, which had been stolen from the Euro-Chemicals plant in Lucan. The chemicals included sulphuric and nitric acid as well as ammonium nitrate and sodium hydrochloride, all of which could be used in the composition of HMEs. British and Irish officials believed the IRA were responsible for the theft, and 'it was agreed that the theft of the chemicals was a further demonstration of the increasing sophistication and scientific ability of the Provisional IRA.'[12] The total amount of arms, ammunition and explosives seized by gardaí in 1985 and 1986 is shown in Tables 11 and 12 overleaf.

Informers and Alleged 'Collaborators'

The number of arms seizures and the general garda disruption of IRA activity in the South during the 1980s alarmed Southern Command. Significant events, such as the interception of the *Marita Ann* and the ambush of an IRA unit at the home of Galen Weston, pointed to possible intelligence leaks within the organisation. There was considerable speculation in the media

Table 11. Garda seizures of arms, ammunition and explosives, 1985[13]

Quantity	Type
167	Firearms (including rifles, shotguns, machine guns, pistols, revolvers, etc.)
10,786	Rounds of ammunition (assorted)
655	Shotgun cartridges
70	Detonators
47	Magazines
16	Bombs of various types
5	Hand grenades
50lbs	Explosives

Table 12. Garda seizures of arms, ammunition and explosives, 1986[14]

Quantity	Type
353	Firearms (including rifles, shotguns, machine guns, pistols, revolvers, etc.)
33,939	Rounds of ammunition (assorted)
621	Shotgun cartridges
36	Detonators
35	Magazines
4	Bombs of various types
10	Rockets
9	Hand grenades
492lbs	Explosives

in the early months of 1985 about the extent of penetration of the IRA in the South by garda informants. Reference was made to the above garda successes, the discovery of a large arms dump at Lusk, County Dublin, in late 1984, as well as the capture of IRA volunteers believed to be linked to the Brighton bombing.[15] In March of that year, gardaí discovered another IRA training camp, this time in east County Mayo. The discovery was made, whether by chance or not, as a routine garda patrol checking on elderly people living rurally approached a farmhouse off the road between Swinford and Kilkelly. Three men were spotted running from the house as the garda patrol car approached. One of the men ran across fields and disappeared, while the two others drove away in a car parked nearby. The two men later entered the home of a woman near Charlestown and demanded her car. According to the woman, the men announced themselves as members of the IRA 'in a spot of trouble … One of them was well-spoken and seemed to be a concerned type of individual, but the other was a bit of a bully.' The men had 'west of Ireland' accents.[16] Despite roadblocks being set up in Counties Galway, Mayo, Sligo, Roscommon and Donegal, none of the men were apprehended. The owner of the farmhouse, a seventy-five-year-old man, was arrested under Section 30 of the Offences Against the State Act. In a search of the surrounding area, two rifles, ammunition, maps and training manuals were discovered. Several days later, during a follow-up search, eight rifles, eight timing devices, a box of ammunition, a letter-bomb device, a training chart and several Sinn Féin election posters were discovered hidden in a wall at the farmhouse.[17] As reported in the *Western People* newspaper:

> The range of equipment and arms found in the Kilkelly area in the past week or so indicates that rumour and speculation about I.R.A. training camps in the West, and more particularly, in Mayo, have had some foundation in fact. A training camp in the general Ballina area was mentioned in a case some time ago in the Special Criminal Court, while speculation about a sizable I.R.A. presence in the county was found in more recent times by the incident in the Belmullet area, in Claremorris, and now in Kilkelly.[18]

That same month, the IRA shot dead an alleged garda informer near Ballincollig, County Cork. The victim, John Corcoran, a forty-five-year-old father of eight, had been held captive for a number of days during which he was interrogated by his captors before being killed. The IRA contacted a priest attached to the Pro-Cathedral in Dublin with information on where Corcoran's body could be recovered, 'in a green sleeping bag beside old car tyres'.[19] In a statement released through the Sinn Féin headquarters in

Belfast, the IRA claimed that Corcoran had been a garda informer for more than seven years and also named the detective who was allegedly his handler. Among the information they claimed Corcoran provided to gardaí was that which led to the arrest of three IRA volunteers during the attempted armed robbery of the Togher post office in October 1981. The IRA also claimed that the victim was engaged in setting up a bogus robbery worth £25,000 with a named detective in order to ingratiate himself with the republican movement. The IRA subsequently used *An Phoblacht* to offer a fourteen-day amnesty to other informers to come forward.[20]

Four young men, including a solicitor, were arrested as part of the investigation into the killing of Corcoran, but none was charged.[21] Sean O'Callaghan, a former IRA volunteer and garda informer from Tralee, admitted killing Corcoran to British police in 1988 and repeated the claim in two newspaper interviews in the mid-1990s. O'Callaghan claimed to have killed him in order to ensure that suspicions about garda infiltration of the Munster IRA ended with Corcoran and did not continue onto himself. Later, O'Callaghan retracted this version of events, claiming he had no part in the killing and had in fact urged his own garda handler to intervene during the days when Corcoran was being held by the IRA for interrogation. In a series of articles in December 1996 and January 1997, journalist Vincent Browne exposed the contradictions evident in O'Callaghan's multiple versions of events.[22] Neither O'Callaghan nor any other member of the IRA was ever charged in relation to Corcoran's killing, leading some to consider whether the gardaí's need to protect O'Callaghan and thus sacrifice Corcoran qualified as state collusion.[23]

Sean O'Callaghan's role in the IRA – particularly the extent of his seniority, influence and knowledge – have long been a source of dispute. According to his own claims, he eventually rose to become O/C of the IRA's Southern Command. This would have made him privy to top IRA strategy and discussions. During the 1998 libel trial of senior republican Thomas 'Slab' Murphy, O'Callaghan claimed to have attended meetings of the IRA's Southern Command between 1983 and 1985 in the rural County Kildare home of Uinseann MacEoin. MacEoin was a journalist, architect and conservationist who penned several valuable histories and had been interned in the Curragh as a young republican during the Second World War. According to O'Callaghan, the attendees at these meetings included

Pat Doherty (Donegal), Gerard 'Dickie' O'Neill (Belfast/Dublin), Tommy Devereaux (Mayo), Martin Ferris (Kerry), Patrick Corry, Ciarán Dwyer (Dublin – this is as reported at the time, though Dwyer was actually from Limerick), Brendan Swords (Dublin), Kieran Conway (Dublin), Sean Finn and James Kavanagh (Wexford). O'Callaghan also claimed that veteran Kerry republican and former Irish Defence Forces officer Joe Keohane was present at other meetings.[24] His claims about the extent of his own role in the IRA have been rubbished by members of the republican movement at all levels, most notably by Danny Morrison, who was later imprisoned with him in the H-Blocks.

Interviewees for this research offer a more prosaic rationale for O'Callaghan's presence at or knowledge of top-level IRA meetings. According to one account: 'cars were at a premium at these meetings and so he'd be allowed stay and maybe picked up information on the drive back where people might be discussing things'.[25] If true, O'Callaghan's willingness to ferry senior republicans around would inevitably mean he picked up scattered bits of stories and gossip, enough to collate into a later narrative. According to another account, a veteran Kerry republican had long suspected O'Callaghan of being an informer and forbade him from attending Munster or Southern Command meetings, at one point physically chasing him from a meeting. Liam Cotter, a veteran Kerry IRA man, also long suspected O'Callaghan and had approached the Munster O/C with his concerns. According to this account, the IRA investigated O'Callaghan, found reasonable grounds for suspicion and informed the IRA Director of Intelligence seven times. However, as the debates around dropping the policy of abstaining from entering Leinster House were becoming more heated and the Munster O/C was a prominent abstentionist, he claims that his concerns were ignored by the IRA leadership.[26]

Several months after the killing of John Corcoran, sometime on 19 or 20 August, the IRA's Dublin Brigade shot and killed forty-six-year-old Tyrone businessman Seamus McEvoy at his bungalow home in Donnybrook. McEvoy had extensive building interests on both sides of the border, principally supplying Portakabins, many of which were used by the RUC. A week prior to the killing, the IRA had published a warning in *An Phoblacht* directed at building contractors who were 'collaborating' with the British Army and RUC:

Over the past few months our intelligence personnel have compiled accurate and extensive dossiers on all those involved in building or refurbish work for the security forces. As a result of this intelligence, we are now in the position to take effective action if builders do not henceforth desist from playing an active role in support of the Crown forces.

Following the discovery of McEvoy's body, the IRA took responsibility for the killing, claiming he was shot for supplying building materials for 'Crown forces'. The statement went on to claim that 'Mr McAvoy [sic] had been given many, many warnings – by telephone, by letter and by IRA attacks on his premises in Coalisland – about his collaboration with the occupation forces in the North.'[27] According to gardaí and Fr Denis Faul, a close family friend of the McEvoys, McEvoy was shot for refusing IRA extortion demands of between £15,000 and £30,000.[28] Gardaí were also reportedly looking into potential connections between the shooting of Seamus McEvoy and John Corcoran. However, as with the killing of Corcoran, nobody was ever charged with the killing of McEvoy.

A second Tyrone businessman was shot dead by the IRA the following year for supplying material and work to the RUC. John Kyle was killed in July 1986 as he stood at the bar of the Crossroads public house in Greencastle village, twelve miles from Omagh.[29] According to a report in the Provisionals' magazine Iris the following year, such attacks were beginning to have an impact. A number of contractors soon publicly declared that they were ceasing to work with British forces, with Texaco joining the list in July 1987.[30]

Portlaoise and Arrest Increases

On the occasions that gardaí succeeded in capturing and convicting IRA volunteers, they were mostly sent to Portlaoise prison to serve their terms. Unrest over the harsh conditions suffered by prisoners there, as well as of their visitors, remained an issue for republicans in the South throughout 1985. According to Iris, IRA prisoners in Portlaoise had previously accepted the governor's proposals to reform visiting and strip-searching conditions to end a long-running dispute. However, by June of that year the proposals were still not implemented.[31] The issue had been coming to a head for a while, with a spokesperson for the prisoners warning in 1984 that 'there will be a confrontation between Republican inmates of Portlaoise Jail and prison officers, unless the authorities scale down the level of strip-searching and reduce the use of solitary confinement'.[32] According to the republican prison leadership, during this period many prisoners routinely received two beatings during confrontations with prison staff. Prison officers would re-enter cells after a first humiliation and beating knowing that prisoners would react badly to this, allowing them to carry out further 'disciplining'. A committee of family members of Portlaoise prisoners documented the number of strip-searches taking place throughout the first half of the 1980s. Despite prisoner numbers decreasing slightly during that period, the number of strip-searches more than doubled:

Table 13. Alleged strip-searches in Portlaoise prison, 1979–84[33]

Time period	Number of alleged strip-searches conducted
September 1979–August 1980	325
September 1980–August 1981	502
September 1981–August 1982	496
September 1983–August 1984	663

By 1985, there were approximately 120 Provisional IRA members serving prison sentences in Portlaoise, thirteen of whom were serving life sentences. Treatment of this latter group and their families was considered particularly harsh. One of them, Michael Kinsella, had been jailed for the murder of Fine Gael senator Billy Fox in 1974. Kinsella had also taken part in the 1974 mass breakout from Portlaoise, after which he returned to active service before being recaptured three years later. By 1984, however, Kinsella was considered to be mentally broken, a state exacerbated by the treatment of his sixty-seven-year-old mother, who was regularly strip-searched when visiting him. Despite public calls from several prominent psychiatrists to have Kinsella transferred to a hospital, he remained in Portlaoise. A report by *Magill* into his conditions stated: 'the determining factor in Kinsella's case is not medical but political'.[34]

Although the governor of Portlaoise was alleged to have reneged on the deal in June 1985 to reform visiting and strip-searching conditions, two months later *An Phoblacht* could claim progress, stating: 'Last week saw the beginning of open visits in Portlaoise prison after nine years of a visiting system which afforded non-physical contact between prisoners and their relatives.'[35] Years of campaigning by the families of Portlaoise prisoners as well as other activists had finally succeeded in bringing conditions within the prison back to a humane level. Facilities and visiting rights reverted to a standard that republican prisoners had not experienced since the mid-1970s, but it was not to last.

In late 1985, perhaps in part due to the more relaxed new regime, a number of IRA prisoners attempted a breakout from the prison. Just before noon on 24 November, while many inmates and prison staff were attending Mass, a prisoner armed with a gun entered the prison's reception area and forced the attending prison officer to open a gate. Eleven other prisoners then made their way through the gate and several more of the seven prison gates using duplicate keys. Those involved were Martin Ferris, Peter Rogers, Eamonn Nolan, Jimmy Gavin, Sean McGettigan, Peter Lynch, Liam Townson, Tommy McMahon, Angelo Fusco, Robert Russell, James Clarke and John Crawley.[36] Ferris and Crawley had been imprisoned for their part in the *Marita Ann* arms importation attempt while Fusco, Russell and Clarke had all previously escaped from the H-Blocks and been subsequently jailed for various IRA activity south of the border. Lynch was imprisoned for his involvement in the shoot-out with gardaí at the home of Galen Weston. Rogers, Ryan, Townson, Gavin, McGettigan and McMahon were all serving life sentences for murder. Rogers was convicted of the murder of Garda Seamus Quaid. Nolan was serving a life sentence for the murder of bystander Eamon Ryan during a bank robbery in County Waterford in 1979. Townson was convicted of the murder of a British soldier in 1977, McMahon of the murder of Louis Mountbatten and three others in 1979, and McGettigan was jailed for the murder of Senator Billy Fox in 1974. Gavin was imprisoned in 1981 for the murder of alleged garda informant John Lawlor in a Dublin public house four years previously.

Following their escape from the main prison building, the group used explosives to blast the main gate of the prison. However, despite an explosion that was heard around the town, the gates held and the prisoners subsequently surrendered. As they were rounded up, McMahon remarked: 'It was a good try anyway.'[37] The material available to the failed escapees, as revealed during their trial the following May, surely caused prison officials and the government to fear that there were IRA sympathisers among the prison staff. Among the items the prisoners had acquired were two handguns, keys to fourteen prison doors, fake prison officer uniforms as well as explosives and a detonator. An exhaustive garda investigation ultimately could not find the 'mole' within the Portlaoise prison staff. Despite this, they remained convinced that such a person, or persons, existed. One senior security official described it as 'extremely disturbing; we know there is a well-placed IRA mole at the jail, but we have not been able to track him down'.[38] Each of the attempted escapees received two months' solitary confinement as well as three-year prison sentences to begin at the end of their current sentences. One immediate impact of the escape attempt was a reversal of the easing-up policy of the prison officials. Relatives of prisoners set up a picket shortly after this, when they were denied entry to visit those who had not been involved in the escape attempt. The following week, *An Phoblacht* reported on the reintroduction of 'a severe regime of beating and forcible strip-searching of republicans'.[39]

Garda harassment and rough treatment of republicans on the outside continued to be a chief complaint among civil liberties groups and some media. One interviewee recalled:

> Harassment was awful. Our house personally was raided – and I can only talk about my own, our own, what happened in our own house, but I know it happened up and down north Tipp … it went as far as my father and a couple of other people I knew were arrested at their workplace, so that pressure would have been put on their bosses to sack them. Now my father was the father of ten children. One can imagine if the bosses had given in, we would have been on the road, ok? That's the sort of harassment that went on. People were told not to hang around with us, not to have anything to do with us. Harassment was as deep as you can get and was as hard as you can get.[40]

Claims of intimidation were quite commonplace from elected representatives of Sinn Féin during this period. Given the party's increasing public involvement and activism, it may have been a strategy by the state to discourage the public from considering association with its members. In September 1985, Donegal Sinn Féin councillor Liam McElhinney described as 'outrageous' an attempt by members of the Irish security forces to intimidate his constituents. According to McElhinney, he arrived at the home of his election agent (the house served as an advice clinic) to find the building completely sealed off by a large force of armed soldiers. The homeowner had earlier refused to admit two local gardaí to the house when they failed to produce a search warrant. McElhinney claimed that he then challenged the local sergeant to provide an explanation for the harassment. The sergeant left the scene, stating that he would get a warrant. Following this, a helicopter arrived and proceeded to buzz the area for thirty minutes. During the sergeant's absence, 'cars and trucks were stopped and searched outside the house in an attempt to scare locals away from known Sinn Féin homes.'[41] McElhinney, a former member of the Irish Defence Forces and a native of County Tyrone, later served prison sentences for offences committed on two separate occasions: for arms possession in 1986 and incitement to join the IRA at a republican Easter commemoration in 1988. He had three previous convictions, two for IRA membership and one for hijacking a bus in Lifford in 1981.[42]

The following year, *Magill* continued their investigative reporting of harassment and ill-treatment of republican suspects, with some disturbing revelations. They learned of at least one doctor in Clones, County Monaghan, who was warned by gardaí not to get involved with suspects or examine them in custody: 'Dr McGoldrick gave evidence that he was in a toilet of a pub when a Special Branch man came up to him and said that in future, when he examined IRA suspects, he should see no injuries.' One man, originally from Belfast, who was interrogated by gardaí in Clones, later received £25,000 in an out-of-court settlement where gardaí admitted no liability. According to his account, he had sustained a number of rough beatings. In addition: 'they forced me into a metal filing cabinet. They locked the doors. They started banging it and shaking it. It fell to the floor. I was inside.'[43] The previous December, *An Phoblacht* reported on a teenager who was arrested in Monaghan and questioned for hours by gardaí about republicans in the Emyvale area. The young man was told that he would be charged with the theft of a car in the locality if he did not provide satisfactory information, despite having an alibi for the time the car was stolen. The newspaper claimed that the young man was also assaulted and that he still bore the marks of the beating while being interviewed by their reporter.[44] In County Kerry, a man was arrested under the Offences Against the State Act and held for two days before subsequently being admitted to hospital for a week due to the rough treatment he received.[45]

As had happened with the anti-drugs movement, other community and pressure groups also came under increasing garda attention during this period. In 1990, the Irish Council of Civil Liberties reported that one of the most frequent complaints for garda harassment in previous years came from people engaged in campaigns for the release of the wrongfully imprisoned Birmingham Six.[46] And it was not only people who were facing increased scrutiny at this time, but also possible sources of funding for the IRA.

The Mystery of the Meath Business Fund

In February 1985, the Fine Gael–Labour coalition government introduced a hurried amendment to the Offences Against the State Act. The amendment allowed for the seizure of money held in an Irish bank if it was believed to 'be the property of an unlawful organisation'; the only evidence necessary for the government to make this decision was 'the opinion of the Minister for Justice'.[47] In such cases, the money would be lodged with the High Court in Dublin, to remain frozen unless the owner of the money brought proceedings to demonstrate that the money should be legally returned to them, or until six months had elapsed without such an appeal – in which case the money would be forfeited. Speaking to the media following the passing of the legislation, Opposition leader Charlie Haughey stated: 'with regard to the urgency of this Bill, the Opposition are prepared to take the legislation on trust from the Government, and accordingly are prepared to facilitate the passage of the Bill without delay'.[48] The amendment was far-ranging and quite unique. Indeed, in the aftermath of its passage, the British government sought to discover whether equivalent laws targeting terrorist finances existed in any other European Commission (EC) states, as well as Canada and the USA. None of their embassies could report that this was the case.[49]

The amendment was brought in to target a particular deposit of £1.75 million recently made to a Navan bank account by businessman Alan Clancy.

Clancy, an Irish citizen, was a long-time resident of New York, where he owned several public houses. He had returned to live in Ireland, settling in Ardee, County Louth. During his business career in the USA, Clancy had a reputation for making large transactions in cash. He claimed to have used a power of attorney to deposit the money in the Bank of Ireland the previous June under the name of David McCartney. The government maintained that the money was part of an elaborate money-laundering scheme set up by the IRA and that it represented a payment made during the kidnapping of Don Tidey. Clancy vehemently rejected this and claimed that the money was to be used to establish a pork-exporting business for the US market, where he had a number of connections. The chairman of Associated British Foods similarly rejected claims about ransom money. But it was reported in the British media, albeit quoting unidentified US government sources, that Clancy was facing a federal grand jury investigation into allegations that he was involved in laundering the money.[50]

As part of the new law, Clancy had six months to appeal the seizure of his money and challenge the government's actions in court. However, as *Magill* keenly noted of the amendment:

> there is one crucial difference between this recent amending legislation and the amending legislation of 1972 which allowed for a garda of the rank of Superintendent to claim that a person was a member of an illegal organisation, and allowed that opinion to become evidence. The Minister for Justice will be allowed to give evidence by certificate and therefore not be liable to cross-examination. Following that legislation, gardaí gave evidence under cross examination of not knowing anything about particular individuals other than they 'were in the IRA.' On this basis, with the accused positively affirming that they were not members of the IRA, the courts tended towards the accused. Eventually, the legislation fell into disuse. The fact that the Minister may not be liable to cross examination as to his 'means of knowledge' regarding the money in the Navan bank account may leave questions unanswered as to what chain of events led to the sequestration of the money.[51]

Controversy over the seized deposit continued, with the vice president of the New York branch of Bank of Ireland categorically denying that he was the target of a federal grand jury investigation or was in any way linked to funding the IRA. Suspicion also fell on insurers Lloyds of London as being the source of the large sum, as a form of 'protection money' against future kidnappings by the IRA on behalf of a number of their clients.[52] Later that year, under pressure from Britain, the Swiss Federal Supreme Court ordered one of its major banks to disclose details about an account believed to contain £2 million in IRA 'protection money', again linked to the 1983 kidnapping of Don Tidey.[53]

However, an investigation by *Magill* provided quite a bit of evidence to support Clancy's claims. The investigation revealed that the sum of money was the 'end product of a long and complicated business deal involving Clancy and David McCartney, a Scotsman who is currently living in Alaska. Clancy had loaned McCartney money, and the money held at Navan belonged to both of them, part of it being the repayment of the loan.' Additionally, Clancy had been in lengthy discussions with the Industrial Development Authority about the intended pork-exporting business. The magazine also questioned why the IRA would transfer such a large sum of money *into* the country, when, if they wanted to use it for the purchase of arms, ammunition or explosives, it would have to be moved out again, and why they would move such a large sum of money in a single amount into a small provincial bank, where it was bound to attract attention.[54]

Despite the passage of the Act being supported across the house, the government was worried that its constitutionality would be challenged.[55] However, Clancy ultimately failed in his bid to have the cash returned to him, and the government never had to provide evidence to support their suspicions as to the source of the money. In 2008, it was formally handed over to the state, having been kept in a holding account since 1985. By that time, Alan Clancy was deceased, there were no outstanding claims by his estate, or the estate of David McCartney, and the sum was then worth €5.9m.[56]

A side note to this saga relates to the expulsion of leading Belfast republican Ivor Bell from the IRA in 1985, for allegedly attempting to organise a coup against what he perceived to be the emasculation of the IRA and the diversion of resources and finances from that organisation into Sinn Féin. He and those around him blamed the apparent reduction in IRA activity in Belfast on Sinn Féin's reluctance to authorise attacks that had the potential to cause political embarrassment in the run-up to elections.

In addition, there were serious concerns over the clear moves towards recognising Leinster House.[57] As part of the fallout from this near split in the republican movement, some within the organisation accused the leadership of informing authorities about the Clancy money in order to further still slow down IRA activity.[58] While these rumours cannot be verified, it seems clear that Bell was seeking to organise enough support within the republican leadership to engineer a takeover. One interviewee claimed that he had been holding up shipments of Libyan weaponry until he had enough support to move, while there are also indications that he had been setting up a parallel financial structure in advance.[59] Several months prior to Bell's expulsion, he and a woman were arrested at the County Louth flat of Bernadette Sands, sister of Bobby Sands. During a search of the flat, gardaí discovered sums of US and British cash: $10,000 and £5,000. Bell's co-arrested claimed in court that the money was from Green Cross (a republican prisoner support organisation) collections and they were delivering it to the organisation's headquarters in Belfast. The district court in Dundalk ordered that the cash be handed over to the Minister for Finance.[60] The provenance of the money seized in Dundalk remains unknown, nor is it known what it was intended for. Given Bell's position at the time on the political–military paradigm within the Provisionals, it's unlikely that it was for Sinn Féin, however. The party had experienced considerable growth across the island since the 1981 hunger strike, but all the campaigning, electoral registration and maintenance had a sizeable financial cost, and yet more elections were on the horizon.

Political Events and Developments

In June 1985, voters in the Republic of Ireland went to the polls to vote in local elections. Despite high expectations, and Gerry Adams declaring himself 'extremely pleased', the result for Sinn Féin did not match party hopes.[61] In total, they had thirty-nine representatives elected: eleven on county councils, twenty on urban district councils and eight town commissioners. Their vote share represented approximately 4 per cent of the total national vote. At the party Ard-Fheis in November, a motion was put forward to end the policy of abstentionism from the Dáil. Earlier in the year, *An Phoblacht* had vigorously denied claims by 'Sunday Times hack Chris Ryder' of a split in the republican movement over this issue of electoral intervention. The report by

Ryder had named several potential dissidents, specifically Dáithí Ó Conaill, Billy McKee, Seamus Twomey, Jimmy Drumm, Joe Cahill and Brendan McFarlane.[62] During the Ard-Fheis debates on the motion, Danny Morrison – a prominent member of the Belfast leadership and formerly Director of Publicity – pointed out that the party would remain isolated in the South unless the policy was abandoned. He later compared the abstentionism policy in the South to making a rod for your own back.[63] Tom Hartley, another member of that leadership, likened abstentionism to handcuffing oneself. Despite these appeals, the motion was defeated by 187 votes to 161, a fairly close-run vote. The defeat was received by prolonged cheering from sections of the attendees. After the vote, Adams and other leading figures left the platform for some time, while pro-abolition delegates from Dublin were reportedly infuriated by the defeat, blaming it on the party's 'old guard'.

One surprise result from the Ard-Fheis was the passing of a motion in favour of recognising a woman's right to choose on the issue of abortion. The motion was passed late on the final day of the Ard-Fheis, when many delegates had left the chamber (it passed by 77 votes to 73) and, as reported, 'was met with whelps of delight, particularly from the women who had spoken in favour of [it]'. While Gerry Adams and Danny Morrison voted against the motion, it is not known if Martin McGuinness did. McGuinness had expressed his support for abortion in certain circumstances in an interview with *Hot Press* the previous month. Minister for Justice Michael Noonan condemned Sinn Féin's new position, stating that 'their support for abortion is a clear indication of the type of society which they seek to impose'.[64] The position was dropped the following year after an intervention by party leadership and was rejected as a motion at the 1987 Ard-Fheis.[65]

A fortnight after Sinn Féin's 1985 Ard-Fheis, the British and Irish governments represented by Taoiseach Garret FitzGerald and Prime Minister Margaret Thatcher signed the Anglo-Irish Agreement. The agreement provided for the Irish Republic to have a limited advisory role in the governance of Northern Ireland in certain minor areas, while affirming the principle of unity by consent. It was criticised by both republicans and loyalists. From the time of the signing of the agreement, the Irish government began taking a less hesitant approach to the thorny issue of extradition. Between 1982 and 1985, there had been a small number of approvals for extradition requests, and much internal debate in government parties for each approval. Following the signing of the Anglo-Irish Agreement, however, extradition requests seem to have been approved more quickly, with internal opposition being far more muted.

In March 1986, a suspected IRA member from Belfast, Eibhlin Glenholmes, was arrested in Dublin. Glenholmes had been on the run for over a year after being named by the British *Sunday Times* as a person of interest in a number of bombings in London in 1981. At the time of the publication of the news article, an arrest and extradition warrant had already been issued for her. That *Sunday Times* article claimed that Glenholmes was living openly in Dundalk, with the gardaí seemingly unconcerned about her status as a person of interest in Britain; nor were they concerned about the extant warrants out for her. In an interview in *Morning Ireland*, it was put to one of the journalists involved in the story that Scotland Yard had leaked the story to the press about garda inaction regarding Glenholmes. In the words of the presenter, David Hanly: 'the British police find that they are getting nowhere in the wake of the Brighton bombing and that this is a ploy to distract attention from their own incompetence and to imply that it is the Irish Gardaí who are being bloody minded and holding them up in their enquiries'.[66] This assertion was strongly rejected by the journalist. Following her arrest in Dublin in March 1986, it emerged that the warrants previously issued for Glenholmes contained several basic errors, including the failure to state the location of an alleged offence for which she was sought.

Glenholmes was released from custody after this disclosure but was rearrested in Dublin on another warrant issued by the British. She was again released, by District Judge Peter Connellan, who ruled that this new warrant was also defective. In total, nine defective warrants were issued by British police in pursuit of Glenholmes. In the aftermath of one of her court appearances, where yet another extradition warrant was thrown out, Glenholmes and her legal counsel attempted to leave the packed courtroom but were physically prevented from doing so by a number of uniformed and plain-clothes gardaí, despite them having no legal right to hold her. A series of extraordinary scenes followed. Glenholmes' solicitor first brought her into the judge's chambers and members of the Special Branch attempted to follow. She was eventually hurried out of a back entrance of the Four Courts in Dublin via a series of corridors, pursued by journalists and gardaí. According to a contemporary news report:

[Glenholmes] was then escorted into a waiting red Toyota car and there were further disturbing scenes as two unmarked Garda cars accelerated into groups of Sinn Fein supporters, who attempted to unsuccessfully block their path. A high-speed chase continued up the quays. During it, gardaí attempted to requisition private vehicles to block the red Toyota and Sinn Fein members moved cars out of the way.[67]

As the chase was going on, gardaí were awaiting another extradition warrant from British police. Glenholmes and a number of supporters – now on foot on Henry Street, having abandoned the vehicle – were corralled by members of the Garda Special Branch as they sought to walk to the nearby Sinn Féin offices. Glenholmes then entered a shop and, as the crowd grew larger on the street, a garda detective fired several shots from a handgun over the heads of Sinn Féin supporters, journalists and shoppers. Glenholmes was rearrested in the shop on foot of the freshly issued warrant, while the shots in the street dispersed some of the crowd. Following yet another release from an Irish court due to a defective extradition warrant, Glenholmes disappeared from public view. An investigation into the unregulated use of the detective's firearm was deemed a 'whitewash' by Fianna Fáil, and it later emerged that this detective was promoted while the investigation was underway.[68]

Another high-profile extradition case that year concerned Owen Carron, who had been elected to the parliamentary seat of Fermanagh–South Tyrone in 1981 following the death of incumbent Bobby Sands. A Fermanagh native, Carron, along with a passenger acquaintance, was arrested near Enniskillen in December 1985 when an AK-47 assault rifle was found in the car he was driving. Carron was granted bail and subsequently fled across the border, settling in County Leitrim. He lived there for two years until he was arrested by gardaí in neighbouring Sligo on foot of a British extradition request. That request followed on from the Irish government's recent ratification of the European Convention on the Suppression of Terrorism, which had been a commitment made during the Anglo-Irish Agreement negotiations. As part of that ratification, a 1987 amendment was made to the 1965 Extradition Act, which included a section exempting certain activities such as bombing and the use of automatic weapons from being labelled as 'political' crimes.[69] Speaking in the Dáil chamber during the debate on the amendment, TD Neil Blaney asserted that the law was 'wrong a month ago, is wrong today and will be wrong next month'. Blaney claimed that the passing of the amendment had a rushed feeling due to three recent events: the Enniskillen bombing, the high-profile kidnapping of a dentist and the capture of the *Eksund* (all covered in Chapter 6). He pointed to the last time the chamber had passed a similar law in haste:

> We fell into the same trap a considerable number of years ago. Some Deputies will recall the [1972] Dublin bombings when many people were killed. That night a vote in this House was altered radically because of that event. We know what happened, that the result of the vote in this House was different because of the bombing. The repeated mentioning of these three happenings in recent times can be dangerously misleading because while in themselves they are horrific acts they are not a basis on which we can justify allowing to become law, legislation which is intrinsically bad, dangerous and unfair to Irish citizens.[70]

Carron appealed his arrest and extradition, arguing that his was a political offence, but this appeal was rejected by the High Court. The unanimous decision of the three judges was that, as Carron had also claimed to have been unaware that his passenger had a gun, 'it was not open to him to assert that, had he been aware of that fact, he would have committed a "political" offence'. In addition, Carron claimed that he would not face a fair trial in Northern Ireland if extradited, citing harassment by British forces in previous years. This too was rejected by the judges, as accounts he gave of ill-treatment in 1981 differed from an affidavit he had signed during that period.[71] Carron then appealed the decision of the High Court and, in April 1987, after two-and-a-half years' detention, he was freed on foot of a Supreme Court decision that his offence had indeed been a 'political' one. The court's decision also ultimately led to the release of two other republicans who were among the 1983 H-Block escapees: James Pius Clarke and Dermot Finucane, brother of assassinated Belfast solicitor Pat Finucane.[72] The release of Clarke, who had been imprisoned in the North for the killing of a UDR man in 1977, would later be credited as contributing to the political downfall of Charlie Haughey. During the appointment process of Dr James McDaid as Minister for Defence in 1991, it emerged that he had once provided an alibi for Clarke. A press photo from the day of Clarke's release also showed a smiling McDaid among the crowd of supporters outside the courthouse in Dublin.[73] The failure of Haughey to have his preferred candidate appointed as minister emboldened his rivals within the Fianna Fáil party and arguably signalled the beginning of the end of his tenure as party leader.

'Troubles'-related cross-border activities led to two particularly heated incidents in County Monaghan in 1986. In late April, IRA volunteer Seamus McElwaine was killed while on active service in neighbouring Fermanagh. McElwaine was the son of a former Sinn Féin county councillor for Monaghan and had risen to the position of O/C of the Fermanagh IRA at the age of nineteen. While serving a life sentence for the murder of a British soldier and a police reservist, he was one of the nineteen IRA prisoners who escaped from the H-Blocks in 1983. McElwaine had declined the offer of an escape route to the USA and returned to active service shortly thereafter. On the night he was killed, he and another IRA volunteer, Sean Lynch, were preparing an ambush on a British Army patrol when they were in turn ambushed by the SAS. McElwaine was wounded in the attack and subsequently shot dead following an interrogation. Lynch was arrested, having also been wounded.

Two days prior to McElwaine's funeral, four IRA volunteers fired a volley of shots over his coffin outside his parents' farmhouse near Scotstown. No gardaí were present at the time. Due to McElwaine's standing in the IRA, the government was anticipating tense scenes at the funeral. Monaghan IRA leader Jim Lynagh had recently been released from prison and was one of those expected to attend. As well as many locals, senior republicans from the North including Gerry Adams, Joe Cahill, Martin McGuinness and Danny Morrison were also to attend. As a result, 150 gardaí – many of them in riot gear – were drafted in to police the event, where an estimated 3,000 mourners had gathered. This policy of a heavy garda presence at republican funerals was implemented in earnest the previous year, at the funeral of Raymond McLaughlin. McLaughlin had served a lengthy prison sentence in England for explosives offences and died in a swimming accident in County Clare shortly after being released from prison. The extent of the garda presence at his funeral led An Phoblacht to remark that the security forces of the South had begun to mimic RUC tactics: the RUC had recently enacted a policy of zero tolerance towards republican trappings at IRA funerals and used large numbers of police in riot gear to enforce that policy.[74]

As the coffin of Seamus McElwaine left his family home, another volley of shots was fired by three masked and uniformed men, who then disappeared into the crowd. Black flags and tricolours at half-mast flew along the four-mile route to the graveyard. Mourners formed a human chain on each side of the cortège to prevent gardaí reaching the coffin and its IRA guard of honour as it entered the church grounds. However, no further incidents took place. The gardaí acted with restraint and Adams urged the crowd to 'leave the guards be. You're at a funeral now. Take it easy.'[75] The IRA guard of honour changed into civilian clothing in one of the church aisles during the funeral Mass and blended in with the crowd of mourners as they emerged from the church.[76]

The other notable incident occurred in August 1986, when up to 500 loyalists – including future DUP leader Peter Robinson – rampaged through the border town of Clontibret in a bizarre 'invasion' to protest the Anglo-Irish Agreement. Two gardaí were injured when attempting to make arrests and restore order. Robinson was subsequently charged in a Dundalk court with unlawful assembly. Despite 500 gardaí being present in the town during the trial, a full-scale riot erupted, with the windows of fifteen cars belonging to supporters of Robinson being smashed and a number of petrol bombs thrown at him and Ian Paisley.[77] Robinson appeared in the Special Criminal Court in November 1986 to face the unlawful assembly charge and ultimately received a fine of £17,500. Prior to this later court appearance, he appealed to his supporters not to travel to Dublin for the trial. Interestingly, Robinson's own journey south for his trial coincided with the annual Sinn Féin Ard-Fheis, for which a large Northern contingent of republicans made their way to Dublin in anticipation of a major clash over the much-debated abstentionism policy.

Prelude to the 1986 Ard-Fheis

At a Sinn Féin Coiste Seasta (standing committee) meeting shortly after the 1981 election, Dáithí Ó Conaill acknowledged the difficulty in explaining abstentionism to the broader population. The Provisional republican movement had long struggled with this issue. The principal flaw was not that the people of Ireland, particularly in the South, did not understand the abstentionist policy. Rather, whenever they did give it any thought, in terms of national representation and legislation, they simply viewed Sinn Féin as toothless. On occasion, as during the hunger strikes or the IRA's border campaign of 1956–62, republicans were elected to the Dáil in small numbers, but these were fleeting protest votes. Perspectives of Sinn Féin and their abstentionist policy among the broader population were summed up by Christy Burke in reference to the 1982 budget vote:

> I remember one woman saying to me, 'Christy, you're a nice fellow and you're hard working, and I know all your family but if you get elected to the Dáil and there's a vote on VAT on children's shoes – what good would you be to me if you weren't in there?' I pointed out to her that I could be vocal outside the chamber but she wasn't buying it. She said, 'That's fine Christy but you wouldn't be there for the vote.'[78]

Sinn Féin's irrelevance to the Irish people on crucial matters of national legislation was guaranteed by their abstentionist policy. Although the leadership had previously been composed of a broadly even divide among proponents of abstentionism and those who wished to abandon it, many of the former, men such as Ruairí Ó Brádaigh and Dáithí Ó Conaill, had resigned leadership positions in Sinn Féin in recent years. This followed on from piecemeal changes to other long-standing Sinn Féin policies strongly associated with these men; the federalism of Éire Nua and the running of candidates in European elections, for example. In moving against Dáil abstentionism, the clique centred around Gerry Adams and Martin McGuinness attempted a two-pronged approach.

At some point in late September or early October 1986, the IRA held its first General Army Convention since the spring of 1970. The convention allegedly took place in Navan under the cover of an Irish-language conference, an allegation strongly denied by Sinn Féin, the Meath-based Seán MacStiofáin, who took part in that *Slógadh* conference, and the *Slógadh* conference organisers themselves.[79] Wherever it took place, upwards of seventy IRA delegates attended the convention and it passed off without attracting any garda attention. At the convention, IRA delegates voted by more than the required two-thirds majority to remove the ban on IRA volunteers discussing or advocating the ending of abstentionism with regard to Leinster House. An IRA spokesperson later affirmed to reporters that 'there will not be a split in the movement'.[80] The delegates also upheld General Standing Order No. 8, which prohibited military action against the administration and security forces of the South, as well as making the IRA's constitution non-sexist. A compromise on the abstentionist policy was reached during the election of a new Army Council, where several prominent people holding dual army–political membership stood aside. It was, according to one account, 'the trade-off which avoided a walk-out by the tough, faceless men'.[81] According to another account, by this stage however, every O/C in every county was a Belfast man (in terms of where their support lay): 'So they were controlling the Army and then they went for Sinn Féin. The only group that they didn't control was the Executive of the Irish Republican Army'.[82]

Despite the convention favouring abandonment of abstentionism in the South, internal IRA opposition continued. The Cork Brigade, the second largest under the Southern Command, had opposed the motion at the army convention, as had units in Kerry and Limerick, and individual volunteers across the country.[83] Overall IRA support for the dropping of abstentionism was clinched due to several factors. The purging of potential dissidents eliminated one difficulty. According to The Phoenix magazine: 'the cities and townlands of the North are filled with Provos who have been purged since 1975 … Among them are top "operators" some of whom only got the chop as late as last year'.[84] According to that publication, this purge was enabled by Dáithí Ó Conaill 'sulking in self-imposed exile, while his opponents consolidated their position'.[85] Ó Conaill was certainly held in esteem by many IRA volunteers – far more so than Ó Brádaigh – and may have been influential in arguing for a continuation of the abstentionist policy, though this seems doubtful. At best, it would have been a rearguard action. Following the convention, Magill was confident that the IRA would not split, conceding only that 'some older members of Sinn Féin would drop out' if the party also abandoned the policy at the Ard-Fheis. However, the publication also warned that 'if the abstentionist policy goes, which the IRA leadership would claim was designed for a short war, it will bring in its wake unavoidable tensions within the movement'.[86]

Ultimately, the arguments of the IRA leadership in 1986 rested on two pillars: pragmatism and tradition. Pragmatism in that the IRA claimed the move was a means to an end and that there would be no moderation of the armed struggle. As Pat Doherty pointed out, the Provisionals would be 'the first attending republican group who [are] avowedly and unequivocally supporters of armed struggle'.[87] Tradition in that, despite rhetoric from Ó Brádaigh and others about the legitimacy of the Second Dáil, the IRA predated any Dáil. Their mandate rested less on the outcome of the 1918 or 1921 UK general elections, which returned a majority of Sinn Féin candidates in Irish constituencies, and more on the IRA's constitution, which asserted that the moral right to engage in warfare rested on three principles. The first two principles were 'the right to resist foreign aggression' and 'the right to revolt against tyranny and oppression'.[88] The third was that the IRA was a direct successor to the Provisional Government of 1916 and the First and Second Dáils of 1919 and 1921 respectively. As the formation of the Irish Volunteers (later to become the IRA) and the 1916 insurrection occurred before either the 1918 or 1921 election, however, the position was that mandates for engaging in armed conflict were applied – not sought – retrospectively.[89] Further, such a mandate, the leadership argued, could be achieved at some stage in the future. This circled the argument back to pragmatism: taking seats in Leinster House was a tactic to help achieve victory, and the mandate could be achieved after that victory.

As far as militant republicans were concerned, the IRA's existence rested principally on the assertion of Irish sovereignty and thus to militarily challenge the British occupation of Ireland which breached that sovereignty. Much of the debate surrounding abstentionism during the 1980s focused on whether recognition of the Dáil removed one of the three moral rights for engaging in armed conflict, and thus the legitimacy of the IRA to exist. For some, abstentionism was therefore a fundamental principle, as Ó Brádaigh was to argue at the 1986 Ard-Fheis. For others it was an outdated tactic, one whose removal would not undermine the other two principles the IRA maintained for their campaign. Ultimately, the latter argument won out at the General Army Convention and, within the wider republican movement, it was dedication to the IRA that held the republican movement together up to and largely after 1986.

In response to the IRA's not-altogether surprising announcement of October 1986, several statements of condemnation appeared in the media from individual republicans and other republican organisations. Cumann na mBan, the female paramilitary wing of the republican movement, equated the abandonment of abstentionism to support for 'special courts, internment camps and all the other trappings of collaboration and repression'.[90] At a leadership level, the relationship between Cumann na mBan and the IRA had long been strained. The decision to allow women to join the IRA as full-time volunteers in the early 1970s was resented by Cumann na mBan, who felt that they were losing some of their best recruits to the larger organisation.[91] Tom Maguire, veteran IRA leader and last surviving member of the Second Dáil, also came out in condemnation. Several days later, a letter appeared in *The Irish Press* signed by a number of well-known republicans – including Gearóid MacCárthaigh, Seán Keenan and Paddy Mulcahy – opposing the move.[92] MacCárthaigh's personal experience of the years leading up to 1986 were of imposed isolation from the republican movement. He had been appointed training officer for Cork during the late 1970s at the request of the brigade O/C, but when that man was replaced, MacCárthaigh's offer of services for either Sinn Féin or the IRA were met with silence. For several years, his only news of the conflict came through the newspapers, although for a brief period he was kept updated on developments by on-the-run volunteer Mick Burke. In 1985, MacCárthaigh was invited to present the Munster award at an annual event recognising those from the four provinces and the USA who had dedicated their lives to the republican movement. Following this ceremony, MacCárthaigh was again isolated. One night, two young Cork IRA volunteers invited him out for a drink, to his great delight. He went along, only to discover that they were essentially sounding him out on his position on abstentionism. 'They obviously didn't know my record,' he said of it.[93]

Those opposed to the dropping of abstentionism were not the only ones writing letters at this time. Pat Magee, a respected IRA volunteer imprisoned in England, wrote to *An Phoblacht* calling for the policy to be dropped.[94] Brian Keenan, one of the most influential IRA leaders, later reflected:

The split in 1986 was inevitable, necessary as far as building Sinn Féin was concerned in the 26 Counties. To make headway with the political project it was necessary to recognise the institutions of the 26-County state. I wrote a letter to the Sinn Féin Ard Fheis that year because I was angry that some people were using IRA martyrs as a reason for not trying to open up a new front in developing Sinn Féin. No living person can say how Pearse, Connolly or Bobby Sands would have reacted to different events.[95]

Following the IRA's announcement, it remained to be seen if Sinn Féin would follow suit.

The 1986 Sinn Féin Ard-Fheis

By the time of the Ard-Fheis in early November, anticipation regarding the abstentionism policy changes had peaked. Backroom discussions took place throughout the weekend of the Ard-Fheis. Des Long, a senior republican from Limerick, later recalled:

> At the Ard Fheis they said that they wanted to see myself, Ruairi O'Bradaigh and Joe O'Neill, and we could bring one other, but we couldn't bring O'Conaill, that was the stipulation. So Joe brought Pat Ward and … it was very acrimonious. Now O'Bradaigh would never use language, but in the end anyway Pat Ward said, and it wasn't me I have a walking stick now, but I didn't have it then. Pat Ward hit the table with the walking stick and he said, 'if I was in my health I would wear this stick off you.' 'Ah no Pat, we know you, you're alright, you're a hundred percent.' So going out of the meeting Slab Murphy said to Ruairi 'now Ruairi don't be starting anything' … So there was no showing of bullets but Slab Murphy and him [Micky McKevitt] were there to be heavies and we just showed that we weren't afraid of them.[96]

As well as accounts of unspoken threats, there were also allegations of dirty tricks played on delegates. Seán Keenan, who almost single-handedly built up the Provisionals in Derry city following the death of Thomas McCool in June 1970, and who lost a son to a British Army bullet, was barred entry to the Ard-Fheis. So too was Tony Ruane, Sinn Féin Treasurer for decades and Honorary Vice President for life.[97] Gearóid MacCárthaigh, who attended the Ard-Fheis as a visitor, spoke of how people were turned away at the doors on the grounds that their delegate cards had already been received, i.e. that people inside were impersonating them.[98] Leinster House, where the Ard-Fheis took place, was packed. An estimated 1,200 people, a mix of delegates and observers, attended as the debate over taking seats in the Dáil veered back and forth.

As discussed earlier, electoral participation in the South was nothing new to the Provisionals. Sinn Féin had had elected representatives participating in local politics in the South for decades. Among them were Joe O'Neill of Donegal and Frank Glynn of Galway, who both attended the 1986 Ard-Fheis. Ó Conaill and Ó Brádaigh had long advocated for local representative participation, as those bodies did not claim sovereignty over the territories they administered, unlike the Dáil. However, many republicans could not see a major difference between taking seats in county councils and taking them in Leinster House.[99] Ó Brádaigh, who supported running candidates in general elections so long as they boycotted the parliament, seemed to misunderstand or ignore the mundane factors which ensured limited support for such a position. For example, he claimed that censorship rather than abstentionism was primarily responsible for Sinn Féin's previous electoral limits in general elections.[100] However, Sinn Féin had experienced electoral growth at a local level and Ó Brádaigh did not draw the connection between the party's support at a local level and their policy of participating in local politics. He thus refused to contrast this with the party's unwillingness to participate in Leinster House politics and their dire performance in general elections (1981 excepted).

Proponents of abstentionism maintained many of the arguments that had been used in 1969–70 regarding the legitimacy of the IRA and armed struggle. Principally, they argued that recognition of Leinster House would undermine the IRA's moral right to engage in armed conflict and that the dilution of long-held principles would ultimately lead to recognition of Stormont and the legitimacy of the Northern state. This was the path followed by those who formed the other side of the debate in 1969–70, a grouping that went through several incarnations during this period, from Official Sinn Féin and the Official IRA to the Workers' Party and Group B. This latter debate did, however, differ from that previous schism in a fundamental way. During the 1986 Ard-Fheis, the leadership advocated the ending of abstentionism for the Southern parliament only; that of a state which the IRA was prohibited from using force against and whose courts they recognised. At the IRA convention the previous month, the leadership had banked on its membership in Northern Command viewing Southern abstentionism as largely irrelevant, so long as the military campaign continued. Frances Mackey, a Tyrone republican who left the Provisionals in 1997 due to their involvement in the peace process, is a case in point. He stated: 'at a personal level I disagreed with going into Leinster House, but it wasn't a significant enough issue to create a major split in the republican movement'.[101] However, as one prisoner argued logically:

> What I felt was a contradiction as well, how do you recognise one partition parliament and refuse to recognise the other? You are giving a notion of credibility to a section of the Irish people in a partitionist section of Ireland, and you are not giving that equal credibility to people living in the rest of the island of Ireland, that is the North, the Six Counties.[102]

Ó Brádaigh himself argued that the movement could not ride two horses in opposite directions, the constitutional and the revolutionary. Speaking at the Ard-Fheis as a normal delegate, he quoted from mainstream newspapers, the editorials of which anticipated 'enmeshing [the Provisionals] in the constitutional system'. Ó Brádaigh then addressed the delegates beseechingly:

> in God's name, don't let it come about that tomorrow, the next day or the day after, that Haughey, FitzGerald, Spring, and those in London and Belfast who oppose it so much, can come out and say, 'Ah, it took 65 years, but we have them at last', and those in Leinster House who have done everything, the firing squad, the prison cells, the internment camps, the hunger strike, the lot, and weren't able to break this movement, that they can come and say at last we have them towing the line. It took us 65 years, but they come in from the cold, they come in from the wilderness and we have them now.[103]

Ó Brádaigh also addressed the question of whether abstentionism represented a principle or a tactic, arguing: 'the sovereignty and unity of the republic are inalienable and non-renounceable. In other words, they can't be given away and are not a matter for reconsideration. They are absolute. We were told last night that we can agree to disagree on fundamentals, how in the name of heavens can we do that?'[104] Ó Brádaigh's position rested on his support for abstentionism until such time as the number of elected abstaining republicans reached a parliamentary majority in a given jurisdiction. This would then allow them to enter and subvert the existing political structures. However, Ó Brádaigh's detractors were able to simplify or distort this argument, claiming this position rested on arithmetic rather than principle.

Across the organisation, there was a lack of consensus on dropping abstentionism, sometimes even within the same area. Joe Cunningham from Sligo and John Joe McGirl from Leitrim used a similar argument in opposing ways. The former argued that dropping abstentionism would indefinitely lengthen the struggle while the latter stated that not to do so would be to 'hand down [this] struggle to another generation'.[105] Limerick city delegates had been instructed by their cumainn to oppose any motion calling for an end to Southern abstentionism.[106] Des Long had received short shrift from the leadership two months prior to the Ard-Fheis, highlighting Martin McGuinness' disingenuous statement that nobody had been 'squeezed out' of the movement. Long was elected head of the Comhairle Limistéar (regional committee) for North Munster in September 1986. A noted abstentionist and member of the old guard, the Ard Comhairle deemed him 'unacceptable' and refused to acknowledge the results of the election. In protest, the local organisation dissolved itself and, when Dublin representatives arrived down and reconvened the association, they again voted Long in unanimously.[107] In a surprise move at the Ard-Fheis, one South Armagh delegate supported the resolution to drop abstentionism, stating that the local unit, which represented the people, were firmly behind the move.[108] However, another delegate from that area condemned the move, calling it a betrayal of the 'Irish Republic'.[109]

It was McGuinness who was chosen to deliver the key speech in favour of abandoning Southern abstentionism. He struck a tone that was part criticism of the past leadership, part warning of irrelevancy and part offering of reconciliation. He told delegates:

> ... issues have been raised by some of the defenders of abstentionism that need to be confronted and challenged. They argue that some TDs entering Leinster House will make it impossible to conduct armed struggle against British rule in the 6 counties. They tell you that it is

inevitable certainty that the war against British rule will be run down. These suggestions deliberately infer that the present leadership of Sinn Fein and the leadership of the Irish Republican Army are intent on edging the republican movement on to a constitutional path. To bolster their arguments, they draw a comparison between a pre-1970s leadership of the republican movement which had surrendered before the war began, and the present leadership of this movement.

Shame. Shame. Shame …

This Ard Fheis and you, the delegates, deserve to know the whole story of this debate. In fact, what you're witnessing here is not a debate over one issue, but two – abstentionism and the leadership of the republican struggle. The two issues should not be confused and those who are considering leaving along with members of the former leadership should consider carefully what I am about to say. The reality is that the former leadership of this movement has never been able to come to terms with this leadership's criticism of the disgraceful attitude adopted by them during the disastrous 18 months ceasefire in the mid-1970s. Instead of accepting the validity of our case, as others who have remained have done, they chose to withhold their wholehearted support from the leadership which replaced them …

If you allow yourself to be led out of this hall today, the only place you're going is home. You will be walking away from the struggle. Don't go, my friends. We will lead you to the republic.[110]

As the motion's votes were counted, it was clear that the abstentionist policy was soundly defeated. Delegates voted by 429 to 161 in favour of dropping the policy in the Republic of Ireland. Following the vote, Ó Conaill, Ó Brádaigh and a number of other delegates and attendees walked out of the Ard-Fheis. They reconvened at a pre-booked hotel convention hall, where they declared the establishment of Republican Sinn Féin, reaffirming the policies of Éire Nua and abstentionism. In a separate meeting held later that evening, the decision was taken to establish an armed wing called the Continuity IRA, with Dáithí Ó Conaill serving as Chief of Staff.[111] Among those who left the Sinn Féin Ard-Fheis were a number of prominent republicans from the Republic, including Frank Glynn, Joe O'Neill and Paddy Mulcahy. Seamus McElwaine's father also ultimately joined Republican Sinn Féin. Many of those who walked out on 2 November were not delegates to the Ard-Fheis, but rather observers. This included Ó Conaill and Gearóid MacCárthaigh. There is no clear consensus on the numbers that left that day. The lowest estimates on the walkout are Peter Taylor's 'around twenty' and Joe Cahill's 'fewer than thirty people'.[112] Cahill, of course, was not an objective bystander in the 1986 Ard-Fheis debates and so his figure must be read with a degree of caution. Other contemporary reports put the number at approximately forty, while subsequent books have used terms such as 'a small number' or 'a small group'.[113] Larger projections of the number of people that left range from 'fewer than 100' and 'about 100' to 'about 130'.[114] However, these numbers seem to be based on a reporting of the first meeting of Republican Sinn Féin, held an hour or so after the walkout. As Pat Walsh noted, 'after the decision was announced, about 40 delegates, including O Bradaigh [sic], left the hall, followed by about 70 or so supporters from the public gallery'; adding that perhaps 100 of these attended the subsequent foundation of Republican Sinn Féin.[115] It is likely that works which put a high figure on delegates who walked out are based on an erroneous reading of contemporary newspaper reports, many of which cite the figure of '130' attending that later meeting.[116] However, even this is open to dispute: it was Republican Sinn Féin themselves who furnished the figure of 130 to the media following the establishment of the party.[117]

Amidst all the claims, what is clear is that the number of delegates who walked out was much less than the 161 who had voted to retain abstentionism. Many of those, such as the majority of the Limerick delegates, did not walk out following their defeat in the motion. As one delegate stated:

Eighty-six was a lot more complex than people put it down to, I actually was against dropping abstentionism, you know … I wouldn't take that stance now, but that's the stance I took then. But we always had the position, the cumann here in the town, there was a number of cumann at the time, but we always had the position at the time, a lot of us, myself, the two delegates in my cumann had the position of … one was supporting the drop, one was against it. We were both mandated to oppose it. But we were also both committed to staying with the party. We weren't going to split.[118]

It has been alleged that 'paper' cumainn played a part in ensuring the abstentionism resolution was passed. Ed Moloney stated that the numbers at the 1986 Ard-Fheis were almost double those at the previous year's convention and reverted to normal levels again in 1987.[119] Moloney also quotes an unnamed former Sinn Féin official as saying that:

> They went about it in two ways. Over a two-year period beforehand released IRA prisoners loyal to Adams were ordered to join Sinn Féin cumainn and take them over ... The other way was that they just invented Sinn Féin cumainn. All you needed was five names, and you got two delegates to the Ard Fheis. They were set up all over the country and in Belfast.[120]

In fact, there were 'over 400' delegates at the 1985 Ard-Fheis, with 628 delegates attending the following year.[121] Arguably, the increase in delegates at ardfheiseanna as the 1980s progressed parallels the political growth of Sinn Féin, as well as the very public approach the party took to increasing political representation. As Danny Morrison noted, there was a surge in the number of cumainn following the hunger strikes. In many areas, Anti H-Block committees simply 'turned overnight into cumainn'.[122] At the 1984 Ard-Fheis, for example, Ard Comhairle member Sean Crowe proudly noted that the number of cumainn in Dublin had increased from twenty-five to thirty-five over the past twelve months. Crowe attributed this in large part due to the party's high-profile participation in the Dublin Central by-election and European Parliament election. Both these elections also capitalised on the participation of Sinn Féin members in local campaigns, such as the anti-drugs and Moore Street traders' campaigns.[123]

Following the 1986 Ard-Fheis, Dáithí Ó Conaill received a letter from a H-Block prisoner who was unhappy with the direction the movement had taken. The letter stated that even those prisoners who did not support the Adams leadership remained unconvinced 'that yourself and Rory [Ó Brádaigh] (whom they don't know of course) would be any better'.[124] It is striking that Ó Brádaigh, who was a virtual unknown to many if not most of the young IRA prisoners in the North in 1986, delivered the most prominent speech at the Ard-Fheis opposing the motion to abandon Southern abstentionism. The letter also suggested that support for any leadership was conditional rather than unquestioning, as one interviewee pointed out of the contemporary leadership.[125]

Since the number of delegates who left the venue to establish Republican Sinn Féin was significantly less than those who voted against the abstentionist motion, one must assume the policy was not a deal-breaker for the majority of those opposed. In the years leading up to 1986, there were regular media portrayals of tensions within the republican leadership on several axes: old–young, left–right, conservative–revolutionary, North–South. These views were often encouraged by the new Northern leadership, who took the ascendancy following the 1975 ceasefire. Danny Morrison's portrayal of the leadership struggle as being one of young, northern leftists versus old, conservative nationalists was particularly influential in having the mainstream media repeat the mantra during the 1980s.[126] However, few of the dichotomies that were encouraged by that leadership to reflect the internal struggles of the republican movement survive serious scrutiny. That a prisoner group in the H-Blocks called the 'League of Communist Republicans' considered linking up with Republican Sinn Féin following the 1986 Ard-Fheis highlights how implausible this simplistic portrayal of the leadership clash along ideological lines was.[127] Moreover, Pat Ward, one of the founders of Republican Sinn Féin and a past member of the Communist Party, was considered 'hard left'.[128] Any left–right distinctions were as simplistic as they had been sixteen years previously. Old versus young can hardly be measured publicly, at least for the IRA, given its status as a proscribed organisation. With regard to Sinn Féin, however, the 'young guns' of 1986 were not above using prominent and elderly individuals to sway dissent at the Ard-Fheis; men like John Joe McGirl and Joe Cahill.

The North–South assertion has some minor validity, though primarily post-hoc and judged by events subsequent to the split. Both contemporary reports and accounts from former IRA members attest to the purging of traditionalists that occurred in the North prior to 1986. It is likely that the relative safety of the Southern state allowed for more formalised opposition to the new leadership and direction to form post-1986, where in the North there might have been a genuine fear of violent reprisal from former comrades. One study quotes a Continuity IRA spokesperson who stated that 65 per cent of their volunteers were from the South and had joined the Provisionals during the 1970s. This, at least, gives some partial insight into the young–old axis. It is claimed that four of the seven members on the Provisionals' initial Army Council later fulfilled the same function for the Continuity IRA. The seven men on the former were Seán MacStiofáin (Meath), Ruairí Ó Brádaigh (Roscommon), Joe Cahill (Belfast), Dáithí Ó Conaill (Cork/Donegal), Seán Treacy (Laois), Paddy Mulcahy (Limerick) and Leo Martin (Belfast). Joe Cahill remained with the Provisionals with five of the remaining six men being Southerners.[129] Returning to the North–South assertion, then, this composition indicates a strong Southern representation for the Continuity IRA. Similarly, the organising committee of Republican Sinn Féin was strongly Southern-focused.[130] However, this simply indicates that at a leadership level, the clash could be perceived as North vs South and does not reflect the reality that the majority of grassroots republicans across the island supported the new leadership which, by 1986, happened to have a majority Northern representation.

The split in the republican movement in late 1986 was predominantly over the issue of leadership and strategic direction. While abstentionism was ostensibly the deciding factor, as with 1969–70 it was primarily used as an engine for schism, but the leadership battle had been won long before the crucial Ard-Fheis took place.

Aftermath of the Split

Politically, Republican Sinn Féin was stronger in the Republic than in Northern Ireland.[131] This is reflected in the composition of its leadership. Its first executive had just two Northerners out of twenty-one members.[132] In the immediate aftermath of the 1986 Ard-Fheis, arrangements for cumainn to affiliate with Republican Sinn Féin were reportedly made in Counties Kerry, Limerick, Tipperary, Roscommon, Galway, Donegal, Fermanagh, Longford, Cavan, Monaghan, Down and Leitrim.[133] There doesn't seem to have been a significantly political split in County Kerry initially, despite the new direction being met with strong opposition there prior to 1986. However, at a meeting several weeks after the Ard-Fheis, up to fifty people from the county transferred their allegiances from Provisional to Republican Sinn Féin.[134] Martin Ferris, who was in Portlaoise prison at the time, was one of those affected by the split, losing several 'very good friends'.[135] In Leitrim it was reported that the entire Sinn Féin structure in the north of the county, as well as the Drumsna cumann, declared for Ó Brádaigh and Republican Sinn Féin. Two months after the split, there were two separate commemorations in Limerick city for Sean South. The Provisionals' event was attended by approximately 300 'mainly young people' and led by Martin McGuinness, while the Republican Sinn Féin event was attended by about 150 people.[136]

A financial report for Republican Sinn Féin several years after the split demonstrated the glaring absence of income from the north of Ireland (both the Northern state and the northern counties of the Republic of Ireland):

Table 14. Republican Sinn Féin income, May 1990[137]

Region	Amount (Irish punts)
USA	£460
England	£202
Ulster (Monaghan)	£100
Leinster (Kildare)	£50
Munster (Cork, Tipperary, Kerry)	£300, £100, £100
Connacht	£100

The level of Republican Sinn Féin activity in the South relative to the North might thus seem to justify the assertion that geography had been a source of division within the movement prior to 1986. However, the plausibility of this rests on turning a blind eye to the Northern purges and the threats allegedly issued to those 'dissidents' who might have contemplated initiating their own military campaign.[138] As Joe O'Neill recounted: 'The next thing anyway, myself and O'Bradaigh was [sic] called to a meeting in Sligo and we were threatened by McGuinness and Pat Doherty and they had two henchmen outside the door, and told that we would be shot if another army was set up.'[139] O'Neill was not the only person to allege that threats were made. One of the committee members of the commemorative National Graves Association, which was largely opposed to dropping abstentionism, said that in the aftermath of the 1986 army convention, two IRA volunteers, one male and one female, made threats that the organisation was to toe the mainstream republican policy line.[140] Reports of the existence of the Continuity IRA (or 'Continuity

Army Council') only emerged around the time of the 1994 ceasefire despite that organisation existing since 1986.[141]

Republican Sinn Féin continued to express support for the IRA's campaign, if not for the politics of the Provisional republican movement. At the establishment of the party in the West County Hotel, it was reported that Dáithí Ó Conaill 'emphasised, to applause from the audience, that they supported the members of the IRA in their actions'.[142] Pat Ward, the principal speaker at their Bodenstown commemoration in 1987, praised the eight IRA volunteers killed by the SAS at Loughgall the previous month. Through their newspaper *Saoirse*, the organisation also expressed their sympathies to the families of the deceased, and the funerals of all those killed at Loughgall were attended by Republican Sinn Féin members.[143] One of those funerals, that of Pádraig McKearney, was the scene of some friction between the Provisionals and Republican Sinn Féin, when Gearóid MacCárthaigh, a member of the latter, was asked to deliver the oration.[144] The McKearney family had strong roots in Roscommon and were close to the Ó Brádaighs.[145] Pádraig's brother, Tommy, was imprisoned in the H-Blocks during this period and his name featured in the December 1989 issue of *Saoirse*, with Christmas greetings being extended to him.[146] Claims that the IRA volunteers at Loughgall were considering breaking away from the Provisional republican movement months after the 1986 IRA army convention cannot be verified and are likely exaggerated views of genuine discontent.[147] As Danny Morrison remarked, they were 'part of the mainstream republican movement and knew exactly what was going on'.[148]

It is not possible to ascertain just how many prisoners aligned with Republican Sinn Féin during the late 1980s, although the lack of specific Christmas well-wishes in issues of *Saoirse* might indicate that there were not many.[149] According to Tommy McKearney:

> I'd say there probably was – see, numbers fluctuated – I'd say there was thirty or forty. But there might have been, at one time there might have been up to seventy or eighty had resigned. But then a lot of them drifted back. There's an enormous pressure when you're within a prison, you know … But, as I say, probably thirty or forty people that might have, at the end of the day, left or resigned. There was more than that thirty.[150]

In Portlaoise, few if any prisoners seem to have left the Provisionals following the Ard-Fheis. However, one must be wary of accepting that all prisoners approved of the Provisional leadership during this period. According to MacCárthaigh, following the 1986 Ard-Fheis, Republican Sinn Féin requested that two of their members be represented on the committee of the prisoner support organisation, An Cumann Cabhrach. This request was denied and prisoners who aligned with Republican Sinn Féin were allegedly threatened with having their aid cut off. Danny Morrison strongly denies this claim.[151] The Prisoner Dependants' Fund, the Northern prisoner support organisation, continued to provide aid to republican prisoners regardless of alignment.[152]

The Libyan Shipments

The perceived commitment of the contemporary leadership of the republican movement towards armed struggle was a key factor in their successful removal of the abstentionism policy. This was the fundamental difference between 1986 and the 1969–70 period, when the Provisionals were established. Then, there was widespread discontent and distrust regarding the leadership's aims, intentions and attitudes towards militancy. Forming part of the debates during 1986 was the leadership's reminder that they had been prosecuting an armed campaign for more than fifteen years, the longest sustained campaign against the British in Irish republican history, and had no intention of stopping. Major arms importations, even unsuccessful ones such as the *Marita Ann*, served to remind potential waverers of that commitment. In addition to recent failed attempts, over the course of 1985–86 four arms shipments of ever-increasing size had successfully arrived into Ireland from Libya. Organised by the quartermaster department, the operation was kept so secret that even the IRA's Director of Intelligence was not aware of it at the time.[153] The shipments were landed from the main transport ships by inflatable boats off Clogga Strand near Arklow, County Wicklow. The coast of Wicklow had previously been used as a landing point for IRA weaponry during the early 1970s.[154] Four importations included over 1,000 AK-47s (and variants), RPG-7 rocket launchers, DShK heavy machine guns capable of shooting down helicopters, flamethrowers, pistols and sub-machine guns, as well as several tons of Semtex plastic explosive. Such was the extent of the loads that a large articulated truck was used to bring sections of it to various 'master dumps' around the country. The IRA in south Leitrim brought one such consignment to their local area.[155] Another was brought to west Limerick, where it was distributed among several specially built dumps.[156] One final importation, equivalent in quantity to the four previous consignments combined, was scheduled for the autumn of 1987. Although all of these importations were highly secretive, to those who knew it was an assurance of the leadership's intentions to continue prosecuting – and even scale up – the armed campaign. For others, the stated commitment to the armed struggle made by the IRA leadership following the General Army Convention in the autumn of 1986 was sufficient. A string of attacks on UDR patrols and RUC stations in the border counties in the preceding two years were also firm evidence of that commitment, part of a strategy that would reach a climax the following year.

6

The IRA Could Start a Civil War with That Lot: 1987

The leadership of the Provisional republican movement moved quickly and ruthlessly wherever it perceived rising dissent during the period from the ending of the 1975 ceasefire to the 1986 abandonment of Southern abstentionism. The speed with which they moved in this regard, as with Ivor Bell in 1985, can be contrasted with how gradually the actual politicisation process developed. What is remarkable is how little the movement spilt during this period of intense internal upheaval, and how no clashes similar to the Official–Provisional feuds of 1971, 1975 and 1977 erupted. This was a testament, perhaps, to the Machiavellian skill of the leadership of the period.

It was with no small degree of concern that the Southern establishment had been eyeing the Provisionals' continued political growth and manoeuvring throughout the decade. More than ever, Sinn Féin activists were subject to arrests under Section 30 of the Offences Against the State Act along with their IRA counterparts. While overlap certainly existed between the two organisations, garda attention was due more to Sinn Féin's political activities, such as its involvement in the anti-drugs movement, than to any real concern that its members were involved in militant subversive activity.

In May 1987, the rural strategy of some Northern IRA units to establish 'liberated zones' on the Tyrone–Monaghan border collided dramatically with a British policy of shoot-to-kill in these more active republican areas. An entire unit of the IRA's East Tyrone Brigade was wiped out in a joint RUC–SAS ambush at the small Armagh village of Loughgall.[1] Among those killed was prominent Monaghan republican and former Sinn Féin councillor Jim Lynagh. Tensions ran high at his removal and funeral as gardaí maintained their zero-tolerance policy towards paramilitary displays. Elsewhere, garda measures against republicans continued to be punitive, as when late in the year a Sinn Féin activist was jailed for possession of a poster which was openly on sale at the party's office in Cork city.

Public tolerance for this type of abuse of the judicial system can perhaps be understood in the context of attacks like the Enniskillen bombing of November 1987, where the IRA detonated a 40lb bomb at a Remembrance Day ceremony killing eleven people and wounding scores more. Condemnation was swift and widespread. Just a few days later, the last and largest of the Libyan arms importations was intercepted off the French coast. Elation among British and Irish authorities was quickly replaced by horror at the realisation that multiple shipments had already successfully gotten through. For the IRA, the interception of this shipment removed the element of surprise critical to a planned offensive, though they remained determined to make optimal use of their new weaponry in subsequent years.

Political Events

The opening months of 1987 were dominated by political events in the South, when, in January, the Labour Party withdrew from a coalition with Fine Gael in a budget dispute, leading to the collapse of the government and the calling of a general election. As their first opportunity to participate in an election in the South since removing the abstentionism policy, Sinn Féin ran twenty-seven candidates in twenty-four constituencies. As the votes were counted on 17 February, it quickly became clear that the party had failed to win any seats, with only three of their candidates retaining their deposits. While expressing disappointment at the result, party leaders pointed to the censorship of Section 31, as well as panic among voters at a potential Fine Gael–Progressive Democrats coalition unexpectedly boosting Fianna Fáil's vote, as the principal factors contributing to their poor showing. The party did see an overall increase in votes over the November 1982 election, however. In Dublin and Leinster, their support increased by 2.2 and 1.6 per cent respectively. One of Sinn Féin's best results in the election came from Dublin Central, where Christy Burke received over 2,500 first preferences votes or 5.3 per cent of the total.[2] Across the state as a whole, the party's vote increase was 1.9 per cent.

According to a detailed study of the election conducted later that year, 'Northern Ireland was not considered an important issue by many.'[3] Indeed, Charlie Haughey, who returned as Taoiseach of a minority Fianna Fáil government, fought the campaign largely on economic issues. The election saw the replacement of Labour by the relatively newly formed Progressive Democrats as the state's third-largest party. The Progressive Democrats had formed in 1985 out of a factional dispute within Fianna Fáil and were considered economically to be to the political right of that party, as well as being anti-republican. However, as with all political parties in the Republic, fiscal or other factors that determined one's voting allegiances in no way precluded support for militant republicanism. As former IRA volunteer Matt Treacy wrote of his time on the run in the late 1980s:

> The sort of people who gave us shelter explains the resilience of the IRA over 30 years and more. Few of them were even Sinn Féin voters, and among them were members of Fianna Fáil, Labour, the Workers Party, the Communist Party and a couple who voted for the Progressive Democrats in the June 1989 general election ... because the candidate had done them a favour.[4]

Republicans continued to decry state treatment of Sinn Féin political activists during this year. An article in *An Phoblacht* late in 1987 entitled 'State attacks on Sinn Fein representatives continue' noted the case of party member Don O'Leary, a father of two from Cork. O'Leary had been one of the party's candidates in the February election, running in the Cork North Central constituency. He was sentenced to five years' imprisonment on an IRA membership charge by the Special Criminal Court for possession of posters which had been on sale in the party's offices in the city since 1985.[5] In contrast to this sentencing, in 1979 two members of Sinn Féin in Dublin were given three-month prison sentences for possession of 'incriminating posters'.[6] While O'Leary denied being a member of the IRA, the presiding judge deferred to the testimony of Garda Chief Superintendent Laurence McKeown. McKeown told the court that it was his belief, based on confidential information relayed to him, that O'Leary was involved in subversive activity. The Court of Criminal Appeal subsequently reduced O'Leary's sentence to four years.[7] O'Leary's sentencing spurred a political campaign in the South for his release, which would lead to several more arrests and imprisonments of republican activists over the following years.

Loughgall

In May 1987, the IRA suffered their greatest loss of personnel 'since the Tan War', when an entire ASU of the East Tyrone Brigade was ambushed and killed in a joint RUC–SAS operation on the outskirts of the small Armagh village of Loughgall.[8] The unit was composed of a number of highly experienced volunteers, including Jim Lynagh. As discussed, Lynagh was well known to gardaí and the RUC at the time of his death and had operated at different times with the IRA's Monaghan and East Tyrone Brigades.[9] He served a five-year jail sentence in Long Kesh in 1973, having been arrested when a bomb exploded prematurely in a car in which he was travelling. In 1979, he was elected to Monaghan District Urban Council and, the following year, was charged with IRA membership and held in Portlaoise prison. He was acquitted after being charged under the Criminal Law (Jurisdiction) Act but was rearrested again several months later and charged with the murder of a British soldier before again being acquitted. Lynagh served a three-year prison sentence in Portlaoise, after being caught with bullets in County Monaghan in 1982, and was released in April 1986.

Given the frequent clashes between gardaí and republicans from Tyrone and Monaghan in and around Monaghan town over the years, it is perhaps no surprise that many gardaí welcomed news of the Loughgall ambush. A British memo reported that Garda Chief Superintendent Pat Doocey and Superintendent Jim McHugh referred to it as 'a good day's work' in private conversation with a British liaison.[10] At Loughgall, the intended IRA target had been the village's RUC station. This was part of a strategy being pursued by republicans in the area of destroying isolated strongholds in order to create a 'liberated zone' akin to areas of South Armagh. It is unknown, outside of tight security circles, how the British acquired the intelligence that enabled them to be lying in wait to ambush the IRA unit that evening. There were strong suspicions of a high-level informer in the east Tyrone area, or at IRA GHQ.[11] An alternative explanation is that the East Tyrone Brigade's strategy of the preceding years enabled the British to shortlist the next potential targets and that they combined this with increased surveillance

on known IRA members in the region, allowing them to identify Loughgall
RUC station as the target.

   Although the ambushed volunteers were armed with relatively modern
assault rifles (including FN FALs and Heckler & Koch G3s), no Libyan
AK-47s were discovered at the scene of the ambush. This was due to the
organisation deliberately keeping back these weapons until all the arms
shipments had arrived. However, given the effectiveness of the East Tyrone
Brigade at this time, there was disquiet among some volunteers at the
perceived lack of material support they had received from GHQ in preceding
years. According to one account, Lynagh had to travel to Munster to source
ammunition shortly before Loughgall as the quartermaster department had
seemingly been holding back supplies from the brigade. Handguns were also
at a premium as, several years earlier, 'Munster was stripped of shorts ... Some
bollocks about the QM [quartermaster].'[12] A loss on the scale of Loughgall
for the IRA led to considerable blame and anger within the organisation,
and there was widespread rioting across the North as news of the ambush
emerged. In Dublin, up to 300 protesters were prevented from reaching the
British Embassy on 11 May by gardaí in riot gear at a barrier on the Merrion
Road. The protesters included two colour parties with musicians and were
led by eight women carrying black crosses. After discussion between them
and gardaí, two of the women were allowed through to hand in a letter of
protest to the embassy. One of those was Margaret McKearney, sister of
Pádraig McKearney, who was killed at Loughgall.[13]

   The funerals of the eight IRA volunteers took place across Counties
Tyrone, Armagh and Monaghan over the following days and drew crowds
ranging from 500 to several thousand. The funeral of Seamus McElwaine
the previous year indicated the approach the state would take to any
subsequent IRA funeral, and hundreds of additional gardaí were drafted
into Monaghan town and Clones in advance of the funeral of Jim Lynagh.[14]
There were serious clashes between republicans and gardaí several days
earlier, as his body passed through the village of Emyvale in a tricolour-
draped coffin. According to the account of Minister for Justice Gerry
Collins to the Dáil:

   When this procession reached the end of the village the cortege stopped
   and immediately the crowd, estimated to be in the region of 700,

tightened in close around it and linked arms. At this, three men in battle dress and black 'balaclavas' and carrying what appeared to be high-powered rifles, quickly emerged from a nearby laneway. They lined up at the side of the coffin, fired some single shots followed by a burst of shots before retreating through the crowd, which broke into cheers, facilitated the retreat of the gunmen and obstructed the Gardaí, who were close to hand, from pursuing them.

Two Garda detectives, who were manning a car patrolling a side road, observed the fleeing gunmen who were being followed by uniformed Gardaí. The detectives' car was observed by the crowd to be blocking the road and preventing the gunmen's escape. The crowd surrounded the car, in which one of the detectives was sitting, and proceeded to heave it over a two feet high wall, to drop it about four feet lower than the road, into a stream about five feet wide and a foot deep … The detective who remained outside the car, called on the crowd to stop their attack on the car with his colleague inside. As the crowd ignored his call and in view of the imminent danger to his colleague, he then fired six or seven bursts of automatic fire from his submachine gun over the heads of the crowd.

The detective who was in the car which landed on its roof in the stream, succeeded in extricating himself by breaking out through the rear car window. As he emerged from the car he, with two other uniformed Garda who had been pushed into the stream, were showered with stones by the violently aggressive crowd. The detective who had fired the earlier shots, at this stage drew his handgun and fired one further shot over the heads of the crowd in an effort to make them disperse and to save his colleagues and himself from possible serious injury. The crowd then withdrew, the armed men having by this time made good their escape.[15]

Lynagh's funeral took place in Monaghan town several days later, on 13 May. There were a few minor scuffles between gardaí and some of the several thousand-strong mourners as the coffin left Lynagh's flat. At that point, nine masked and uniformed IRA volunteers, seven men and two women, stepped out from the flat and saluted the coffin. No weapons were produced, and the cortège then proceeded to St Macartan's Cathedral in the town. Gardaí were present outside the service, though by prior agreement, as with the funeral of McElwaine the previous year, the tricolour was removed from the coffin before entering the church. Referring to the death of Lynagh's brother, Michael, in custody several years earlier, Sinn Féin county councillor for Monaghan Pat Treanor stated at the funeral: 'He [Jim Lynagh] was continually targeted by the Gardaí for surveillance and harassment, continuous arrests and beating down through the years. When these tactics failed to intimidate Jim they turned their attention to the rest of the Lynagh family. Their vindictiveness led to the death of Jim's brother, Michael.'[16]

The lack of any reference to the manner of Jim Lynagh's death by the officiating priest caused considerable anger. At the graveside oration, Gerry Adams said one might think Lynagh had died of pneumonia rather than being shot dead. Adams attended the funeral with Joe Cahill and Martin McGuinness while, separately, Ruairí Ó Brádaigh also attended.[17] As noted in the previous chapter, the garda policy of zero tolerance towards republican paramilitary displays mirrored that introduced by the RUC. Traditionally, at the funerals of IRA volunteers, the coffin was draped in a tricolour, with black gloves and a beret placed atop the flag. For those killed on active service, a volley of shots was fired over the coffin, either at the funeral or some other opportune time. On such occasions, during several recent funerals of Northern IRA volunteers, there had been multiple injuries among the mourners as the opposing policies of republicans and the police led to clashes.[18] Owing to this, the Provisionals conducted an internal policy review in early 1988. They published the results of this in *An Phoblacht*, which reported: 'RUC attacks on republican funerals have resulted in scores of people being injured and have caused distress to families and friends. The IRA on Monday night, January 18th, issued a lengthy statement saying that, in future, no shots will be fired during funeral processions.'[19]

Jim Lynagh's funeral took place prior to this policy change, and gardaí did not quickly forget the assault on their members at Emyvale. More than a year after the funeral, five men from County Monaghan were tried in the Special Criminal Court on charges ranging from riotous assembly to assault and obstructing a garda, as well as causing damage to a garda car. Found guilty, three of the men received sentences of between five and six years' imprisonment in a case republicans referred to as 'bitter revenge for [garda] humiliation'.[20]

IRA Attacks in the South and around the Border

Whether an informer was the source of British intelligence for the Loughgall ambush has never been exposed, but the issue of informers remained an ongoing one for the IRA. In 1987, three men suspected of such activity were shot dead. Two of the victims were from Northern Ireland: Thomas Wilson (35), a member of the Workers' Party, and Charles McIlmurray (30), an IRA volunteer from Belfast. The body of the third man, Dubliner Eamonn Maguire (33), was found near the South Armagh village of Cullaville at the end of August. An IRA statement in *An Phoblacht* claimed:

> The IRA executed an informer in South Armagh stating that it has a responsibility to 'protect our membership from infiltration and from death and imprisonment'. Eamonn Maguire, from Finglas, Dublin was recruited by the Special Branch in Dublin in 1979 after he was found in possession of IRA documents. Since then he had regular meetings with a Special Branch officer in Dublin for which he received small amounts of cash on a regular basis. The IRA announced an amnesty to all informers in the 26 Counties, provided they come forward within two weeks.[21]

Maguire had been charged with IRA membership in 1979, with a garda superintendent providing testimony against him. However, in the absence of any supporting evidence, he was acquitted. At the time of his death, he was separated, with two children and a third on the way. Information provided by him allegedly led to the arrest and imprisonment of at least two IRA volunteers. It is claimed that Martin 'Doco' Doherty from Finglas, who had joined the IRA in the wake of the hunger strikes, was set up by Maguire in 1982. Doherty and another man, Gerard McGrath of Ballymun, were sentenced to seven years' imprisonment for firearms possession linked to an attempted armed raid on a security van delivering wage packets at Phibsborough.[22] Doherty was shot dead by loyalists in Dublin city centre in 1994 as he sought to prevent them from planting a bomb at a republican social function.

According to the IRA's former Director of Intelligence, Maguire was certainly acting as a garda informant and had been 'sniffed out' by the IRA's intelligence officer in Belfast after a long period of suspicion.[23] Maguire's family vigorously disputed the IRA's claims, alleging that his killing was the result of a 'personal vendetta' and that the IRA had 'acted on the bases of suspicion, rumour and innuendo befitting an organisation which ... operates like the Mafia'. In addition, the gardaí claimed that Maguire was a 'totally insignificant figure within the Republican movement'.[24] The media pointed to the lack of detail in the IRA's statement, unusual for a statement justifying the killing of an informer, noting that it 'refers to a number of incidents eight years ago and a robbery at the Ranks Flour Mills in Dublin, which have been closed for some time. It also claims that Maguire informed on a relative and other Republicans in Dublin, but none of these assertions are supported by precise details'.[25] Nearly 1,000 people attended Maguire's funeral, and the attendant publicity was acutely embarrassing for the IRA, which had a strong presence in the north Dublin area. As the killing of Maguire had evidently taken place outside of garda jurisdiction, the gardaí stated that the investigation would be handled by the RUC. They did intend, however, to interview a Dublin woman and a recently released IRA member. Ultimately, no charges were ever brought forward over the killing of Eamonn Maguire.

Informers were not the only targets that year for the IRA. On the afternoon of 2 June, they shot and killed a member of the RUC from County Donegal in what gardaí described as a 'well-planned attack'. Constable Samuel McClean (40), a twenty-year veteran of the force, was working on a small farm he had recently purchased near to the home of his parents, just off the Ballybofey to Letterkenny road. According to reports, a blue van drove into the farmyard and two men got out wearing balaclavas, shooting him at point-blank range with a handgun and shotgun as he sought to defend himself with a shovel. According to gardaí, McClean had been warned by them on several occasions that his life was in danger as he was known to travel regularly to visit his parents on his days off. Amidst heavy security provided by gardaí and the Irish Defence Forces, the RUC Chief Constable John Hermon and approximately 100 of his officers attended McClean's funeral in Stranorlar.[26]

The following month, there were tense discussions between the British and Irish governments on border security following a one-shot IRA sniper attack on an eight-man British Army foot patrol, which left a soldier dead. The victim was shot as his patrol walked along the main street of the Country Fermanagh village of Belleek, and the weapon used was believed to be a .303 Lee Enfield rifle with a telescopic sight. The RUC claimed that the fatal shot came from a scrub-covered hillside overlooking the village on the Donegal side of the border. The following day, the Northern Ireland Secretary of State Tom King told BBC radio that the border was 'a great resource' to the IRA as a means of escape after attacks, as well as a hub for transiting weapons to the North.[27] The following year, Belleek native and self-employed haulage contractor Michael Joseph Herron (19) was acquitted of the killing in Dublin, having been tried under the Criminal Law (Jurisdiction) Act. The prosecution was dropped and, according to a note in the Irish government records: 'No reason was given at the Special Criminal Court, but official sources said it was because prosecuting lawyers believed there was insufficient evidence.'[28] This caused considerable anger on the British side.

British allegations that the Republic of Ireland was a place of refuge for the IRA was a periodically recurring theme of the 'Troubles'. It was most commonly claimed in the early 1970s, particularly by rogue members of the Conservative Party and the Unionist parties of Northern Ireland. One of Tom King's predecessors, James Prior, aroused considerable anger in Dublin government circles during his tenure as Secretary of State in 1982, when he claimed in Westminster that cross-border attacks made up 40 per cent of all IRA attacks. Later that year, speaking to a US radio station, he described how 'fugitive terrorists' regularly found a 'safe haven' in the Republic of Ireland, prompting an official complaint from the Irish government.[29]

Late in 1987, gardaí were actively pursuing former IRA and INLA member, Dessie O'Hare, in a manhunt lasting several weeks and akin to the search for Dominic McGlinchey four years earlier. O'Hare had originally been part of the IRA's South Armagh Brigade before defecting to the INLA in the late 1970s. He was acquitted in the 1978 shooting of a British soldier at his wedding in County Meath but was imprisoned in Portlaoise from 1979 to 1986 for arms possession following a high-speed chase in which another car passenger was killed. Following his release and the chaotic dissolution of the INLA into rival factions during the mid-1980s, O'Hare formed a small gang that kidnapped a Dublin dentist, John O'Grady, and subjected him to extreme ill-treatment and torture while attempting to extract a ransom payment. The victim's father-in-law, the head of a profitable medical research company, had been the intended target but was not present when the kidnap gang arrived at his home, so O'Grady was taken instead. As with the McGlinchey manhunt, and general IRA activity, gardaí lamented the skewed perceptions of the conflict that benefited republicans. The officer leading the kidnapping investigation 'complained bitterly that too many people regard people like the "Border Fox" [O'Hare's nickname] as the Robin Hood of today ... "They were given support, food, shelter by many many people," he said in a radio interview.'[30] A British report from their Dublin embassy noted: 'morale in gardaí is rock-bottom' and that the structure in place for major cases like the O'Hare manhunt was wholly deficient, as case officers were assigned based on area divisions not issues.[31] Eventually, O'Hare and an accomplice, Martin Bryan, were traced to the midlands. At a joint garda–army roadblock outside Urlingford, County Kilkenny, the car in which they were travelling was halted. In the ensuing gun battle, Bryan was killed and O'Hare and an Irish soldier were injured. O'Hare subsequently received a forty-year jail sentence.[32]

The above-mentioned break-up of the INLA degenerated into a series of deadly feuds during this period, with a number of killings in 1986–87 in Northern Ireland and County Louth. One victim was Mary McGlinchey, wife of Dominic. On one occasion, the brother of an INLA hunger striker travelled down to Munster in an attempt to assassinate a prominent member of a rival faction. As a result of this feuding, many INLA members defected to the Provisional IRA, partly to come under that larger organisation's protection. This included several men who would later play significant roles in the IRA's Southern Command.[33]

IRA Fundraising Activities

O'Hare's ransom attempt may have reflected previous IRA activities, but in 1987 the IRA was moving on to new revenue sources. In that year, the British Home Office estimated the IRA's annual income at just over £3 million. On armed robberies, they noted that while this activity netted the organisation 'in excess of £100,000 per annum, there is some indication that they are moving away from this risky method of raising money except when they are very short of cash'.[34] Just two years earlier, the British estimated that up to 60 per cent of the IRA's income derived from armed robberies North and South.[35] Overseas contributions, predominantly the US-based NORAID, but also smaller sums from Australia and 'some irregular foreign donations such as from the Libyan Government', brought in an estimated £200,000 annually.[36] The shift from regular armed robberies to more sophisticated or less risky ventures became more apparent from the mid-1980s onwards. For example, during this period the IRA exploited the growing popularity of video cassette players by producing and distributing pirate or counterfeit films.[37] In a study on IRA financing, Max Taylor and John Horgan quote a statement in the possession of the gardaí that they had been given access to from an alleged Southern Command meeting (*c.* 1985), which stated:

> The Southern Command obtained finance through armed robberies but these often went wrong. The result was that it was costing PIRA to support the families of members imprisoned for armed robbery offences … [D] gave an example of a robbery in Tralee which had obtained £92,000 and compared it to a pub bought for £17,000 which was then worth £200,000.[38]

By the end of this decade, a garda spokesman suggested that twenty-five pubs in Dublin and twelve outside the capital were suspected of operating as IRA fronts, though this is impossible to verify.[39] Given the need for extreme prudence with regard to expenditure, the Provisionals rigorously weighed up the benefits of any significant potential investment. One interviewee spoke of an example concerning a republican sympathiser, a farmer who sought to build a slatted shed in a field on his land. A deal was worked out with the local IRA command whereby they paid for the construction of the shed, the supplies and labour. In return, the farmer consented to an arms storage bunker being built underneath it. To allay suspicion, the farmer took a loan from the bank and simply used that money to pay back the monthly loan instalments, interest notwithstanding. He gained a solid shed for little financial cost while the IRA, with a little investment, gained a durable and covert storage bunker.[40]

The IRA was still willing to carry out large-scale raids for financing if they felt the gain was outweighed by the potential risk. In May 1987 such an operation backfired badly, leading to the capture and arrest of six IRA volunteers in County Louth. The men had approached the security guard at a liquor warehouse and demanded entrance, intending to take a lorry loaded with £50,000-worth of alcohol. This was to be sold, with the proceeds going to the republican movement. However, armed detectives surrounded the warehouse while the men were still inside. They were found hiding in the attic and arrested. During their trial, Detective Superintendent Patrick Culhane told the court that the men were all members of the IRA and had 'been actively involved with leading members of the organisation'.[41] All six received seven-year prison sentences on burglary and arms possession charges. It is not clear where gardaí received their intelligence about the raid.[42]

In August, three men went on trial at the Special Criminal Court for an armed robbery the previous year at a cash-and-carry in Listowel, County Kerry, in what gardaí referred to as a 'well-planned, professional operation'. According to court accounts, three armed and masked men burst into the cash-and-carry owner's home in Lixnaw on the night of 27 August 1986. He was put on the ground at gunpoint and the men demanded the keys to the building as well as information on how the alarm system worked. The owner was then brought to the premises and forced to deactivate the alarm. He later recalled that a number of other men wearing balaclavas and boiler suits backed a lorry into the yard of the store. The lorry was loaded with more than £80,000-worth of spirits, tobacco and electrical goods before the raiders made their escape. Gardaí later arrested a number of known republicans in the area. One of those, Maurice Prendergast – a prominent local republican with a previous IRA membership charge – was accused of assaulting a member of the gardaí when they arrested him at his home. It was alleged that he tried to goad the garda into hitting him back so he could feign illness. One man received a prison sentence for his part in the raid: Nicholas Buckley (32) of Castlemaine was sentenced to seven years' imprisonment for armed robbery. Prendergast was sentenced to twelve months for assault and resisting arrest, although he was cleared on an armed robbery charge. Timothy Galvin (45), a farmer and father-of-six, also from Castlemaine, pleaded guilty to receiving stolen goods and received a five-year suspended sentence.[43] Such examples of a loss of manpower for the IRA were mirrored later that year in a most significant loss of arms.

Arms Discoveries

On 27 January, gardaí searched the County Meath farm of a middle-aged father-of-seven, Sean Anthony Healy. According to Detective Superintendent Patrick Culhane, the man had been 'known to members of the gardaí to be actively involved with the Provisional IRA for a number of years.'[44] In a search of the home, they discovered grenades, gelignite, shotgun cartridges, timing devices and detonating cord. Under the floorboards of the house, a red canvas bag was found containing four homemade grenades, several packets of modified shotgun cartridges and more detonating cord. A brown paper parcel containing 10lbs of gelignite was found in the garage. 'Derry' had been written on the wrapper. In a follow-up raid in nearby Trim, gardaí found live ammunition and a roll of fuse wire in a house. The homeowner, Noel McCabe, a twenty-nine-year-old married father-of-three, was arrested. Healy was subsequently sentenced to seven years' penal servitude while McCabe received three years.[45] Although little was made of the homemade grenades discovered on Healy's farm, these weapons were prototypes of the IRA's drogue bomb, which was soon to acquire a fearsome reputation among the RUC and British Army deployed in Northern Ireland.

In April, there were two significant explosives finds within twenty-four hours. On 22 April, gardaí discovered a concealed bunker on the lands of a farmer at Mullaghmore, Virginia, County Cavan. The bunker contained approximately half a ton of nitrobenzene and HME mixture. The following day, gardaí discovered 240lbs of HME hidden in a bog at Bunbeg, County Donegal. A snapshot of a British report on arms discoveries in the Republic of Ireland during just one month in 1987 illustrates the regularity of small-scale discoveries across the state:

Table 15. Arms and military paraphernalia discoveries in the Republic, March 1987[46]

Division	Date	Location	Seizure
Cavan/ Monaghan	5.3.87	Agheeshal, Broomfield, Castleblayney, Co. Monaghan	Firearms cleaning equipment 1 dagger with sheath

Division	Date	Location	Seizure
Donegal	1.3.87	Carnowen, Castlefin, Co. Donegal	1 shotgun
Dublin Metropolitan Area	2.3.87	Campion's Public House, Balgriffin, Raheny, Dublin	1 hand grenade
Dublin Metropolitan Area	24.3.87	12, Charleville Mall, North Strand, Dublin 3	21 rounds of ammunition 1 paramilitary uniform 1 short fair-haired wig 3 car reg. plates Assorted electronic equipment 1 set of handcuffs 1 baton
Dublin Metropolitan Area	25.3.87	44, Greenfort Ave., Quarryfield, Clondalkin	1 .22 rifle 4 rounds of ammunition
Dublin Metropolitan Area	28.3.87	76, Seatown Villas, Swords, Co. Dublin	1 shotgun 1 cartridge
Louth/Meath	6.3.87	Mullacrew, Louth, Co. Louth	2 two-way radios
Louth/Meath	25.3.87	A ditch between Fairways Hotel and the Main Dublin/ Belfast Road	1 .45 revolver
Louth/Meath	31.3.87	44, O'Hanlon Park, Dundalk, Co. Louth	1 bomb 1 timing device

Division	Date	Location	Seizure
Leix/Offaly	2.3.87	The Lochs, Rahan, Tullamore, Co. Offaly	1 .22 rifle
Limerick	6.3.87	Convent St., Limerick	1 shotgun 2 cartridges
Mayo	14.3.87	4, Collins Close, Ballina, Co. Mayo	1 air pistol
Mayo	31.3.87	Creagh Road, Ballinrobe, Co. Mayo	1 shotgun 1 cartridge
Roscommon/ Galway	3.3.87	Newtownmorris, Tuam, Co. Galway	1 shotgun 1 rifle 18 cartridges 38 rounds of .22 ammo

In November 1987, a young Dundalk man, Anthony Taafe (18), walked free from the Special Criminal Court following his acquittal on a bomb charge. Taafe had been found not guilty of possession of 'explosive substances', specifically, a modified transistor radio and a modified walkie-talkie. He had been arrested in a laneway in Dundalk after gardaí on foot patrol saw a man they believed to be a member of an illegal organisation carrying a parcel. During his trial, a ballistics expert told the court that the radio and walkie-talkie that were discovered in the parcel were modified in such a way that they could be used to set off remote-controlled bombs at distances up to 800 metres. The judge ultimately ruled that, while it was possible Taafe had been recruited to deliver the parcel by a subversive organisation, 'there was some doubt as to whether Taafe knew the parcel contained bomb-making equipment'.[47]

That same month, another Dundalk man was remanded in custody on charges dating back to his alleged possession of explosives at Grangebellew, Dunleer, in 1980, while a County Monaghan man was jailed for five years for running a 'bomb factory' at a derelict house at Mullacroghery in the county. Sean Tierney (39), an agricultural contractor, was arrested near the derelict house where three beer kegs with boiled-down fertiliser had been discovered by gardaí. Timing devices were also found in the vicinity. During his trial, Tierney told the court that he had met a man, Fergal McGrath, in a pub at Smithboro and agreed to give him a lift. During the trip, McGrath asked Tierney to pull into the side of the road, where he collected the three kegs and put them in the boot of the car. McGrath, who was not in court as he had jumped bail, allegedly told Tierney he was 'helping a man to make poitin'.[48]

In July, gardaí discovered an IRA training camp on the Malin peninsula, though no arrests were made, and during a routine search operation outside Ravensdale in County Louth, a steel-lined bunker that contained a ton of HME, as well as over 1,000 rounds of assorted ammunition was uncovered.[49] According to a British report on the Malin discovery:

> The arms and explosives found were in a plastic pipe and the find consisted of 1 Thompson sub-machine gun, 1 pistol, 4 rifles (one of which was an armalite AK 47 [sic]), 165 rounds of assorted ammunition, 5 magazines and cleaning equipment. All the weapons were in good condition and the Gardaí believe [they] may have been put there recently. Target boards were also found in the area.[50]

The British had additional grounds for optimism in 1987. For much of the past five years, they had sought to co-ordinate with the Irish government the research and manufacturing of a fertiliser that could not be easily converted into HME. That is, the ammonium nitrate ratio would be reduced and the extraction of it made more difficult. As per a British report on HME:

> Ammonium Nitrate has explosive properties and in its pure form mixed with fuel oil it is the common quarry blasting explosive known commercially as ANFO. When controls on commercial explosives were tightened in 1970 the terrorist immediately turned to other materials for his bombs, principally to high-grade (up to 100%) AN fertilisers, customarily in conjunction with fuel oil both of which he [the terrorist] was able to obtain without difficulty and inconspicuously. In 1972 'high-grade' AN fertiliser was banned in both NI and the ROI and farmers

were restricted to fertilisers with a lower maximum AN content of 79%. It was thought at the time that this was sufficient to prevent the use of AN in HME but unfortunately the terrorist turned to processing the available lower-grade AN fertilisers to 'recover' higher content AN material. The explosive was produced by mixing the recovered AN with fuel oil, adding a booster charge of more sensitive explosive, and initiated by detonating fuse and detonator. This recovery process was invariably carried out in 'kitchens' located in the Republic.[51]

While the British put considerable funding into research on new fertilisers, they were concerned that the initiative would lack impact if the Irish did not also agree to produce the new product. For their part, the Irish expressed concern at the economic impact of such a fundamental manufacturing change, particularly in cash-strapped production factories in the South. There had already been significant economic and production-line impacts as a result of changes to the composition of fertiliser during the previous decade. In 1984, an agreement was reached, with the Irish offering the facilities of the Institute of Industrial Research and Standards and the Department of Agriculture to help in the research programme. Shortly after this, however, they became unresponsive to communication from their British counterparts. British frustration at the lack of co-operation from their Irish counterparts was apparent in an internal memo in December 1986: 'The Irish line was, I'm afraid, a complete smoke screen ... To date, we have had no reply, despite letters, phone calls, and personal contacts. On my visit to Dublin on 4 December, my hosts said that they hoped I could take a paper back with me. They failed to achieve this, and I still have not received it.'[52]

Despite this, the British could announce in 1987 that research carried out by a team of British and Irish scientists had identified a new ammonium nitrate-based fertiliser, where that component was significantly reduced and 'urea with suitable non-detonable fillers has been added'.[53] In addition, a new coating on the granules made it much more difficult to extract the explosive components. One caveat was noted in the report, however: 'Any industrial equipment, when handling the granules, is likely to cause some wearing down of the coating, or some cases where the coating falls off the granule, or where the granule is split, exposing uncoated materials.' The

IRA quickly discovered these shortcomings and adapted their process for extracting the explosive components, rendering futile years of massively funded research. Discussing the processing of the new fertiliser, an interviewee recalled:

> ... they [the IRA] actually started going from the boiling of it to the grinding of it in that period. They were using the grinders to grind it up, which was near enough the same thing. You know things for grinding, mangles and all that? They were using those, but they were these big industrial coffee grinders sort of thing, but they'd wear out after a certain amount of time ... They bought these coffee grinders, and they were using those to grind the mix ...[54]

Ultimately, there was no material impact on the ability of the IRA's Southern Command to supply Northern units with HME. Indeed, an *Irish Times* report in October 1987 noted: 'So far this year the RUC has recovered some 5 tonnes of explosives, the largest quantity since 1976.'[55] This followed on from the RUC discovery of a 3,000lb bomb in County Tyrone, the largest ever constructed by the IRA. The bomb was made up of fertiliser-based HME packed into fifty-eight plastic bags and stored on a slurry spreader. Several weeks earlier, a 500lb device had been discovered in a van in Derry. In the South, gardaí also had their largest explosives find of the conflict to date: 2,040lb of HME were uncovered near Dundalk in July.[56]

On Sunday, 8 November 1987, an IRA bomb exploded at the Enniskillen cenotaph during a Remembrance Day ceremony. Eleven people were killed and scores more injured, many with life-impacting injuries. A twelfth victim died after years in a coma. The bomb was planted by members of the IRA's South Fermanagh Brigade, having allegedly been assembled outside Ballinamore and transported across the border by multiple volunteers operating in relays. The IRA claimed that the bomb had been intended as an attack on members of the security forces who were to assemble near the cenotaph. One account claimed that, if the bomb had managed to strike security force members primarily, the inevitable civilian casualties would hopefully have been small enough to be deemed acceptable collateral.[57] Claiming responsibility for the bombing, an IRA statement alleged that it was to be triggered by remote control, but that a British Army high-frequency scanning device had set the detonator off prematurely. The army rubbished these claims, stating that pieces of a timer were found in the wreckage of the explosion. If the bomb was set to be detonated by a timer, there could be no guarantee that it would not explode when civilians were in immediate proximity. Shortly after the explosion, another Fermanagh IRA unit reportedly abandoned attempts to detonate a bomb in the village of Tullyhommon. This second bomb was approximately 140lbs of explosives contained in a beer keg and plastic container, with a command wire running across the border to County Donegal. While the Tullyhommon bomb was composed of HME, the bomb that exploded at Enniskillen was allegedly a mixture of HME and Semtex.

Those involved in the Enniskillen bombing were based on both sides of the border and gardaí in Monaghan, suspecting that something was afoot on the morning of the attack, had actually arrested several republicans – primarily Tyrone men on the run and living in Monaghan. Gardaí and police in Northern Ireland believed the operation was led by a young local female IRA leader based in Monaghan.[58] The Enniskillen bombing horrified many in the South, perhaps in a way no other IRA attack had since the 1978 La Mon Hotel bombing, which killed twelve people. Writing in the aftermath, one Belfast journalist identified Southern hostility to Northerners as being due to a complex set of issues, but that ultimately it boiled down to 'ignorance and shame'. He added that 'southerners don't understand the conflict in the north but they do know they are deeply ashamed of it'.[59] The 1987 amendment to the Irish 1965 Extradition Act was introduced several weeks after the Enniskillen bombing. Given the vocal opposition to this amendment in the weeks leading up to its passage – within and without the Dáil – the public outrage over the Enniskillen bombing likely eased its eventual passage. In a poll conducted in the South in the aftermath of the bombing, 40 per cent of those questioned were in favour of the amendment, 23 per cent wanted it postponed and 20 per cent were opposed.[60]

Eksund and Operation Mallard

Compounding the impact of the Enniskillen bombing was the fact that across Britain and Ireland, people were still reeling from the discovery of the largest ever IRA arms importation just a short time earlier. In the early hours of Saturday 31 October, French naval vessels intercepted the Panamanian-registered ship, the *Eksund*, in the Bay of Biscay, after it had been spotted moving in an erratic fashion. On board the ship were five Irishmen, including the captain, an experienced sailor named Adrian Hopkins, and Gabriel Cleary, one of the most senior members of the IRA's GHQ staff. Also on board was James Doherty from County Donegal, who was suspected of organising and running an IRA training camp that was discovered by gardaí on Cruit Island in 1981.[61] Hopkins had previously been a merchant seaman and the founder of a holiday firm, Bray Travel, which went into liquidation in 1980, leaving over 600 Irish travellers stranded on the Canary Islands. Less than three months later, he was preparing to re-enter the travel business as a chartered boat operator using his own personal wealth of £250,000 as start-up money.[62]

While the five men on board the *Eksund* were arrested, brought to the French mainland and held in prison, French officials were initially unclear as to their identities or the intended destination of the cargo. Part of the issue was that several of the crew were using false passports, part of the batch stolen by the IRA from the Irish Department of Foreign Affairs in 1984. It was quickly determined, however, that this was likely an IRA operation, despite Hopkins having no previous known republican connections. As the ship's cargo was inventoried and details released, the shocking scale of the importation attempt became apparent. On board was somewhere between 120 and 150 tons of arms, explosives and military equipment. The cargo included anti-aircraft missiles and heavy machine guns, both of which were capable of shooting down British military aircraft. Also discovered were 1,000 AK-47s, a dozen RPG-7s, hundreds of grenades, thousands of fuses and electrical detonators, flamethrowers and two tons of the Czech-made plastic explosive Semtex. Semtex was then one of the most sophisticated explosives available. It was composed of a thin, malleable material, highly unreactive and unable to be detected by the types of X-ray bomb detectors that were installed in British and Irish airports.[63]

The *Eksund* shipment represented the last of the major arms importations from Libya to the IRA during the 1980s and the weight of its cargo was equivalent to the four previous shipments combined. A British official who bumped into the Fine Gael Press Secretary Peter White immediately after news of the capture of the *Eksund* emerged reported that White had confided to him that one senior party member muttered, upon hearing the news, 'Christ – the IRA could start a civil war with that lot. And win.'[64] In a statement released in the aftermath of the seizure, Minister for Justice Gerry Collins referred to a threat 'to the very safety and security of the State. The power of those highly sophisticated weapons to maim, destroy and kill was on a scale we have never before encountered.'[65]

While suspicion fell on Colonel Gaddafi's Libya as the source of the arms, that regime was quick to refute the notion. However, throughout the last quarter of 1986, Gaddafi had become increasingly indiscreet in speeches about his rediscovered support for the IRA. As early as April and May 1987, newspapers had been speculating that the IRA had acquired Semtex. The explosive was only used by the militaries of a small number of countries, including Libya, narrowing the field of suspects.[66] Although the AK-47s captured by gardaí in the north-west of the country in January 1986 had been Romanian-made, they were discovered alongside boxes clearly bearing Libyan markings. The Irish beef export industry to Libya, at that time worth tens of millions of pounds to the Irish economy, likely played a part in the government's unwillingness to look too closely into the Libyan connection.

During a discussion between a representative of the British Embassy and the new Garda Commissioner Eamonn Doherty, the latter admitted that gardaí believed the AK-47 arms finds in early 1986 represented the totality of an IRA importation operation and that they had halted a planned IRA winter offensive. He and the rest of the force were therefore very shaken at news of the *Eksund,* as well as subsequent UK estimates of what had already gotten through. In the days following the *Eksund's* capture, as the realisation sank in among the British and Irish governments that this was not the only shipment, dots were joined and connections made: bayonets discovered alongside automatic rifles in Sligo the previous year matching other rifles discovered in Chester, England; the 'Libyan armed forces' and 'destination Tripoli' markings on the Sligo boxes; multiple reports of the IRA having acquired Semtex during the previous twelve months.[67] Later garda and RUC estimates of the pre-*Eksund* shipments amounted to the following, in addition to huge quantities of Semtex:

Table 16. Security estimates of Libyan shipments successfully landed in Ireland[68]

Quantity	Type
1200	AK-47s
40	General purpose machine guns
26	DShK heavy machine guns
10	Surface-to-air missiles
130	RPG-7 missiles
33	RPG-7 launchers
10	Flamethrowers
130	Webley revolvers
275	Hand grenades
50	9mm pistols

While upwards of 100 tons of Libyan arms, explosives and military equipment had already been successfully landed prior to the interception of the *Eksund*, a major IRA offensive planned for the North was being held back until the last of the arms arrived safely. The armaments that had been successfully landed over the previous two years were stored in 'master dumps'. All the 'big stuff' was put into storage south of the Galway–Dublin line, and overseen by the IRA's quartermaster department. These dumps were large, sophisticated underground bunkers built inside farm buildings and under silage pits on land owned by republican sympathisers. When and as required, parts of their contents were broken up and transported north to border areas, from where they were then brought into Northern Ireland. South Tipperary was considered the beginning of this 'line', a geographical area under the remit of the quartermaster department. No training camps or other IRA activity that might draw unwanted garda attention were permitted to take place in that vicinity.

Each AK-47 in the shipments came with a bayonet, magazines, cleaning kit and scabbard. Since the IRA had already established an efficient cleaning system for their weaponry years before, and the bayonets were 'useless' in modern insurgency, almost all of this was discarded, with huge quantities of bayonets simply dumped in rivers across the South.[69] According to a former member of the quartermaster department, the weapons came from Libya 'without any strings attached, as long as they were used'. The interviewee continued: 'They were important at the time, as I said, that's what kept a lot of people in the movement. It gave us a better armament. It didn't put us on par with them, but it put us where we were there or thereabouts, like, you were able to use the same weapons as the Brits.'[70] Semtex was particularly valued. Although grinders could mitigate British and Irish developments to make fertiliser less useful to the IRA, the acquisition of Semtex represented the first time since the early 1970s that the IRA had commercial explosives in any significant quantity. The amount that came in was 'ten tons plus ... but it wasn't hundreds of tons', therefore the IRA's engineering department 'made the best use of it as they could ... they actually refined everything down, and they used very small amounts'. Semtex would be used by the IRA 'in the main as a booster, or "up-and-unders" they'd use it, you know, or the mortars. And even in some of the bigger mortars they'd use the mix and the Semtex as a booster.'[71] The reference to 'boosters' meant the Semtex would be used in small amounts, as a primary explosive, to detonate much bigger HME bombs. Examples of this kind of bombing include the 1992 Baltic Exchange bombing and the 1996 Docklands bombing, both in London.

On 24 November, Minister for Justice Gerry Collins confirmed in the Dáil that the government strongly suspected that 'four separate cargoes of arms and ammunition may have been landed' already.[72] The previous morning, the Irish security forces embarked on what the *Irish Independent* reported as being 'the biggest security operation ever mounted' by the state.[73] By the end of the first day of searches, small quantities of arms and ammunition had been discovered, but nothing substantial. During the course of this so-called 'Operation Mallard', which ran until 29 November, 7,000 gardaí and soldiers searched over 50,000 homes across the state, including on Tory and Inisboffin islands. The searches also extended to 164 cruisers on the River Shannon and 775 caravans across the country, and all of these were conducted without a warrant. Over 85 per cent of the house searches were also carried out without a warrant.[74] Despite this, as Minister Collins pointed out on 11 December, only thirty-six formal complaints had been made by members of the public (though this had risen to over 300 by Christmas). The cost of the operation was estimated to be £2m, which, when combined with the search operation following the O'Grady kidnapping earlier in the year, put the garda budget significantly in the red.[75] One Dublin republican publication alleged that, during the raids – which included raids on 'members of Fianna Fail, Labour, Fine Gael and Sinn Fein' – gardaí searched through personal letters, with many copied or simply taken away.[76]

One Munster interviewee, who served a prison sentence during the 1970s for IRA activity, recalled the searches:

> I was away back in [location redacted], I missed them all; the fishermen, everybody was raided. Loads of people were raided, anyone and everyone was raided … But I remember coming in, walking into the house, I came in the back door into the house, the house was very close to the road. But, Jesus, I spotted this fella, big trench coat and he'd an Uzi stuck straight in my father's face, I'll never forget it … What was a seventy-eight-year-old man going to do to him, you know … But then they took away a load of stuff. They brought it all back again, the local sergeant brought it back. I said, 'Why didn't the fella who brought it away bring it back?' 'Check it now there and make sure it's all there,' he said, 'you wouldn't trust them,' he said, you know.[77]

Criticism of the massive search operation from the opposition benches within the Dáil was muted. There was a general consensus on the validity of Minister Collins' earlier statement that 'the IRA's arsenal of weapons was of such power and sophistication that it could render the Gardaí powerless and seriously threaten the army'.[78]

Operation Mallard uncovered an array of sophisticated facilities designed and constructed in anticipation of large-scale arms importations. On the Clare–Galway border – the location of several significant arms discoveries in the previous decade, and near the home of the former Clare IRA quartermaster – gardaí discovered two empty purpose-built bunkers. As the *Irish Independent* reported on 28 November:

> The Gardaí were last night rating the discovery of the concealed bunker, in an open field at Barna, Tubber, as of 'major significance' in the huge nationwide hunt for IRA arms … similar bunkers may now be discovered

in other strong republican areas of the country. Gardaí revealed that the bunker, uncovered in South Galway, contained a room about 20ft by 10ft by 8ft high – from which there was a 112ft long tunnel ending in another bunker of about 6ft by 4ft ... One garda told the newsmen: 'The whole structure looked very professional and elaborate – it had all the hallmarks of being suitable as an arms workshop or a secret hideout for fugitives or Libyan arms.' ... Special Branch sources said last night that the areas earmarked for attention focused particularly on strong republican locations.

Two days previously, fifteen detonators, five rounds of ammunition and a pistol were discovered at Ballinamore, while seven rocket launchers were found in a dugout at Clara, County Offaly.[79] At Clogga Strand near Arklow, believed to be the landing place for the successful Libyan importations, a 55ft-long bunker was found on the land of a known republican. Again, it was empty. Following its discovery, The Phoenix reported on how permission for its construction had been:

> submitted to the Department of Agriculture, complete with full plans, in 1984 in order to avail of a 33% grant. The 'bunker' was situated next to a cow byre, and was intended to be used as 'a cattle slurry pit' – fulfilling all regulations in that regard. The 'secret tunnel side-entrance' was also included in the submitted plans. A 'drainage hatch'.[80]

The following month, another bunker was discovered at Ballinalee, County Longford. This bunker was also on farmland and was reported to be fifteen feet long, built with concrete and equipped with a cooker and lighting. It was accessed through a manhole. By the end of the year, four elaborate bunkers and sixteen dugouts had been located by the gardaí and army. Much of the intelligence that led to the discovery of the underground bunkers came from British aerial reconnaissance (they had recently been given permission to conduct these flights in the South), as well as British-supplied metal detectors. The arrangement to exchange equipment in this way had been a provision of the Anglo-Irish Agreement.[81] However, because of the lack of weapons discovered in the bunkers, gardaí admitted it was unlikely anybody would be charged in relation to their discovery.

Considering the scale of the search, and the quantity of weapons available to be discovered, the operation was a disappointing failure for the security forces. The search had been focused particularly on strong republican locations. Despite this, the returns were minimal: 'small quantities of arms and ammunition', 'fifteen detonators, five rounds of ammunition and a pistol', 'seven rocket launcher devices', for example.[82] It is likely that the lack of major discoveries was due to the arms still being stored in the 'master dumps', bunkers so well hidden that they would not be picked up by aerial reconnaissance or metal detectors.[83] Initially, Garda Commissioner Doherty was hopeful that because Operation Mallard faced 'a relative lack of success' – as bunkers were empty but primed for use – this meant most of the Libyan arms had been on the *Eksund*. He later acknowledged that this was not the case.[84] A British official noted in a report to Whitehall that Doherty appeared to have a 'green streak' in him, implying that he was quite naïve about IRA capabilities.[85]

Three of the five men captured on board the *Eksund* – Gabriel Cleary, James Doherty and James Coll – were held on remand in French prisons until 1991 before being tried. Adrian Hopkins and Henry Cairns were both released on bail in early 1990. Hopkins took the opportunity to flee the country and was arrested in Limerick in July of that year. Despite French authorities stating that they would not issue an extradition warrant, Hopkins was tried in absentia in a French court and sentenced to seven years' imprisonment. He also faced trial in Ireland, in the Special Criminal Court, on arms-smuggling charges, where he received an eight-year prison sentence with five of those suspended for co-operation with the authorities, as well as time already spent in prison awaiting trial.[86] Back in France, Cleary, Doherty and Coll received five-year sentences on arms-smuggling charges, while Henry Cairns was given the same sentence but with two years suspended. The four men were also forbidden from returning to France for five years after their sentences expired. As they were led from the dock to applause from relatives and supporters, one of them remarked, 'It could not be better.'[87]

One unexpected result from Operation Mallard was the inadvertent discovery of several 1983 H-Block escapees. Paul Kane and Dermot Finucane were arrested by gardaí near Granard, not far from Ballinalee, during the operation. Gardaí also discovered a bunker in that location the following month.[88] A long extradition battle saw different results for these two men. Kane was eventually extradited to Northern Ireland in 1989, being flown there by helicopter. A founding member of Fianna Fáil, Commandant Martin McEvoy, quit the party following this extradition, claiming: 'the party is straying from the principles set down in 1926'.[89] The extradition request for Finucane and another man were turned down by the Irish courts amidst claims of brutality by Northern Irish prison warders against prisoners, as well as admissions of widespread perjury by the warders. This extradition refusal was seen by the British press as having a major negative impact on Anglo-Irish relations.[90] Two other H-Block escapees, Anthony Kelly and James Joseph Clarke, were arrested in the Dublin suburb of Kilbarrack during a garda search of the home of a married couple. As noted in the previous chapter, Kelly had been arrested by gardaí at a 'bomb factory' in County Donegal in 1985, but he had jumped bail and been on the run since then. Both men would go on trial at the Special Criminal Court in January 1988.

By any measure, 1987 was a bad year for the Provisional republican movement. Their first electoral outing in the Republic since ending the abstentionism policy was a disaster. Not only did Sinn Féin face an embarrassing result, but the forfeiture of twenty-three candidate deposits meant a cost of several thousand pounds. The loss of a number of experienced IRA volunteers in the Loughgall ambush had an operational impact regionally, but also led to a lingering fear that there was an informer at large in the east Tyrone area. This poisoned the atmosphere among surviving members of the brigade and its support base for some time. The public anger in Finglas over the killing of an alleged informer was a significant embarrassment for the IRA in north Dublin, long a stronghold of militant republican support, while the targeting of Samuel McClean in County Donegal caused considerable local anger. The Enniskillen bombing continues to be regarded as one of the worst atrocities committed by the IRA during the 'Troubles'. That this came so soon after the capture of the *Eksund* put the Provisionals on the back foot for some time. And, while they were lucky to emerge from the South's Operation Mallard relatively unscathed in terms of loss of arms and matériel, the army and garda discoveries of many of their bunkers were certainly a blow. More than that, they had now lost the element of surprise in launching an offensive, something that was as valuable as the arms themselves. With the capture of the *Eksund*, and the British and Irish governments' relatively accurate estimations of what weaponry had gotten through, the movement began to waver in deciding their next steps.

7

A Sign of Respect
for the Flag: 1988–89

While Operation Mallard yielded very little in terms of IRA weaponry, garda and army searches continued into the following years, albeit at a reduced intensity. These search operations led to a number of significant arms seizures in 1988 and 1989. Indeed, during these two years, gardaí could claim credit for the capture of 450 firearms, nearly one and a half tons of explosives and over 130,000 rounds of ammunition. During this period, the IRA in Munster were left reeling from two major events. In May 1988, an experienced member of Southern Command was shot dead by gardaí following an aborted post office robbery in rural County Clare. Later that year, Kerry IRA officer and long-time garda informant Sean O'Callaghan walked into a police station in England and confessed his role in a range of IRA activities. His disappearance three years earlier had led to a panicked shifting of arms and armaments from dumps in the Munster area. The state continued to extradite, or attempt to extradite, IRA volunteers to Northern Ireland and Britain to face trial throughout this period. In the case of Robert Russell, the months leading up to his extradition – and the campaign North and South to prevent it – increased tensions considerably. Russell's eventual extradition in August 1988 led to a weekend of violence across the North reminiscent of some of the worst of the early years of the 'Troubles'. Conversely, in the case of Southern IRA member and former priest Patrick Ryan, the Irish government refused to extradite him to Britain, despite considerable evidence of his involvement in militant activity in continental Europe.

Along the border, the IRA continued to pose problems for the

British in the latter years of the 1980s. While civilian casualties led to the disbandment of a Fermanagh IRA brigade, that county witnessed one of the most audacious IRA attacks of the conflict, at Derryard checkpoint in December 1989. Earlier in the year, the killing of two senior RUC officers in Armagh led to long-running claims of collusion between gardaí and the IRA in the Louth–Armagh area. The publication of an exhaustive inquiry into the matter in 2013 failed to prove or disprove the allegations conclusively.

Mallard Continued: Explosives and Arms Captures

The state's extensive search for the IRA's Libyan weaponry officially ended in late November 1987. However, the gardaí and Irish Army continued to hunt for these weapons well into 1988. Through a combination of surveillance, tip-offs and scrambled IRA plans, a substantial amount of weaponry and explosives was recovered in the early months of the year. Beginning in January, gardaí in Donegal discovered a major IRA arms dump, while, across the border near Lisburn, the RUC intercepted a truck carrying similar weaponry. The Donegal cache was discovered at the Five Fingers beach on Malin Head and consisted of 100 automatic rifles, several general-purpose machine guns as well as a significant amount of ammunition, grenades and explosives. The weapons had been stored in two oil tanks and buried under sand at the beach. The beach itself is quite remote and surrounded by sand dunes and hills. According to one account, the weapons had been brought there from central storage in Munster in four loads containing twenty-five automatic rifles, one general-purpose machine gun and attendant paraphernalia. Each of these typical weapons loads would be stored near the border before being brought across at an opportune time and passed to the quartermaster of a local IRA unit in the North. It was standard operating procedure that loads were never to be stored together once they left a 'master dump'. However, despite the Donegal unit responsible assuring the quartermaster department that they had several storage areas ready to receive weapons loads, this turned out to be untrue and when the loads arrived, they hurriedly chose a remote location and buried them all together. There was, therefore, considerable anger within the IRA at the loss.

Given the disruption caused by information passed to the RUC by the Derry IRA quartermaster Frank Hegarty in previous years, there were fears of another informer in the area. The IRA's quartermaster department held an internal inquiry and determined that the discovery was 'purely accidental'. They concluded the most likely cause was that passers-by had witnessed the weapons being cached and contacted the gardaí. According to one interviewee:

> We brought it all up to them – and like we brought up four different loads – we brought up twenty-five and one GPMG [general-purpose machine gun], and they all lumped it into the one dump. And they were seen by people, and people reported them to the police and the cops came upon it that way, you know. Like, I don't think there is anything more devious about giving it away or anything. The previous one, where your man Frank [Hegarty] was involved, and British intelligence, that was where eighty rifles got caught – where they followed him over from Cavan or Monaghan. British intelligence had actually been operating in the South and they informed the guards.[1]

Compounding the Donegal loss, another large load of weapons was intercepted several days later outside Lisburn. There, the RUC stopped and searched a refrigerated lorry or ice cream van (reports vary) coming from south Tipperary and driven by a Belfast republican known to them. Inside the vehicle they found two RPG-7 rocket launchers with over a dozen rockets, twenty grenades, fifteen automatic rifles and one GPMG. In addition, there were thousands of rounds of ammunition and bomb-making paraphernalia, including fuses for the IRA's new homemade drogue bombs. It was believed that this consignment was being transported to the IRA's Belfast Brigade, to be broken up upon arrival.[2] Another load was captured in Derry city in September 1988, consisting of Semtex, a mortar and eleven mortar bombs, a grenade launcher, an AK-47, the barrel of a GPMG, a large quantity of heavy-calibre and armour-piercing rounds, several litres of nitrobenzene, timing units, detonating cord and other bomb-making paraphernalia. The rest of that month brought a litany of bad news to the Provisional IRA as arms dumps were located in several counties.

Following their success in Donegal, on 23 February, gardaí uncovered a substantial weapons cache in a hayshed near the Portmarnock harness-racing track in County Dublin. The find consisted of two dozen automatic rifles, ninety-one blocks of Semtex, dozens of grenades, tens of thousands of rounds and a number of warheads for RPG-7s. The rifles had been wrapped in heavy-duty polythene plastic, leading gardaí to believe that they were ready for immediate dispersal. One man was arrested. The weapons were close in serial number to those discovered in Sligo and Roscommon in 1986 and gardaí reported that the dump was not as elaborate as previously discovered IRA arms bunkers. This led them to believe that many of the weapons were being moved in haste to smaller, older dumps to avoid the kind of large seizures as happened at Malin Head, and in Sligo the previous year.[3]

A few days later, a number of weapons and 20,000 rounds of ammunition were found in a cache behind a hedge running alongside a secondary road between Ballivor and Mullingar in County Meath. In the next few weeks, there were further weapons finds in Counties Limerick, Cavan and again in Donegal. In two locations outside Patrickswell, County Limerick, gardaí found dumps containing among other things automatic rifles, bayonets, ammunition and telescopic sights. One man was arrested. On St Patrick's Day, gardaí uncovered another dump, this one in a 500-gallon milk tank buried in a field near the village of Finea, County Cavan. Inside were four rifles – including two sniper rifles – an anti-tank gun, ammunition and explosives, as well as assorted military paraphernalia, such as flak jackets, army radios and rangefinders. The following day, in premises in Letterkenny, gardaí recovered detonators, ammunition and assorted bomb-making equipment. Another man was arrested.[4]

In mid-July, a walker on the banks of the River Nore just outside Borris-in-Ossory in County Laois found a Russian-made DShK heavy machine gun and reported it to gardaí. The weapon had been hidden in undergrowth on the banks of the river, with the gun barrel and firing mechanism wrapped in plastic. Three rifles, a shotgun and two rockets had been discovered in the same location a short time earlier.[5] The previous month, the IRA's South Armagh Brigade deployed one of the Libyan-acquired DShK heavy machine guns for the first time, in an anti-aircraft capacity, successfully shooting down a British Army helicopter.[6] Also in July, gardaí made a significant arrest and discovery when they searched a van driven by Patrick Flanagan (48) outside Borris-in-Ossory. According to court accounts, they were searching a farmyard in the townland of Derrin when Flanagan drove his van into the yard. Detectives noticed a lump in the back of the van covered by a blanket, which Flanagan, an unemployed painter, explained away as 'old paint stuff'. When the van was searched, it was found to contain several assault rifles, a sawn-off shotgun, a .22 rifle, an RPG-7 rocket launcher with two rockets, as well as plastic bags containing over 2,000 rounds of ammunition. Flanagan was not understood to be a member of the IRA, but gardaí were aware that he had travelled to the border during the 1970s with known IRA members to fill in roads that had been cratered by the British Army. In sentencing him to ten years' imprisonment, Mr Justice Barr said: 'It goes without saying that the destructive power of these armaments was very great indeed.'[7]

There were serious concerns in Dublin and London at the lack of arrests and prosecutions in the wake of some of these significant arms seizures. As was explained to one staff member at the British Embassy in Dublin, the Director of Public Prosecutions was reluctant to proceed with cases where arms were discovered on a person's land as it was difficult to prove that they were aware of it.[8] In June, a substantial quantity of mortars, bayonets and detonators were discovered by gardaí in yet another underground concrete bunker at Ballivor. The site was less than a mile from where gardaí had found weapons and nearly 20,000 rounds of ammunition earlier in the year. The 11ft-long bunker was found below a hayshed on a 130-acre farm. When gardaí pumped out a large amount of water from the bunker, they found six homemade mortars, eight bayonets, twenty-two detonators, one pistol, assorted ammunition, one grenade, fuse wire and other bomb-making equipment. The owner of the farm, a forty-two-year-old local man, was arrested under Section 30 of the Offences Against the State Act.[9]

A major IRA HME supply chain was disrupted later in the year when gardaí arrested a man at a house in Kells, County Meath. Members of the Security Task Force and local gardaí had conducted a week-long surveillance operation on a lorry container that was parked off the main Dublin to Derry road, just outside Kells. Suspecting that the container would soon be transported north, they seized it and arrested the driver: James Anthony Murphy, a twenty-nine-year-old married man originally from Belfast but living in Dundalk. In the container, gardaí found 380 gallons of nitrobenzene, capable of making 800 mortar bombs. Later court testimony heard how Murphy had picked up the material in Amsterdam and brought it via Rosslare to the location where gardaí seized it. Murphy said he was not a member of the IRA – a point not disputed by the garda present in court, Detective Sergeant Corrigan – and that he had done the job for money, thinking it was 'an ordinary smuggling operation'. He was sentenced to six years' imprisonment.[10]

In August 1988, gardaí uncovered another supply route, this one used by the IRA to import radio equipment for detonating bombs. This equipment was capable of protecting IRA signals from radio scanners introduced by the British Army in recent years to set off bombs prematurely, something that had significantly impacted the IRA's ability to mount ambushes on British forces in the North. Three radio transmitters, which included encoders and decoders, were discovered at a post-office box in the Finglas area of Dublin, having originated in Amsterdam. At the same time as the Finglas discovery, gardaí found a small quantity of arms and ammunition concealed in a wall at a forest outside Newcastle, County Wicklow. The find consisted of two sub-machine guns, four carbine rifles, one AK-47, a pistol, a revolver and a sawn-off .22 rifle. The cache also included two 7lb tins of assorted ammunition. The previous December, four guns and several hundred rounds of ammunition had been found in the same locality, prompting speculation from the gardaí that there may have been a paramilitary training camp in the area.[11] It was perhaps these suspicions that led gardaí to mistakenly raid a camping trip organised by Na Fianna Éireann, the youth wing of the republican movement, in March 1989. Ten teenage members of the organisation were arrested by gardaí at a campsite on the Powerscourt House estate in County Wicklow on that occasion, with the media reporting it as the disruption of a significant IRA training camp. All those arrested were released without charge the same day.[12] In November, *An Phoblacht* reported on the case of two members of Na Fianna Éireann, aged fourteen and seventeen, who were allegedly assaulted by gardaí following their arrest in Dublin city centre. According to the report:

> The two had just completed a collection in a city centre pub, with the permission of the barman, when a garda grabbed them … On their

arrival in the Bridewell they demanded to see a doctor and a solicitor. Both requests were refused. They also requested receipts for the collection tins which were confiscated – that too was refused. They were then taken into a room by a number of gardaí where they were kicked, punched and slapped for a number of minutes.[13]

An Irish government report in March 1988 on arms seizures noted that, since the beginning of 1987, more than 800 firearms had been recovered by security forces on both sides of the border. In addition, some 18,000lbs of explosives – including nearly 900lbs of commercial explosives – and nearly 180,500 rounds of ammunition had been recovered. The report noted, however, that 'it is not possible to determine precisely what proportion this represents of the firearms and explosives currently available to terrorists'.[14]

Despite having acquired substantial modern armaments from Libya, the IRA continued to experiment with homemade weapons. While the Libyan importations were a considerable windfall, the organisation had long been accustomed to matériel-lean years, and thus was always seeking ways to maximise what supplies it had. In April 1985, IRA units in the cities of Belfast and Derry began experimenting with a new weapon in attacks on British Army and RUC armoured vehicles: a homemade grenade launcher. The weapon, developed and tested by IRA engineers in the South, fired an improvised warhead primarily consisting of conventional explosives, usually Semtex. There was considerable recoil from the weapon, so IRA volunteers typically used a 'cushion' at the shoulder support. This could be a folded-over packet of J-cloths or a packet of biscuits fitted into the tube. Wholemeal oat biscuits were preferred for their density.[15] A republican report on the use of homemade weaponry appeared in a July issue of *An Phoblacht*: 'The ability of the IRA to design, develop and construct new weapons in its struggle against the Brits has been ably demonstrated during the last year. Browning 50s mounted on trucks, new handheld grenade launchers, radio-controlled bombs, and a more accurate mortar-bomb system have all successfully been used against crown forces.'[16]

In the latter half of 1987, IRA units in urban areas of Northern Ireland introduced another deadly homemade weapon to the theatre of conflict. Usually referred to in mainstream media as the 'drogue bomb', republicans referred to it as an 'impact grenade' and it looked similar to a First World

War-era German stick grenade. It was made up of a tin can stuffed with plastic explosives with a wooden handle attached and a parachute device (for example, a bin liner) at the end of the handle to guide the grenade. A copper cone was attached to the top of the can to concentrate the explosive blast. The parachute ensured that the copper tip was the first point of contact when the bomb struck a target and the heat generated by the blast vaporised the copper into extremely hot gas capable of penetrating the armoured vehicles used by the RUC and British Army. The ease with which these weapons could be manufactured, as well as concealed, made them ideal for attacks in urban areas where they could be thrown at passing mobile patrols from an alley, or dropped from a block of flats.

Drogue bombs were used dozens of times in the autumn of 1987 and caused their first fatality, RUC officer Constable Colin Gilmore, in Belfast in January of the following year. Following this incident, British forces began an urgent review of the protective capabilities of their armoured vehicles.[17] In the aftermath of the killing of Constable Gilmore, An Phoblacht referred to the 'battered morale' of 'crown forces' and their becoming 'increasingly alarmed at the effectiveness of the IRA's new impact grenade ... perfected by IRA engineers'.[18] The relatively small blast radius of the drogue bombs was suited to urban areas, not just for the proximity it allowed IRA units to get to their target, but also as a way of reducing the possibility of civilian casualties. This was of increasing consideration during the 1980s as the Provisionals pursued a dual political–military strategy. In contrast, in rural areas, the tactic of attacking patrols or convoys of British soldiers and RUC with large roadside bombs continued as before, as these bombs – usually made up of several hundred pounds of HME – were detonated by line-of-sight, meaning they could be called off if civilians were approaching. In August 1988, the IRA in Tyrone ambushed a British Army transport near Ballygawley with such a bomb. Eight soldiers were killed and nearly thirty more injured. This attack was unusual, however, in that the bomb used was made entirely of Semtex – upwards of 200lbs – without any HME.

In his annual report for 1988, the new Garda Commissioner Eugene Crowley listed the total number of arms, ammunition and explosives seized by gardaí that year (see Table 17).

Table 17. Garda seizures of arms, ammunition and explosives, 1988[19]

Quantity	Type
327	Firearms (including rifles, shotguns, machine guns, pistols, revolvers, etc.)
108,396	Rounds of ammunition (assorted)
2,741	Shotgun cartridges
72	Detonators
302	Magazines
16	Bombs of various types
15	Rockets
124	Mortar bombs
30	Barrels of nitrobenzene
1	Bazooka
5	Telescopic sights
3,075	Fuse wire (metres)
105	Bayonets
82	Hand grenades
1,116lbs	Explosives (homemade and commercial)

Among the commercial explosives seized in 1988 were several hundred pounds of Semtex.[20] It was vital for the police and armies of both states on the island to acquire samples of this explosive to attempt to implement detection measures. The explosive was undetectable by existing scanners at ports and airports in Britain and Ireland as it had virtually no smell and could be moulded into any shape, so was easily hidden in luggage or vehicle frameworks. After a relative lull during the late 1970s, the IRA had begun targeting England again during the 1980s in bombing campaigns and it was no more difficult for its volunteers to smuggle Semtex into Britain to maintain this campaign than any other arms or explosives. Semtex was found in the car used by three IRA volunteers killed by the SAS in Gibraltar in March 1988, demonstrating this ability to transport the explosive even from Ireland to continental targets. A British report on sniffer dogs discussed the need to detect Semtex that might be smuggled into Northern Irish prisons, noting:

'It is however possible to train dogs to detect the substance (some better than others) and to this end, the RUC are including Semtex in all Initial and Refresher explosive courses carried out on our behalf.'[21] The report goes on to note that, with any explosive, 'once the initial course is completed, handlers are issued with a small sample of the substances to enable them to keep their dog familiar with the smells involved'. There were difficulties in acquiring such samples, due to bureaucratic restrictions. This caused severe frustration on the part of the report's author:

> Despite explaining our case carefully to the RUC, I have been unable to obtain the supply of Semtex H explosive to enable our handlers to maintain the standard achieved on Initial and Refresher Training ... The inability of the RUC to provide us with the substance is not due to any lapse on their part. As the correspondence shows, they do not have enough for their own, never mind for other agencies' use. Quite simply, because Semtex is an illegal substance, there is no legal source for them to approach to obtain it ... The puzzling aspect of this situation is that the Army can and do obtain Semtex following incidents and finds both here and on the mainland. Why the RUC cannot obtain supplies from the Army, when they are in the front line facing devices made from Semtex is something of a mystery to me. What is quite clear however is that we cannot approach the Army direct, as present legislation demands that all movement of explosives within Northern Ireland must be controlled by and through the RUC explosives section ... The unfortunate truth is that some 2–3 weeks after training, our dogs are no longer able to identify Semtex as they receive no practice whatsoever in its detection. Our flank is completely exposed from this point of view, and is set to remain so unless steps are taken to iron out whatever barriers there are to the release of quantities of Semtex to interested agencies.[22]

Detection of Semtex exercised the minds of both the British and Irish governments and detection technology did exist which could be implemented into scanners. This was, however, very expensive to acquire and maintain. It was not until the Libyan bombing of Pan Am Flight 103 (the 'Lockerbie bombing') in December 1988 that most British and Irish airports – including Dublin and Shannon – began to install such scanners. In many cases, the installation was paid for by US airlines.[23]

IRA Funerals and Informers

The IRA volunteers slain in Gibraltar represented one of several significant personnel losses for the Provisionals in early 1988. Seán Savage, Daniel McCann and Mairéad Farrell were shot dead on 6 March by the SAS at a petrol station in the British colony. Eyewitnesses reported that masked men shot two of them as they lay on the ground having surrendered. All three were highly experienced IRA volunteers. Farrell was one of the Armagh/H-Block candidates during the 1981 general election, where she garnered 2,751 first-preference votes in the Cork North Central constituency. Although not armed at the time of their deaths, the three were on active service, and had planned to attack British forces based in the colony. The bodies of Savage, McCann and Farrell were flown to Dublin Airport by chartered aircraft before travelling by cortège to the border. The decision to fly the bodies direct from Gibraltar to Dublin followed reports that ground staff in Heathrow and Gatwick Airports had signalled their intent to refuse to handle the coffins. Security for the cortège journey was under the personal control of the Garda Commissioner, and a large crowd of republican sympathisers and senior Sinn Féin officials, as well as family members of the victims, awaited the coffins at Dublin Airport. Thousands of people in the Republic turned out to pay their respects along the route of the cortège, including a crowd of 5,000 in Dundalk. The cortège was prevented from crossing the border for an hour as the RUC insisted that the tricolours were removed from the coffins before the hearses could enter Northern Ireland.[24] According to a report in *Magill* the following month, members of the gardaí in Dundalk saluted the coffins as they passed through the town.[25] Deputy Michael McDowell of the Progressive Democrats asked Minister for Justice Gerry Collins in the Dáil whether garda authorities were aware in advance of such actions and whether they approved of the same. While stating that no direction was issued at Garda Headquarters level, Minister Collins went on to explain:

> Deputies will probably be aware that there is a long tradition whereby gardaí in uniform salute funerals, particularly when the coffin is draped

in the national flag … I believe that this practice is, and is intended to be, a sign of respect for the flag and for the dead – not necessarily any sympathy or support for any cause that might be represented by the occasion.[26]

This garda saluting of the coffins would take on major significance following an IRA attack outside the Armagh village of Jonesborough twelve months later.

The killings in Gibraltar unleashed a tragic chain of violent events in Belfast, beginning with the funerals of the three in Milltown Cemetery on 16 March. There, the loyalist Michael Stone attacked the funerary crowd with grenades and a handgun, killing three people and injuring more than fifty others. At the subsequent funeral of one of those victims, IRA volunteer Caoimhín Mac Brádaigh, two British soldiers in an unmarked car and wearing civilian clothing drove at speed towards the funeral cortège. Fearing a repeat of the Milltown attack, the crowd surrounded the vehicle causing the soldiers to draw their weapons. They were pulled from the car, viciously beaten and then shot. Given the significant media presence at the funeral, the attack was caught on camera.

While there was a notable absence of any RUC or British Army presence at the Belfast funerals, two weeks prior to the events at Milltown cemetery two IRA volunteers from South Armagh, Brendan Burns and Brendan Moley, were buried surrounded by hundreds of British soldiers and police, with at least five helicopters also hovering over the graveyard in Crossmaglen. The two men were killed when a bomb they were transporting exploded prematurely near Crossmaglen on 29 February. Both Burns and Morley were experienced IRA operatives, with Burns in particular being sought by the British for suspected involvement in the 1979 Warrenpoint attack and the killing of five British soldiers at Camlough, County Armagh, in May 1981. He had been living in the South after spending two years in Portlaoise prison and beating an extradition attempt in 1985. At the funeral, violent clashes broke out between mourners and the RUC, with the RUC claiming they intervened to prevent a paramilitary display at the graveyard. Locals said that the RUC and army intervention began much earlier, at the home of one of the dead men.[27]

In May, the IRA's Southern Command lost one of their own experienced members, Hugh Hehir, following a bungled armed robbery in County Clare.

Shortly before 8 a.m. on the eighth of that month, Hehir and another man armed with revolvers and automatic rifles, and with their heads covered by balaclavas, knocked on the door of the Caher post office. Just minutes earlier, two members of the gardaí had made a morning delivery of cash to the postmistress there, Mrs Kelly. Believing the gardaí had returned, Mrs Kelly opened the door and was confronted by the armed men. According to a media account, Mrs Kelly shouted loudly and the two men panicked, with one of them dropping his gun. The report continued: 'Mrs Kelly ran after the raider and picked up his gun. She then ran back to the post office door and locked it from the outside so that the raiders would not be able to get in if they returned.'[28] That version of events was disputed by a republican account, which claimed: 'Such was the gentleness of Hughie [Hehir], who could in different circumstances show fierce courage, that rather than assert himself at the post office when the owner raised the alert, the raid was abandoned.'[29]

As the raiders fled or abandoned the robbery, Mrs Kelly ran to a neighbour's home and telephoned the gardaí, who were able to redirect the two detectives who had just dropped off the cash delivery to double back. On a remote road between Caher and Feakle, the patrol car spotted and gave chase to the IRA unit, who were driving a white estate van. According to garda accounts, the van pulled into a laneway, which the gardaí were able to block off with their patrol car. One of the raiders pointed a revolver at the oncoming car, at which point one of the gardaí fired a burst from his Uzi machine gun. A shoot-out then erupted, with both sides firing at each other. At some point one of the raiders escaped, using a handgun and an automatic rifle to cover himself. He then hijacked an articulated lorry on a nearby road, having crossed several fields. Hehir was already slumped over the steering wheel of the van, fatally wounded. The gardaí called for medical and spiritual aid for Hehir and he was taken by helicopter to Cork Regional Hospital, where he was pronounced dead shortly afterwards.[30] Several days after the shooting, *An Phoblacht* published an account of the incident, allegedly passed from the volunteer who escaped to an intermediary of the newspaper. That account is largely similar to the garda account, with some differences:

As they were driving away in an estate van, a garda squad car approached them, then turned and gave close chase. Hughie [Hehir] pulled the van across the road to block the squad car so that they could escape and the second Volunteer got out on the road and trained a rifle on the gardaí whose car had mounted the verge and overtaken the van. A republican source quoted Hughie's comrade as saying: 'All I heard was a burst of machine-gun fire from one of the guards who had jumped out of the car. For a few moments we faced each other and I shouted for them to drive on, drive on. The Task Force guy fired at me again and ordered me to drop my gun. I then fired two shots well to his left and he ducked. He fired another burst and we kept shooting at each other. He tried to shoot me again and I fired one or two more warning shots to either side of him, hitting the boot of the car, and eventually the one with the gun got back in the car and they drove around the corner and I went over to Hughie, thinking he was lying down in the car but he was just covered in blood.'[31]

Hugh Hehir (37), from Clarecastle in County Clare, was the first IRA volunteer to be killed by Irish security forces since Dubliner Tom Smith was shot dead by the army following an escape attempt from Portlaoise prison in 1975. Hehir had joined the IRA shortly after August 1969, having previously served in the Irish local defence force, the Forás Cosanta Áitiúil (FCA). During the early 1970s, he had operated in several locations on the border along with Cork volunteers Anthony Ahern and Dermot Crowley, and was one of the few Southern IRA volunteers to be on active service in Belfast. He was arrested there in the New Lodge Road area along with Belfastman Joe Doherty in early 1974 for possession of explosives and was subsequently sentenced for this and IRA membership and imprisoned in Long Kesh until 1979. At the time, Long Kesh held a number of other Southerners, a mix of interned and sentenced prisoners. Upon his release, Hehir immediately reported back to the IRA. According to *An Phoblacht*, he was 'an extremely popular republican who was known the length and breadth of Ireland, and this was attested by the large number of people who attended the removal'.[32] The oration at Hehir's funeral was delivered by Cyril McCurtain from County Limerick, another Southerner who had been imprisoned in Long Kesh. McCurtain previously shared a prison cell with Bobby Sands and was responsible for teaching him and other Northern IRA prisoners the Irish language.[33]

In the aftermath of the shooting, gardaí conducted raids on a number of homes belonging to members of Republican Sinn Féin in the Munster area. According to a statement by that organisation, this was because the van used in the armed robbery belonged to the Republican Sinn Féin Treasurer and Public Relations Officer (PRO) for Clare. It was allegedly stolen and used by Hehir and his accomplice 'as a deliberate attempt to shift responsibility for the Caher post office raid onto Republican Sinn Féin members'. The statement went on to express sympathy with the widow and children of Hehir.[34]

Several months before Hehir's death, another funeral had witnessed a large turnout of republicans from both sides of the border. Joe Keohane died on 5 January at the age of sixty-nine in his native County Kerry. As noted in the previous volume of this study, Keohane was a household name in the country due to his GAA record and is considered one of the football greats. He had served as an officer in the Irish Defence Forces and, when the attacks on nationalist areas of Northern Ireland took place in August 1969, he was a reserve officer in the FCA. In 1971, Keohane was arrested by Military Intelligence and subsequently court-martialled on thirteen charges including misappropriation of rounds. He was found guilty on nine of the charges, severely reprimanded, discharged and fined.[35] During the following decade he did not play any significant political public role, and his next major public appearances were when he canvassed for H-Block candidate Joe McDonnell in 1981. Obituaries for Keohane appeared in *An Phoblacht* and Republican Sinn Féin's *Saoirse* newspaper, the former taking up most of a page. That obituary noted cryptically: 'From the republican perspective, the enormity of his contribution for the present will have to remain unwritten. But when the time comes to record the deeds of those who have helped in finally securing Irish freedom, the name of Joe Keohane will figure prominently.'[36]

Later that year, IRA informer and fellow Kerryman Sean O'Callaghan walked into a police station in Tunbridge Wells and confessed his role in several IRA killings in County Tyrone during the 1970s. O'Callaghan had disappeared from Tralee in 1985, reportedly spending the interim period in Holland, France, Germany, Australia and America, according to his own account.[37] O'Callaghan was sentenced to several life sentences but was released in 1996 upon being granted a Royal Prerogative of Mercy. Following his release, he collaborated with journalist Liam Clarke on a memoir, *The*

Informer. In that book and subsequent media appearances over the years, O'Callaghan considerably amplified his status in the IRA. It should be noted that he was most likely O/C for Kerry at the time he went missing and his disappearance led to a number of arms dumps being hurriedly moved in the area. According to a former IRA Director of Intelligence, O'Callaghan had a known drink problem and was 'under investigation for missing cash at the time he absconded'.[38] Another account corroborates the claim about O'Callaghan's drinking problem, leading to his not being trusted by many in the area.[39] Given the animosity that any informer generates in republican circles, particularly one who subsequently courted a media profile, the veracity of these claims cannot be confirmed.

Garda Pressure

The unsuccessful post office robbery that led to the death of Hugh Hehir was not the only failed IRA raid in the area in 1988. In October, gardaí foiled an armed robbery at the greyhound stadium on the outskirts of Limerick city. That operation was carried out by a combined unit of Limerick and north Kerry volunteers. According to court accounts, two employees at the track were carrying the night's takings of £7,900 to a safe when they were confronted by armed and masked men. The track employees were struck by the men and shots were fired into the air to disorient and frighten the employees before the cash was taken. As the IRA unit got into an escape vehicle, two garda detectives who were on the scene fired warning shots over the roof of the car. The men exited the vehicle and surrendered, before being arrested. They were later charged with possession of firearms and ammunition with intent to endanger life, and of armed robbery. Three of them received prison sentences, ranging from three to nine years, while a fourth, younger man received a suspended sentence after giving an undertaking that he would sever his connections with subversive organisations. As the sentences were read out, the men shouted 'Tiocfaidh Ár Lá' to cheers and applause from the public gallery. After passing sentence, the presiding judge paid tribute to the gardaí on the scene, remarking that their intervention, against four men who were 'armed to the teeth' was 'an act of extraordinary courage'.[40]

Garda pressure on republican activists continued to extend to members of the Provisionals' political wing during this period. Following the jailing of

Sinn Féin member Don O'Leary the previous year for possession of a poster depicting an IRA volunteer, a 'Release Don O'Leary Campaign' was initiated across the state, being particularly strong in Munster. In March, armed gardaí raided seven homes in Shannon following the painting of fifteen 'Release Don O'Leary' slogans on walls around the town.[41] Locals described the raids as 'an indiscriminate act of revenge'.[42] Those whose homes were raided included the treasurer, secretary and PRO of the local branch of the National Association of Tenants Organisation. In June, a leading member of the campaign in Cork city was arrested and charged with the same offence as O'Leary: possession of an incriminating document. The 'document' was another republican poster, which was being sold openly from the city's Sinn Féin office for several months. Shortly after this, a third member of the campaign was arrested in Cork city on the same charge. According to *An Phoblacht*, legislation was such that the charge of 'possession of an incriminating document' automatically carried a secondary charge of IRA membership. Thus, if charged with possession of an incriminating document, the onus was then on a defendant to beat a charge of IRA membership in court. Also in June, Donegal Sinn Féin councillor Liam McElhinney received a five-year jail sentence for incitement to join the IRA. The charge originated from McElhinney's appearance at an Easter commemoration in Drumboe, County Donegal, in 1987, in which he expressed support for the IRA's campaign. One of the three judges presiding in that case had also presided at Don O'Leary's trial.

The old accusation that gardaí were targeting Sinn Féin organisers in order to fish for information on republican activists returned in 1988. In April, eight armed members of the Garda Special Task Force raided the Nenagh home of Brian Smith, Sinn Féin's North Tipperary Comhairle Limistéar chairperson. Smith was arrested and the Task Force confiscated large amounts of Sinn Féin documents, including names and addresses of party members in the region. In September, over a dozen homes were raided in one Dundalk housing estate over the course of a week. No arrests were made, and no arms or explosives discovered. Earlier in the year, over 400 members of Concerned Parents Against Drugs staged a picket for several hours outside Ronanstown Garda Station in Dublin following the arrest of eleven of its members. Several months later, four of the picketers, all of whom were members of Sinn Féin, received court summonses. In a Dáil response to an opposition request for information on numbers arrested and charged under Section 30 of the Offences Against the State Act, Minister for Justice Gerry Collins stated that over 21,000 arrests had been made under the Act between 1972 and 1986. Charges followed in only 17 per cent of arrests. The increase in arrests year on year continued to be alarming. In 1986 there were 2,387 arrests as compared with 1972, by far the most violent and destructive year of the 'Troubles', when there had been 229 arrests.[43] While questions and concerns regarding the use or misuse of far-reaching legalisation such as the Offences Against the State Act dogged the state throughout all decades of the 'Troubles', there were other misfires on the part of the state regarding action against republican activists.

High-Profile Extraditions and Extradition Attempts

In January 1988, H-Block escapees Anthony Kelly and James Joseph Clarke appeared in the Special Criminal Court on charges of unlawful possession of a pistol with intent to endanger life and of assaulting a garda. The two men had been discovered during a garda search of a house in Kilbarrack as part of Operation Mallard. According to court accounts, Clarke had pointed a gun at Garda Gerard Black and told him, 'I'll blow your fucking head off.'[44] This followed on from what was described as a 'vicious melee' between the two defendants and gardaí in the hallway of the home. At the time of the trial, Kelly was already serving a seven-year jail sentence for possession of a rifle and explosives in County Donegal in 1985. Clarke was sentenced to seven years' imprisonment for possession of the pistol and assaulting a garda, while Kelly received an eighteen-month sentence on the latter charge.[45]

In the same month that Kelly and Clarke appeared in the Special Criminal Court, the Supreme Court in Dublin was processing the case of another H-Block escapee. Robert Russell was arrested in May 1984 when armed gardaí surrounded a house in Ballymun where he had been staying. He had previously been sentenced to three concurrent twenty-year prison sentences in Northern Ireland for charges that included the attempted murder of an RUC superintendent. While imprisoned in the South he challenged an extradition warrant, triggering a legal battle that went on for several years. During this period, Russell took part in the failed 1985 prison escape at Portlaoise. Finally, in January 1988, in a judgment of three to two, the Supreme Court determined that Russell should be extradited to Northern Ireland. As reported by *An Phoblacht* on the front page of that newspaper:

> In an extraordinary judgement this week, the Dublin Supreme Court upheld the extradition order against Belfast republican Robert Russell and ruled that to carry out a policy of re-uniting Ireland without the approval of the Dublin government is to subvert the 26-County Constitution ... This highly controversial ruling was reached by three of the five Supreme Court judges, with the other two dissenting strongly. The decision of the divided court, coming in the wake of last December's Extradition Act, now copperfastens the ending of the political exceptions in extradition cases.[46]

It could be expected that the Provisionals' own publication would challenge this ruling. However, concerns were expressed over the decision in mainstream media too. A 'Special Legal Correspondent' for *The Irish Times* wrote a piece entitled 'Demise of the political offence', noting that the judgment meant:

> ... to take up arms with a view to reintegrating the 'national territory' by this means was to subvert the Constitution. Article 6 provided that all such issues of national policy (which included how, and by what means, the national territory should be re-integrated) were reserved to the Government and Dáil and to take up arms to achieve that end was to violate a democratically arrived national policy and, hence, to subvert the Constitution.[47]

The two dissenting judges did not accept this logic, stating that there was no evidence that Russell intended to subvert the Constitution. Further, the judgment prioritised the organisational membership of a defendant over their actions when reaching a decision. That is, even if Russell had not committed any violent crimes, simply by being a member of the IRA he was subverting the Constitution and thus could not claim political asylum. This was a far-removed ruling from that used to determine Dominic McGlinchey's extradition several years earlier. On that occasion, the decision to refuse to classify McGlinchey's actions as 'political offences' had rested on the extremity of the violence used in those actions.

The *Irish Times* piece pointed out further inconsistencies in the judgment, stating that it would 'result in a curious anomaly whereby members of Loyalist paramilitaries could still avail of the political offence exception … but members of organisations such as the IRA and INLA would be precluded from doing so'.[48] Organisations such as the UVF and UDA carried out violent attacks in the Republic during the 'Troubles', including the Dublin and Monaghan bombings which killed over thirty people. However, those organisations had no expressed policies towards the state and thus were not considered 'subversive'.

Russell's extradition was set for August 1988, on the day when he was due for release from Portlaoise prison. His continued imprisonment there was on foot of the 1985 escape attempt, for which he received a three-year sentence. Over the course of the year, *An Phoblacht* regularly kept a countdown towards the date of Russell's extradition on its front page, noting in a June issue: 'There are now 77 days to go before Robert Russell is handed over to the RUC on his release from Portlaoise. At any point between now and August 25th, Fianna Fail Justice Minister Gerry Collins has the option to release him.'[49] Shortly before the date set for Russell's extradition, another republican, Gerard Harte, was handed over to the RUC at the border. Harte, a native of Lurgan in County Armagh, had just served a four-year prison sentence in Portlaoise for his part in an armed robbery in Dundalk. He was wanted in Northern Ireland for several charges, including possession of firearms, arising out of incidents in 1979 when he was sixteen years old.[50]

A campaign to oppose Russell's extradition gathered momentum over the course of the summer, culminating in a large demonstration in Dublin a week before he was due to be extradited. This demonstration brought the city centre to a standstill for several hours.[51] Meanwhile, IRA units in the North were under their own instructions for the weekend of Russell's extradition. On the day before it was to happen, buses of protestors arrived at Ballymascanlon, north of Dundalk and several miles south of the border crossing of Carrickcarnon, where he was to be handed over. By 2 a.m., the crowd was perhaps 200-strong and included Gerry Adams and local Sinn Féin representative, Jim McAllister. Gardaí in riot gear formed a cordon and at 6 a.m., Russell was taken from a side entrance in Mountjoy prison and spirited to the border via a back road. An RUC helicopter from Jonesborough barracks awaited him. He had been moved to Mountjoy from Portlaoise prison the day before his extradition in a bid to foil attempts by republican activists there to physically block his removal, as well as a planned violent protest by over 100 republican prisoners within Portlaoise. Over the following twenty-four hours, the IRA carried out more than 200 operations across Northern Ireland. Vehicles were hijacked and burnt out in north and west Belfast, there were twenty-seven reported shootings and twenty-one bombings, over 200 attacks on police with five police vehicles and several barracks damaged. Twenty RUC officers and nine civilians were injured, and the police made forty-three arrests.[52]

Four days after Russell's extradition, *An Phoblacht* reported:

> Three more republican prisoners who have already served sentences imposed on them on Britain's behalf in the 26 Counties are now to become victims twice over of the Dublin government's collaboration with Britain. Tony Sloan, Michael McKee and Paul Magee have joined Robert Campbell on the extradition conveyor-belt. All four men are being sought by the RUC to serve long sentences handed down in their absence when they escaped from Crumlin Road Gaol in 1981.[53]

In the case of Michael 'Beaky' McKee, as well as several others, he was tried twice for the same crime. First in the South, under the Criminal Law (Jurisdiction) Act, and then again in the North after extradition, having already served a prison sentence for the crime in Portlaoise.[54]

While the Russell dispute was unfolding, another extradition storm cloud was forming. In late June 1988, Belgian police raided an apartment in Brussels and arrested Patrick Ryan (58), a former Pallottine priest from Rossmore, County Tipperary. The raid was carried out on the apartment of a suspected IRA sympathiser following the killing of three British servicemen in the Netherlands. Inside the flat, police found bomb-making manuals and remote-control detonators. It was reported that Ryan also regularly resided in the Spanish resort town of Benidorm and, when arrested, was found to be carrying a large amount of money in US dollars and German deutschmarks. Ryan had previously worked as a missionary in Tanzania and London but left the Pallottine Order without notification at some point in 1974. He was believed to have lived in numerous European countries, as well as making visits to Libya, between that time and his arrest.

The Belgian government turned down a British extradition request as, under Belgian law, a person could only be extradited if the offence they were facing was also a crime in Belgium. In refusing the extradition request, the Belgian government said that the charges were described 'in a very imprecise manner' and did not 'constitute the offence of belonging to an illegal organisation'.[55] Ryan admitted to collecting money for the relief of Northern Irish nationalists, as well as campaigning on civil rights issues, such as opposition to the RUC's use of plastic bullets as crowd control. Danny Morrison acknowledged Ryan as a republican during this period but denied he was a member of the IRA or a card-carrying member of Sinn Féin.[56]

Although not intending to hand Ryan over to the British courts, the Belgians had no desire to try him in their own country. He was subsequently deported to the Republic of Ireland in November, arriving in a Belgian military aircraft. The British made an extradition request to the Irish government the following month, which was also turned down. In May 1989 Ryan ran as an independent candidate, though with Sinn Féin support, in the European Parliament elections for the Munster constituency. It was reported in *The Phoenix* that the party leadership, as well as Northerners in general, opposed his candidature, but that it had been proposed and supported by republicans in Tipperary and Kerry, who said they would run him with or without party approval. The opposition reportedly stemmed from Ryan's close relationship with Ivor Bell, as well as a number of republicans in the South who had sided with Republican Sinn Féin following the 1986 Ard-Fheis.[57] Although he failed to be elected, Ryan received nearly 31,000 votes, or 6.2 per cent of the total. According to one account, there was a surprise angle to that result, if correct:

> Paddy Ryan went forward for Munster, you know, he got a huge vote. He didn't make it, but it turned out at the time there were a load of guards around Munster voted, because they knew the guards had voted because of the postal vote, you know. And they knew that, somebody figured out that a lot of guards had voted for Paddy Ryan.[58]

In a BBC interview in 2019, the eighty-nine-year-old Ryan admitted to his involvement in 'over a hundred' explosions across Britain and Northern Ireland. He also claimed that he was the main 'channel of contact' between the IRA and Libya between 1973 and 1984, and thus was responsible for the re-establishment of communications between the two sides, which resulted in the massive arms importations during the 1980s.[59] Whether Ryan played as prominent a role as he claimed is unclear. As to that Libyan weaponry, while much of it remained safely cached in 'master dumps', gardaí continued to have some success in disrupting IRA matériel.

Further Explosives and Arms Seizures

Throughout 1989, gardaí made significant arms and explosives discoveries across the state. Early in the year, a major find took place at an isolated farm shed at Cadamstown near Kinnity, County Offaly. The cache consisted of 21lbs of Semtex, thirty-six mortar bombs, two rifles and a quantity of ammunition. That find represented the fourth major seizure in the Laois–Offaly area in recent months. As well as the Nore riverbank and Borris-in-Ossory finds noted earlier, a number of mortar bomb cases had been discovered near Ferbane in County Offaly, while an IRA training camp used for rifle and heavy machine gun practice was discovered in a disused mine at Rossmore on the border of Laois and Carlow. Gardaí believed that all four discoveries were linked to one IRA unit operating in the area.[60] The discovery of mortars in two of the caches was significant, as Northern units of the IRA had recently begun using the latest addition to their homemade mortar arsenal. This most recent version was called the 'Mark VI', being the eleventh iteration of the IRA's mortar development, and was far-removed from the primitive weapons the IRA had first begun experimenting with during the early 1970s. The Mark VI had an effective range of 500 metres and was first used against a British Army observation post in South Armagh in May 1989.[61] That same month, eight mortars were discovered by the RUC during a search of a garden in Dungannon, County Tyrone. Later in the month, gardaí came upon a van near Hackballscross, County Louth. It drew their attention when the occupants ran from it as the gardaí approached. Upon inspection, it was discovered that the van had been converted into a mobile mortar-launching platform, with the mortar tubes welded to the back. Similar improvised mortar platforms were used in the North as well as in an attack on 10 Downing Street in February 1991. Four mortar bombs with propulsion units, as well a range of other explosives, were discovered near Blessington, County Wicklow, also in May. Later that year, on the Wicklow coast five miles south of Arklow, locals found a barrel on the beach in the aftermath of a storm. Inside was a mortar launcher, tripod and ten mortar bombs. A follow-up search by gardaí along the beach led to the discovery of a second cache in the open. This had presumably been buried in the dunes but uncovered by the storm. That second find consisted of three mortar bombs and three launchers. Gardaí believed that, within their original burial places, the armaments would have been deep enough to have escaped detection by metal detectors.

In June, Paschal Burke (25) of no fixed address pleaded not guilty to unlawful possession and control of explosive substances at Ballinastoe, Roundwood, County Wicklow, at what was believed to be a mortar- and explosives-testing ground for the IRA. According to court reports, two gardaí on a routine patrol in this wooded and hilly part of the county discovered a piece of Wavin piping on a hillside about ten feet from the road. Inside the piping they found explosives. As the gardaí were making this discovery, several men emerged from behind a rock nearby and fled. The gardaí unsuccessfully gave chase, but later recognised and arrested Burke. Forensic evidence on his clothing was said to link him to the find, as well as car keys discovered on him which belonged to a car found near the scene. During the trial, it emerged that a garda had allegedly entered Burke's prison cell posing as a solicitor and asked about an incident that occurred in 1984, to which Burke was believed to be linked. Burke received a six-year prison sentence for the Ballinastoe discovery.

In July, four men were arrested following the discovery of fifty mortar component parts in Coolock and, later in the year, Joseph Doolan (44), a farmer from County Offaly, received a five-year jail sentence for unlawful possession of an incomplete mortar bomb, a propulsion unit and powder. According to Doolan, he had been approached by a man who wanted the use of a workshop in the midlands and was willing to pay £80 per week for use of Doolan's sheds.[62]

As well as mortars, gardaí made a number of other arms and explosives discoveries throughout the year. An arms dump discovered in the Manorcunningham area of County Donegal in May was reported to contain five rifles, a military assault shotgun, three handguns, over 2,500 rounds of ammunition, assorted combat clothing, eight drogue bombs, three conventional grenades, two-and-a-half pounds of Semtex, radio equipment and five timers. Several days later, gardaí launched a massive search operation in the north of the county centred on Lough Fern, near Milford, where they believed a large cache of arms explosives had been stored. Although the search was unsuccessful, a small underground bunker and some spent shells were discovered near Letterkenny. Earlier in the year, gardaí uncovered another underground bunker in the same area, reported to be relatively small, measuring six feet by four feet. In the same area, gardaí had already discovered over 1,300 rounds of ammunition hidden in a plastic drum in a car abandoned in a local quarry.[63]

During the same period, up to 100 gardaí backed up by the defence forces in Munster launched an intensive search operation over several days centred on the Woodcock Hill area of Cratloe in County Clare, between Limerick city and Shannon town. A twelve square-mile area was sealed off during the search, with all passing traffic stopped and searched. Historically, the area had been extensively used for IRA training camps and arms dumps stretching back to the 1920s, and it was still used as such during the 1970s. On this occasion, however, nothing of interest was discovered. The search caused some disruption to IRA activity in the area though, and there were fears within the organisation, perhaps exacerbated by the disappearance of Sean O'Callaghan from Kerry, of an informer within the ranks. In the aftermath of the garda operation, the room of a local pub was firebombed by the IRA, who claimed it was being used for garda–informer debriefings. The local IRA then issued an amnesty, calling on any informers to come forward and identify themselves. They claimed to be aware of three additional pubs used by gardaí to debrief informers. Whether or not any informers did avail of the amnesty, or indeed whether the search operation was due to information provided by an informant, is unknown, although there were reports of a man originally from Northern Ireland being held in protective custody in Limerick prison for providing information leading to the Donegal and Clare–Limerick search operations.[64]

While the major searches in these regions may have proved fruitless, in August gardaí claimed a significant victory with the discovery of the biggest bomb ever found in the state following a planned search operation in Omeath, County Louth. The bomb, an ANFO-type HME weighing 1,500lbs, was packed into three forty-five-gallon drums and was stored in a van adjacent to a house and some sheds in a rural area. It was reportedly primed for use against the RUC barracks in nearby Newry. Gardaí also discovered five drogue bombs and several timers in the van.[65] In December, Joseph Patrick Parker (67) was sentenced to three years' imprisonment for possession of the bomb. The presiding judge suspended a further seven years on condition that Parker renounce the IRA and their violence under oath. Parker, a former British soldier and internee, originally from the Ardoyne in Belfast, told the court that he had been approached by two men who claimed to be members of the IRA. The men had told him they were taking over his sheds for a few days and Parker did not object as he feared for the safety of himself and his family. The court also heard that a son-in-law of Parker had been shot dead by British soldiers in Belfast in 1971 and he himself received a suspended sentence in a Belfast court in 1977 for possession of a gun and ammunition.[66]

Border Activity

Elsewhere along the border, in January 1989, the IRA announced that they had 'stood down and disarmed' the West Fermanagh Brigade of the organisation. This followed on from a number of attacks by that brigade which caused considerable public criticism, including the killing of an alleged informer that month, the 'accidental' killing of a young woman in March of the previous year, as well as the Enniskillen bombing of November 1987.[67] Gillian Johnston (21) had been shot dead while sitting in a car with her fiancée outside her family home in March 1988. The IRA expressed regret for her killing, referring to it as 'a mistake' and claiming that her brother, a member of the UDR, was the intended target. When this claim was disputed by the Johnston family, the IRA acknowledged that her brother was not in fact in the UDR. The killing that spurred the disbandment of the unit was that of Harry Keys, a former RUC officer, in January 1989.[68] Keys had resigned from the RUC three years previously but was shot dead by the IRA outside his girlfriend's house in Ballintra, County Donegal. In the aftermath of the killing, *An Phoblacht* reported:

A former RUC man was shot dead by Volunteers of the IRA's Fermanagh Brigade on Sunday night, January 15th. The man who died was shot several times as he left his girlfriend's house in Ballintra, County Donegal at shortly after 8pm. In claiming responsibility for the attack the Fermanagh Brigade said the dead man had been acting in an intelligence-gathering capacity for the RUC and had been using his cross border trips to collect information on republicans in the Donegal area.[69]

This claim was vehemently denied by the victim's family, as well as security forces on both sides of the border. Local media referred to the killing as being the result of 'a personal grudge against [Keys]'.[70] Following the killing, the IRA launched an internal inquiry into the activities and intelligence capabilities of the West Fermanagh Brigade. The brigade, based out of Ballyshannon and Bundoran, reportedly had a core membership of seven men and one woman. It included within its ranks a Limerick man who was believed to be linked to the killings of both Keys and Johnston, and the shooting dead of two elderly building contractors in 1988 as they left Belleek RUC station. This man, based in Ballyshannon, was seen in the Ballintra area shortly before the attack on Keys. The IRA leadership was not satisfied with the explanations provided by the brigade for the killings in 1988 and 1989, and moved to disarm and disband the membership there. An additional factor in the unit's disbandment may have been the unwelcome interest their actions were attracting from gardaí. As reported by *Magill*, 'it is not insignificant that two arms finds took place in remote areas of Donegal in the days immediately after the [Harry] Keys shooting'.[71] Following the IRA's announcement, senior republican sources indicated to media contacts their confidence that the disbanded brigade would not re-emerge in a new form. This claim was treated with scepticism and derision by representatives from various political parties in the locality. In mid-March, there were reports of a new IRA unit being formed in the south Donegal area, though without some of the more rogue elements that had previously been involved.[72]

Concerns about Donegal were quickly overshadowed by an event which stunned the security forces on both sides of the border. On 23 March 1989, the front-page of *An Phoblacht* carried the headline 'RUC Reels', stating in the sub-header: 'The RUC is reeling after the IRA's execution of two of its most experienced and senior commanders in South Armagh.'[73] Around noontime on 20 March, RUC Chief Superintendent Harry Breen and Superintendent Bob Buchanan had travelled to Dundalk's Garda Station to meet with Garda Chief Superintendent John Nolan to co-ordinate on cross-border operations against smugglers. The meeting was not planned in advance, having been set up that morning in a telephone call between Buchanan and Nolan using a direct telephone line to Nolan's office. The two RUC officers arrived at Dundalk Garda Station shortly after 2 p.m. and left Dundalk at approximately 3.20 p.m. in a red Vauxhall Cavalier, a personal car owned by Buchanan. As the car approached the crest of a hill near the Edenappa Road, south of Jonesborough, they encountered an IRA checkpoint manned by members of the South Armagh Brigade. The following is an extract from the Smithwick Report, which investigated potential collusion between gardaí and the IRA in the RUC officers' deaths:

> two men in full combat clothing and carrying rifles got out of the [white] van and took up positions on either side of the road. At approximately 3.40pm one of these gunmen stood up and stopped three vehicles travelling towards the South. The occupants were taken out of their vehicles and made to lie on the road. Almost immediately a red Vauxhall Cavalier drove up and was stopped by the gunman on the road. The white van at this stage was parked about 20 yards down the road towards the border and then drove alongside the Vauxhall Cavalier. At this stage the red Cavalier started to reverse back and stalled in the process. The car was restarted and again the driver attempted to reverse back. Four masked gunmen jumped out of the van and commenced to open fire on the car. The car reversed back and crashed into the hedge. One witness told the Garda that the passenger got out of the car and waved a white handkerchief. A gunman ran down to him. Another witness describes hearing a loud burst of shots, then a pause, then two single shots. Two of the gunmen searched the car and took a briefcase or folder. They also took what appeared to be two small notebooks. All of the gunmen then got into the white van and the driver who never left the van drove north turning left towards the Kilnasaggart Bridge and over the border.[74]

Ballistics analysis later indicated that four weapons were used in the ambush: two Armalite rifles, a Ruger Mini-14 and an AK-47. One of the Armalites had been used in the killing of Dublin man Eamonn Maguire in September 1987. It was believed that the number of people involved in the IRA operation ranged from twenty to seventy volunteers and active supporters.[75]

In the immediate aftermath of the killings, there were concerns and accusations that a tip-off to the IRA from a garda or gardaí based in Dundalk led to the ambush. Within twenty-four hours, the Irish government was preparing to ask garda authorities to launch a top-level investigation into these concerns of collusion. The saluting of coffins containing the dead from the Gibraltar shootings had already led to suspicions about the Louth Division of An Garda Síochána. Of additional concern to security forces on both sides of the border were IRA claims that they had obtained confidential files from the car containing information on a network of informants in nationalist areas of Northern Ireland.[76]

Nobody was ever prosecuted for the killings of Breen and Buchanan, and the contemporary garda investigation did not confirm any collusion between its members and the IRA. However, a number of organisations, politicians, journalists and newspaper columnists continued to maintain that the IRA were acting on a garda tip-off. In 2013, Justice Peter Smithwick published the findings of a tribunal investigation titled: 'Report into the Tribunal of Inquiry into Suggestions that Members of An Garda Síochána or Other Employees of the State Colluded in the Fatal Shootings of RUC Chief Superintendent Harry Breen and Superintendent Robert Buchanan on the 20th March 1989'. The tribunal, led by Justice Smithwick, had been prompted by an earlier scoping report into the killings carried out by Canadian judge Peter Cory. On the publication of the later report, Justice Smithwick stated that he was 'satisfied there was collusion in the murders' of the two men. However, he applied quite an expansive qualification, in that his definition of collusion was:

> meant in the broadest sense of that word. While it generally means the commission of an act, I am of the view that it should also be considered in terms of an omission or failure to act. In the active sense, collusion has amongst its meanings to conspire, connive or collaborate. In addition, I intend to examine whether anybody deliberately ignored a

matter, turned a blind eye to it or pretended ignorance or unawareness of something one ought [to] morally, legally or officially, oppose.[77]

Smithwick's exhaustive tribunal found multiple accounts of garda mal-practice, including the completion of false passport applications, which facilitated three members of the Provisional IRA in obtaining false passports. However, there was no 'smoking gun' of collusion, nor anything close to that understanding in the deaths of the two RUC officers. Among the claims made in the report were those of a former British Army brigadier, who said the level of planning that went into the IRA operation could not have been enacted from a tip-off on the day of the ambush. Further, claims of the telephone line between Buchanan and Nolan being 'tapped' were rubbished in the report. Superintendent Buchanan was a regular traveller to Dundalk Garda Station and drove a distinctive car, making it entirely 'plausible' that the IRA could have mounted the operation solely 'on the basis of an established pattern of travel'. There were also garda reports that the IRA had a total of four roads connecting Dundalk to the border under surveillance for several weeks prior to the attack. This would indicate that they expected Buchanan to travel to a meeting with his garda counterparts at some imminent time, and that there was a finite number of routes he could travel. The higher estimation of seventy IRA members and supporters being involved in the operation was tied to this scenario.[78]

One garda was subject to intense scrutiny during the tribunal hearings and in media reporting of the same. Former Detective Sergeant Owen Corrigan had previously been named by MP Jeffrey Donaldson in the House of Commons, using parliamentary privilege, as the source of the tip-off to the IRA. Justice Smithwick summed up Corrigan as: 'vague, evasive and inconsistent. It is impossible to attach any credibility to his evidence in circumstances where he frequently provided one answer to a question, only subsequently to provide an entirely different answer to the same question.'[79] The RUC had had concerns about Corrigan for several years prior to the ambush on the Edenappa Road. Superintendent Buchanan had himself allegedly passed on warnings to garda counterparts about Corrigan associating with known IRA members in Dundalk. Although Justice Smithwick could find no record of this information being relayed to the gardaí, his report did reveal that a man named John McAnulty was the source of information to the RUC in 1985 about Corrigan allegedly passing information to the IRA.[80] Several months after the killings of Breen and Buchanan, the IRA's South Armagh Brigade killed McAnulty, claiming that he had been an RUC informant since 1972. This was denied by the man's family who said the IRA shot him for refusing to pay 'protection money'.[81]

Corrigan had had an active career with An Garda Síochána, being praised by one Special Criminal Court judge in 1982 for 'extraordinary courage' in tackling and disarming a man armed with an assault rifle after a 100 mph car chase.[82] In later life, he acquired a number of properties, including a public house and commercial property, ostensibly on a garda salary, pension and associated gratuity. For his part, Corrigan entirely rejected the findings of the Smithwick Report, stating that all his 'dealings with the Provisional IRA were for the purpose of gathering information and/or intelligence to support An Garda Síochána in defending this State and its people during the troubles'.[83] It is worth noting that those who had been most vocal in the media about garda–IRA collusion in the Louth–South Armagh area refused to appear at the tribunal, or were forced to significantly tone down previous claims. Toby Harnden, author of a book on the Provisional IRA's South Armagh Brigade, refused to appear at the tribunal. Justice Smithwick noted that he was 'extremely disappointed' with Harnden's decision, adding: 'notwithstanding that he was not prepared to give evidence before the Tribunal, he recently participated in a RTÉ *Prime Time* television report dealing with the subject matter'. Smithwick concluded: 'His non-attendance at the Tribunal means that it would not be appropriate to attach weight to the allegations contained in his book'.[84] Former newspaper columnist Kevin Myers, who previously wrote of 'the IRA mole in An Garda Síochána', was forced to concede at the tribunal: 'I may have stated it in a more authoritative way than I probably should. I probably wrote it as a fact where if I wrote the article now I probably would not write it as a fact'.[85] The earlier Cory Report had also referred to the allegations of Harnden and Myers as 'hypothesis' and 'speculation' and concluded that, 'on the basis of the Garda interviews with the authors and without any cross-examination of the authors these articles have been thoroughly discredited'.[86]

Fears of collusion continued to run strong in the South as the decade closed out. In July 1988 an IRA prisoner produced a pistol in a holding cell on the second floor of the Four Courts building in Dublin in an escape attempt.

The prisoner, Thomas McMahon, was serving a life sentence for the 1979 murders of Louis Mountbatten, Doreen Brabourne, Nicholas Knatchbull and Paul Maxwell. Gardaí were unable to determine how McMahon acquired the weapon, though it was believed to have been deposited in a lavatory at Portlaoise prison. Against protocol, McMahon had been allowed to visit the lavatory after he had been searched but before he and his escort set out for the Four Courts. There was thus speculation in garda circles that security personnel at the jail were in collusion with IRA prisoners.

Following the announcement of an investigation into the incident, the Prison Officers' Association expressed its confidence that its members would be vindicated by an inquiry, noting that prison officers were subject to similar allegations following the failed escape attempt of Martin Ferris and nine others in 1985. An investigation at that time had failed to establish any evidence against members of staff.[87] During this same period, *An Phoblacht* was reporting on rising pressure in Portlaoise, as 'Governor Ned Harkins and his officers continue to implement petty, vindictive and inhumane policies against republican prisoners of war.'[88] Unfortunately for the Prison Officers' Association, their confidence in the anticipated result of the investigation was not entirely borne out. In August 1988, it was reported that a prison officer based in Portlaoise was to be disciplined for his role in the incident involving Thomas McMahon. While there was insufficient evidence to justify criminal charges, the investigation found that the officer had not complied with security procedures at the prison during the transfer of McMahon.[89]

In June of the following year, Dessie Ellis was due to appear in Dublin's Bridewell Court to face an extradition hearing to Britain on explosives charges. On the day of the hearing, gardaí spotted a man sitting at railings outside the courthouse and approached him. James Flood (32) had his left arm covered with a jacket under which gardaí found a small plywood box containing a trigger device with wires running to a small depression in the wall of the building. A pound of Semtex had been buried in the depression. On the other side of the wall was the cell where Ellis was being held. Flood was arrested and, though refusing to speak during a lengthy interrogation, was subsequently sentenced to five years' imprisonment for unlawful possession of the explosive, an electrical detonator, a power unit and detonating cord. The arrest of Flood, a Coolock native, led to a series of garda raids in that part of Dublin the same evening. This led in turn to the discovery of an IRA 'bomb factory' manufacturing mortar components, noted earlier in this chapter.[90] The plan to blast a hole in the Bridewell Court to effect the escape of Ellis was reminiscent of a previous attempt in 1976. On that occasion, an IRA volunteer posing as a tourist with a haversack planted a bomb at an exterior wall of Green Street Court. Another bomb had been smuggled into the courthouse and was detonated, with the two explosions blasting an escape route for several IRA prisoners.[91]

Closing Things Out

By the close of the decade, *The Phoenix* was reporting forlornly on the continuing heroin trade in Dublin: 'With the most effective anti-drugs organisation in the city hampered by the absence of its key members, and the gardaí committed to spending more time and money preventing the CPAD from operating, the drugs problem looks set to continue flourishing.'[92] Inner-city communities as well as outlying estates continued to be ravaged by the drug epidemic. In September 1989, Harry Melia, a prominent drug-pusher and associate of the brother of gangland figure 'The General', was shot at his home in front of his girlfriend and a neighbour. While the shooting was initially believed to be linked to a feud that had begun with a public house affray several weeks earlier, gardaí subsequently turned their attention to the IRA and local anti-drugs movement. Four members of a local anti-drugs organisation, including a spokesperson, were arrested and questioned under Section 30 of the Offences Against the State Act, before being released. Melia and another man were later jailed for ten and eight years respectively for unlawful possession of firearms and possession of stolen jewellery.[93]

That same month, the activities of two IRA members in Munster led to a major manhunt by gardaí, severely disrupting republican activity in the area. On 18 September, two gardaí on mobile patrol spotted a van in a quarry at Birdhill, County Clare. On approaching the van, they saw a motorcycle parked nearby and two men, who proceeded to produce a handgun and machine gun and demand the keys to the garda patrol car, in which they drove off. The van and motorcycle were later identified as having been stolen in Dublin weeks earlier. Minutes after their escape, the two men used the patrol car to flag down a passing vehicle. The driver, James Foley, was tied up at gunpoint and taken with the men in his car on a near hundred-mile journey around the west Munster area lasting ten hours. They later abandoned Foley and his car at Curraghchase Forest Park in County Limerick before making a getaway on foot. Despite an intensive garda search and multiple roadblocks, the two men were not apprehended.

Descriptions of the men provided by Mr Foley led gardaí to believe that at least one of them was a republican from Pallaskenry, near Curraghchase. That man, Patrick 'Packie' Sheehy, was already being sought for questioning by gardaí regarding several armed robberies. In addition, the British had identified him as a person of interest following their discovery of a major IRA 'bomb factory' in south London the previous December. During a raid on a flat in Clapham, the Metropolitan Police discovered 150lbs of Semtex, a number of AK-47s and, hidden in an air vent, a list of the names and addresses of up to a hundred leading British politicians and other figures. Documentation was found leading them to suspect that Sheehy had been an active member of an IRA unit linked to the flat. He had been working in London as a plasterer under an assumed name at the time. When this link first emerged, it came as a surprise to gardaí in west Limerick, who had known him only as a minor Sinn Féin figure who had sold *An Phoblacht* locally. It is unclear what the two men had been preparing for when disturbed at Birdhill. There was speculation that they planned to carry out an armed robbery, while another theory is that they were planning to kidnap an executive from Guinness Peat Aviation, based out of Shannon town. The latter operation would have been unusual for the IRA during this period, as kidnappings had largely been ruled out following the debacles earlier in the decade. The use of a van and motorcycle seem superfluous for an armed robbery, however.[94]

By the end of 1989, garda seizures of arms and explosives were in the same vein as previous years, seemingly with no let-up (see Table 18).

Despite these finds, earlier in the year a number of senior gardaí had confided to the media their belief that the state-wide search for major stockpiles of IRA arms and explosives had 'lost its momentum' since Operation Mallard.[95] According to one account, by the end of the 1980s and despite significant use and seizures, the IRA still possessed half of the Semtex it had received from Libya, so three tons.[96] However, according to

Table 18. Garda seizures of arms, ammunition and explosives, 1989[97]

Quantity	Type
122	Firearms (including rifles, shotguns, machine guns, pistols, revolvers, etc.)
24,712	Rounds of ammunition (assorted)
2,070	Shotgun cartridges
227	Detonators
103	Magazines
85	Bombs of various types
1	Rocket
36	Mortar bombs
44.3 litres	Nitrobenzene
248	Cordtex (metres)
4	Telescopic sights
47	Fuse wire (metres)
12	Bayonets
390	Hand grenades
1,836lbs	Explosives (homemade and commercial, including Semtex)

the account of somebody who was instrumental in facilitating the Libyan importations, the total amount of Semtex that the IRA received was more than ten tons. This would indicate that the amount still available to them going into the 1990s was considerably more than three tons.[98] Significantly, prior to the IRA's arms decommissioning in the early 2000s, British intelligence estimated that they remained capable of building 2,000 bombs equivalent to the one that destroyed the Baltic Exchange in the City of London in 1992. That bomb was the largest explosive detonated in England since the Blitz and damaged over 200 buildings. Its financial cost was 25 per cent more than the total cost of the more-than 10,000 bombs detonated in Northern Ireland since 1969. In the aftermath of the 1992 bombing, insurance and reinsurance markets indicated to the British government that they could not accurately calculate potential loss exposure for any subsequent such attacks within the City.

As a new decade dawned, the IRA's capabilities continued to be formidable. In November 1989, Northern Ireland Secretary Peter Brooke caused outrage and consternation among unionists and the Dublin government when he stated his belief that the IRA could not be defeated militarily. Gerry Adams used the opportunity to claim it was now 'morally imperative that the British Government enters into dialogue, the objective of which should be the resolution of this long conflict'.[99] Brooke's statement followed on from the claim of the recently retired Commander in Chief of British Army land forces, Sir James Glover, that 'in no way can or will the Provisional IRA ever be defeated militarily'.[100]

Several weeks after Brooke's statement, an IRA unit of the South Fermanagh Brigade launched an audacious attack on a British Army outpost at Derryard, a quarter of a mile from the border. The unit first took over a nearby house, before driving a lorry up to a checkpoint adjoining the outpost. A truck fitted out with homemade armour and carrying a number of other members of the unit provided support. As the soldiers stationed at the checkpoint prepared to halt the lorry, several IRA volunteers opened fire, killing a soldier while the lorry continued up to the checkpoint. The driver then abandoned the vehicle, which partially exploded moments later as the driver fled, killing another soldier and seriously injuring a third. An RPG-7 was simultaneously fired at the outpost. A number of weapons from the Libyan shipments were used in this attack, including DShK heavy machine guns, grenades, AK-47s and a flamethrower. After making a concerted attempt to actually enter the outpost in order to plant a large bomb, the IRA unit only began their withdrawal when they came under fire from a returning army patrol. A helicopter accompanying the army patrol was forced to disengage when it came under fire. The IRA unit made their escape in the armoured truck, abandoning it near the border with an undetonated bomb on board. In a statement released after the attack, the IRA said their intention had been to 'wipe out the checkpoint completely'.[101] Several days later, in a new year's message, the IRA referred back to Brooke's statement: 'British ministers not only know in their hearts that they cannot defeat us but have been forced to admit it publicly'.[102] The Derryard outpost had been one of several built by the British Army along the Fermanagh border in the early 1980s in an attempt to curb cross-border IRA attacks in the region. In the aftermath of this and a similar attack at Annaghmartin the following year, the decision was taken to close a number of these forts.[103] The Derryard attack was both a brutal end to the year and a definitive statement by the IRA of its resolve and ability to continue its military campaign.

Conclusion

Difficult to Envisage a Military Defeat

As the 1980s came to a close, approximately fifty members and supporters of the Provisional IRA were serving prison sentences in Portlaoise. This was less than half of the number of republicans imprisoned in the South a decade earlier. In 1979, that number was closer to 130 prisoners. Typically, at any given time during the 'Troubles', the number of IRA prisoners in the prisons of the Republic of Ireland represented 10 per cent of all IRA prisoners.[1] Thus, in 1991, there were 488 IRA prisoners in Britain and Ireland, of whom fifty-six (11 per cent) were in the South. After two decades of violence, the 'Troubles' had already cost 2,965 lives, nearly 800 of those deaths having occurred during the 1980s. Included in this number were eighty-seven members of the IRA, many of whom died in British shoot-to-kill operations. Over the course of the decade, a number of measures were introduced North and South to tackle the IRA, supplementing efforts made during the 1970s. As discussed, legislation was introduced to further undermine republican financing and organisational abilities in the Republic. While still an emotive issue that could guarantee mass demonstrations in the South, extradition was essentially a fait accompli by the end of the decade. However, the outcome of any subsequent trial in Northern Ireland could never be guaranteed, and many republicans were acquitted in Northern Irish courts following extradition. With the threat of extradition now a constant, as well as the risk of being tried in the Republic for crimes committed in the North, Northern IRA members 'on the run' had to be extra careful if choosing the South as a so-called 'safe haven'. This state of affairs was far removed from the early days of the 'Troubles'.

Despite all these challenges, the Provisional republican movement arguably closed out the decade in a greater position of strength than when they had entered it. And not just the IRA. Ten years earlier, Sinn Féin had very much been the poor cousin within the republican movement. Gradual changes initiated in the post-1975 ceasefire restructure period had clearly shifted the balance of the relationship by the end of the 1980s. A measure of the party's strength or influence can be gauged through the lens of its perceived threat to both states on the island. At the beginning of the decade, the hunger strikes, the 1982 Assembly elections and Adams' winning of the Westminster seat of West Belfast were still in the distance. In the South, while the party had several elected councillors at the beginning of the decade, these were often long-standing and accepted members of the local political system, used to doing deals with fellow elected representatives across the political party spectrum. Changes wrought by the mass politicisation on the island as a result of the H-Block protests were viewed with trepidation by both Garret FitzGerald and Charlie Haughey. The election of two IRA prisoners to the Dáil in June 1981 was particularly alarming. Nothing like it had taken place in the South in decades. As FitzGerald later remarked of his own efforts, which contributed to the 1985 Anglo-Irish Agreement: '[It was] the rise of Sinn Féin that led me to contemplate and work towards an Agreement with Britain as the only way, it seemed to me, of blocking the rise of Sinn Féin …'.[2]

The party's ability to identify and seek to address local concerns saw them gain political capital in the Republic throughout the 1980s, most notably, the very visible involvement of members of the republican movement in the anti-drugs campaign in Dublin. The jettisoning of abstentionism in the South was the successful conclusion of a long campaign spearheaded by the predominantly Northern republican leadership, albeit with support from Southern members. From 1986, Sinn Féin's political potential, and the threat it represented to the Southern establishment, became much more real. Although the party did not actually break through to Dáil representation until the following decade, that potential – and threat – was always there. The seeming shift in garda attention to the harassment of Sinn Féin members appears, now as well as then, to have been at least in part a political use of the state's police force. The party was never a plausible existential threat to the state, and the government's swift row back from talks of proscription in December 1983 reflects that.

If the party was not a serious threat to the Southern state, there were very legitimate fears that the IRA could be following the interception of the *Eksund* in 1987. The seizure of the *Eksund* and its cargo caused massive reverberations through the corridors of power. Throughout the 1970s and 1980s, the IRA acquired modern weaponry, sometimes through large shipments, but primarily piecemeal. However, regular garda and army seizures and failed importations ensured that the organisation fluctuated between famine and not-quite-feast in terms of matériel. With the exception of some notable shipments, such as in 1972 from Libya, most IRA arms acquisitions had been quite small. The first of the new Libyan shipments in 1985 was larger than anything the IRA had ever even attempted to acquire to date, larger than the failed shipments of the *Claudia* in 1973 and the *Marita Ann* in 1984. Yet, that 1985 shipment was the smallest of the consignments from Libya in this era. Each successive shipment, up to the *Eksund*, represented an exponential increase in size and equipment. It was not simply the amounts that were significant either. Included in the shipments was the extremely powerful and virtually undetectable plastic explosive Semtex, as well as an array of weaponry capable of downing British Army helicopters. Given the size of the consignments, the South as a hinterland for the IRA was more important than ever. Put simply, the amount of Libyan weaponry was too vast to even be stored in dumps across Northern Ireland in its entirety.

As well as the threat the IRA represented in terms of sheer military capability, the danger it posed to the integrity of the state was demonstrated through its counterfeiting attempts, as well as an unknown but significant degree of infiltration of bodies such as the Irish civil service. It seems unlikely that the theft of 100 passports from the Department of Foreign Affairs in 1984 could have taken place without some assistance from within, for example. And while questions remain regarding the involvement of members of An Garda Síochána in the killing of RUC officers Harry Breen and Bob Buchanan in 1989, there were a number of other incidents where the state could rightfully suspect collusion. The theft of garda uniforms from Fenit in 1983 serves as one example. At the beginning of the 1990s, the Irish Army conducted an internal investigation into suspected IRA sympathisers within the force. One outcome was that a soldier based in the Dublin area was discharged for passing information on garda–army border activity to the Provisionals. In September 1991, a serving garda based at Henry Street in Limerick city was arrested and charged with passing information to the IRA regarding several imminent garda raids on arms dumps and training camps in the Limerick–Tipperary area.[3] Regardless of potential, however, the IRA never sought to represent or be, in practice, an existential threat to the Irish Republic. Even operations such as the 1983 counterfeiting attempt were intended to fill IRA coffers, not undermine the economic integrity of the state. Interestingly, in their own publication of 1990, the gardaí concluded that 'violent crime has not been a major feature of Irish life'.[4] The IRA's General Standing Order No. 8 specifically forbade its members from engaging militarily with the forces of the Southern state although, as detailed in this study, there were some terrible and tragic incidents when that order was disregarded. Nevertheless, hundreds of IRA volunteers were arrested and imprisoned in the South throughout the 'Troubles' without attempting violent resistance. This was a purely practical consideration.

The financial costs to the Republic of Ireland during the 'Troubles' were immense. While the state was just as eager to quash the IRA as their British counterparts, the difference was the environment in which they had to work. The legacy of the state's own celebration of its violent revolutionary past, as well as a sizeable population who continued to support or tolerate militant republicanism, meant they had to tread more carefully. The South had to increase staffing in the prison, army and police forces, maintain a heavy and costly border security presence, and compensate business and property owners for damaged property in a number of instances. Figures released in 2021 revealed that the financial cost of the 'Troubles' to the Irish state was far higher than it was to Britain. By the mid-1990s, security was costing the Irish state £200 million per annum, proportionately three times higher than the annual costs to the UK.[5] Despite all efforts at containment or destruction, however, North and South the IRA persisted. Indeed, as the 1990s dawned, they seemed as capable of maintaining their military campaign as at any other time since the early 1970s. The Provisionals' political nous and representation was also stronger than it had been ten years previously. What's more, the British seemed resigned to publicly acknowledging the futility of pursuing a solely military strategy of defeating the IRA. All of these changes would lead to a decade of momentous change for all sides in the conflict.

ENDNOTES

Introduction

1   https://cain.ulster.ac.uk/cgi-bin/tab3.pl (accessed: 20 January 2022). The cross-tabulation on the archive erroneously gives '13' for 1974, when thirty-four people were killed.

2   Gearóid Ó Faoleán, *A Broad Church: The Provisional IRA in the Republic of Ireland, 1969–1980* (Dublin: Merrion Press, 2019). See Chapter 2.

3   Paul Gill and John Horgan, 'Who were the Volunteers? The shifting sociological and operational profile of 1240 Provisional Irish Republican Army members', *Terrorism and Political Violence* 25:3 (2013), p. 439.

4   Allen Feldman, *Formations of Violence: The Narrative of the Body and Political Terror in Northern Ireland* (Chicago: University of Chicago Press, 1991), p. 222.

5   Raymond Murray, *Hard Time: Armagh Gaol, 1971–1986* (Cork: Mercier Press, 1998), p. 79.

6   *The Irish Times*, 28 August 2014; Brendan Walsh, 'When Unemployment Disappears: Ireland in the 1990s', Centre for Economic Research – Working Paper Series, www.ucd.ie/economics/research/workingpapers/2002/WP02.29.pdf (accessed: 16 January 2022).

7   *The Irish Times*, 8 October 1986.

8   Micheál MacGréil, *Prejudice and Tolerance in Ireland* (Dublin: National College of Ireland Press, 1977), pp. 127 and 247.

9   E.E. Davis and Richard Sinnott, 'The controversy concerning attitudes', *Irish Quarterly Review*, vol. 69, no. 274 (Summer 1980), p. 191. See also: MacGréil, *Prejudice and Tolerance*, p. 247.

10 Pádraig O'Malley, *The Uncivil Wars: Ireland Today* (Boston: Beacon Press, 1997), p. 260.

11 W.H. Van Voris, 'The Provisional IRA and the Limits of Terrorism', *The Massachusetts Review*, vol. 16, no. 3 (Summer 1975), p. 426.

12 K.J. Kelley, *The Longest War: Northern Ireland and the I.R.A.* (London: Zed Books, 1990), p. 57.

13 J.B. Bell, *The IRA 1968–2000: Analysis of a Secret Army* (London: Routledge, 2000), p. 38.

14   Desmond Fennell, *Heresy: The Battle of Ideas in Modern Ireland* (Belfast: Blackstaff Press, 1993), p. 198.

15   *An Phoblacht*, 18 July 1981.

16   Fionnuala O'Connor, *In Search of a State: Catholics in Northern Ireland* (Belfast: Blackstaff Press, 1993), p. 224.

17   *Hibernia*, 30 March 1973.

Chapter 1

1   www.irishstatutebook.ie/eli/1965/act/17/enacted/en/print (accessed: 25 July 2021).

2   *The Irish Times*, 5 and 8 February 1980.

3   Ó Faoleán, *A Broad Church*, p. 85.

4   Sean O'Mahony Collection, 12A 2980 (NLI).

5   www.newulsterbiography.co.uk/index.php/home/viewPerson/1791 (accessed: 26 June 2021).

6   *Hibernia*, 17 January 1979.

7   *The Irish Times*, 21 February 1980.

8   *An Phoblacht*, 28 June 1980.

9   *Hibernia*, 13 March 1980.

10   *An Phoblacht*, 15 March 1980.

11   *The Irish Times*, 3 December 1980.

12   An Garda Síochána Annual Reports, 'Report on Crime 1980', www.garda.ie/en/about-us/publications/annual%20reports/an-garda-siochana-annual-reports/1980-commissioner-s-report.pdf (accessed: 25 October 2021).

13   *The Irish Times*, 8 April 1980; *Hibernia*, 19 June 1980.

14   *Irish Independent*, 4 March 1980.

15   Foreign & Commonwealth Office, 87/1013 (The National Archives, Kew, UK – hereafter, TNA).

16   *The Irish Times*, 3 and 25 April 1980.

17   *The Irish Times*, 6 June and 2 July 1980; *The Irish Press*, 2 July 1980.

18   *The Irish Times*, 8 September, 17 October and 11 and 12 December 1980.

19   *The Irish Press*, 15 September 1980; *The Irish Times*, 17 September 1980; *Sunday Independent*, 14 September 1980.

20   An Garda Síochána Annual Reports, 'Report on Crime 1980', www.garda.ie/en/about-us/publications/annual%20reports/an-garda-siochana-annual-reports/1980-commissioner-s-report.pdf (accessed: 25 October 2021).

21   *The Tuam Herald*, 23 August 1980.

22   *Western People*, 6 August 1980; *The Irish Times*, 30 July 1980; *Western Journal*, 28 May 1982.

23   *The Connaught Telegraph*, 2 May 1984.

24   *The Irish Times*, 30 July 1980, 25 May and 24 July 1982.

25   Interview with 'interviewee A', Clare, 1 April 2011; 'Five days in an IRA training camp', *Iris: the republican magazine*, no. 7 (November 1983) (hereafter 'Five days'). See also: 'The IRA Speak Full Version', www.youtube.com/watch?v=HCenYr2VOMk (accessed: 13 July 2021).

26   *The Phoenix*, 13 January 1989.

27   'Five days'.

28   Ibid.

29   *The Irish Times*, 16 September 1988.

30   Interview with 'Tipperary republican', Tipperary, 18 February 2011.

31   *The Irish Times*, 6 August 1980. A garda spokesman in Carrickmacross later stated that there was 'no evidence found to suggest that the area was used to train men, nor had anyone been spotted running away from the scene, as a report had suggested', *Dundalk Democrat*, 9 August 1980.

32   Evelyn Brady, Eva Patterson, Kate McKinney, Rosie Hamill and Pauline Jackson (compilers), *In the Footsteps of Anne: Stories of Republican ex-Prisoners* (Belfast: Shanway, 2011), p. 189.

33   *The Irish Times*, 30 September, 5 and 11 December 1980; *The Irish Press*, 1 October 1980; *In the Footsteps of Anne*, p. 190.

34   *The Irish Times*, 19 June 1980.

35   An Garda Síochána Annual Reports, 'Report on Crime 1980', www.garda. ie/en/about-us/publications/annual%20reports/an-garda-siochana-annual-reports/1980-commissioner-s-report.pdf (accessed: 25 October 2021).

36   *The Irish Times*, 5 June 1980.

37   *The Irish Times*, 22 May 1980.

38   *The Irish Times*, 21 June and 15 July 1980.

39   *The Irish Times*, 16 September, 15 and 17 October 1980 and 28 January 1981. At one point, Grew was suspected of involvement in five armed robberies across the state.

40   *Garda ar Lár* (Garda Seamus Quaid), RTÉ One. Broadcast on 26 January 2009. Available at www.youtube.com/watch?v=7G9qGH5PhVY (accessed: 29 June 2021); *The Irish News*, 31 July 2013; *Irish Mirror*, 12 October 2014.

41   www.garda.ie/en/about-us/our-history/roll-of-honour/roll-of-honour-description/quaid-seamus.html (accessed: 1 July 2021).

42   Liz Walsh, *The Final Beat: Gardaí Killed in the Line of Duty* (Dublin: Gill & Macmillan, 2001), p. 102.

43   Interview with Mick O'Connell, Clare, 27 March 2010.

44   'Gaelic Athletic Association official guide', www.gaa.ie/api/pdfs/image/upload/wyb4qbqzii6vstod1ygg.pdf (accessed: 16 May 2021).

45   Desmond Fahy, *How the GAA Survived the Troubles* (Dublin: Merlin, 2001), p. 14.

46   Barry Flynn, *Soldiers of Folly: the IRA Border Campaign, 1956–1962* (Cork: Collins Press, 2009), p. 120; *The Irish Times*, 7 January 1957.

47   *The Irish Times*, 7 January 1957.

48   Ruán O'Donnell, *From Vinegar Hill to Edentubber: The Wexford IRA and the Border* (Wexford: Cairde Na Laochra, 2007) p. 49.

49   Ó Faoleán, *A Broad Church*, pp. 93–4.

50   Interview with Donal O'Siodhachain, Limerick, 16 March 2011.

51   Interview with Martin Ferris, Kerry, 22 June 2010.

52   Mike Cronin, Mark Duncan and Paul Rouse, *The GAA: A People's History* (Cork: Collins Press, 2009), p. 168.

53   *Irish Independent*, 25 March 1980.

54   *The Irish Times*, 9 February 1979.

55   *The Irish Times*, 16 August 1979.

56   *An Phoblacht*, 31 May 1980.

57   *The Irish Times*, 28 January 1980; *Irish Independent*, 5 January, 31 January, 29 March 1980.

58   *Irish Independent*, 24 January 1980; *Hibernia*, 24 January 1980; *Irish Press*, 31 March 1980.

59   *An Phoblacht*, 19 January 1980.

60   *The Irish Times*, 15 January 1980.

61   *The Irish Times*, 21, 23, 25, 26 and 31 January 1980 and 7 October 1985.

62   Foreign & Commonwealth Office, 87/1013 (TNA).

63   *Evening Press*, 9 November 1981.

64   *The Irish Times*, 27 October 1980.

65   *The Irish Times*, 4 November 1980.

66   *An Phoblacht*, 15 November 1980; *The Irish Press*, 31 October and 1 November 1980.

67   *The Irish Times*, 30 June 1980; *The Anglo*-Celt, 4 July 1980. The victim's surname is given in different sources as 'Elliot' and 'Elliott'.

68   Edgar Graham, 'Ireland and Extradition: A protection for Terrorists' (Belfast: The Universities Press, 1982).

69   *The Irish Times*, 4 August 1980 and 28 May, 29 May, 30 May and 4 and 5 June 1981.

70   *An Phoblacht*, 5 January 1980.

71   *The Irish Times*, 12 February 1980.

72   *The Irish Times*, 5 and 6 September 1980. *An Phoblacht* ran a story on the killing of Ross Hearst under the heading: 'Informer Executed', 13 September 1980.

73   Graham, 'Ireland and Extradition'; *The Irish Times*, 7 December 1983.

74   *An Phoblacht*, 9 December 1979; *The Irish Times*, 14 February 1980, 2 November 1981 and 16 March 1995.

75   *The Guardian*, 11 October 2010.

76   *Hibernia*, 22 May 1980; *Irish Independent*, 24 January 1980.

77   *Hibernia*, 15 May 1980.

78   *An Phoblacht*, 17 December 1981.

79   *An Phoblacht*, 8 May 2008.

80   Feldman, *Formations of Violence*, p. 161.

81   *An Phoblacht*, 22 December 1979. The official name for this organisation in time became the 'H-Blocks/Armagh Committee'. Throughout this book, the official name is used interchangeably with 'Anti H-Block'.

82   *An Phoblacht*, 8 March 1980.

83   *An Phoblacht*, 14 June, 9 August, 27 September and 8 November 1980; *The Irish Times*, 10 November 1980.

84   *The Irish Times*, 21 November and 8 December 1980.

85   *Irish Independent*, 11 and 18 December 1980.

86   Leonard Figg, 'Republic of Ireland: Annual Review for 1980', https://cain.ulster.ac.uk/proni/1981/proni_CENT-1-10-13_1981-01-21.pdf (accessed: 22 March 2021).

Chapter 2

1   https://northernsong.wordpress.com/2012/05/09/the-glover-report/ (accessed: 26 July 2021).

2   *The Irish Times*, 23 January 1981.

3   *The Irish Times*, 23 and 24 January 1981 and 9 May 2001.

4   Roinn an Taoisigh, 2014/105/461 (National Archives of Ireland, Dublin – hereafter, NAI).

5   *The Irish Times* 10, 11 and 14 December 1985. Quote taken directly from 14 December edition of *The Irish Times*.

6   Home Office, 4/4643 (TNA).

7   *The Irish Times*, 8 and 22 May 1981.

8   Home Office, 4/405 (TNA).

9   *The Irish Times*, 12 February 1981.

10   Roinn an Taoisigh, 2011/127/1120 (NAI).

11   *The Irish Times*, 7, 9 and 12 February 1981, 24 February and 6 March 1982.

12   Home Office, 4/4050 (TNA).

13   Roinn an Taoisigh, 2015/89/31 (NAI).

14   See, for example: *The Cork Examiner* and *The Daily Telegraph*, 17 July 1982.

15   Roinn an Taoisigh, 2012/90/1068 and 2015/89/31 (NAI).

16   Roinn an Taoisigh, 2015/89/31 (NAI).

17   Home Office, 4/4050 (TNA).

18   *An Phoblacht*, 31 December 1981.

19 *The Irish Times*, 20 April 1981.

20 Home Office, 4/4164 (TNA).

21 *Irish Independent*, 1 May 1981.

22 *The Irish Times*, 23 April and 2 May 1981.

23 *The Irish Times*, 25 March 1981.

24 *Irish Independent*, 18 December 2005.

25 Foreign & Commonwealth Office, 87/1126 (TNA).

26 There is no consensus on whose idea it was to nominate Bobby Sands for the Fermanagh–South Tyrone election, some claiming it was Jim Gibney of Belfast and others insisting it was Dáithí Ó Conaill. Gibney himself spoke of it being his idea in the 2016 documentary *66 Days*, but this is fiercely disputed by other republicans. See, for example, the discussion in Chapter 12 of Robert White, *Out of the Ashes: An Oral History of the Provisional Irish Republican Movement* (Dublin: Merrion Press, 2017).

27 Danny Morrison (ed.), *Hunger Strike: Reflections on the 1981 Hunger Strike* (Dingle: Brandon Press, 2006), pp. 135–41.

28 Ed Moloney, *A Secret History of the IRA* (London: Penguin, 2003), p. 209.

29 *The Irish Times*, 6 May 1981.

30 *Evening Herald*, 6 May 1981; *The Irish Times*, 7 May 1981.

31 *The Irish Times*, 7 May 1981.

32 *Irish Independent*, 7 and 8 May 1981; *The Irish Times*, 7 May 1981.

33 Interview with 'interviewee C', Limerick, 25 March 2011.

34 *The Irish Times*, 16 October 2009.

35 *Irish Independent*, 14 May 1981.

36 *Irish Independent*, 12 and 14 May 1981; *The Irish Times*, 16 and 18 May 1981.

37 *Evening Herald*, 13 May 1981.

38 *Hibernia*, 24 January 1980.

39 Interview with 'Limerick republican', Limerick, 17 September 2010.

40 'The fight goes on': tape-recorded memoir of Gearóid MacCárthaigh, Glucksman Library, University of Limerick 10tape_sideA01_T006.

41 Ó Faoleán, *A Broad Church*, pp. 62–3.

42 *Magill*, June 1981. Please note that due to funding issues *Magill* was sometimes published bi-weekly and sometimes just monthly. When monthly, the publication would only list the month of publication. This explains the inconsistency in referencing for this publication.

43 *The Irish Times*, 3 January and 30 March 1981.

44 *The Irish Times*, 31 March and 29 July 1981.

45 See *The Irish Times*, 4 August 1981. The Dungiven hurling team is now named after Kevin Lynch.

46 *The Irish Times*, 29 March 1982.

47 *The Irish Times*, 20 October 1982.

48 Fahy, *How the GAA Survived the Troubles*, p. 80.

49 Colm Toibín, *Walking Along the Border* (London: Queen Anne Press, 1987), p. 76.

50 Collated from Gerard Magee, *Tyrone's Struggle for Irish Freedom* (Omagh: Tyrone Sinn Féin Commemoration Committee and Gerard Magee, 2011).

51 Sean O'Mahony Collection, 12A 2980 (National Library of Ireland – hereafter, NLI).

52 Eamon Sweeney, *Down, Down, Deeper and Down: Ireland in the 70s & 80s* (Dublin: Gill & Macmillan, 2010), p. 233; Daniel Finn, *One Man's Terrorist: A Political History of the IRA* (London: Verso, 2021), p. 150.

53 Interview with Seán O'Neill, Limerick, 30 March 2011.

54 Interview with 'Midlands republican', Tipperary, 9 January 2011.

55 *An Phoblacht*, 4 April 1981.

56 *Evening Herald*, 13 June 1981.

57 *The Irish Times*, 3 August 1981.

58 *The Irish Times*, 16 July, 4 and 5 August 1981.

59 Dan Harvey, *Soldiering Against Subversion: The Irish Defence Forces and Internal Security During the Troubles* (Dublin: Merrion Press, 2018, Kindle edition), location: 2974–2978.

60 According to a later garda report, eighty-one members of the force were injured during two protest marches at the embassy. See: An Garda Síochána Annual Reports, 'Report on Crime 1981', www.garda.ie/en/about-us/publications/annual%20reports/an-garda-siochana-annual-reports/1981-commissioner-s-report.pdf (accessed: 25 October 2021). Dan Harvey claims 200 people were injured during the riot, with 75 per cent of these being gardaí, but provides no source. Harvey, *Soldiering Against Subversion*, location: 2510.

61 *The Irish Times*, 20 July 1981.

62 Ibid.

63 *An Phoblacht*, 17 December 1981.

64 See, for example: *The Irish Press*, 22 and 30 June 1983; *Irish Independent*, 10 December 1981, 29 June and 9 December 1983.

65 Agnes Maillot, *New Sinn Féin: Irish Republicanism in the Twenty-first Century* (London: Routledge, 2005), p. 76.

66 Brian Hanley and Scott Millar, *The Lost Revolution: The Story of the Official IRA and the Workers Party* (Dublin: Penguin, 2009), p. 427.

67 Interview with 'interviewee C', Limerick, 25 March 2011.

68 Interview with Kieran Conway, Dún Laoghaire, 25 September 2016.

69 *The Irish Times*, 14 May 1981.

70 *The Irish Times*, 25 July 1981, 27 and 29 April 1982.

71 *The Irish Times*, 27 May and 22 October 1981.

72   *The Irish Times*, 7 October 1981.

73   *The Irish Times*, 31 March 1982.

74   *The Irish Times*, 5 December 1981.

75   *The Irish Times*, 1 and 5 December 1981; *Evening Herald*, 1 December 1981.

76   *The Irish Times*, 5 and 11 December 1981.

77   Home Office, 4/5319 (TNA).

78   *An Phoblacht*, 26 January 1980.

79   *An Phoblacht*, 5 July 1980.

80   Ibid. This issue of *An Phoblacht* contained photos of bruising on the man. See also: *An Phoblacht*, 29 March and 30 August 1980 and 19 April 1984.

81   *The Irish Times*, 2, 6 and 7 November 1985.

82   *An Phoblacht*, 15 June 2006.

83   An Garda Síochána Annual Reports, 'Report on Crime 1981', www.garda. ie/en/about-us/publications/annual%20reports/an-garda-siochana-annual-reports/1981-commissioner-s-report.pdf (accessed: 25 October 2021).

84   Ibid.

85   Sean O'Callaghan, *The Informer* (Reading: Corgi, 1999), p. 149.

86   *The Irish Times*, 24 December 1981.

87   Roinn An Taoisigh, 2012/90/782 (NAI).

88   Compare: A.J. Wilson, *Irish America and the Ulster Conflict, 1968–1995* (Belfast: Blackstaff Press, 1995), p. 190 with Kevin Rafter, *Sinn Féin 1905–2005* (Dublin: Gill & Macmillan, 2005), p. 190.

89   Ó Faoleán, *A Broad Church*, p. 120.

90   Tim Pat Coogan, *The I.R.A.* (London: Harper Collins, 1995), p. 522; *The Irish Times*, 17, 21 and 23 October 1981.

91   Pat Magee, *Where Grieving Begins: Building Bridges after the Brighton Bomb – a Memoir* (London: Pluto Press, 2021), p. 78.

92   Interview with 'Limerick republican', Limerick, 17 September 2010.

93   Rafter, *Sinn Féin*, p. 115.

94   *The Irish Times*, 24 October 1977.

95   O'Mahony Papers, MS 44/169/2 (NLI).

96   *An Phoblacht*, 28 January 1980.

97   *The Irish Times*, 2 November 1981.

98   *The Irish Times*, 26 November 1981.

99   Interview with Pat Magee, Limerick, 11 October 2010.

100   *An Phoblacht*, 3 December 1980.

101   *The Irish Times*, 17 February 1982; *Irish Examiner*, 22 June 1982; *Leitrim Observer*, 26 June 1982.

Chapter 3

1   *The Irish Times*, 4 February 1982.
2   Ó Faoleán, *A Broad Church*, p. 83.
3   *Magill*, September 1984.
4   *The Irish Times*, 15, 16 and 20 February 1982.
5   *Belfast Telegraph*, 15 March 1982. Five years later, the South Armagh IRA successfully attacked and damaged the British Army base at Glassdrummond with mortars.
6   *The Irish Times*, 4 and 7 January 1982.
7   *The Irish Times*, 19 December 1979 and 8 March 1982. In 1984 Tuite reportedly received a particularly brutal assault in his prison cell during a search by warders: *An Phoblacht*, 14 February 1984.
8   *The Irish Times*, 13 November 1982.
9   *The Irish Times*, 6 and 7 January, 4 February, 6 March, 3, 8, 9, 10 and 16 December 1982.
10   *Magill*, 30 October 1982.
11   *The Irish Times*, 11 March 1982 and 25 May 1996.
12   *The Irish Press*, 25 March 1982.
13   Roinn An Taoisigh, 2012/90/820 (NAI) and *The Irish Times*, 18 March 1982.
14   Roinn An Taoisigh, 2012/90/820 (NAI).
15   *Evening Press*, 18 March 1982.
16   Interview with 'Tipperary republican', Tipperary, 18 February 2011.
17   Ó Faoleán, *A Broad Church*, pp. 54–6.
18   *Evening Press*, 17 March 1982.
19   *Saoirse*, June 1989.
20   *The Irish Times*, 30 August 1982.
21   Home Office, 4/5141 (TNA).
22   Ibid.
23   *Evening Herald*, 21 June 1982; *The Irish Press*, 30 July 1982.
24   Northern Ireland Office, 12/525A (PRONI); *The Irish Times*, 22 and 28 January 1983.
25   An Garda Síochána Annual Reports, 'Report on Crime 1982', www.garda.ie/en/about-us/publications/annual%20reports/an-garda-siochana-annual-reports/1982-commissioner-s-report.pdf (accessed: 25 October 2021).
26   Home Office, 4/5319 (TNA).
27   *The Irish Times*, 15 and 16 August 1983.
28   Harvey, *Soldiering Against Subversion*, location: 3593.
29   *The Irish Times*, 20 and 26 February 1982.
30   *The Irish Times*, 27 February 1982.
31   The party changed its name from Sinn Féin–The Workers' Party to simply Workers' Party in 1982.

32 *Magill*, 31 May 1982.

33 *An Phoblacht*, 7 March 1981.

34 *Magill*, October 1984 and 9 November 1983.

35 Gene Kerrigan, *Hard Cases: True Stories of Irish Crime* (Dublin: Gill & Macmillan, 1996), p. 130.

36 Ó Faoleán, *A Broad Church*, pp. 164–5.

37 *Magill*, November 1984.

38 Brendan Ryan, *Keeping Us in the Dark: Censorship and Freedom of Information in Ireland* (Dublin: Gill & Macmillan, 1995), p. 51.

39 Dáil Éireann, Written Answers, Offences Against the State Act, vol. 341, no. 2, 16 March [March] 1983.

40 *Magill*, August 1986.

41 *Magill*, 30 May 1985.

42 *The Irish Times*, 26 July 1983, 4 and 13 February 1988.

43 *Magill*, April 1986; *The Irish Times*, 26 January, 11 and 14 June 1983.

44 *The Irish Times*, 5 March 1983.

45 *The Irish Press*, 1 November 1983; *Irish Independent*, 1 November 1983; 'Portlaoise Prison, for security reasons ...' (Portlaoise Prisoners Relatives Action Committee, 1985), 1A 734 (NLI).

46 'Portlaoise Prison, for security reasons ...'.

47 *An Phoblacht*, 31 May 1984; *The Irish Times*, 26 May and 28 November 1984.

48 *The Irish Times*, 29 March 1983.

49 Walsh, *The Final Beat*, p. 125.

50 *The Irish Times*, 10 August 2013.

51 *Irish Independent*, 9 August 2013.

52 *The Irish Times*, 30 April 1984.

53 England-based units had sought GHQ permission to shoot warders following the death of hunger striker Michael Gaughan in 1974, though this request was denied. Ruán O'Donnell, *Special Category, The IRA in English Prisons, Vol. 1: 1968–1978* (Dublin: Irish Academic Press, 2012), p. 200. The Southern government also claimed to have received warnings that prison warders' lives were at risk in 1973, though none were attacked. See: Roinn An Taoisigh, 2004/21/05 (NAI).

54 *An Phoblacht*, 6 September and 1 November 1984, 7 March and 30 May 1985.

55 *The Irish Times*, 13 January, 10 February and 28 April 1982.

56 O'Callaghan, *The Informer*, p. 274.

57 *The Irish Times*, 17, 18 and 19 November 1982.

58 Tim Pat Coogan, *The Troubles* (London: Penguin, 1996), p. 229.

59 Home Office, 4/5568 (TNA).

60 *The Irish Times*, 9, 10 and 12 March 1983.

61 *The Irish Times*, 19 February and 18 December 1982.

62   *Sunday Tribune*, 9 August 1981. See also: Walsh, *The Final Beat*, pp. 184–5.

63   Rafter, *Sinn Féin*, p. 196.

64   *The Irish Times*, 5 February 1983; interview with 'Limerick republican', Limerick, 17 September 2010.

65   Northern Ireland Office, 12/525A (PRONI).

66   *The Irish Times*, 13 and 21 January 1983.

67   Interview with Seán O'Neill, Limerick, 30 March 2011.

68   *The Irish Times*, 9 June 1983.

69   *The Irish Times*, 11 April 1986.

70   *The Guardian*, 13 March 2004.

71   *The Irish Times*, 12 and 25 February 1983.

72   *The Nationalist and Leinster Times*, 8 April 1983.

73   *The Irish Times*, 15, 16 and 25 February 1983.

74   O'Callaghan, *The Informer*, p. 194.

75   Moloney, *A Secret History of the IRA*, p. 242.

76   Coogan, *The I.R.A.*, p. 523.

77   Interview with 'interviewee A', Clare, 1 April 2011.

78   Walsh, *The Final Beat*, p. 135.

79   *Magill*, 18 April 1985; interview with 'Limerick republican', Limerick, 17 September 2010.

80   *Irish Independent*, 15 April 1983.

81   *Evening Echo*, 14 April 1983.

82   *Magill*, 18 April 1985.

83   *The Irish Times*, 9 May 1983.

84   Interview with 'Limerick republican', Limerick, 17 September 2010.

85   Collated from *Magill*, 18 April 1985 and interview with 'Limerick republican', Limerick, 17 September 2010.

86   *The Irish Times*, 28 April 1983.

87   *The Irish Times*, 29 June 1983 and 10 July 1984; *The Anglo Celt*, 13 July 1984.

88   *Magill*, 18 April 1985.

89   *The Irish Times*, 9 May, 29 June, 10 July, 18 and 19 November, 6 December 1983.

90   Interview with Kieran Conway, Dún Laoghaire, 25 September 2016.

91   *The Irish Times*, 30 April and 14 May 1983.

92   *The Irish Times*, 16 August and 2, 5 and 7 November 1983.

93   Coogan, *The I.R.A.*, p. 257.

94   Foreign & Commonwealth Office, 87/1853 (TNA).

95   *The Irish Times*, 6 December 1982 and 27 September 1983.

96   Interview with 'Limerick republican', Limerick, 17 September 2010.

97   *Irish Independent*, 21 September 2003.

98   *The Phoenix*, 1 February 1985.

99   *The Irish Times*, 15, 18, 19 and 28 November 1983.

100   *The Southern Star*, 3 December 1983.

101   *The Kerryman*, 2 December 1983.

102   *The Irish Times*, 10 October 1984; *Leitrim Observer*, 24 December 1984.

103   *The Irish Times*, 26 November 1983.

104   *The Irish Times*, 11 October 1984.

105   *The Irish Times*, 30 November 1983.

106   See, for example, *An Phoblacht*, 19 January 1980, for a report on a series of raids and general harassment in the area.

107   A.J. Davidson, *Kidnapped: True Stories of Twelve Irish Hostages* (Dublin: Gill & Macmillan, 2003), p. 120; *Magill*, January 1984; Cormac Ó Suilleabhain, *Leitrim's Republican Story, 1900–2000* (Leitrim: Cumann Cabhrach Liaotrama, 2014), p. 359.

108   Uinseann MacEoin, *The IRA in the Twilight Years, 1923–48* (Dublin: Argenta, 1997), p. 578.

109   Davidson, *Kidnapped*, p. 121.

110   Harvey, *Soldiering Against Subversion*, location: 1410–1417.

111   *The Irish Times*, 21 December 1983.

112   *Irish Independent*, 15 February 2009.

113   Ó Suilleabhain, *Leitrim's Republican Story*, p. 162.

114   *The Irish Times*, 19 December 1983; *Magill*, January 1984; Davidson, *Kidnapped*, p. 123; Ó Suilleabhain, *Leitrim's Republican Story*, p. 375.

115   Foreign & Commonwealth Office, 87/1854 (TNA).

116   *Leitrim Observer*, 31 December 1983.

117   Ó Suilleabhain, *Leitrim's Republican Story*, pp. 373–5.

118   *The Irish Times*, 21 December 1983.

119   McGing's occupation is variously described in different newspapers as a teacher and a civil engineer who worked for several county councils.

120   *An Phoblacht*, 12 December 1984; *The Irish Times*, 2 November 1984.

121   Home Office, 4/5568 (TNA).

122   *Evening Press*, 16 February 1984.

123   *The Irish Times*, 10 May and 2 November 1984.

124   *The Irish Times*, 21 and 22 December 1983.

125   *The Irish Times*, 19 December 1983.

126   Walsh, *The Final Beat*, p. 146.

127   *Irish Examiner*, 17 June 2008; Walsh, *The Final Beat*, p. 152.

128   *Magill*, January 1984; Eunan O'Halpin, *Defending Ireland: The Irish State and its Enemies since 1922* (Oxford: Oxford University Press, 1999), p. 340.

129   *The Irish Times*, 30 December 2021.

130   *Garda ar Lár* (Garda Gary Sheehan).

131   Interview with Seán O'Neill, Limerick, 30 March 2011.

132 *The Irish Times*, 9 November 1987.
133 Matt Treacy, *A Tunnel to the Moon: The End of the Irish Republican Army* (Dublin: Brocaire Books, 2017), p. 44.
134 *Magill*, January 1984.
135 Interview with Kieran Conway, Dún Laoghaire, 25 September 2016.
136 *The Irish Times*, 2 and 20 December 1985.
137 *The Irish Times*, 20, 21, 26 and 27 June 1985.
138 MacCárthaigh, 'The fight goes on', 9Tape_SideB01_T006.
139 *The Irish Times*, 21 and 27 June 2008 and 11 September 2010.
140 *Irish Independent*, 17 December 1983.
141 Ó Faoleán, *A Broad Church*, p. 120.
142 *The Irish Times*, 21 December 1983.
143 *Irish Examiner*, 20 December 1983.
144 *Evening Press*, 20 December 1983; *The Irish Press*, 20 December 1983.
145 *The Irish Times*, 24 January 1984.
146 *Irish Independent*, 17 December 1983.
147 *The Irish Times*, 19–22 December 1983.

Chapter 4

1 *An Phoblacht*, 2 and 9 February and 1 March 1984.
2 *Magill*, September 1984.
3 *Evening Press*, 26 January 1984.
4 Foreign & Commonwealth Office, 87/1854 (TNA).
5 Foreign & Commonwealth Office, 87/1344 (TNA).
6 *An Phoblacht*, 2 February and 22 March 1984.
7 This man, John Hartnett, was later found guilty of falsely imprisoning gardaí. *Evening Echo*, 17 March 1984. Interview with Seán O'Neill, Limerick, 30 March 2011.
8 Interview with 'Tipperary republican', Tipperary, 18 February 2011. See also *Evening Echo*, 17 March 1984, where it states: 'Gardaí confirmed that McGlinchey was reported to have been seen in the Nenagh area.'
9 Margie Bernard, *Daughter of Derry: The Story of Brigid Sheils Makowski* (London: Pluto Press, 1989), p. 164; *Irish Independent*, 19 March 1984; interview with Seán O'Neill, Limerick, 30 March 2011.
10 *The New York Times*, 19 March 1984.
11 Interview with Danny Morrison, online, 13 September 2021.
12 *An Phoblacht*, 22 March 1984.
13 Roinn an Taoisigh, 2014/105/461 (NAI).
14 Roinn an Taoisigh, 2012/90/782 (NAI).

15   See: 'Letters to the Editor', *The Irish Times*, 20 April 1998; Alpha Connelly, 'Ireland and the Political Offence: Exception to Extradition', *Journal of Law and Society*, vol. 12, no. 2 (Summer 1985), pp. 153–82.

16   Roinn an Taoisigh, 2014/105/461 (NAI).

17   *An Phoblacht*, 2 August 1984.

18   Roinn an Taoisigh, 2014/105/461 (NAI).

19   *Magill*, 1 October 1985. Quinn was a Ballina native who passed off more than £10,000 in travellers' cheques in London; the money was then passed on to an INLA member.

20   Roinn an Taoisigh, 2014/105/461 (NAI).

21   Roinn an Taoisigh, 2012/90/782 (NAI).

22   Sweeney, *Down, Down, Deeper and Down*, p. 247; Sean Flynn and Padraig Yeates, *Smack: The Criminal Drugs Racket in Ireland* (Dublin: Gill & Macmillan, 1985), p. 108.

23   Rosita Sweetman, *On Our Knees: Ireland, 1972* (London: Pan Special, 1972), p. 37.

24   *Irish Independent*, 7 March 1980.

25   *Hibernia*, 19 June 1980.

26   Flynn and Yeates, *Smack*, p. 155; André Lyder, *Pushers Out: The Inside Story of Dublin's Anti-Drugs Movement* (Victoria: Trafford Publishing, 2005), p. 14; Barry Cullen, *Community and Drugs: A Discussion of the Contexts and Consequences of the Community Drug Problems in Ireland, 1976–2001* (Dublin: TCD Addiction Research Centre, 2003), p. 26.

27   *The Irish Times*, 23 September 1982 and 15 February 1984; 'The Press and the People in Dublin Central: Ronan Sheehan Talks to Tony Gregory, Mick Rafferty & Fergus McCabe', *The Crane Bag*, vol. 8, no. 2, Media and Popular Culture (1984), p. 45.

28   Flynn and Yeates, *Smack*, p. 157.

29   Ibid., p. 158; Hanley and Millar, *The Lost Revolution*, p. 448; *Irish Independent*, 6 October 1982.

30   *The Irish Times*, 28 March 1984; Flynn and Yeates, *Smack*, p. 234.

31   *The Irish Times*, 9 November 1982.

32   *Magill*, March 1984.

33   *Evening Echo*, 20 March 1984.

34   *Irish Independent* and *The Irish Times*, 1 March 1984.

35   *An Phoblacht*, 26 July and 9 August 1984. See also: *We Say You Have To Go*, RTÉ radio documentary, https://www.rte.ie/radio/doconone/1151050-we-say-you-have-to-go (accessed: 18 September 2022).

36   *The Irish Times*, 21 and 22 February 1984.

37 *Inner City Republican*, November 1983.

38 Lyder, *Pushers Out*, p. 41.

39 *Evening Press*, 15 March 1984.

40 *The Irish Times*, 14, 23 and 24 March 1984; Lyder, *Pushers Out*, pp. 51–2.

41 *The Irish Times*, 23 and 24 March and 28 July 1984.

42 *Irish Independent*, 21 July and 26 October 1985.

43 *The Irish Times*, 6 December 1983; *Irish Independent*, 16 December 1983.

44 Hanley and Millar, *The Lost Revolution*, p. 373.

45 Bill Rolston and David Miller (eds), *War and Words: The Northern Ireland Media Reader* (Dublin: Beyond the Pale Publication, 1996), p. 235.

46 *Magill*, Christmas 1986/7; *The Irish Times*, 20 November 1987.

47 Home Office, 4/5415 (TNA).

48 *The Irish Times*, 27 March 1984.

49 Lyder, *Pushers Out*, p. 50.

50 'The Press and the People in Dublin Central', p. 46.

51 *The Irish Times*, 28 March 1984.

52 See, for example, all February 1984 issues of *An Phoblacht*.

53 *An Phoblacht*, 22 March 1984.

54 *Magill*, March 1984; Flynn and Yeates, *Smack*, p. 255.

55 *An Phoblacht*, 5 April and 28 June 1984.

56 *Ballymun Bulletin*, November 1991.

57 Interview with 'Dublin republican', Dublin, 30 September 2010.

58 *The Irish Times*, 27 July 1985.

59 'Meeting Room and the Dublin anti-drugs movement of the 1980s', http://anarchism.pageabode.com/andrewnflood/meeting-dublin-anti-drugs-movement-cpad (accessed: 30 August 2021).

60 An Garda Síochána Annual Reports, 'Report on Crime 1983', www.garda.ie/en/about-us/publications/annual%20reports/an-garda-siochana-annual-reports/1983-commissioner-s-report.pdf (accessed: 25 October 2021).

61 *An Phoblacht*, 22 November 1984 and 7 March, 11 April, 5 September and 24 October 1985.

62 Cullen, *Community and Drugs*, p. 28 and interviews with 'Dublin republican', 30 September 2010 and Dessie Ellis, 1 October 2010.

63 Interview with Dessie Ellis, Dublin, 1 October 2010.

64 Lyder, *Pushers Out*, p. 312.

65 *Magill*, July 1983.

66 Gerry Adams, *Free Ireland: Towards a Lasting Peace* (Kerry: Brandon Press, 1995), p. 155.

67 Flynn and Yeates, *Smack*, p. 312.

68 *The Irish Times*, 19 June 1999.

69   'Republican Left', internal document, http://cedarlounge.files.wordpress.com/
      2010/08/rep-left.pdf (accessed: 30 August 2021).
70   Flynn and Yeates, *Smack*, p. 252.
71   Rafter, *Sinn Féin*, p. 204.
72   *Sunday Tribune*, 13 April 1986.
73   Interview with Kieran Conway, Dún Laoghaire, 25 September 2016.
74   *The Irish Press*, 30 January 1984.
75   *The Irish Times*, 30 January and 7 June 1984, 6 February 1985.
76   *The Irish Times*, 20 February 1985.
77   *The Irish Times*, 11 April 1984, 15 January and 4 July 1986.
78   *The Irish Times*, 29 March 1985.
79   Ibid.; Walsh, *The Final Beat*, pp. 169–70.
80   *The Irish Times*, 16 August 1984.
81   Until 1990, the death penalty was still applied in cases of 'capital murder', which
      included the murder of on-duty gardaí.
82   *The Irish Times*, 24 April 1986.
83   *The Irish Times*, 21 December 1984 and 9 April 1986.
84   *The Irish Times*, 1 March 1984.
85   *Magill*, November 1985.
86   Tom Inglis, *Truth, Power and Lies: Irish Society and the Case of the Kerry Babies*
      (Dublin: UCD Press, 2003), p. 120; *Magill*, October 1984.
87   Interview with Mick O'Connell, Clare, 27 March 2010 and 'Limerick Republican',
      Limerick, 17 September 2010. Joanna's mother's maiden name was Fuller, see:
      Report of the Tribunal of Inquiry into 'The Kerry babies case' (Dublin: Stationery
      Office, 1985), p. 13.
88   MacEoin, *The IRA in the Twilight Years*, p. 558.
89   Inglis, *Truth, Power and Lies*, p. 157.
90   The tribunal of inquiry into this case refused to equate garda prevarication with the
      'barefaced lies' of the Hayes family, instead referring to their mistruths as 'gilding
      the lily, or wishful thinking elevated to the status of hard fact'. *Report of the Tribunal
      of Inquiry into 'The Kerry babies case'*, p. 61. Adding to the civil war-legacy element
      to this case, Justice Lynch's father (also a judge) was a pro-Treaty TD and senior
      officer in the National Army during the Civil War who served in Kerry. *Kerry Baby*,
      The Mick Clifford Podcast, https://soundcloud.com/mickcliffordpodcast/kerry-
      baby (accessed: 18 September 2022).
91   *The Irish Times*, 30 November and 5 December 1984. Tensions were so high that
      one of the boarding crew actually fell overboard while getting onto the *Marita Ann*
      and had to be rescued by Ferris and Browne. John Crawley disputes the claim that
      there were grenades on board.

92   *The Marita Ann Story*, www.youtube.com/watch?v=JAa0_209kJw (accessed: 15 December 2021).

93   Mark Urban, *Big Boys' Rules: The SAS and the Secret Struggle Against the IRA* (London: BCA Books, 1993), p. 129.

94   *The Irish Times*, 21 June 1986.

95   *The Irish Times*, 18 April 1986.

96   J.J. Barrett, *Martin Ferris: Man of Kerry, The Authorised Biography* (Kerry: Brandon Press, 2005), pp. 156–60.

97   Foreign & Commonwealth Office, 87/1867 (TNA).

98   *The Marita Ann Story*, www.youtube.com/watch?v=JAa0_209kJw (accessed: 15 December 2021).

99   Interview with Kieran Conway, Dún Laoghaire, 25 September 2016.

100 O'Callaghan, *The Informer*, pp. 244–7.

101 *The Irish Times*, 19 May 1984.

102 Roinn an Taoisigh, 2018/68/59 (NAI); Toby Harnden, *Bandit Country: The IRA & South Armagh* (London: Coronet, 1999), p. 320.

103 *The Irish Times*, 20 June 1985.

104 *The Irish Times*, 28 November 1984 and 10 May 1985.

105 An Garda Síochána Annual Reports, 'Report on Crime 1984', www.garda.ie/en/about-us/publications/annual%20reports/an-garda-siochana-annual-reports/1984-commissioner-s-report.pdf (accessed: 25 October 2021).

106 *The Irish Times*, 22 December 1984.

107 Interview with Kieran Conway, Dún Laoghaire, 25 September 2016.

108 *The Irish Times*, 5 November 1984.

109 *The Irish Times*, 6 November 1984.

110 Eamon Collins, *Killing Rage* (London: Granta Books, 1998), p. 211.

111 Interview with Kieran Conway, Dún Laoghaire, 25 September 2016.

Chapter 5

1   Magee, *Tyrone's Struggle*, p. 318.

2   *The Irish Times*, 2 March and 20 February 1986.

3   *The Irish Times*, 13 February 1986.

4   *Sligo Champion*, 31 January 1986.

5   *Leitrim Observer*, 19 July 1986. A 2017 obituary for Richard 'Dick' Cryan, brother of Samuel, notes: 'Two of Dick's brothers, Sam and Pádraig, suffered imprisonment for their involvement with the Republican Movement throughout the 60s, 70s and 80s': *Saoirse*, November 2017.

6   *The Irish Times*, 20 June and 18 July 1986.

7   *Irish Independent*, 24 January 1986; *The Irish Times*, 27 January 1986.

8   *The Irish Times*, 27 May 1986.

9   *The Irish News*, 29 December 2017.

10   Home Office, 4/5141 (TNA).

11   Northern Ireland Office, 3/42A (PRONI).

12   Home Office, 4/7094 (TNA).

13   An Garda Síochána Annual Reports, 'Report on Crime 1985', www.garda. ie/en/about-us/publications/annual%20reports/an-garda-siochana-annual-reports/1985-commissioner-s-report.pdf (accessed: 25 October 2021).

14   An Garda Síochána Annual Reports, 'Report on Crime 1986', www.garda. ie/en/about-us/publications/annual%20reports/an-garda-siochana-annual-reports/1986-commissioner-s-report.pdf (accessed: 25 October 2021).

15   *The Irish Press*, 25 March 1985.

16   *The Irish Times*, 19 March 1985.

17   *The Irish Times*, 18 and 25 March 1985; *Mayo News*, 20 March 1985 and *Western People*, 27 March 1985.

18   *Western People*, 27 March 1985.

19   *The Irish Times*, 8 January 1997.

20   *Evening Echo*, 25 March 1985; *An Phoblacht*, 28 March 1985.

21   *Evening Echo*, 17 April 1985.

22   *The Irish Times*, 8 January 1997.

23   *Irish Examiner*, 26 August 2017.

24   *The Irish Times*, 30 April and 6 May 1998.

25   Interview with 'Interviewee A', Clare, 1 April 2011.

26   Interview with 'Limerick republican', Limerick, 17 September 2010.

27   *An Phoblacht*, 22 August 1985.

28   Foreign & Commonwealth Office, 87/2057 (TNA).

29   *The Irish Times*, 21 August 1986.

30   *Iris*, October 1987.

31   *Iris*, July 1985.

32   *The Irish Times*, 18 April 1984.

33   'Portlaoise Prison, for security reasons ...'.

34   *Magill*, 1 October 1984.

35   *An Phoblacht*, 1 August 1985.

36   *An Phoblacht*, 28 November 1985.

37   *The Irish Times*, 30 May 1986.

38   *The Irish Times*, 25 November 1985, 14 February and 30 May 1986 and 5 October 1988.

39   *An Phoblacht*, 28 November 1985.

40   Interview with Seamus Morris, Tipperary, 26 May 2010.

41   *An Phoblacht*, 5 September 1985.

42 *The Irish Times*, 22 October 1986 and 25 June 1988.

43 *Magill*, August 1986.

44 *An Phoblacht*, 19 December 1985.

45 *The Phoenix*, 15 February 1985.

46 *Magill*, June 1990.

47 www.irishstatutebook.ie/eli/1985/act/3/enacted/en/print.html (accessed: 21 September 2021).

48 *The Irish Times*, 20 February 1985.

49 Home Office, 4/7092 (TNA).

50 *Associated Press*, 26 February 1985; *The Irish Times*, 21 and 25 February 1985.

51 *Magill*, 1 May 1985.

52 *The Irish Times*, 25 and 26 February 1985.

53 *The Irish Times*, 21 November 1985.

54 *Magill*, 1 May 1985.

55 Home Office, 4/6333 (TNA).

56 *The Irish Times*, 15 March 2008.

57 *The Irish Times*, 27 April 1985; Tommy McKearney, *The Provisional IRA: From Insurrection to Parliament* (London: Pluto Press, 2011), p. 159; Moloney, *A Secret History*, pp. 244–5.

58 *The Irish Times*, 23 and 27 April 1985.

59 Interview with Kieran Conway, Dún Laoghaire, 25 September 2016.

60 *The Irish Times*, 21 February 1985.

61 *The Irish Times*, 22 June 1985.

62 *An Phoblacht*, 25 April 1985.

63 Interview with Danny Morrison, online, 13 September 2021.

64 *The Irish Times*, 11 October, 4 and 6 November 1985.

65 *The Irish Times*, 2 November 1987.

66 Roinn an Taoisigh, 2014/105/461 (NAI).

67 *The Irish Times*, 24 March 1986.

68 *The Irish Times*, 24 March, 2 and 9 April 1986.

69 As late as 1984, the Irish government had refused to ratify the convention and the civil service drafted a briefing note for government ministers explaining the reasons for non-ratification. Namely: 'because of doubts that the Convention agrees with generally accepted principles of international law relating to non-extradition for political offences': Roinn an Taoisigh, 2014/105/461 (NAI).

70 Dáil Éireann debate, Tuesday, 1 December 1987, vol. 376, no. 1. Both the act and amendment were voted into the statute book and Carron's arrest was one of the first to follow on from that.

71 *The Irish Times*, 17 March 1989.

72 *The Irish Times*, 7 April 1990.

73   *The Irish Times*, 14 and 15 November 1991.

74   *An Phoblacht*, 19 September 1985.

75   *The Irish Times*, 29 April 1986.

76   *The Anglo-Celt*, 1 May 1986.

77   *The Irish Times*, 15 August 1986.

78   Rafter, *Sinn Féin*, p. 144.

79   *Meath Chronicle*, 25 October 1986. There are some unconfirmed reports that the IRA held a General Army Convention sometime in 1974. See, for example: *The Irish Press*, 4 October 1986.

80   *The Irish Press*, 4 and 15 October 1986.

81   *The Phoenix*, 8 May 1987. See also, *An Phoblacht*, 16 October 1986.

82   John F. Morrison, *The Origins and Rise of Dissident Irish Republicanism: The Role and Impact of Organisational Splits* (London: Bloomsbury Academic, 2013), p. 126.

83   Interview with 'Limerick republican', Limerick, 17 September 2010; MacCárthaigh, 'The fight goes on', 10tape_sideA01_T006; David Sharrock and Mark Devenport, *Man of War, Man of Peace: The Unauthorised Biography of Gerry Adams* (London: Macmillan, 1997), p. 246.

84   *The Phoenix*, 7 November 1986.

85   *The Phoenix*, 21 November 1986.

86   *Magill*, July 1986.

87   'The Politics of Revolution', p. 18. Sinn Féin document, 1986, www.leftarchive.ie/workspace/documents/827-politics-of-rev-sf-86-2.pdf (accessed: 25 September 2021).

88   Text of Irish Republican Army (IRA) 'Green Book' (Book I and II), https://cain. ulster.ac.uk/othelem/organ/ira/ira_green_book.htm (accessed: 20 August 2022).

89   'The Politics of Revolution', p. 31.

90   *The Irish Times*, 29 October 1986.

91   Interview with Kieran Conway, Dún Laoghaire, 25 September 2016.

92   *The Irish Press*, 1 November 1986.

93   MacCárthaigh, 'The fight goes on', 10tape_sideA01_T006 and 10tape_sideB01_T006.

94   Interview with Pat Magee, Limerick, 11 October 2010; *An Phoblacht*, 28 August 1986.

95   'Brian Keenan, 1941–2008: A Republican Legend' (Dublin, 2008).

96   Morrison, *The Origins and Rise of Dissident Irish Republicanism*, pp. 141–2. Pat Ward had been left with permanent debilitating physical damage from his participation in a hunger strike in Portlaoise during the 1970s and died at an early age. Some accounts mistakenly attribute to Des Long the hitting of the table with a walking stick, hence the clarification in this account.

97   Robert W. White, *Ruairí Ó Brádaigh: The Life and Politics of an Irish Revolutionary* (Indiana: Indiana University Press, 2006), p. 302.

98   MacCárthaigh, 'The fight goes on', 10tape_sideA01_T006.

99   Interview with Martin Ferris, Kerry, 22 June 2010.

100 Henry Patterson, *The Politics of Illusion: A Political History of the IRA* (London: Serif, 1997), p. 188.

101 P.M. Currie and Max Taylor, *Dissident Irish Republicanism* (London: Continuum, 2011), p. 20.

102 Rogelio Alonso, *The IRA and Armed Struggle* (New York: Routledge, 2007), p. 122.

103 Speech by Ruairí O'Bradaigh, former President of Sinn Féin, opposing the motion on abstentionism (resolution 162), Sinn Féin Ard-Fheis, Dublin (2 November 1986), https://cain.ulster.ac.uk/issues/politics/docs/sf/rob021186.htm (accessed: 26 September 2021).

104 Ibid.

105 'The Politics of Revolution', pp. 12 and 20; *The Phoenix*, 8 May 1987.

106 Interview with Maurice Quinlivan, Limerick, 10 May 2010.

107 *The Phoenix*, 25 September 1986.

108 O'Mahony Papers, MS44/161/8 (NLI).

109 *The Irish Times*, 3 November 1986.

110 Speech by Martin McGuinness, then vice president of Sinn Féin, on the issue of abstentionism (Resolution 162), Sinn Féin Ard Fheis, Dublin, (2 November 1986), https://cain.ulster.ac.uk/issues/politics/docs/sf/mmcg021186.htm (accessed: 26 September 2021).

111 Interview with 'Limerick republican', Limerick, 17 September 2010.

112 Peter Taylor, *The Provos: the IRA and Sinn Féin*, (London: Bloomsbury, 1998), p. 338; Brendan Anderson, *Joe Cahill: A Life in the IRA*, (Dublin: O'Brien Press, 2003), p. 336.

113 *Leitrim Observer*, 3 November 1986; *The Irish Times*, 3 November 1986; Patrick Bishop and Eamonn Mallie, *The Provisional IRA* (London: Corgi, 1988), p. 448; Moloney, *A Secret History*, p. 289; Brendan O'Brien, *The Long War: IRA and Sinn Féin, 1985 to Today* (Dublin: O'Brien Press, 1993), p. 130.

114 Paul Bew and Gordon Gillespie, *Northern Ireland: A Chronology of the Troubles, 1968–93*, (Dublin: Gill and Macmillan, 1993), p. 202; Rafter, *Sinn Féin*, p. 133; R.W. White, *Provisional Irish Republicans: An Oral and Interpretative History* (Westport: Praeger Publishers Inc., 1993), p. 157.

115 Pat Walsh, *Irish Republicanism and Socialism* (Belfast: Athol Books, 1994), p. 238.

116 See: *The Irish Times*, 3 November 1986; *Leitrim Observer*, 3 November 1986.

117 *The Irish Press*, 3 November 1986.

118 Interview with Maurice Quinlivan, Limerick, 10 May 2010.

119 Moloney, *A Secret History*, p. 296. There are no sources in Moloney's book to support this claim. Moloney also does not explain the high numbers at ardfheiseanna during the 1970s.

120 Ibid.

121 *An Phoblacht*, 7 November 1985; *The Irish Times*, 3 November 1986.

122 Interview with Danny Morrison, online, 13 September 2021. The National H-Block/ Armagh Committee formally wound down in the autumn of 1982. Finn, *One Man's Terrorist*, p. 153.

123 *The Irish Times*, 5 November 1984.

124 O'Mahony Papers, MS44/162/5 (NLI).

125 Interview with 'interviewee C', Limerick, 25 March 2011.

126 *The Phoenix*, 6 July 1986, for example. Ed Moloney, who wrote for *Magill* in the years prior to the Ard-Fheis, acknowledged being duped by Morrison in this sense. See his introduction to White, *Ruairí Ó Brádaigh*.

127 O'Mahony Papers MS44/162/5 (NLI).

128 Interview with Tommy McKearney, Monaghan, 30 July 2013.

129 Andrew Sanders, *Inside the IRA, Dissident Republicans and the War for Legitimacy* (Edinburgh: Edinburgh University Press, 2011), pp. 201–2. M.L.R. Smith, *Fighting for Ireland? The Military Strategy of the Irish Republican Movement* (London: Routledge, 2002), p. 113.

130 *The Irish Times*, 3 November 1986.

131 An examination of the Easter commemorations for 1987 reveals that attendance was significantly higher at events in the Southern state as opposed to the North. See *Saoirse*, May 1987.

132 *The Irish Press*, 3 November 1986; *Leitrim Observer*, 8 November 1986; White, *Provisional Irish Republicans*, p. 157. Similarly, on the first Provisional Sinn Féin caretaker executive, just one of its twenty members was from the North; L. Slevin of Fermanagh. See *The Irish Press*, 12 January 1970.

133 *The Irish Press*, 10 November 1986.

134 *The Kerryman*, 7 and 28 November 1986.

135 Interview with Martin Ferris, Kerry, 22 June 2010.

136 *Leitrim Observer*, 8 November 1986; *The Irish Times*, 5 January 1987.

137 O'Mahony Papers, MS44/168/4 (NLI).

138 Interview with 'Limerick republican', Limerick, 17 September 2010. The Provisional IRA would issue such threats again eleven years later when the movement split over acceptance of the Mitchell principles. Interview with 'interviewee C', Limerick, 25 March 2011.

139 Morrison, *The Origins and Rise of Dissident Irish Republicanism*, p. 144.

140 Interview with NGA committee member, Dublin, 10 September 2010.

141 Interview with 'Limerick republican', Limerick, 17 September 2010. A *Sunday World* article shortly after the 1986 split reported that an unnamed former IRA Director of Operations, sacked after the kidnapping debacles of 1983, would become head of a new IRA. *Sunday World*, 23 November 1986.

142 *The Irish Times*, 3 November 1986. Republican Sinn Féin treasurer Joe O'Neill also reiterated this soon after the 1986 Ard-Fheis, *Donegal News*, 8 November 1986.

143 *Saoirse*, June and July 1987; interview with NGA committee member, Dublin, 10 September 2010.

144 *The Phoenix*, 22 May 1987; O'Brien, *The Long War*, p. 152.

145 *Saoirse*, June 1987; Magee, *Tyrone's Struggle*, p. 198. Gearóid MacCárthaigh also had close links to Tyrone, having operated as a Training Officer there during the 1970s.

146 *Saoirse*, December 1989.

147 See, for example, Moloney, *A Secret History*, pp. 314–16.

148 Interview with Danny Morrison, online, 13 September 2021.

149 See *Saoirse*, December 1991, where only a small number of prisoners are named directly.

150 Interview with Tommy McKearney, Monaghan, 30 July 2013.

151 MacCárthaigh, 'The fight goes on', 10Tape_SideA01_T006; interview with Danny Morrison, online, 13 September 2021.

152 Interview with Tommy McKearney, Monaghan, 30 July 2013.

153 Interview with Kieran Conway, Dún Laoghaire, 25 September 2016.

154 Ó Faoleán, *A Broad Church*, p. 80.

155 Ó Suilleabhain, *Leitrim's Republican Story*, p. 388.

156 Interview with 'interviewee C', Limerick, 25 March 2011.

Chapter 6

1 One history of the SAS's operations in Ireland notes the significant rise in shoot-to-kill operations following the collapse of the supergrass trials. It is possible British policy shifted in extremity following the failure of those trials. See, Urban, *Big Boys' Rules*, p. 162.

2 Rafter, *Sinn Féin*, p. 150.

3 Michael Laver, Peter Mair and Richard Sinnott (eds), *How Ireland Voted: The Irish General Election 1987* (Dublin: Poolbeg Publishers, 1987), pp. 67 and 126.

4 Treacy, *A Tunnel to the Moon*, pp. 44 and 47.

5 *An Phoblacht*, 31 December 1987.

6 *An Phoblacht*, 15 December 1979.

7 *An Phoblacht*, 31 December 1987. See also, *The Irish Times*, 20 November 1987 and 30 July 1988.

8   *An Phoblacht*, 31 December 1987.

9   Magee, *Tyrone's Struggle*, p. 362.

10   Foreign & Commonwealth Office, 87/3007 (TNA).

11   Ed Moloney dedicates a chapter to the Loughgall ambush and theories as to British intelligence on same. See, 'Death in Tyrone' in Moloney, *A Secret History of the IRA*. Mark Urban, in his history of the SAS claims that the informer was a local woman from a nationalist background, who was subsequently disowned by her husband and neighbours. Urban, *Big Boys' Rules*, pp. 236–7.

12   Interview with 'interviewee A', Clare, 1 April 2011.

13   *The Irish Times*, 12 May 1987.

14   *The Irish Times*, 11, 13 and 14 May 1987.

15   Department of Foreign Affairs, 2017/4/71 (NAI). See www.oireachtas.ie/en/debates/debate/dail/1987-05-13/3/?highlight%5B0%5D=collins&highlight%5B1%5D=cortege&highlight%5B2%5D=cortege (accessed: 8 September 2022).

16   *The Northern Standard*, 14 May 1987.

17   Compilation funeral and riot footage, www.youtube.com/watch?v=TdK6edhNV-k (accessed: 12 October 2021).

18   See, for example, the funerals of Derry IRA volunteers, Edward McShaffrey and Patrick Deery, where the RUC fired plastic bullets at the mourners and nine people were hospitalised: *The Irish Times*, 3 November 1987.

19   *An Phoblacht*, 21 January 1988.

20   *An Phoblacht*, 24 October 1988 and 23 June 1989.

21   *An Phoblacht*, 31 August 1987.

22   'That's the Sort of Me, Volunteer Martin "Doco" Doherty, 1958–1994', p. 5. For a report on their sentencing, see: *Evening Echo*, 8 March 1983.

23   Interview with Kieran Conway, Dún Laoghaire, 25 September 2016.

24   *The Irish Times*, 5 September 1987.

25   *The Irish Times*, 3 September and 2 November 1987.

26   *The Irish Times*, 3 and 5 June 1987.

27   *The Irish Times*, 21 and 22 July 1987.

28   Roinn an Taoisigh, 2018/28/2799 (NAI).

29   Roinn an Taoisigh, 2012/90/782 (NAI).

30   *Irish Independent*, 9 November 1987.

31   Foreign & Commonwealth Office, 87/2503 (TNA).

32   *The Irish Times*, 28 November 1987.

33   Interview with 'Tipperary republican', Tipperary, 18 February 2011.

34   Home Office, 4/7092 (TNA).

35   *The Irish Times*, 20 February 1985.

36   Home Office, 4/7092 (TNA).

37   Interview with 'interviewee C', Limerick, 25 March 2011.

38   John Horgan and Max Taylor, 'Playing the 'green card' – financing the provisional IRA: part 2', *Terrorism and Political Violence*, 15:2 (2003), pp. 1–60.

39   *The Independent*, 28 September 1992.

40   Interview with 'Tipperary republican', Tipperary, 18 February 2011.

41   *The Irish Times*, 17 July 1987.

42   *The Irish Times*, 15 May 1987.

43   *The Irish Times*, 19, 24 and 25 June 1987

44   *The Irish Times*, 6 May 1987.

45   *The Irish Times*, 30 January, 6 and 13 May 1987.

46   Home Office, 4/6926 (TNA).

47   *The Irish Times*, 5 November 1987.

48   *The Irish Times*, 4 and 8 April and 27 November 1987.

49   *The Irish Times*, 27 July 1987.

50   Foreign & Commonwealth Office, 87/2569 (TNA).

51   Home Office, 4/5141 (TNA).

52   Home Office, 4/7501 (TNA).

53   Ibid.

54   Interview with 'interviewee C', Limerick, 25 March 2011.

55   *The Irish Times*, 20 October 1987.

56   *The Irish Times*, 19 and 20 October 1987; *The Irish News*, 20 October 1987.

57   *Sunday Tribune*, 28 October 2007.

58   *The Irish Times*, 8 November 1997.

59   *Fortnight*, December 1987.

60   *Irish Independent*, 15 November 1987.

61   *The Irish Times*, 25 July 1991.

62   *Magill*, 31 March 1981.

63   *The Irish Times*, 24 November 1987.

64   Foreign & Commonwealth Office, 87/2509 (TNA).

65   *The Irish Times*, 24 November 1987.

66   Roinn an Taoisigh 2018/28/2175 (NAI); *Sunday News*, 26 April 1987; *The Phoenix*, 8 May 1987.

67   *The Irish Times*, 24 November 1987.

68   *Magill*, 1 June 1998. *Magill* refers to the AK-47 assault rifles as AKMs, a more modern version of the AK-47, but the latter term is used throughout this work as the general principle of both weapons is the same and the IRA possessed both.

69   Interview with 'Tipperary republican', Tipperary, 18 February 2011.

70   Interview with 'interviewee C', Limerick, 25 March 2011.

71   Ibid.

72   Dáil Éireann private notice questions, arms search by security forces, 1987 (375/1987), 24 November 1987.

73   *Irish Independent*, 24 November 1987.

74   *The Irish Times*, 25 December 1987.

75   *The Irish Times*, 25 and 11 December 1987.

76   *Saoirse – South City Republican*, January 1988.

77   Interview with Mick O'Connell, Clare, 27 March 2010.

78   *Irish Independent*, 24 November 1987.

79   *Irish Independent*, 28 November 1987.

80   *The Phoenix*, 18 December 1987.

81   Foreign & Commonwealth Office, 87/2503 (TNA); *The Phoenix*, 23 September 1988; *The Irish Times*, 22 December 1987.

82   *Irish Independent*, 25, 27 and 28 November and 11 December 1987.

83   A.R. Oppenheimer, *IRA, The Bombs and Bullets: A History of Deadly Ingenuity* (Dublin: Irish Academic Press, 2010), p. 143.

84   Foreign & Commonwealth Office, 87/2503 (TNA).

85   Foreign & Commonwealth Office 87/2503 (TNA).

86   *The Irish Times*, 26 August 2015.

87   *United Press International*, 6 March 1991.

88   *The Irish Times*, 25 November 1987.

89   *The Irish Times*, 18 April 1989.

90   *The Irish Times*, 4 March, 14 March and 14 April 1989, 15 March 1990 and 8 June 1992.

Chapter 7

1   Interview with 'interviewee C', Limerick, 25 March 2011.

2   Department of Foreign Affairs, 2018/28/2799 (NAI); *The Irish Times*, 4 February 1988.

3   *Irish Independent*, 25 February 1988; *The Irish Times*, 24 and 25 February 1988.

4   *The Irish Times*, 29 February, 11, 18 and 19 March 1988.

5   *The Irish Times*, 16 July 1988.

6   *An Phoblacht*, 30 June 1988.

7   *The Irish Times*, 16 November 1988.

8   Foreign & Commonwealth Office, 87/3007 (TNA).

9   *The Irish Times*, 9 June 1988.

10   *The Irish Times*, 16 November 1988 and 15 February 1989.

11   *The Irish Times*, 8 August 1988.

12   *An Phoblacht*, 3 March 1989.

13   *An Phoblacht*, 2 November 1989.

14   Department of Foreign Affairs, 2018/28/2799 (NAI).

15   Interview with 'Tipperary republican', Tipperary, 18 February 2011.

16   *An Phoblacht*, 4 July 1985.

17   *The Irish Times*, 27 January 1988.

18   *An Phoblacht*, 28 January 1988.

19   An Garda Síochána Annual Reports, 'Report on Crime 1988', www.garda. ie/en/about-us/publications/annual%20reports/an-garda-siochana-annual-reports/1988-commissioner-s-report.pdf (accessed: 25 October 2021).

20   Roinn an Taoisigh, 2018/68/59 (NAI).

21   Northern Ireland Office, 8/3/4A (PRONI).

22   Ibid.

23   *The Irish Times*, 29 March 1989.

24   *The Irish Times*, 12 and 14 March 1988.

25   *Magill*, April 1988.

26   Written Answers, Saluting at Funerals, Dáil Éireann debate, Tuesday, 19 Apr 1988, vol. 379, no. 6.

27   *The Irish Times*, 1 and 7 March 1988; *Magill*, 1 October 1985.

28   *The Irish Times*, 7 May 1988.

29   *An Phoblacht*, 12 May 1988.

30   *The Irish Times*, 7 May and 5 October 1988.

31   *An Phoblacht*, 12 May 1988.

32   Ibid.

33   Denis O'Hearn, *Bobby Sands: Nothing but an Unfinished Song* (London: Pluto Press, 2006), p. 72.

34   *Saoirse*, June 1988.

35   Ó Faoleán, *A Broad Church*, pp. 62–3.

36   *An Phoblacht*, 14 January 1988.

37   *The Kerryman*, 2 December 1988.

38   Interview with Kieran Conway, Dún Laoghaire, 25 September 2016. O'Callaghan had been in contact with journalist Ger Colleran prior to surrendering to British police specifically to deny this embezzlement accusation.

39   Interview with 'Limerick republican', Limerick, 17 September 2010.

40   *The Irish Times*, 15 and 16 December 1988.

41   *Irish Examiner*, 27 February 1988.

42   *An Phoblacht*, 3 March 1988.

43   *An Phoblacht*, 14 and 28 April, 23 and 20 June, 7 July and 18 September 1988, 9 February 1989.

44   *The Irish Times*, 11 March 1988.

45   Ibid; *An Phoblacht*, 14 January 1988.

46   *An Phoblacht*, 21 January 1988.

47   *The Irish Times*, 23 January 1988.

48   Ibid.

49   *An Phoblacht*, 9 June 1988.

50   *The Irish Times*, 6 September 1986; *An Phoblacht*, 25 August 1988.

51   *An Phoblacht*, 25 August 1988.

52   *The Irish Times*, 27 and 30 August 1988.

53   *An Phoblacht*, 31 August 1989.

54   Interview with Danny Morrison, online, 13 September 2021.

55   *The Irish Times*, 6 July, 28 and 29 November 1988.

56   *The Irish Times*, 15 December 1988.

57   *The Phoenix*, 5 May 1989; *The Irish Times*, 28 November 1989.

58   Interview with Mick O'Connell, Clare, 27 March 2010.

59   *Belfast Telegraph*, 19 October 2019. Other accounts attribute this connection to Ivor Bell, which may explain the pair's closeness.

60   *The Irish Times*, 6 January 1989.

61   Tony Geraghty, *The Irish War: The Hidden Conflict Between the IRA and British Intelligence* (Baltimore: Harper Collins, 1998), p. 192.

62   *The Irish Times*, 2, 10 and 12 May, 9 June, 1 July, 22 November and 19 December 1989.

63   *The Irish Times*, 25 January, 1 and 5 May 1989.

64   *The Phoenix*, 5 May 1989; *Irish Examiner*, 5 May 1989; *The Irish Press*, 5 May 1989; *The Irish Times*, 5 May 1989.

65   *The Irish Times*, 29 August 1989.

66   *The Irish Times*, 13 December 1989; *The Irish Press*, 13 December 1989.

67   The Enniskillen bombing was allegedly primarily the work of the South Fermanagh Brigade, though the West Fermanagh Brigade did help bring the bomb across the border. See, *Sunday Tribune*, 28 October 2007.

68   The victim's surname is spelled variously as 'Keys' and 'Keyes' in different media.

69   *An Phoblacht*, 19 January 1989.

70   *Fermanagh Herald*, 28 January 1989.

71   *Magill*, February 1989.

72   *The Irish Times*, 25 January 1989; *Donegal Democrat*, 27 January and 10 March 1989; *Irish Independent*, 29 January 1989. It should be noted that ballistics tests on weapons found on the dead IRA volunteers at Loughgall indicated that they were used in every IRA killing in Counties Fermanagh and Tyrone in 1987. It may be that multiple IRA units were using the same arms dump, or perhaps those killed at Loughgall had previously played a role in the IRA in Fermanagh. If so, that role might have been one of relative restraint, or greater due diligence, given that the most egregious attacks by the Fermanagh IRA took place following the Loughgall ambush. See, *The Irish Times*, 29 December 2017.

73   *An Phoblacht*, 23 March 1989.

74   'Report into the Tribunal of Inquiry into Suggestions that Members of An Garda Síochána or Other Employees of the State Colluded in the Fatal Shootings of RUC Chief Superintendent Harry Breen and Superintendent Robert Buchanan on the 20th March 1989' (hereafter 'The Smithwick Report'), http://opac.oireachtas.ie/AWData/Library3/smithwickFinal03122013_171046.pdf (accessed: 25 October 2021), pp. 71–2.

75   'The Smithwick Report', pp. 107 and 439.

76   *The Irish Times*, 21 and 23 March and 27 June 1989.

77   'The Smithwick Report', p. 16.

78   Ibid., pp. 14, 89, 98 and 102–4.

79   Ibid., p. 353.

80   Ibid., pp. 141–2, 332 and 339.

81   *The Irish Times*, 20 July 1989.

82   *The Irish Times*, 5 February 1982.

83   *Drogheda Independent*, 10 June 2013; *The Irish Times*, 5 December 2013.

84   'The Smithwick Report', p. 212.

85   Ibid., p. 219. See *The Irish Times*, 12 November 1999, for Myers' original piece on the killings.

86   Cory Collusion Inquiry Report, https://cain.ulster.ac.uk/issues/collusion/cory/cory03gibson.pdf (accessed: 25 November 2021), pp. 38 and 43.

87   *The Irish Times*, 21, 22, 23 July and 3 August 1988.

88   *An Phoblacht*, 7 January 1988.

89   *The Irish Times*, 3 August 1988.

90   *The Irish Press*, 30 June and 1 July 1989; *Irish Examiner*, 2 November 1989.

91   Ó Faoleán, *A Broad Church*, p. 130.

92   *The Phoenix*, 30 June 1989.

93   *Irish Examiner*, 23 September 1989 and 14 July 1990; *The Irish Press*, 29 November 1990.

94   *The Irish Times*, 20 September and 3 October 1990; *Irish Examiner*, 5 January 1991.

95   *The Irish Times*, 6 January 1989.

96   Oppenheimer, *IRA, The Bombs and Bullets*, p. 85.

97   An Garda Síochána Annual Reports – 'Report on Crime 1989', www.garda.ie/en/about-us/publications/annual%20reports/an-garda-siochana-annual-reports/1989-commissioner-s-report.pdf (accessed: 25 October 2021).

98   Interview with 'interviewee C', Limerick, 25 March 2011.

99   *The Irish Press*, 4 November 1989.

100   *Belfast Telegraph*, 1 March 1988.

101   *Irish Independent*, 14 December 1989; *Fermanagh Herald*, 23 December 1989.

102   *Irish Independent*, 30 December 1989

103   *The Irish Times*, 5 December 1990.

Conclusion

1   Joe Joyce and Peter Murtagh, *Blind Justice* (Dublin: Littlehampton, 1984), p. 329; *The Irish Times*, 2 December 1989.

2   Sweeney, *Down, Down, Deeper and Down*, p. 348.

3   *The Irish Times*, 21 October 1991 and 1 February 1992.

4   Gemma Hussey, *Ireland Today: Anatomy of a Changing State* (London: Viking Press, 1995), p. 132.

5   *The Irish Times*, 29 December 2021.

BIBLIOGRAPHY

Archives and Libraries

The National Archives of Ireland, Dublin (NAI)
Department of Foreign Affairs
Roinn an Taoisigh

National Library of Ireland, Dublin (NLI)
Sean O'Mahony Collection

The National Archives (UK), Kew (TNA)
Home Office
Foreign & Commonwealth Office

Public Records of Northern Ireland, Belfast (PRONI)

Glucksman Library, University of Limerick
'The fight goes on': tape-recorded memoir of Gearóid MacCárthaigh

Dáil Éireann Parliamentary Minutes

Official Publications and Reports

An Garda Síochána Annual Reports, 1980–89
Report of the Tribunal of Inquiry into 'The Kerry babies case' (Dublin: Stationery Office, 1985)
Report of the Tribunal of Inquiry into suggestions that members of An Garda Síochána or other employees of the state colluded in the fatal shootings of RUC Chief Superintendent Harry Breen and RUC Superintendent Robert

Buchanan on the 20th of March 1989, set up pursuant to the Tribunals of Inquiry (Evidence) Act 1921–2004
Cory Collusion Inquiry Report: Lord Justice Gibson and Lady Gibson

Author Interviews

Interview with Mick O'Connell, Clare, 27 March 2010
Interview with Maurice Quinlivan, Limerick, 10 May 2010
Interview with Seamus Morris, Tipperary, 26 May 2010
Interview with Martin Ferris, Kerry, 22 June 2010
Interview with NGA committee member, Dublin, 10 September 2010
Interview with 'Limerick republican', Limerick, 17 September 2010
Interview with 'Dublin republican', Dublin, 30 September 2010
Interview with Dessie Ellis, Dublin, 1 October 2010
Interview with Pat Magee, Limerick, 11 October 2010
Interview with 'Midlands republican', Tipperary, 9 January 2011
Interview with 'Tipperary republican', Tipperary, 18 February 2011
Interview with Donal O'Siodhachain, Limerick, 16 March 2011
Interview with 'interviewee C', Limerick, 25 March 2011
Interview with Seán O'Neill, Limerick, 30 March 2011
Interview with 'interviewee A', Clare, 1 April 2011
Interview with Tommy McKearney, Monaghan, 30 July 2013
Interview with Kieran Conway, Dún Laoghaire, 25 September 2016
Interview with Danny Morrison, online, 13 September 2021

Newspapers and News Agencies

An Phoblacht
Associated Press
Ballymun Bulletin
Belfast Telegraph
Donegal Democrat
Donegal News
Drogheda Independent
Dundalk Democrat
Evening Echo
Evening Herald

Evening Press
Fermanagh Herald
Fortnight
Hibernia
Inner City Republican
Iris
Irish Examiner
Irish Independent
Irish Mirror
Leitrim Observer
Limerick Leader
Magill
Mayo News
Meath Chronicle
Saoirse
Saoirse – South City Republican
Sunday Independent
Sunday Tribune
Sunday World
The Anglo-Celt
The Connaught Telegraph
The Guardian
The Independent
The Irish News
The Irish Press
The Irish Times
The Kerryman
The Nationalist and Leinster Times
The New York Times
The Northern Standard
The Phoenix
The Sligo Champion
The Southern Star
The Tuam Herald
United Press International

Western Journal
Western People

Journals and Pamphlets

'Brian Keenan, 1941–2008: A Republican Legend' (Dublin, 2008)

Edgar Graham, 'Ireland and Extradition: A Protection for Terrorists' (Belfast: The Universities Press, 1982)

Irish Quarterly Review

Journal of Law and Society

'Portlaoise Prison, for security reasons ...' (Portlaoise Prisoners Relatives Action Committee, 1985)

'Republican Left'

Terrorism and Political Violence

'That's the sort of me, Volunteer Martin "Doco" Doherty, 1958–1994'

The Crane Bag

The Massachusetts Review

'The Politics of Revolution', Sinn Féin document, 1986

Books

Adams, G., *Free Ireland: Towards a Lasting Peace* (Kerry: Brandon Press, 1995)

Alonso, R., *The IRA and Armed Struggle* (New York: Routledge, 2007)

Anderson, B., *Joe Cahill: A Life in the IRA* (Dublin: O'Brien Press, 2003)

Barrett, J.J., *Martin Ferris: Man of Kerry, The Authorised Biography* (Kerry: Brandon Press, 2005)

Bell, J.B., *The IRA 1968–2000: Analysis of a Secret Army* (London: Routledge, 2000)

Bernard, M., *Daughter of Derry: The Story of Brigid Sheils Makowski* (London: Pluto Press, 1989)

Bew, P. and G. Gillespie, *Northern Ireland: A Chronology of the Troubles, 1968–93* (Dublin: Gill & Macmillan, 1993)

Bishop, P. and E. Mallie, *The Provisional IRA* (London: Corgi, 1988)

Brady, E., E. Patterson, K. McKinney, R. Hamill and P. Jackson (compilers), *In the Footsteps of Anne: Stories of Republican ex-Prisoners* (Belfast: Shanway, 2011)

Collins, E., *Killing Rage* (London: Granta Books, 1998)

Coogan, T.P., *The I.R.A.* (London: Harper Collins, 1995)

—, *The Troubles* (London: Penguin, 1996)

Cronin, M., M. Duncan and P. Rouse, *The GAA: A People's History* (Cork: Collins Press, 2009)

Cullen, B., *Community and Drugs: A Discussion of the Contexts and Consequences of the Community Drug Problems in Ireland, 1976–2001* (Dublin: TCD Addiction Research Centre, 2003)

Currie, P.M. and M. Taylor, *Dissident Irish Republicanism* (London: Continuum, 2011)

Davidson, A.J., *Kidnapped: True Stories of Twelve Irish Hostages* (Dublin: Gill & Macmillan, 2003)

Doherty, D., *Will You Murder My Husband? Catherine Nevin and the IRA* (Cork: Mercier Press, 2000)

Fahy, D., *How the GAA Survived the Troubles* (Dublin: Merlin, 2001)

Feldman, A., *Formations of Violence: The Narrative of the Body and Political Terror in Northern Ireland* (Chicago: University of Chicago Press, 1991)

Fennell, D., *Heresy: The Battle of Ideas in Modern Ireland* (Belfast: Blackstaff Press, 1993)

Finn, D., *One Man's Terrorist: A Political History of the IRA* (London: Verso, 2021)

Flynn, B., *Soldiers of Folly: the IRA Border Campaign, 1956–1962* (Cork: Collins Press, 2009)

Flynn, S. and P. Yeates, *Smack: The Criminal Drugs Racket in Ireland* (Dublin: Gill & Macmillan, 1985)

Geraghty, T., *The Irish War: The Hidden Conflict Between the IRA and British Intelligence* (Baltimore: Harper Collins, 1998)

Hanley, B. and S. Millar, *The Lost Revolution: The Story of the Official IRA and the Workers Party* (Dublin: Penguin, 2009)

Harnden, T., *Bandit Country: The IRA & South Armagh* (London: Coronet, 1999)

Harvey, D., *Soldiering Against Subversion: The Irish Defence Forces and Internal Security During the Troubles* (Dublin: Merrion Press, 2018, Kindle edition)

Hussey, G., *Ireland Today: Anatomy of a Changing State* (London: Viking Press, 1995)

Inglis, T., *Truth, Power and Lies: Irish Society and the Case of the Kerry Babies* (Dublin: UCD Press, 2003)

Joyce, J. and P. Murtagh, *Blind Justice* (Dublin: Littlehampton, 1984)

Kelley, K.J., *The Longest War: Northern Ireland and the I.R.A.* (London: Zed Books, 1990)

Kerrigan, G., *Hard Cases: True Stories of Irish Crime* (Dublin: Gill & Macmillan, 1996)

Laver, M., P. Mair and R. Sinnott (eds), *How Ireland Voted: The Irish General Election 1987* (Dublin: Poolbeg Publishers, 1987)

Lyder, A., *Pushers Out: The Inside Story of Dublin's Anti-Drugs Movement* (Victoria: Trafford Publishing, 2005)

MacEoin, U., *The IRA in the Twilight Years, 1923–48* (Dublin: Argenta, 1997)

MacGréil, M., *Prejudice and Tolerance in Ireland* (Dublin: National College of Ireland Press, 1977)

Magee, G., *Tyrone's Struggle for Irish Freedom* (Omagh: Tyrone Sinn Féin Commemoration Committee and Gerard Magee, 2011)

Magee, P., *Where Grieving Begins: Building Bridges after the Brighton Bomb – a Memoir* (London: Pluto Press, 2021)

Maillot, A., *New Sinn Féin: Irish Republicanism in the Twenty-first Century* (London: Routledge, 2005)

McGladdery, G., *The Provisional IRA in England: The Bombing Campaign 1973–1997* (Dublin: Irish Academic Press, 2006)

McKearney, T., *The Provisional IRA: From Insurrection to Parliament* (London: Pluto Press, 2011)

Moloney, E., *A Secret History of the IRA* (London: Penguin, 2003)

Morrison, D. (ed.), *Hunger Strike: Reflections on the 1981 Hunger Strike* (Dingle: Brandon Press, 2006)

Morrison, J.F., *The Origins and Rise of Dissident Irish Republicanism: The Role and Impact of Organisational Splits* (London: Bloomsbury Academic, 2013)

Murray, R., *Hard Time: Armagh Gaol, 1971–1986* (Cork: Mercier Press, 1998)

O'Brien, B., *The Long War: IRA and Sinn Féin, 1985 to Today* (Dublin: O'Brien Press, 1993)

O'Callaghan, S., *The Informer* (Reading: Corgi, 1999)

O'Connor, F., *In Search of a State: Catholics in Northern Ireland* (Belfast: Blackstaff Press, 1993)

O'Donnell, R., *From Vinegar Hill to Edentubber: The Wexford IRA and the Border* (Wexford: Cairde Na Laochra, 2007)

—, *Special Category, The IRA in English Prisons, Vol. 1: 1968–1978* (Dublin: Irish Academic Press, 2012)

Ó Faoleán, G., *A Broad Church: The Provisional IRA in the Republic of Ireland, 1969–1980* (Dublin: Merrion Press, 2019)

O'Halpin, E., *Defending Ireland: The Irish State and its Enemies since 1922* (Oxford: Oxford University Press, 1999)

O'Hearn, D., *Bobby Sands: Nothing but an Unfinished Song* (London: Pluto Press, 2006)

O'Malley, P., *The Uncivil Wars: Ireland Today* (Boston: Beacon Press, 1997)

Ó Suilleabhain, C., *Leitrim's Republican Story, 1900–2000* (Leitrim: Cumann Cabhrach Liaotrama, 2014)

Oppenheimer, A.R., *IRA, The Bombs and Bullets: A History of Deadly Ingenuity* (Dublin: Irish Academic Press, 2010)

Patterson, H., *The Politics of Illusion: A Political History of the IRA* (London: Serif, 1997)

Rafter, K., *Sinn Féin 1905–2005* (Dublin: Gill & Macmillan, 2005)

Rolston, B. and D. Miller (eds), *War and Words: The Northern Ireland Media Reader* (Dublin: Beyond the Pale Publication, 1996)

Ryan, B., *Keeping Us in the Dark: Censorship and Freedom of Information in Ireland* (Dublin: Gill & Macmillan, 1995)

Sanders, A., *Inside the IRA, Dissident Republicans and the War for Legitimacy* (Edinburgh: Edinburgh University Press, 2011)

Sharrock, D. and M. Devenport, *Man of War, Man of Peace: The Unauthorised Biography of Gerry Adams* (London: Macmillan, 1997)

Smith, M.L.R., *Fighting for Ireland? The Military Strategy of the Irish Republican Movement* (London: Routledge, 2002)

Sweeney, E., *Down, Down, Deeper and Down: Ireland in the 70s & 80s* (Dublin: Gill & Macmillan, 2010)

Sweetman, R., *On Our Knees: Ireland, 1972* (London: Pan Special, 1972)

Taylor, P., *The Provos: the IRA and Sinn Féin* (London: Bloomsbury, 1998)

Toibín, C., *Walking Along the Border* (London: Queen Anne Press, 1987)

Treacy, M., *A Tunnel to the Moon: The End of the Irish Republican Army* (Dublin: Brocaire Books, 2017)

Urban, M., *Big Boys' Rules: The SAS and the Secret Struggle Against the IRA*

(London: BCA Books, 1993)

Walsh, L., *The Final Beat: Gardaí Killed in the Line of Duty* (Dublin: Gill & Macmillan, 2001)

Walsh, P., *Irish Republicanism and Socialism* (Belfast: Athol Books, 1994)

White, R.W., *Out of the Ashes: An Oral History of the Provisional Irish Republican Movement* (Dublin: Merrion Press, 2017)

—, *Provisional Irish Republicans: An Oral and Interpretative History* (Westport: Praeger Publishers Inc., 1993)

—, *Ruairí Ó Brádaigh: The Life and Politics of an Irish Revolutionary* (Indiana: Indiana University Press, 2006)

Wilson, A.J., *Irish America and the Ulster Conflict, 1968–1995* (Belfast: Blackstaff Press, 1995)

Podcasts, Television and Radio Documentaries

Garda ar Lár (RTÉ)

Vol Seamus McElwaine IRA (YouTube)

The Marita Ann Story (YouTube)

We Say You Have To Go (RTÉ)

Kerry Baby (Soundcloud)

INDEX